Madonna

Books by Mark Bego

The Captain & Tennille (1977)
Barry Manilow (1977)
The Doobie Brothers (1980)
Michael! [Jackson] (1984)
On the Road with Michael! [Jackson] (1984)
Madonna! (1985)
Rock Hudson: Public & Private (1986)
Sade! (1986)
Julian Lennon! (1986)
The Best of "Modern Screen" (1986)
Whitney! [Houston] (1986)
Cher! (1986)
Bette Midler: Outrageously Divine (1987)
The Linda Gray Story (1988)
TV Rock [The History of Rock & Roll on Television] (1988)
Aretha Franklin: Queen of Soul (1989)
Between the Lines [with Debbie Gibson] (1990)
Linda Ronstadt: It's So Easy (1990)
Ice Ice Ice: The Extraordinary Vanilla Ice Story (1991)
One Is the Loneliest Number [with Jimmy Greenspoon of Three Dog Night] (1991)
Madonna: Blonde Ambition (1992)
I'm A Believer: My Life of Music, Monkees and Madness [with Micky Dolenz of the Monkees] (1993)
Country Hunks (1994)
Country Gals (1994)
Dancing In The Street: Confessions of a Motown Diva [with Martha Reeves of Martha & the Vandellas] (1994)
I Fall To Pieces: The Music & the Life of Patsy Cline (1995)
Bonnie Raitt: Just in the Nick of Time (1995)
Rock & Roll Almanac (1996)
Alan Jackson: Gone Country (1996)
Raised On Rock: The Autobiography of Elvis Presley's Step-Brother [with David Stanley] (1996)
George Strait: The Story of Country's Living Legend (1997, 1998 & 1999)
Leonardo DiCaprio: Romantic Hero (1998)
LeAnn Rimes (1998)
Jewel (1998)
Matt Damon: Chasing a Dream (1998)
Will Smith: The Freshest Prince (1998)
Vince Gill (2000)
Madonna: Blonde Ambition [Updated Edition] (2000)
Rock Rules (2000)
Cher: If You Believe (2000)

Madonna

Blonde Ambition

Updated Edition

Mark Bego

Cooper Square Press

To Ann Bego
"Well now, lassie!"

First Cooper Square Press edition 2000

This Cooper Square Press paperback edition of *Madonna* is an unabridged republication of the edition first published in New York in 1992, with the edition of a new chapter and updated appendices. It is reprinted by arrangement with the author.

Published by Cooper Square Press,
An Imprint of Rowman & Littlefield Publishing Group
150 Fifth Avenue, Suite 911
New York, New York 10011

Distributed by National Book Network

Library of Congress Cataloging-in-Publication Data

Bego, Mark.
    Madonna : blonde ambition / Mark Bego.—updated ed.
      p. cm.
    "First cooper Square Press edition"—T.p. verso.
    Includes bibliographical references and index.
    ISBN 0-8154-1051-4 (pbk. : alk. paper)
    1. Madonna, 1958- 2. Singers—United States—Biography. 3. motion picture actors and actresses—United States—Biography. I. Title.

ML420.M1387 B44 2000
782.42166'092—dc21   00-030717
[B]

Contents

Madonna: "I have a long range plan."

Mark Bego: "Where do you see yourself in the future?"

Madonna: "At the Betty Ford Hospital. It's where all the famous people go!"[1]

Introduction

The afternoon I finished writing this book, I went to a cocktail party to celebrate. When I arrived there, the host said to me, "Congratulations! There's just one thing I want to know. At the end of the book, how does Madonna come across—is she a bitch, or is she a goddess?"

After thinking for a moment I replied, "Actually, both."

"How marvelous!" my friend exclaimed. "A bitch goddess!"

In a very simple way, the term "bitch goddess" cuts to the essence of the subject of this book. Madonna represents different things to different people. As her career progresses and she slowly peels away various layers of camouflage, new dimensions of her personality are exposed. She is often so revealing that her attentive audience is treated like voyeurs in a church confessional. Among other things, she is a hard-as-nails workaholic, an egotistical mistress of media manipulation, and a progressive-thinking iconoclast who will do and/or say anything to shock people.

Since I was born in Pontiac, Michigan—the city Madonna grew up in—to me she will always be a pushy local-girl-made-good. Although I didn't know her at the time, like Madonna I too moved to New York City in search of fame. We met on several occasions in the early eighties, when she was at the beginning of her singing and acting career and I was enjoying the initial success of my writing career.

At the time, as a magazine writer, I was meeting and interviewing lots of singers who had hit records, including Madonna. However, the second I was introduced to her, I knew that she was different. After an hour of talking to her, I knew that, whatever it took, she was somehow destined to become a star.

Since that time I was amazed at how many of my friends in the music business went on to work with her. While writing this book, I had the unique opportunity of being able to turn to my own personal phone book to get in touch with them. In my conversations with Madonna's co-workers and friends, I found that they each had one outrageous story or another that has never appeared in print, which added a fresh facet to her story.

In 1984 I was asked by a book publisher to propose a biography about someone at the forefront of the music scene, keeping in mind a release date of the following spring. When I proposed doing a book on Madonna, the editors loved the idea. I had just interviewed Madonna, only weeks after her prime-time television debut on the first annual MTV Awards. During our interview, we laughed about the cameramen who had angled the camera shots up her dress while she performed "Like a Virgin." She was brash and bratty even then, but when she talked about her career, she was clearly focused. There was no doubt in my mind that she was going places.

A couple of weeks later I visited her on the set of *Desperately Seeking Susan* and watched her film the scenes that took place outside the fictitious Magic Club. I was also one of the invited guests at her "Like a Virgin" party at Private Eyes, which is described in this book.

As I predicted, in 1985 Madonna became the hottest new star of the year. When the book I had written about her, *Madonna!*, was released, it went on to sell a million copies. Since then I have kept tabs on her every move. I knew that the day would eventually come when I would write a much more detailed book on the life of Madonna. In 1989 I realized that that time had come, and I began work on this book.

The term "blonde ambition" was used in a 1985 magazine article about Madonna. When I first proposed writing this book, it seemed like a perfect title. After Harmony Books gave me a contract to do so, Madonna announced that her 1990 concert tour was going to be titled "Blonde Ambition" as well. It certainly seemed to be a favorable omen. It would be sheer egomania for me to say "great minds think alike," but when you're dealing with a subject like Madonna, modesty should never enter the picture.

Madonna is a pushy bitch, an egotist, and an accomplished dominatrix at the art of self-promotion. Yet, underneath all of her accomplishments, there still lies a rebellious Catholic girl from Pontiac, Michigan, willing to do anything for attention. I am mesmerized by her, admire her creative talent, salute her hard work, and believe in her humanistic politics. There has never been a popular singer who has so totally captured the ears and eyes of the world, and who uses her power to make changes in our consciousness. While she has the spolight, she slaps the bigoted and narrow-minded masses around her for being homophobic, racist, and misogynistic. Not only has she become the biggest star in the show business galaxy, she's also determined to change the way we look at ourselves.

I've been following Madonna's career since the early days when she was showcasing herself at clubs in New York City like Paradise Garage and Studio 54. The book that you are holding in your hands is a product of several years of research. It is about a determined little girl from my hometown, who clawed, pushed, and finagled her way to the top of the entertainment world. She's the ultimate bitch goddess, and her name is Madonna.

MARK BEGO

One

If I weren't as talented

Everyone's

as I am ambitious, I would be

Favorite

a gross monstrosity.[2]

Pop

—Madonna

Dominatrix

It is four A.M., New Year's Day 1991, and Madonna has just awakened in her luxurious Manhattan apartment, groggy from a drunken sleep. The previous night she had hosted a party for a circle of her friends, plus an invited fortune-teller. When the soothsayer read the singer's palm, she informed Madonna that her current relationship was nothing more than a passing fancy, and that she would never bear children. Upset, Madonna showed the fortune-telling woman the door, slugged down two martinis on an empty stomach, and passed out on the marble floor of her bathroom. This was highly uncharacteristic

1

behavior for Madonna, a legendary control freak who works hard at never losing her composure.

The following morning her head is spinning. One of the things on her mind is the fact that in the past three years, her personal life has left her unfulfilled. The love life that she once had complete control over has turned suddenly sour. How can this be? Madonna is the steel-cold paragon of self-love, the hard-as-nails "boy toy" who has used love like a tool and tossed aside men like yesterday's newspapers. She's the "Material Girl" with every possession money can buy, the all-controlling star who supposedly "fucked her way to the top." Yet, now that she sits at the summit of wealth and accomplishment, she sits there alone.

Welcome to the upper-stratosphere world that Madonna lives in— a gilded cage at the pinnacle of fame and fortune. Now that she has everything she has ever desired—everything except someone to share it with—is she really happy? To compensate, she has taken upon herself the task of blatantly shocking as many people as she can with her pronouncements and her behavior.

"Have you ever been butt-fucked?" Madonna asks one of her openly gay dancers in her candid documentary film, *Truth or Dare: On the Road, Behind the Scenes, and In Bed with Madonna*. In another scene, Madonna visits with one of her high school chums. She reminisces with a girlfriend, who she claims "finger-fucked" her when they were teen-agers. Also in the film are "Candid Camera"–like scenes of Madonna simulating fellatio on a phallic-shaped Evian water bottle. These were just a few behind-the-scenes events, taped amid Madonna's 1990 concert tour, a show featuring on-stage masturbation and cross-dressing as two of the evening's themes. This is the Madonna of the 1990s: everyone's favorite pop dominatrix.

The mere mention of Madonna's name conjures strong reactions: she is the kind of girl you either love, hate, or love to hate. Rarely does she elicit a blasé response. Brash, bratty, rude, shocking, stunning, controversial, glamorous, and unpredictable—Madonna is the biggest international star of the nineties. Singer, dancer, actress, movie star, pin-up girl, and outrageous celebrity-for-all-seasons, she is the self-created product of shameless media manipulation.

She is a mass of contradictions. The images she so masterfully projects are displays of total extremes. One time she may come across as vulnerable and sincere. The next time she appears crude, abrasive, downright slutty. She is an extremist, and all of the extremes are true. Neither boundless in artistic scope nor wealthy in natural talent, she is undeniably brilliant at working within the range of her limitations and turning everything she touches into classic pop art.

Although she is virtually transparent in her desire and drive to become famous simply for the sake of fame, the public just can't seem to get enough of her. Recordings, magazines, calendars, and concert tickets sell out in record numbers when her name or likeness is on them. In a business that is as fickle as the weather, it seems that Madonna is always in season.

According to *Forbes* magazine, she is the wealthiest and highest paid woman in show business today, and neither scandal nor controversy can touch her rock-solid hold on the public's attention. In less than ten years, she has elevated herself to that rarefied state of celebritydom where the minutiae of her private life have become even more newsworthy than her commercial products.

She is not the most beautiful singer or actress in show business, but Madonna has an indefinable star quality that causes all attention to focus on her when she walks into a room. In fact, anyone who has sat next to her when she is wearing minimal makeup immediately realizes that she has very little natural beauty. Her eyebrows are uncontrollably bushy, her unadorned eyes are rather plain, and the shape of her luscious mouth is as painted on as the strategically placed Marie Antoinette beauty mark penciled on her upper lip. However, when she is made up correctly, with porcelain white skin and ruby red lips, she can look undeniably dazzling.

In a world littered with dozens of flash-in-the-pan media stars, Madonna has a mesmerizing allure which is unstoppable. Censored music videos, nude photos in *Playboy* and *Penthouse*, crude language, marriage to an obnoxious punk, rumors of lesbian affairs, the Pope's ban on her performing in Italy, three bomb movies in a row, lousy reviews on Broadway, and scandals with members of both sexes could spell the end to any normal star's career—but not Madonna! On the contrary, giving her bad publicity is like trying to put out a fire with gasoline.

Whenever we get used to one look, sound, or career path, an unpredictable Madonna simply shows us a new side to herself. Not since

David Bowie has a pop star been more a chameleon. We've come to know her as a bohemian bare-midriffed waif, a blonde bombshell, a disco tart, a *Cosmopolitan* cover girl, a leather-clad biker girl, the empress of Metropolis, a Brooklynese con artist, a flapper, and a cartoon chanteuse. Every move she makes, and every persona change she goes through, only makes for more front page news. Her combination of seductive warmth and steel-cold aggressive drive has the world transfixed. Hers is the most calculated career romp of the century, and none of the competition—male or female, black or white, gay or straight—can touch her.

From the rarefied heights she has attained in the entertainment business, she has few competitors. Her original rival, Cyndi Lauper, has watched her own ship sink after a long series of ill-chosen career moves. Bruce Springsteen perpetually seems to be kicking back. Whitney Houston suffers from a case of style over substance and massive media overexposure. And, while immature and childlike Michael Jackson is busy playing with his zoo animals, Madonna goes straight for the crotch, toying with everyone's libido.

Instead of getting into a rut, Madonna simply continues to reinvent herself. By constantly changing her persona and image, no matter what moves she makes, the public will eagerly eat it up. With anticipation we all stand in awe—waiting for that next move. One moment she's dressed trashy, with crucifixes dangling from every appendage, the next minute she is chic and glamorous. As soon as you get used to one look or sound from her, *voilà!*—she's changed her fashion, her hair color, her lover, and/or all of the above.

As the eighties ended Madonna was at the top of everyone's media sensations list: *Time*'s top ten "Faces of the Decade," *Billboard*'s "Top Ten Recording Artists"; she was even named by *Musician* magazine as the undisputed "Artist of the Decade."

Although she is clearly a product of the "Me Generation," Madonna is also a champion of her personally selected causes. While in her songs and videos she serves up sex with the ease of someone scooping ice cream, she is also very up-front in declaring that the sex she advertises is "safe sex." She is second only to Elizabeth Taylor in her aggressive public stance in support of the war on AIDS. She has turned several of her concerts into AIDS fundraisers, inserted safe-sex pamphlets into her albums, cassettes, and compact discs, and admonished her live audiences with "Don't be silly, put a rubber on your willy!"

Apart from the videos, the headlines, and the fashion statements, what is it that makes Madonna tick? And what aspect of her does the public find so fascinating? As a singer she doesn't have a very versatile vocal range. She is often too stiff and cardboard as an actress. In fact, her film career may go down in history as the world's longest and costliest on-the-job training session since the movies were invented.

Her most fully realized screen role is that of a unidimensional cartoon character—Breathless Mahoney. As a sex symbol she isn't the most voluptuous or the most breathtakingly beautiful girl around. In the charm department she's neither gracious nor tactful. Often she comes across like a precocious little girl who lifts her dress over her head for attention.

What fuels her drive and makes her a legend while other women in the music business merely reign as flavor of the month? *Rolling Stone* has called her "the most notorious living blonde in the modern world." And, although she occasionally dyes her hair back to its natural brunette, they're absolutely correct. Maybe it's just some sort of magical combination of all of her attributes, thrust before the public in a frank, shameless, sex-kitten-in-heat style. She is the first to admit, "Manipulating people, that's what I'm good at."[3]

In the 1930s it was platinum blonde Jean Harlow who oozed sex, and who caused the then-uncensored movie business to establish the Hayes Code to restore "moral decency" to the screen. In the 1950s, Marilyn Monroe became Hollywood's reigning blonde bombshell with her seemingly innocent and purring sexuality. In the 1990s we have Madonna. Times have changed since Harlow and Monroe, but our hunger for movie star glamour has not.

If the unique niche Madonna has carved for herself is any indication, the world craves a sex goddess who is streetwise, smart, and liberated. Madonna isn't some studio-manufactured doll with blonde hair and a pretty smile. She's a gutsy young woman who is entirely in control of her every move. Who else could get away with simulated masturbation on stage one minute and promoting her role in a Disney film the next?

She's clearly got her finger on the pulse of what the public wants—even if that pulse point is in the groin. She is one smart cookie who has, in the words of Bette Midler, "pulled herself up by her own bra straps."[4]

Her gutsy determination and flamboyant style have charmed the world, even if her controversies have shaken it up a bit from time to time. While people scoff when comparisons are made to Marilyn Monroe, Madonna has the staying power and the drive to stand uniquely on her own. She uses the blonde temptress image when it works to her advantage. Although she occasionally enrages feminists with her sex-as-a-weapon antics, it's clear that she is in control of her destiny at all times. As the head of three of her own corporations, she has proven that she can play hardball with the big boys—matching them tit for tat in the corporate boardroom.

Her entire career is one well-orchestrated combination of business politics and bedroom politics. Her affairs with powerful and influential men who can help her are more and more carefully calculated as time goes on. She used one boyfriend to get a record deal; she used another to obtain a hit sound; she used her husband to ensconce her firmly in Hollywood; and she used Warren Beatty to gain credibility in the film world. On the one hand, she used men long enough to fulfill her purpose and then she dumped them. On the other, those men never received so much publicity and media fame as when they were on Madonna's arm. The role that Sean Penn will best be remembered for is that of Madonna's husband.

Madonna isn't so much a star as she is a headline-grabbing media manipulator extraordinaire. The *National Enquirer*, the *Star*, and Britain's the *Sun* aren't her adversaries, they're her personal playgrounds. MTV, *Time*, *Forbes*, *The New Republic*, "Nightline"—there's no media outlet that hasn't succumbed to her ability to sell copies, gather viewers, or draw advertising dollars. More of a public performer than a respected singer and actress, Madonna is a star—which for her is a role unto itself. She has become media philosopher Marshall McLuhan's worst nightmare: a woman with supreme control over both the medium and the "massage."

When it comes to social climbing, there is no one like Madonna. It's common knowledge that the best way to get something from someone is to have them fall in love with you. To say that Madonna resorted to her sexual charms early in her career sounds a bit careless now, especially from the perspective of the nineties. However, life in Manhattan from 1978 to 1982 was far from prudish, and Madonna didn't do anything more outrageous or loose in the morals department than anyone else at that time. If she slept her way to the top, so what? She was simply better at calculating her moves than the rest of the pack who were trying to claw their way up the ladder of success.

When she moved to Manhattan in 1978 and was disastrously bombing out in a dance career, she "just happened to" move in with musician Dan Gilroy, who gave her a crash course in musical training. When she was eating out of garbage cans in the Music Building and lacked direction, she "just happened to" move into her manager Camille Barbone's apartment, where she was taught all about the business of managing a band. When she needed someone to plug her into the record business, she "just happened to" charm disc jockey Mark Kamins into getting her a deal at Sire Records. When she needed someone to sharpen her musical sound and find a hit record, she "just happened to" start dating aspiring record producer Jellybean Benitez, who introduced her to the movers and shakers in the music production business. When she longed to break into film, Madonna "just happened to" marry movie star Sean Penn. When her movie career was floundering, she "just happened to" start dating superstar Warren Beatty. Madonna's personal life from 1978 to 1985 represents creative dating at its finest.

Her instinctive and admirably calculating self-education has extended beyond the bedroom as well. When she wanted to learn about how to promote a record in the dance clubs, she pumped record company executive Bobby Shaw for all that he could teach her. When she wanted to learn the ropes about publicity, she quizzed people in the know, including Jellybean's publicist, David Salidor, for tips on how to do it correctly. When she needed a high-powered manager to pull all of her business together, she went right to the top, and pushed herself into the office of Freddy DeMann.

Madonna is one smart cookie. She didn't stumble into the spotlight, she pushed her way into it. She knew where she wanted to go, and she did everything in her power to get herself there. This sounds cold and calculating, but in reality, it is 100 percent true. To her credit, she has never stabbed anyone in the back to get what she wanted. She never has had to. She is kind to and appreciative of people who are loyal to her. However, when she is finished with anyone who has been useful, she feels no remorse about turning the corner and leaving them in her dust. If you can't keep up with Madonna when she is ready to make one of her career moves, the bus is simply going to leave without you. She carries no excess baggage, and anyone who can't keep the pace suddenly finds themselves left behind, wondering: "What happened?"

She is a strong, self-determined woman who has conveniently used her relationships with men to help her get what she wants. But, who can help her now?

Underneath the bleached blonde hair, the missile-cone breasts, the bustier, the crucifixes, and the spoiled attitude, several questions remain unanswered: Who is Madonna? What does she want? What is the secret of her control and calculating self-confidence? Now that she has it all, is it lonely at the top? And, more important, why do we all care so damn much? Like a cleverly constructed piece of origami art, the mystery of Madonna has just begun to unfold. . . .

Two

From the start

Think

I was a very bad girl.[5]

of

—Madonna

Me

When Madonna first arrived on the popular music scene in the early eighties, her songs were delivered from a stance of playful partying ("Everybody"), heated sex ("Burning Up"), greed ("Material Girl"), and narcissism ("Think of Me"). Single-mindedly her underlying message was the command "Look at me." However, as time went by, piece by piece she began to reveal different aspects of her complex personality and the deeply ingrained obsessions that were left by strict parental authority and a devout Catholic upbringing.

Madonna's initial image was more a case of style than of substance. But once she'd achieved objective number one, fame itself, and the public spotlight was focused on her, she began exorcising childhood demons with her pen. There were songs of sibling rivalry ("Keep It Together"), paternal rebellion ("Papa Don't Preach"), resentment of religious authority ("Like a Prayer"), and feelings of desertion ("Promise to Try").

Her aggressiveness is probably the single key element of her success, and this is clearly traceable to Madonna's childhood. She admits, "Coming from a big family had something to do with it. There's that competitiveness that you have when there's a whole bunch of you and you want your parents' attention, and you don't want the hand-me-down clothes. You wanna stand out, you wanna be treated special. And then also my mother dying when I was six and a half, I think that had a lot to do with me saying—after I got over my heartache—'Well, I'm gonna be really strong and if I can't have a mother to take care of me, then I'm gonna take care of myself.' "[6] Taking care of herself has since proven more of a lifelong plan than a simple goal.

Looking back on her childhood, Madonna explains, "I had a very middle-, lower-middle class sort of upbringing, but I identify with people who've had, at some point in their lives, to struggle to survive. It adds another color to your character."[7]

Another touchstone of identification in Madonna's life is her ethnic makeup. While she is half Italian and half French Canadian, it is her attachment to her family roots in Italy that she most often speaks of. In the New York music circles where she first gained notoriety, one of the most asked questions was, "Where on earth did she come from?" Indeed, to comprehend what Madonna is all about is to understand her struggles within her family, her willfulness, her childhood scars, and her need to distance herself from pain.

Madonna's Italian ancestry dates back to the 1800s in Pacentro, in the province of Abruzzi. The village of Pacentro has a population of less than 1,600 people and is located about eighty miles from Rome. It was here that her paternal great-grandfather, Nicola Pietro Ciccone, was born in 1867. According to those who remember him, he was a tall, handsome, well-built man who learned to read and write at an early age. In 1893, at the age of twenty-six, he married a local girl named Anna Maria Mancini, and rarely ever strayed far from his hometown.

Nicola and Anna Maria had a son named Gaetano, who was born in 1901 and became Madonna's grandfather. Since Pacentro was a small village with little opportunity for upward mobility, Nicola was insistent that his young son go to school to learn to read and write so that he could improve his lot in life.

Madonna's great-grandmother Anna Maria had a best girlfriend named Concetta, with whom she had grown up. Concetta had two daughters, Bambina and Michelina. As children, Gaetano, Bambina, and Michelina would play together in the sunny streets of Pacentro. When the three children grew up to be teenagers, love blossomed between Michelina and Gaetano. Fearing that their parents would disapprove, the couple kept their affection a secret for a long time. Finally, unable to mask their love, they announced their adoration for each other to their families. While their respective parents found no objection, there was the question of how they would support themselves if they indeed intended on getting married. The advent of World War I only further complicated the situation.

Bambina, who was then a young girl of sixteen, recalls, "After the First World War, Nicola, seeing that there was no life for Gaetano in Pacentro, asked the local priest to write to America to his brothers— who were factory workers in Pittsburgh, Pennsylvania—to find work for his son."[8] Gaetano departed Italy for America, vowing to Michelina that he would return to marry her and bring her back with him. At the age of eighteen, two years later, he did return and fulfill his promise. They had an intimate family wedding in the small Pacentro church, then they both left for Pittsburgh, Pennsylvania.

Theirs was a storybook romance. Now married, the childhood sweethearts boarded a ship bound for America. They ventured across the Atlantic Ocean to live the life that Gaetano had set up for them. Immigrating to the United States, as so many Europeans were doing during that same era, they looked forward to their new life together in the land of opportunity.

Today, Madonna's great aunt Bambina and her family still live in Pacentro. Bambina, who corresponded regularly with her sister, to this day recalls that Michelina had her first child, Mario, in 1930. Four years later she gave birth to Silvio, Madonna's father. In the next six years, Michelina and Gaetano had four other children—all boys.

"My grandparents came from Italy on the boat," says Madonna. "They went to Pennsylvania, a town right outside of Pittsburgh, because the steel mills are there and there was a lot of work."[2] They lived in an all-Italian neighborhood, and her grandfather found a job in one of the steel mills. When Michelina and Gaetano arrived in America, they spoke no English. When Madonna was young she saw them frequently. To her they represented an old lifestyle that her father wasn't interested in. He wanted to assimilate his family. He went on to college where he received an engineering degree. He eventually moved to Michigan to work in the automotive industry.

Silvio, whose nickname is Tony, was the only one among his brothers who obtained a college degree. He was grateful for the rewards and security that his formal education afforded him. It became an important point to him, and he in turn was very insistent that his children take advantage of the opportunities that schooling brought.

"He was in the air force," says Madonna of her father, "and one of his best friends was my mother's oldest brother."[2] He fell in love with her immediately. She was French Canadian and a native of Bay City, Michigan. Not only was she unforgettably beautiful, but she had a unique first name. It was "Madonna."

Explaining her mother's unusual name, the vogueing rock star we now know by that moniker says, "My mother is the only other person I have ever heard of named Madonna."[2] When the young singer first became involved in the music industry, everyone assumed that she had taken it as a stage name.

Silvio "Tony" Ciccone and the attractive young woman named Madonna Fortin married and settled in Pontiac, Michigan, in the heart of automotive country U.S.A. Tony worked as an engineer, holding down a job at the nearby Chrysler Corporation, working on defense systems. Eager to start a family, the young couple soon had two sons, Anthony and Martin, who were born a year apart.

Early the following year, Madonna Ciccone discovered that she was again pregnant and expecting her third child in late summer. In August of that year the family was vacationing in Bay City when the expectant mother suddenly went into labor. On August 16, 1958, she gave birth to her first daughter, whom she and Tony gave her own unique name: Madonna Louise Ciccone.

"The reason I was born in Bay City is that we were at my grandmother's house," the singing star explains.[2] According to Madonna, her given name is special. "It means virgin, mother, mother of Earth, someone who is very pure and innocent, but someone who's very strong."[9]

Speaking disparagingly of her birthplace has gotten her into some hot water in the past. In 1987, after she became the famous singing sensation she is now, Madonna told Jane Pauley on NBC's "Today" show that Bay City was a "smelly little town in northern Michigan."[10] Bay City was not amused by its most famous daughter's remark on national television, and she was blasted by the local paper—only weeks before a scheduled Michigan concert appearance. From the stage of the Pontiac Silverdome she apologized to the crowd, explaining that her remark referred to the Dow Chemical plant near her grandmother's house, not the people of Bay City.

After the birth of little "Nonnie"—as Madonna was called as a child—the family returned to their home off Featherstone Road, not far from where the Pontiac Silverdome stands today. Even at the height of the city's popularity, Pontiac was never very glamorous, but it was a hub of activity from the thirties to the fifties. With several lakes in the vicinity, the area is a haven for both winter and summer sports. Located just north of Detroit in Oakland County, Pontiac is rich in history. In the eighteenth century Chief Pontiac of the Ottawa tribe was based in the vicinity, and later the city—and the car that is manufactured there—took his name. During the twenties people flocked to Pontiac to work in the automotive plants: Pontiac Motors, Fisher Body, and General Motors Truck & Coach. However, by the late fifties Pontiac saw its downtown area begin to disintegrate. When the Pontiac Mall stole the need for a traditional Main Street–type of urban shopping district and the county courthouse moved to an outlying area, the once bustling Pontiac downtown began to resemble a crime-ridden ghost town. Attempts were made to revitalize the Pike Street area, but the parade of time simply passed Pontiac by; all of the major stores have long since relocated to suburban shopping centers.

Madonna's childhood was nothing out of the ordinary. She played with her dolls, fought with her two older brothers, and learned how to vie for attention in her growing family. Becoming the center attraction was a justifiable goal in the Ciccone family, because every year for the next three years, almost like clockwork, Madonna Ciccone, Sr., gave birth to another baby. In rapid succession came Paula, Christopher, and Melanie to give little Nonnie some competition in the attention department.

It wasn't long before Nonnie learned how to succeed at drawing all eyes to herself. "From when I was very young, I just knew that being a girl and being charming in a feminine sort of way could get me a lot of things, and I milked it for everything I could,"[3] she explains. "I was always very precocious as a child, extremely flirtatious."[11]

"I grew up in a really big family and in an environment where you had to get over it to be heard. I was like the she-devil!" says Madonna. "It was like living in a zoo, kind of. You have to share everything. I slept in a bed for years—not even a double bed—with two sisters."[1]

Madonna remembers that she would go to any extreme to get all of the attention in the family. She brazenly proclaims that, "I would even hurt myself, like burn my fingers deliberately, just to get attention."[12]

According to Madonna, her earliest memories go back to when she was about four or five years old. They're mainly memories of her beautiful mother. She remembers not being able to sleep at night. So she would go into her parents' bedroom and climb into bed with them. She laughingly proclaims, "I wanted to sleep with 'the A-Team.'"[13]

Madonna says that her second memory conjures feelings of regret. It was the first time she was deliberately cruel to someone else. She recalls sitting on the driveway to her house, when a young neighborhood girl came waddling up to her with her diapers on. She looked up at Madonna, handed her a dandelion, and Madonna promptly pushed her down. Madonna recalled being mad because she was being punished at the time and her first instinct was to lash out at someone who was more helpless. "I saw in her innocent eyes the chance to get back at some authority," says Madonna.[13]

She claims that the dandelion enraged her as well because they're weeds that grow out of control in people's yards. She professes only to like things that are cultivated. From an early age she had already learned to be the obsessive control freak that she is today.

When she was a child she always thought that the world was hers. It's not that her views have changed since she was a child, it's just that the world that was her realm has grown and expanded beyond the confines of Pontiac, Michigan.

Some of Madonna's adult role-playing manifested itself at an early age. In her play world, Madonna's Barbie doll set the record straight with her Ken doll from the very start. No one was going to set up rules for Barbie to live by, and in later years Madonna would follow the doll's lead. "I played with my Barbie dolls all the time," she recalls. "I definitely lived out my fantasies with them. I dressed them up in sarongs and miniskirts and stuff. They were sexy, having sex all the time. I rubbed her and Ken together a lot. And man, Barbie was *mean*."[14]

From a very young age, one of Madonna's playmates was a neighborhood girl, Carol Belanger. To this day Carol remembers how she and Madonna got into trouble with Carol's mother one afternoon. It seems that Madonna and Carol had stripped the dolls' clothes off and placed them on top of each other in Barbie's bed. Carol's mother was quite *un*amused at finding Ken attempting to have sex with Barbie with their frustratingly anatomically incorrect plastic bodies.

"I was never a Girl Scout," Madonna recalls, "but I was a Campfire Girl and a Brownie. Campfire Girls had a cooler uniform." She was never good at being part of an organization, she further explains. "I'd camp out with the boys and get into trouble."[15]

Of all the childhood memories that come to her, thoughts of her mother seem to come most often. "I remember her being a very forgiving, angelic person," says Madonna of her mother. "I have a memory of my mother in the kitchen scrubbing the floor."[2]

Madonna remembers that her parents were quite permissive, and, within certain parameters, they allowed their six kids to run rampant around the neighborhood. The family's house was on the outskirts of the urban center of Pontiac, and there were undeveloped lots and fields, with woods and trees to play in. Her parents angered a lot of the neighbors because they had so many undisciplined kids. Madonna's two unruly older brothers would play with fire and break things around the house. They would never be fiercely punished, only spoken to mildly about their behavior.

"When I was a little girl, I wished I was black. All my girlfriends were black," says Madonna of the integrated neighborhood that her family lived in.[16] She views it as a positive growing experience. She was fascinated with the braided hairstyles her black girlfriends had, and she fell in love with the rhythm and blues and soul music that they would listen to together on the radio.

As time progressed, Madonna made several unsuccessful attempts to make her own hair stick up in tight braids. She also found herself jealous of her neighborhood girlfriends' more lenient upbringing. They were allowed to bring their portable record players outside and play music until late in the evening. Madonna's free time was far more structured.

When Tony Ciccone came home from work, it was time for the kids to come in for dinner and to do their chores and/or homework. Madonna used to envy the neighborhood girls whose parents let them stay out late playing in their yards while Madonna and her sisters and brothers were corralled in the house.

Madonna was especially jealous of the fact that the neighborhood girls didn't have the structured life of a strict Catholic upbringing. "I envied them. They didn't have any rules," Madonna still recalls.[17]

With her strong sense of independence, and the fact that she is as aggressive as any of the men she regularly competes with in show business today, one would think that Madonna must have been quite an unfeminine hellion as a child. However, she was quite the opposite. Her sister Paula was really considered the tomboy of the family, while she was more the "sissy." In fact, Madonna used her feminine wiles to get what she wanted.

Instead of being the type of child who was always getting away with something and trying to hide it from her parents, she was the clan's primary stool pigeon. She had her father wrapped around her finger, she confesses. Whenever her brothers would skip school or do anything else they weren't supposed to, little Nonnie would "rat" on them. Of course— as in all sibling fights—her brothers extracted their own revenge. They would all pick on her, and she in turn tattled on them to their father. "Or," she recalls, "they'd pin me down on the ground and spit in my mouth. All brothers do that, don't they?"[2]

By all accounts—in spite of Tony Ciccone's efforts—Madonna was spoiled rotten, and that's basically how she's always been. As the first girl in the family, she was fawned over at an early age and treated special. To this day, if she doesn't have everyone's attention, she simply does or says something to be noticed.

"I wasn't quiet at all," she admits. "I remember always being told to shut up everywhere: at home, at school."[2] For her, mouthing off has always come naturally.

Tony and his wife were pretty strict about what their six children could and could not do. Television and candy were two of the things on the "limited access" list. Since candy was very rarely found in the

Ciccone household, when Madonna grew up and left the house, she indulged in all sorts of junk food to make up for the lack of sugar in her childhood diet—especially since it was at one time forbidden to her. Forbidden things only make her want them more zealously.

Although she didn't get to watch very much television while she was growing up—her father didn't approve of it—she did watch lots of old movies and recalls fantasizing about the glamorous images she saw up on the screen. Show business was a realm she had yet to encompass as a pre-teenage girl growing up in the industrial Pontiac area.

"The only remotely entertainment-oriented dream I ever had," she says, "was one where I dreamed I kissed Robert Redford."[18] At the time, she was in the sixth grade, and the dream has yet to come true.

When she was allowed to watch TV, it was either Saturday morning cartoons or other harmless teenage fare like "The Partridge Family" or "The Monkees." When she was in junior high school, she would sneak over to girlfriends' houses to catch episodes of "Dark Shadows" on the sly.

"I used to try to copy Shirley Temple when I was a little girl," she says, remembering still another cinematically inspired image.[19] She would turn on the family record player and dance in the basement. Sometimes she danced alone, other times she would give dance lessons to her girlfriends.

According to Madonna, it was her mother who first introduced her to dance. "She taught me my love of dancing," says Madonna. "I learned by watching her dance to Chubby Checker records."[20]

Reaching the ripe old age of five meant that it was time for Madonna to start attending school. Instead of going to the local public schools like the rest of the kids in the neighborhood, the Ciccone children were bused to the local Catholic schools. Nuns, identical school uniforms, and mysterious religious imagery suddenly became a dominant influence.

At first Madonna was fascinated by the serene beauty of the nuns. At one point during her childhood, she actually considered becoming a nun when she grew up. But it wasn't long before she grew to resent the regimentation that Catholic school presented. Rationalizing, she explains, "The reason I'm not a nun is because you can't take your own name. How could I change my name? I have the most holy name a woman can have."[21]

"I went to three Catholic schools as a child, with uniforms, and nuns hitting you over the back with staplers," Madonna was later to reminisce with a certain lack of reverence.[5] The three parochial schools that she attended in the Pontiac area were St. Andrew's, St. Frederick's, and Sacred Heart Academy.

With six kids in the family, Tony Ciccone made certain that his children didn't have a lot of unstructured time on their hands in which to get into trouble. Madonna explains, "My father was a real disciplinarian, very strict, and you'd get up every morning and go to church before you go to school. You'd wear a uniform and, when we'd get home from school, we'd change our clothes and do our chores. We did our homework."[22] After dinner the Ciccone children weren't allowed to watch TV. Their lives were regimented until they were older. Their father was a hard worker who frowned on his children having idle time. If they didn't have schoolwork to do, he found projects for them around the house.

As Madonna grew older, her relationship with him was often strained. "My father was very strong," she says in retrospect. "I don't agree with some of his values, but he did have integrity, and if he told us not to do something he didn't do it either."[2] A lot of parents who tell their children not to smoke cigarettes actually smoke cigarettes themselves. Madonna's father also had strong beliefs about sex. He believed that making love was a sacred thing reserved for marriage.

Instead of immediately rebelling, Madonna learned to work around her father's authority. "I was my father's favorite," she insists, "I knew how to wrap him around my finger."[2]

In school, Madonna was a very good student who got all A's on her report cards. Her father would reward his children for good grades. He gave them quarters for every A. This family ploy of being paid for the best grades trained Madonna to become competitive at an early age. If she wanted special privileges, she would simply employ some special talent or accomplish some task more proficiently than anyone else. If she failed to win a competition, she was never entirely defeated—she simply pushed herself harder the next time around.

All of the kids in the neighborhood recall that Madonna's mother always had a smile on her face. In spite of the fact that she had six kids of her own running through the house like a band of hellions, she always welcomed her children's friends in the house as well.

"If you wanted to send a few more kids over to her house it was always okay," remembers family friend and neighbor Patrick McFarland.[23] His daughter, Moira, was one of Madonna's playmates and a frequent visitor to the Ciccone ménage.

Madonna pioneered new ways to get noticed on the school playground: "We had to wear uniforms to school, so I would put bright panty bloomers underneath and hang upside down on the monkey bars at recess."[24] From an early age she took a cue from Shakespeare's *As You Like It* and made all the world her stage.

Most people who were raised Catholic will agree that Catholicism is based as much in authority and fear as it is in adherence in the Ten Commandments. The double standards that it imposes are quite inconsistent, and Madonna was quick to realize that there were going to be some severe differences of opinion between her, the nuns, the church, and her father.

"So often I would be confused about who I was worshiping, God or my father," she says in her typically haughty fashion. "Then, as I got older, I hated the idea that I had to go to church all the time."[11]

In addition, she found the Catholic Church to be extremely sexist in its edicts. Her Barbie doll rewrote all the rules to fit her needs—why shouldn't Madonna perform the same task? "I also remember being really annoyed that I couldn't wear pants to school or church," she says. "My brothers could, and that seemed to me all locked up with the religion." When she questioned her father, his answer was always, "Because I said so."[11]

As an adult she would look back on Catholicism with some disdain: "You know how religion is," she ponders, "guys get to do everything. They get to be altar boys. They get to stay out late. Take their shirts off in the summer. They get to pee standing up. They get to fuck a lot of girls and not worry about getting pregnant. Although that doesn't have anything to do with being religious."[18]

She did, however, glean some positive lessons from the church. It taught her the importance of family, which is something deeply ingrained in her. "I was also raised to believe that when you marry someone, you marry him for life."[11]

When she was five years old, something tragic occurred in Madonna's young life: her beautiful mother died. The tragedy left an emotional scar on the young girl, which she is still struggling to deal with as an adult.

"I knew she was sick for a long time with breast cancer," recalls Madonna.[2] As the disease progressed, her mother grew very weak, but she continued to do the things she had to do. Because she was so fragile she would often stop during the day to rest. Madonna was disappointed she couldn't play with her like before.

Throughout the ordeal Madonna's mother tried to keep her feelings inside and not alarm her children. Despite constant pain, she never complained. One day when she was sitting on the couch, Madonna remembers climbing on her back and demanding, "Play with me, play with me," but her mother couldn't, and she started to cry. Madonna remembers pounding on her back with her fist, not understanding what was going on. Then she realized her mother was crying. "I stopped tormenting her after that. That was the turning point when I knew. I think that made me grow up fast."[2]

In retrospect, Madonna realized how much strength her mother had. "I don't think she ever allowed herself to wallow in the tragedy of her situation. So in that respect I think she gave me an incredible lesson."[11]

When things took a turn for the worse, Madonna's mother spent several months in the hospital. It was devastating for Madonna and her siblings to watch this happen to their mother, and it was also very disturbing to watch their father live through the anguish as well. Says Madonna, "It is awful to see your father cry. But he was very strong about it."[2] He would take his children to the hospital to visit their mother. She was often cracking jokes, which made the visits easier.

Her mother died on December 1, 1963. Madonna remembers that right before she died one of her last requests was for a hamburger. This struck Madonna as funny. After her mother died, everything changed; the family was often split up and the kids had to go stay with relatives.

"Once you get hurt really bad when you're young, nothing can hurt you again," says Madonna.[25] Witnessing the slow death of her mother left a profound mark on the girl's life. That period when Madonna realized that her mother wasn't fulfilling her role has a lot to do with her current zest for life. "It left me with an intense longing to fill a sort of emptiness," she confesses.[7]

Uncontrollably, her innocent world of Barbie dolls and Shirley Temple dance lessons was shattered by the reality of death and loss. For the first time in her life she had to look death in the eye and try to comprehend it. "I think the church pretty much stays with you," she says contemplatively. "Whatever was drilled into you when you were growing up, whatever your picture of God was, I think you die with that image in your head."[26]

Like many children who have to face the death of a parent, Madonna's mourning and sorrow were accompanied by a deep sense of guilt. "I haven't resolved my Elektra complex," she recently admitted, referring to the psychological syndrome that defines those exact feelings.[27] A cloud of guilt hangs over her head to this day because she acted cruelly toward her mother, though in reality Madonna's hurtful action was merely a childish outburst. Unfortunately, her mother's death left scars that not even time has healed.

One of her neighborhood girlfriends, Moira McFarland, recalls the death of Madonna, Sr., and its effect on the little girl. Says Moira, who lived two houses away from the Ciccones, "I remember feeling really bad when her mother died, but it probably made [Madonna] stronger because she hurt so bad."[23]

After the funeral was over and the reality of the tragedy sank in, it was time for the family to deal with several changes that had to be made. Tony Ciccone still had to work to support his family, so for several weeks following the death of Madonna, Sr., the six children were farmed out to relatives.

Madonna has a lifelong knack for prospering, even in the face of tragedy or disaster. Instead of letting a negative situation defeat her, somehow it ends up making her stronger. At an early age she learned how to get special privileges. She was good at getting into situations where, say, she was the hall monitor and reported classmates who weren't behaving. Often the nuns would forgive her for misbehavior. Their rationalization was, "Well she doesn't have a mother and her father isn't there a lot."[28]

Before long Tony found a solution to his housekeeping/child-raising dilemma. He began hiring housekeepers. Unfortunately the six rambunctious Ciccone kids proved quite a handful to look after, so they went through quite a few hired hands before they found a compatible and compassionate one.

After Madonna's mother's death, the little girl felt as if she was "the main female of the house."[29] Since there was no adult woman in the household, Madonna felt that she should naturally be the second in command.

Eventually Tony found a pretty, energetic, and exuberant woman named Joan who was able to corral the Ciccone clan and wasn't overwhelmed by them or the housework. The real surprise came when the six children discovered that their father was not only pleased with her cooking and cleaning proficiency—he had fallen in love with her. Madonna was especially dumbfounded by her father's announcement that Joan was going to be their new mother. Bruised feelings and emotional resentment were the children's initial response.

"My father's marriage was a surprise to us," says Madonna, "because we all thought he was going to marry someone else who looked very much like our mother." According to Madonna, Joan was "really gung-ho, very strict, a real disciplinarian."[3]

Madonna, still embittered, recalls how difficult it was to accept her new stepmother, both as a figure of authority and as the most important female in her father's life. "My father wanted us to call her 'Mom,' not her first name," she said.[29] The whole experience turned out to be a painful one. Madonna missed her mother, and took it out on her stepmother.

"I don't really want to talk about my stepmother," is often how Madonna responds when she is asked about Joan Ciccone, in spite of the fact that her father's second marriage took place three decades ago.[2]

Madonna felt that her stature in the family as the oldest girl should buy her prestige and privilege. Instead she found herself saddled with responsibilities, like baby-sitting and diaper changing. Madonna resented the duties delegated to her as the oldest girl. While her friends and neighborhood children were out playing, she had to act responsibly. "I think that's when I really thought about how I wanted to do something else and get away from all that," Madonna recalls.[2] She viewed herself as Cinderella, burdened by a stepmother and lots of work. All she really wanted was to go out and wear pretty dresses.

She further complains, in her spoiled Catholic schoolgirl tone, "I didn't resent having to raise my brothers and sisters as much as I resented the fact that I didn't have my mother."[11] Madonna's picture-perfect vision of family life was ruined, and she and her brothers and sisters weren't very happy about it.

According to her, the thing that she hated the most about Joan was her taste in clothes she purchased for her young stepdaughters. "My stepmother had a thing about buying. She'd go out and buy us all the same thing—the same fucking outfits. Then I had to wear uniforms to school. I was dying for some individuality," she proclaims like a petulant child.[1] Madonna tried everything in an effort to look different than her brothers and sisters, from odd-colored socks to bows in her hair. This may well have been the beginning of the Madonna style.

In her own mind, by remarrying, her father had somehow betrayed her. She recalls turning her animosity on him. "For years I resented him. You see, when my mother died, I attached myself to my father."[16] Madonna felt deserted, as though her stepmother had taken her father away.

Even among her siblings, Madonna felt like a loner. In large families distinctly different personalities often emerge. According to Madonna, some of her siblings were extroverts while others were very shy. As a child Madonna didn't feel close to anyone at home. As in most large families there is often competition between sisters and brothers, and in the Ciccone family, each child actively vied for the attention of their father. Madonna's method for winning his approval was through school: "I was a straight-A student, and they all hated me for it because I did it more for the position I was going to have in my father's eyes than for whatever I was going to learn by studying."[11]

For the three years before her father remarried, Madonna virtually clung to him, emotionally and physically. She claims, "Like all young girls, I was in love with my father and I didn't want to lose him."[11] With the loss of her mother, it became more and more important for Madonna to know that her father was there for her. When Mr. Ciccone married her stepmother, Madonna, hurt by the lack of attention, realized she could get by without anyone. Unwilling to open herself to more heartbreak, at a young age she learned to stand confidently on her own.

Like a stranger in a strange land, Madonna felt as though her existence had been turned upside down after her mother's death. It looked as if her whole world had ended. And though it didn't, it would never be quite the same.

At the age of seven, Madonna and Moira McFarland dug Moira's mother's wedding dress out of the closet, and put on a play in the backyard. The girls fought over who would play the leading role. "She was the prettiest girl I ever knew," says Moira.[23] Naturally Madonna ended up with the starring role. The price of admission for the show was set at a competitive ten cents. This was to go on record as the most economical ticket in her performing career.

In 1966 she made her First Communion, and when she was confirmed, chose the name *Veronica* to add to her own birth name. She was now Madonna Louise Veronica Ciccone.

According to Madonna, St. Veronica "wiped the face of Jesus and then carried around the cloth with his blood and sweat on it."[14] She was attracted to her strange passion. Like St. Veronica, Madonna was destined to become legendary for doing things that were both passionate and weird.

In order to keep his kids occupied and using their minds, Tony Ciccone insisted that they all learn to play a musical instrument. Madonna ended up taking piano lessons after school. She claims that she absolutely hated the lessons, so she came up with a plan. She convinced her father that dance lessons were a good idea and much more creative than piano.

There is a song from the Broadway show *A Chorus Line* called "At the Ballet." In the song three girls sing about escaping painful childhood experiences by taking dance classes. The moral of the song is that in spite of unhappy home lives and traumatic realities, everything was somehow "beautiful" at the ballet. For Madonna, it was like this. She could forget about her stepmother, the nuns at school, her sibling rivalries, even the death of her mother, for hours at a time during her dance lessons.

The year 1967 was dubbed the "Summer of Love" in pop cultural terms. It was the year that Madonna first began developing her own musical taste. Her three favorite records—which she owned as 45 rpm singles—were the Strawberry Alarm Clock's "Incense & Peppermints,"

Gary Puckett and the Union Gap's "Young Girl," and the Box Tops' "The Letter."

Imagine, if you will, the sight of Madonna and her two older brothers—Anthony and Martin—fighting over the use of the family turntable. Even at the age of eight Madonna was fighting a heated battle to control the stereo, insistent that *her* music get played.

"When I was growing up, my older brothers were into hard rock and I hated it," Madonna says. "They would purposely scratch the needle across my pop records, like my 'Incense and Peppermints' record, and my Gary Puckett 'Young Girl (Get Out of My Mind)' record."[5] Then the fights would start. "My brothers listened to heavy metal all the time," she recalls, "and weird fusion jazz—Mahavishnu Orchestra. I hated that!"[1]

"A lot of Motown," is what she remembers on the airwaves. "All the AM stations in Detroit, that's all they played. I heard it all the time."[1] It was impossible to grow up in the Detroit area in the sixties without being touched by the sound of Motown music. Local AM radio stations like CKLW and WXYZ played the sounds of "the Motor City" almost nonstop in those days. According to her, "I grew up loving innocent child voices like Diana Ross, while she was with The Supremes, and Stevie Wonder when he was young."[30]

Another of her musical influences was Frankie Lyman of the Teenagers. She especially liked the distinctively high-pitched sound of his voice. It was an adolescent pop quality she would later mimic on record. As far as the trashy girl-gone-bad stance that some of her music would later take, Madonna claims that this is attributed to another of her idols from the sixties: Ronnie Spector of the Ronettes.

It was also during the summer of 1967, while Madonna was eight years old, that the Detroit and Pontiac race riots took place. For anyone living in the area, they were frightening occurrences never forgotten. The sounds of sirens, breaking glass, and gunfire—in usually docile Pontiac—were especially terrifying for children to witness and hear. The Ciccones were one of the few Caucasian families in a racially mixed neighborhood. During the 1967 riots Madonna recalls that the streets were pretty rough. In the midsixties, several more black families had moved into the same neighborhood, and many white families left. Madonna's was one of the white families who didn't move. However, Madonna survived that ordeal unscathed, and time marched on.

"I discovered boys when I was about nine," She recalls, despite the fact that her father told her to stay away from them.[31] Not content just to flirt coyly, Madonna took a more aggressive stance when it came to the opposite sex: "I remember I wanted to chase after boys on the playground, and the nuns told me I couldn't, that good Catholic girls didn't chase boys."[11] Madonna didn't take the nuns' warnings too seriously and often wound up being punished for her flirtatious behavior.

Recalling the first object of her prepubescent affections, she confesses, "The first boy I ever loved was Ronny Howard in my fifth-grade class. He had real white-blond hair and sky-blue eyes. He was so beautiful, I wrote his name all over my sneakers and on the playground I used to take off the top part of my uniform and chase him around!"[9] Obviously, little Nonnie was coming out of her shell—in a big way.

There was also a boy named Tommy, who she recalls running after on the playground. For added speed, Madonna first removed her blazer and blouse. The nuns grabbed her and informed her that good Catholic girls don't take off their clothes in public and chase boys. "He had terrible teeth, but I wanted him," she remembers about Tommy.[23] The following day she and Tommy sneaked into the convent and it was there that she received her first kiss—which to this day she remembers as being "incredible."[32]

Other girls didn't care for Madonna because her direct approach with boys was quite different than what they expected. "I didn't play the cat-and-mouse game," she recalls with pride.[25]

Meanwhile, on the home front, her father's second marriage brought about several changes, including two more children in the family to compete with. When Madonna was nine, her stepmother gave birth to Jennifer, and the next year, gave birth to Mario. As the family competition for attention grew stronger, Madonna learned to escape more and more into her own rebellious world.

Things just weren't going according to her plans. Never one to suffer in silence, Madonna began to protest openly against school, church, and her parents' authority. This phase coincided with her discovery of boys. "It was at the same time that I started to rebel against religion, to be conscious of what I consider to be the injustices of my religious up-bringing."[11]

She adds, "I certainly wanted really badly either to find out my parents weren't my real parents—so I could be an orphan and feel sorry for myself—or wanted everyone to die in a car accident so I wouldn't have parents."[33]

Often punished for her behavior, Madonna would throw temper tantrums, slamming her door and muttering under her breath that she hated her father. She claims that had her mother not died while she was still a young girl, she might have grown up to become an entirely different person. Watching her young mother suddenly disappear from her life, she realized how short life really was: too short to settle for anything less than everything you desire. Had her childhood taken a different path, she might never have blossomed into the high-priestess of rebellious self-expression that we have come to know as Madonna.

Three

The angriest time in my life —

Express

I'd have to say that was in

Yourself

my teen years.[28] *—Madonna*

When Madonna was ten years old, things started to change both within and around her. It was then that the Ciccone family moved from Pontiac to the nearby suburb of Rochester, Michigan. It was also around this time that Madonna began to question everything that she had been taught or told about life. There seemed to be a vast difference of opinion between her father, the nuns, and her own will. It was at this age of ten that she began making her own decisions about life.

As a small child, her picture of earthly perfection was the life of the nuns, because it seemed that they were divine untouchables. She had dreams of becoming a nun. "Then, when I realized that nuns didn't have a sex life, I was incredibly disenchanted."[11]

In an effort to discover what made the nuns tick, she and her cohort in crime, a neighborhood friend named Carol Belanger, went on a spying expedition, inquisitively peeking through the windows of the convent. Their mission was to see what was beneath the nuns' habits.

When the subjects of sex and boys entered the picture, Madonna found herself even more confused. It seemed that the more she pondered, the more perplexed she became. Madonna's family was a strict one, and when she was a child her grandmother often preached to her that it was best to love Jesus and to stay away from boys. "I grew up with two images of a woman—the virgin and the whore."[24]

She claims, "Your parents give you false expectations of life. All of us grow up with completely misguided notions about life and they don't change until you get out into the world."[34]

Madonna suddenly realized that she would have to find out what life was all about for herself. Step number one in her program of exploration called for breaking all of the previous rules that had been imposed upon her. "I wanted to do everything everybody told me I couldn't do," she proclaims of her own preteen declaration of independence.[3]

At the age of ten, Madonna's childish attention-getting ploys successfully garnered her the all-eyes-on-me effect she desired. Her favorite stunt was still the tried-and-true hanging upside down from the gym equipment on the playground so that all the boys could see her panties. Little did the appalled nuns know, but fifteen years later, Madonna Ciccone was to become world famous for a slight variation on that same theme, wearing a brassiere as an outer garment. Even as a fourth-grader she was perfecting her craft as an exhibitionist!

A new way of life called for new role models. This time around it was the world of pop music and the movies. Her early idols included Nancy Sinatra (go-go boots, miniskirts, blonde hair, and all), Marilyn Monroe (of course), Jean Seberg in *Joan of Arc*, and Brigitte Bardot, particularly in the film *Contempt*, in which Bardot seemed obsessed with her looks, as was Madonna.

"When I was growing up, I was religious, in a passionate, adolescent way. Jesus Christ was like a movie star, my favorite idol of all."[15] Even as a child, Madonna's perception of the world had always been a tug of war between the profane and the sacred.

Madonna also seemed to embrace the wisdom of Oscar Wilde when he said, "To love oneself is the beginning of a life-long romance."[35] From that point on, she launched herself on a campaign of self-discovery. Bending the rules to fit her needs, she cleverly devised ways to *appear* to be obedient to her father's many edicts. Remembering this era, Madonna explains, "When I'd go to school I'd roll up my uniform skirt so it was short, I'd go to the school bathroom and put makeup on and change into nylon stockings I'd bought. I was incredibly flirtatious and I'd do *anything* to rebel against my father."[3]

In 1969, as a fifth-grade schoolgirl, she nearly gave her father heart failure with one of her onstage appearances. It was during a St. Andrew's school talent show. Ever on top of a trend, Madonna's concept was to perform a go-go dance like she had seen Goldie Hawn do on TV's "Laugh-In." Gyrating to a song by The Who, there on-stage stood Madonna— wearing a bikini bathing suit and covered from top to bottom with psychedelic swirls of fluorescent green paint. From where Tony Ciccone sat in the audience, it appeared that his ten-year-old daughter was stark naked! He was so mad he nearly hit the ceiling.

"My father grounded me for two weeks," she recalls. "Oh, he was so horrified. 'How could you do that to me?' he said."[32]

Having her dad angry at her was something that she just had to get used to, because she was constantly doing something to piss him off. Madonna remembers, "He wanted me to have more humility, more modesty."[36] It became a never-ending battle between them.

The following year, while in junior high school, to get involved in an after school activity that would keep her out of the house, Madonna became a cheerleader. For her it was just another outlet for her hyperactivity. Cruising the boys was just the first of her rebellions. Around the same time, she began rebelling against the church in earnest. In addition, she was maturing physically at a much faster rate than the rest of the girls in her class. "They hated me," Madonna recalls. It was at this time, that she became more aware of sex. "About its presence, not about what I was going to do about it."[11]

It was blond-haired Colin McGregor who shared some of Madonna's first physical experiences with the opposite sex. Colin met Madonna when they were both nine years old at St. Andrew's in Rochester. He never paid much attention to her until their hormones started flowing at the age of twelve, when they were both in seventh grade.

"She kept wearing scanty panties and the shortest miniskirts in the school to make the boys notice her," Colin recalls of the sudden maturing of Madonna.[37]

In an effort to see the panties of the girls on the cheerleading squad, Colin and a group of his friends begged to see them perform their cheers. All but one of the girls on the squad refused, knowing full well what the boys were after. But Madonna went on to show them her act, performing cartwheels, and ultimately showing off her red underwear.

Although Madonna was forbidden to go to the movies, she managed to make plans to meet Colin and catch a film. Advanced for his age, Colin had other objectives on his mind when he asked his rebellious classmate to the screening. There was no hesitation when she accepted the young Romeo's invitation. In teenage terms, his goal was to get her alone in the dark and "cop a feel."[37]

"It happened after I persuaded Madonna to go to a spooky movie— *The House of Dark Shadows*," says Colin, as if the incident were yesterday. "She was very well developed for her age and her breasts were her best assets."[37]

From that point on Colin and Madonna would meet on the sly for "make-out sessions." There was a wooded area behind the school that the kids used to call "the swamp."[37] Between classes Madonna and the aggressive McGregor boy would rendezvous.

Up until this point Madonna professes that she was quite a loner. Although she hung out with Carol Belanger, she pretty much stuck to herself. "I never had a group of friends in school," she remembers. "I kept to myself and did what I wanted to do."[3]

Even in high school Madonna sensed there was something more to life, while her classmates plodded through school days and social activities perfectly contented. Her inability to be completely satisfied with high school life made it difficult for young Madonna to identify with most of her peer group. "As far as friendships go, I sort of hung around on the outside of things and befriended [those] who other people thought were the class nerds," she recalls.[13]

In seventh grade, Madonna continued to experiment with the boys. "I remember this girl named Katrina who was really blonde and pretty, and everybody liked her, and her boyfriend started flirting with me."[32] The interaction between Katrina's boyfriend and Madonna led to hard feelings, and eventually Katrina slapped Madonna in front of "everybody."[32]

To this day Madonna feels that she was grossly misjudged. She recalls that her unjustified reputation as school slut made it difficult to make friends. The girls in her class avoided her because of her terrible reputation, while the boys in the class wouldn't date her because it wasn't cool to go out with someone perceived of as a slut. "I was called those names when I was still a virgin," she claims.[38]

In addition to occasionally sneaking off to the movies, there were also school dances that Madonna went to. Moira McFarland recalls going with her to one of the after-school dances. "When she started to dance," says Moira, "everybody cleared off the dance floor and started watching."[23] Madonna's actions were so unrestrained that even though she was only twelve, people around her looked to her as an inspiring, liberating influence. It was to remain one of her most essential charms.

At house parties the kids would bring their favorite dance music singles. Records would spin on the stereo, and Madonna and Carol, and several of their other friends, would give each other dance lessons while Sly and the Family Stone or The Rolling Stones would play. Madonna remembers when she gave her first lesson to a boy. "I was really sexy—right—like stomping, grinding."[19]

Carol Belanger laughingly remembers Madonna as a buxom and strikingly attractive girl: "She teased the boys by going to parties wearing a full-length figure-hugging bodysuit to protect her virginity."[39]

When she was in the eighth grade, thirteen-year-old Madonna made her movie-acting debut. It was a school project, directed by one of her classmates. Filmed with a Super-8 camera, Madonna's role called for her to have an egg fried on her stomach. Even then her performances were deemed to be in questionable taste.

In 1971, the summer between eighth and ninth grade, Madonna went up to Bay City to stay with her grandmother for several weeks. Staying at Grandma's was always a treat for Madonna. While her parents were assured that she was properly chaperoned, Madonna was busy breaking all the rules that her parents laid down. To her, it felt as if she was on her first adult vacation. Describing Grandma, Madonna recalls, "She wasn't an extreme disciplinarian like my parents, so I loved going there."[13]

Another fun aspect of going to spend time in Bay City was that she got to hang out with her uncles. Her mother's brothers were only a couple of years older than her brother Anthony. Not only were they a treat to be with, but they also had their own band. The young girl was immediately impressed with their fun-loving lifestyle, which was so different from the atmosphere she was raised in. Madonna describes her uncles with much fondness. "I was watching my uncles' rock and roll band—wearing tight jeans for the first time in my life. I smoked a cigarette—not too successfully. I started feeling like, 'Yeah, this is it, I'm *cool!*' "[13]

She came back from her sojourn away from her parents and for the first time felt like a real grownup. But her dream was quickly shattered when her stepmother took one look at Madonna in mascara and rouge and told her to her painted face that she looked like a cheap "floozy" and to wash the makeup off before her father saw her. This became a private joke between Madonna and her friend Carol Belanger. Plotting personal revenge, Madonna and Carol decided that if they were going to be branded as "floozies," then they would really play the part to the hilt—at least on film.

Their famous floozy afternoon was staged only because they knew that their parents didn't approve. Madonna says, "We got dressed to the nines. We got bras and stuffed them so our breasts were over-large and wore really tight sweaters—we were sweater-girl floozies. We wore tons of lipstick and really badly applied makeup and huge beauty marks and did our hair up like Tammy Wynette."[13] To this day Carol has the "floozy" snapshots.

Another of Madonna and Carol's revels involved going to church together, dressed in long overcoats—and totally naked underneath. There were also shoplifting competitions to see who could get away with the most merchandise. Three guesses who won. Bingo: Madonna by a landslide!

Madonna's conflicts with her stepmother reached a greater frequency after the girl reached puberty. Joan informed her that she was absolutely forbidden to wear anything during her period except sanitary napkins. "My stepmother said [tampons were] like intercourse," complains Madonna.[18]

Madonna says it was Moira McFarland who showed her how to correctly insert a tampon. Since her stepmother told her not to wear one, she was determined to learn how on her own. The lesson in tampon insertion led to some adolescent same-sex experimentation. In Madonna's *Truth or Dare* film she talked about being manually masturbated by Moira. McFarland also taught Madonna how to properly smoke a cigarette. Even as a teenager, there were few things that Madonna wouldn't try.

In the autumn of 1973 Madonna found herself in a new and more liberal atmosphere. She convinced her parents to allow her to attend public school, Rochester Adams High School. No more Catholic schoolgirl uniforms, and it was a chance to stretch out a bit more and define her own personality. Among the extracurricular activities she became involved in were cheerleading and the drama club.

On the pages of the school's yearbook, the *Highlander,* Madonna is seen as a member of the Junior Varsity cheerleading squad. The caption read: "Can you imagine what life at Adams would have been like without our JV cheerleaders?"[40]

One of the photos of the Junior Varsity cheerleaders shows Madonna and the girls greeting the cheerleading squad from nearby Groves High School. Another shot shows the octet of Adams cheerleaders in a pyramid formation. There in the top row stands Madonna Veronica Louise Ciccone with her flowing, shoulder-length brunette hair. The photos depict a parade of pleated skirts and pom-poms.

She also remembers the little cliques in which high school kids congregate. Madonna didn't identify with any one particular group. The hippies were too lazy, and although Madonna was a cheerleader for a little while, she quickly realized that high school athletes' only interests were sports, drinking, and chasing girls. Somehow it just wasn't Madonna's scene.

That same year she made one of her initial stage appearances, in the "Homecoming" assembly. Whenever there was an opportunity to perform, Madonna participated. "*Cinderella* and *The Wizard of Oz* and *Godspell* and *My Fair Lady*—the ingenue role was always mine."[2] Although she also admits that if there were a need for a bad girl, all eyes would turn to her.

Talent shows represented Madonna's chance to really show people what she was all about: high drama and theatrics. They were also a great outlet for her energy. She would plan the event from concept to costumes. "I would try to get other girls involved, so I could tell everybody what to do and push them around . . . I've always been a control freak," she says.[25]

While she was expanding her creative horizons, the ever-present titillation of the final taboo—sex—loomed overhead. It was at the age of fifteen in her first year of high school, on a cold, windy night in December of 1973, that she went "all the way" with a handsome seventeen-year-old classmate named Russell Long. Madonna liked him because he was older and more mature. He even smoked marijuana. He had longish brown hair and a broad smile, and he drove a light blue 1966 Cadillac, which she loved.

The car, however, was not the scene of the main event. Since, according to Russell, "Madonna wanted her first time to be special," they waited until a particular night when his parents had left town for the weekend.[41] That fateful night the high school couple went to the movies and to a local Rochester burger joint. After finishing their hamburgers, they sat in the eatery finishing their Coca-Colas and stared longingly into each other's eyes. Long confesses that he was wondering how he was going to maneuver getting his date home and into bed.

But he didn't have to maneuver at all because Madonna, always the aggressive one, suggested the two head back to his place. "I was so nervous I couldn't get her bra strap undone," says Russell. But that wasn't a problem either. Madonna undid the strap and helped Russell find what he was looking for. Then, according to Russell, Madonna said, "Do you want to do it or not?"—as though she had decided in advance that this would be the day on which she would lose her virginity.[41]

After that night at Russell Long's parents' house, Madonna would meet her young Lothario with his eight-cylinder steed. According to Long, of all the places that the two of them made love the backseat of his Cadillac was her favorite place.

Shielded from the outside by the steamed-up windows of the Cadillac, Madonna was not inhibited about quickly taking off all her clothes—except her bra and panties. Then she'd curl up in the backseat while Russell took off his shoes and pants. Then the two would talk, cuddle, and, according to Long, write their initials in the steam on the windows. Madonna would talk about how difficult her home life was. How her mother had died at the age of thirty, and how she worried that her brothers and sisters didn't like her.

"She was always saying how she was going to show them—she was going to show everyone. I guess that's why she threw herself into everything at school—cheerleading, dancing, acting, school choir," surmises Long.[41]

Years later, after her song "Like a Virgin" hit Number One, an obvious question Madonna was frequently asked concerned whether or not she mourned the loss of her own virginity. She flippantly replied, "Oh, no. I thought of it as a career move."[3]

Meanwhile, back at Rochester Adams High School, news of Madonna's affair with Russell worked its way through the gossip grapevine. Madonna and Russell's classmates referred to his Cadillac as the "passion wagon."[41]

Another schoolmate, Mark Brooky, remembers that Madonna had "a reputation" around school. "I remember seeing her go up and down the hall," says Brooky—who would avidly watch her. "We used to have a rating system for all the girls, and we had a 'Top Ten,' all of us guys. I think she got a nine out of a possible ten!"[42]

In addition to observing her between classes, Mark recalls catching one of Madonna's early performances. Every year, Rochester Adams High School held what they called Winter Carnival Week. Among the other festivities, the school put on a talent show, in which Madonna participated.

Showing off his yearbook, Brooky explains, "There's a picture of her in one of these where she's dancing. She's got a white thing on, and black knickers, and she's dancing. It has a dumb little caption on it. It was a talent show. I think she sang, and it didn't seem like anyone was impressed. She didn't bomb out, but I don't think that anyone was real impressed. We didn't know that she was going to sell a million records!"[42]

The photo shows Madonna doing a dance onstage in the high school gym. She was wearing black satin knickers, white socks, and on her feet are a pair of Mary Jane dance shoes. The caption that accompanies the photo reads: "Honest, it's really me . . . cross my heart."[40]

The much-talked-about romance between Madonna and Russell didn't last beyond his high school graduation the following spring. However, her passion for performing only grew further. She liked having all eyes centered on her, and she quickly discovered that the more outrageously she behaved or dressed, the more attention she received.

During the same school year she made some decisions about her future. While she enjoyed the dance class she was taking, she realized that she had outgrown it, and needed to get involved with a more challenging and more professional dance program. "When I was in the tenth grade I knew a girl who was a serious ballet dancer," Madonna explains.[28]

Always looking for a way to the next break, Madonna attached herself to the girl, who took her to a ballet class at the Christopher Ballet studio in Rochester. It was there that she would meet the man who was to become her mentor. His name was Christopher Flynn, and he was responsible for shaping Madonna from an ambitious but uncertain girl with raw talent into a uniquely confident performer.

"That's where I met Christopher Flynn, who saved me from my high school turmoil," says Madonna.[28] Flynn's ballet school catered to more serious dancers. At this point, Madonna had only studied jazz, so in order to keep up she had to work twice as hard. Flynn was impressed with her disciplined work ethic.

At first Madonna found Flynn to be very strict, compared to the dance lessons she had been taking. "He was very Catholic and disciplined," is how she describes him.[3]

After several weeks of hard work, however, she realized that it was going to pay off, and she could successfully compete with the other aspiring profesionals in the group.

Flynn claims that he was genuinely impressed by her drive and discipline. He also recalls that she had an indefinable quality that set her apart from the rest of his students. According to Flynn, Madonna was one of the best students he ever taught. "A very worldly sort of woman even as a child."[24]

"I really loved him," says Madonna. Flynn was the first person she'd met who embodied what she thought was an artistic spirit. He complimented her beauty, which few had done before. "I knew I was voluptuous for my age, but I'd never had a sense of myself being beautiful until he told me," she says.[2]

Prior to her dance training, Madonna recalls feeling awkward physically. She simply wasn't comfortable with her body. As she really worked at perfecting her craft, she not only found that her body was in better shape, but that her self-esteem was improving as well. "Before I started feeling devoted to dancing, I didn't really like myself very much," she confesses. "When I started having a dream, working toward that goal, having a sense of discipline, I started to really like myself for the first time."[13]

Her attitude toward, and relationship with, her siblings suddenly ceased to be strained. She was finally enjoying something that she was doing—immensely. At first it was merely a pressure release for her to let off steam. Then, suddenly her outlook and her perspective changed. She grew closer to her brothers (her younger brother even attended dance class with her) although she was still quite competitive with her sisters.

This is not at all to say that Madonna had begun to conform. Quite the contrary. This is the point where she began growing, experimenting, and finding her own signature style—in what she did, how she looked, how she carried herself, and how she dressed. Her high school classmate Mary Conley Belote remembers Madonna's sudden change from varsity cheerleader to artistically temperamented dancer.

In high school everything is measured in popularity. Recalling Madonna's ranking in that department, Mark Brooky says, "As the years progressed there, from a cheerleader as a sophomore, she seemed to be more popular. By senior year, she seemed to be less popular. She cut her hair, and seemed to be more withdrawn."[42] What she was doing was withdrawing from the high school social circle and entering into a whole new dimension of expression that most of her classmates didn't even know existed. Madonna mellowed as high school progressed. She had a goal, and despite the pressures of family, friends, and church, it seemed much more important than anything as superficial as high school popularity. She recalls, "There's a lot of pressure to fit into the group."[28] She didn't give a damn if she fit into any of her high school peer groups. She was too busy plotting her own personal lifestyle renovation.

Even among her ballet classmates, she was blossoming into a unique creation. Most students would wear the standard black leotards and white tights to class, but not Madonna. She had short hair while most girls wore their hair long. She would rip her tights and cut and safety pin her leotard. "Anything to stand out from them and say 'I'm not like you, OK?"[43]

As a junior, Madonna helped to found Rochester Adams High School's Thespian Society. She acted in several skits, and she had a starring role in the troupe's production of *Dark of the Moon*. She was also a member of the "Help-a-Kid" program to tutor younger children. She made sure that she always had a project to throw herself into.

When Madonna turned sixteen, she got her driver's license and her first car—a red Mustang convertible, which her father bought for her.

This opened up all sorts of new avenues of opportunity for the continuing misadventures of Madonna and Carol Belanger. "Sometimes I'd literally put my hand over her mouth to shut her up," says Carol, remembering the day the pair drove over to a nearby lake in Madonna's racy new car. When a group of rough-looking bikers began hurling firecrackers at them, Madonna opened her smart mouth and yelled at them to knock it off. "The next thing I knew one of the biker girls came down and started hitting her in the mouth," says Carol.[24] Madonna went home with a black eye and a sore cheek.

Another one of Madonna's routines involved announcing on Sunday mornings that she and Carol were on their way to church. She would pick up Carol, and they *would* drive to the church—just to grab a church bulletin as evidence that they had been there. They would then proceed to spend the next hour in the local donut shop.

Madonna also remembers journeying to dangerous downtown Detroit to see her first rock concert—David Bowie at Cobo Hall. "Oh, it was the most marvelous thing I'd ever done in my life," she recalls.[9] But when she returned home, she was punished.

Another awakening came via Christopher Flynn, with whom she had become fast friends and who was exposing her to a more so-phisticated world. At first it was just to cultural events. "He educated me; he took me to museums and told me about art. He was my mentor, my father, my imaginative lover, my brother, everything, because he understood me," she says.[2]

As they got to know and trust each other, Flynn told her he was gay, then began to show her a whole new underground world that fas-cinated her. She was introduced to the gay discos of Detroit. "Men were doing poppers [amyl nitrate] and going crazy. They were all dressed really well and were more free about themselves."[29] Madonna had such a presence at the discos that people would simply stand and watch her dance.

"She was always trying to be better, always positive, always filled with urgency, always making the most of it, and she had this tremendous thirst for everything, insatiable," says Flynn.[32]

On one of their trips to downtown Detroit to boogie, Madonna entertained Flynn with a nonstop barrage of "knock-knock" jokes. "I was so caught up I missed my exit, which meant miles and miles of more knock-knock jokes."[32] Among the gay clubs they would frequent were Menjo's and Bookie's on Six Mile Road.

After the clubs, somehow high school dances were never quite the same. French teacher Carol Lintz remembers seeing Madonna in the middle of the dance floor, without a partner. "She'd be in the front of the cafeteria, just really letting loose," says Lintz. "The other kids would walk up to me and say, 'Who's Madonna dancing with?' "[44] When the music would start, Madonna didn't mind dancing alone because it was the music that was important to her, not the social aspect of the dance.

After Madonna had gotten a taste of the exciting outside world, she really knew that she could be somebody. Stoked by the new awareness that she could make positive changes in her life, she also saw that she had the ability within herself to set her dreams in motion. Dancing truly liberated her creative energy. From that point on she made certain she kept her goals lofty. What she really wanted was to be a star. She really wasn't too concerned about what it was that she was going to star in— she could work out those details along the way.

"I wanted to be a movie star," she recalls, "but when you grow up in some hick town in Michigan, there's nothing you can do that will make you feel like you're going to be a movie star."[1] Perhaps it was dancing that would be the vehicle to take her out of Pontiac. Complete with a painter's palette of goals, Madonna took careful inventory of her options.

"I was always the lead in every musical and every play in high school. When I graduated I got the Thespian Award. That's my claim to fame," she says, summing up her high school years. On the other side of the coin, she admits that, "I was a rebel in school. I didn't really fit in. I hung out with all the misfits and freaks that nobody wanted to hang out with."[1]

When Madonna began dancing, the crowd she spent time with was much older. "I felt superior," she says.[3] She belonged in a special world, unlike in high school when she played the outcast. It was obviously time for Madonna to move on, and, she decided, it was dance that was going to be the catalyst to her next step.

Her choir teacher, Tim Lentz, distinctly remembers Madonna. According to him, "She dared to be different."[44]

Nancy Ryan Mitchell was Madonna's counselor at Rochester Ad-
High, and she recommended that Madonna should apply for a scholarship
at the University of Michigan because she was bright and very mature.
The counselor's recommendation on Madonna's application utilized the
adjectives "extremely talented, dedicated, motivated, sparkling personality."[45]

Because of her academic grades, and her moxie, she was indeed
offered a scholarship to study dance at "U of M" in Ann Arbor. This
proved to be her launching pad out of Michigan and the trajectory to
her ultimate target: multimedia stardom.

Mitchell recalls Madonna's drive by explaining, "She knew she was
good and wanted to be famous and would work hard to make it."[45]

While Madonna moved on toward her ultimate metamorphosis, what
became of her childhood friends? Colin McGregor's family moved to
Scotland when he was sixteen. Today he is a successful businessman
in London. Moira McFarland is now Moira Messina and is a housewife
living with her husband and children in Pinehurst, North Carolina. Mark
Brooky is a disc jockey and lives with his wife in Florida. Carol Belanger
still lives in the Pontiac area. Of all her friends from the past, Carol
and Moira are the only ones with whom Madonna maintains occasional
contact.

Russell Long, who was Madonna's first lover, is now married and
has children. Russell drives a truck for United Parcel Service. "I wonder
if he still loves me," Madonna wonders. "He probably does."[18]

According to her, "Ever since I was small I wanted to be the girl
who stole everybody's heart."[20] She was like that in high school, and to
this day Madonna remains obsessed with an ever-thirsty desire for ad-
ulation. By the end of her senior year in high school, the thing she was
most excited about was getting her life further down the path toward her
dreams.

And

of instinct

You

just like an animal.[46]

Can

—Madonna

Dance

I t was the beginning of 1976, and seventeen-year-old, academically accelerated Madonna Ciccone was graduating from Rochester Adams High School a semester early. Continuing her dance classes with Christopher Flynn, a path quickly laid itself out before her like Dorothy's yellow brick road. Almost simultaneously with Flynn's announcement that he was leaving his studio to become an instructor in the dance department at the University of Michigan in Ann Arbor, Madonna was granted her scholarship to the same college. Like Merlin and young King Arthur, the student and her mentor uprooted themselves for their creative reign in a new kingdom.

The move to college killed several birds with a single stone. Besides providing her with valuable training, attending the university pleased Madonna's father and allowed her to leave her hometown and her family behind her. Escaping from a life under her father's thumb excited her, yet she had the security of having Flynn along to challenge, guide, and direct her.

Mr. Ciccone placed a lot of stress on the importance of his children's schoolwork. He wanted them to use their intelligence to get the most out of their lives. As Madonna reflects, "My father never brought me up to get married and have kids. We utilized our intelligence."[22]

Not only did her scholarship represent a fantastic opportunity, it also afforded her the freedom to make several new choices about what she wanted to do with her life. The first thing she eliminated from her existence was the repressive influence of religion. Although Madonna missed her family, leaving home—and Sunday morning church services—wasn't difficult.

In the fall of 1976 Madonna resided in a dormitory room at the U of M's Stockwell Hall. She quickly made friends with several of the other girls in her dance classes, and in order to have spending money she landed a job at Miller's Ice Cream Parlor. She became fast friends with another dance student who scooped ice cream at Miller's, Whitley Setrakian. Also during that year, Madonna became friends with another girl from her dance classes, Linda Alaniz, and took a job as a bar waitress at a local college hangout called Dooley's.

Madonna and Linda would study classical dance by day, and by night they would dance their butts off at Ann Arbor clubs, including the Blue Frogge and the Ruvia. Linda recalls, "We'd dance six hours at school, then go home and eat, then dance another four hours at night. The woman just loved to dance!"[45]

The University of Michigan is known as a party school, and Madonna immediately got into the swing of things. When she got out on the dance floor of a local club, people cleared out of her way as though she were a whirling dervish.

One night while she was boogieing at the Blue Frogge, Madonna spotted a black waiter who looked as if he was more fun than the rest of the patrons. "He was real cute," she recalls, "someone all soulful and funky looking you couldn't help but notice. First time in my life I asked a guy to buy me a drink."[29] The man's name was Steve Bray, and at the time he was also the drummer in a local band.

Madonna didn't realize it at the time, but in Bray she had just met someone who was destined to become a lifelong friend and cohort in music. Footloose and brazen Madonna and even-tempered Bray were destined to become lovers.

During the first semester of her sophomore year, Whitley asked Madonna if she wanted to share an apartment in University Towers. "One of the first things I noticed," says Setrakian of Madonna, "was she really said what was on her mind. We filled needs for each other. I felt like she just needed somebody to accept her, no questions asked."[45]

After Madonna moved into the University Towers apartment with Whitley, they found that they shared a lot in common. They both loved dance, and both read poetry. Madonna was still amid her initial vegetarian kick, and she would live on granola and popcorn. Whitley had her own nickname for her nonconformist roommate. She would refer to her as "my little bowl of bear mush,"[45] a name coined for Madonna's eating habits at the time.

In July 1978 Madonna was one of the students from the University of Michigan's dance department who traveled to Durham, North Carolina, to participate in the annual summer dance festival at Duke University's East Campus. During a break between performances, Madonna stepped outside the auditorium and sat munching granola she had mixed into a carton of Dannon lemon yogurt.

At the time, Richard Maschal was a thirty-four-year-old reporter with the *Charlotte Observer*. Covering the dance festival, he was eager to interview one of the dancers when he stumbled into nineteen-year-old Ms. Ciccone. According to Maschal, "She had a beautiful face, the image, I immediately thought, of a Renaissance madonna. As writers will do, I began composing a story in my head about a dancer as beautiful as a madonna. We sat on a bench, and I asked her name. 'Madonna,' she said." He found the girl to be "remarkably self-possessed for a teenager and incredibly self-absorbed."[47]

"She spoke to me about wanting to quit school in Michigan, and heading for New York to audition for the Pearl Lang dance company," Maschal recalls of his chance meeting with the future pop music siren. She complained to him about the lack of nightlife in Durham and described her tenure as a dance student as "pretty draining and demanding. You spend all your time dancing, every day—day in and day out."[47]

Maschal says it was her facial features that most impressed him; he felt she had the kind of face that belonged in a fresco on a church ceiling: "Round eyes, arched eyebrows, finely drawn mouth—Da Vinci would have loved it."[47]

After she returned to Ann Arbor following the Duke dance festival, Madonna began to formulate a new plan: she was going to blow off college, take the money she saved from her bar tips, and head for New York City to seek her fortune. This was not a plan she arrived at solely by herself; it grew out of seeds that Christopher Flynn had been constantly and consistently planting in her fertile young mind. "He encouraged me to go to New York," Madonna recalls. "He made me push myself."[29]

With Flynn's nurturing encouragement, that very summer Madonna put her ambitious new plan into action. The real stumbling block was her fear of her father's reaction. Could she really toss the scholarship aside and run off to New York City? "I was torn between taking the grant and going to New York," she says, recalling her dilemma at the time. "University meant pleasing my parents and getting money and security."[48] Finally, she figured she had nothing to lose—and everything to gain.

With this new goal in mind, Madonna began to store up her tips from waitressing at Dooley's. She had a book about the New York Ballet Company, and in it she would stash her extra cash. Linda Alaniz remembers Madonna showing her the money she kept in the book for her eventual trip to New York.

After a year and half of college, Madonna announced her plan to her father and stepmother. Predictably, Tony Ciccone totally freaked out when he heard what his oldest daughter was planning. He wanted her to go to college. Dancing, in his mind, was a hobby, not a profession.

It was one of those now-or-never situations. In her mind, if she stuck around Ann Arbor until she graduated she was going to lose her momentum. When she danced, she felt as though she could conquer the world.

"Before I started dancing, I felt really physically awkward," she proclaims, "not comfortable with my body." Dancing satisfied two needs in her life: for mental and physical strength. "I feel superior. I feel like a warrior."[11]

warrior was about to take on Manhattan and the world of
ial dance. Madonna recalls her college days with fondness, but
wnen it was time to leave, she was more than ready to go. She had saved
enough money to purchase a one-way ticket to New York City, and in
spite of how much protesting her father did, she was going. In July 1978
Madonna boarded a plane at Detroit Metropolitan Airport, and she has
never regretted it for a moment. When she boarded the jet—for the first
airplane ride of her life—she basically left Steve Bray and all her other
school friends in the dust.

"Looking back," says Madonna of Bray, "I think I probably did
make him feel kind of bad, but I was really insensitive in those days.
I was totally self-absorbed."[29] Although Steve Bray recognizes that Madonna is talented and a friend, he says, "With her, being polite and
ladylike gets left behind."[49]

Madonna departed from the Wolverine State: next stop Manhattan
Island.

When she got off the plane, she hailed a taxi and instructed the
driver to take her "to the middle of everything."[2] He gladly complied—
and dropped her off in the center of Times Square: neon lights, Broadway
theaters, pimps, hustlers, prostitutes, con men, and porno palaces. At
the time, she had her life savings in her pocket: $35. How far did she
think that amount of money would go?

Madonna was overwhelmed by the tall buildings. Wandering down
Lexington Avenue in her winter coat, suitcase in hand, she met a man
who offered to let her stay in his apartment. While most would hesitate
before moving in with a stranger, Madonna stayed with him for two
weeks. "He showed me where everything was, and he fed me breakfast.
It was perfect."[2]

Like Tennessee Williams's character Blanche DuBois, Madonna
relied on the kindness of strangers. However, her streetcar was named
"ambition," not "desire."

With no means of supporting herself but her looks and pushy
charm—sometimes confused with moxie—Madonna set about looking
for work.

The closest she could come to her much desired big break was
when she auditioned for the prestigious Alvin Ailey Dance Theater. She
didn't end up with a real paying gig, but she did land a work-scholarship,

which basically meant that she could study dance with the third-string company without having to pay them. It sounds impressive, and was inarguably a foot in the door, but there remained one minor flaw: the matter of needing money to buy food with.

Madonna found the largely black, multiracial dance company a fascinating experience. For once she found herself in a room full of people as aggressive as she was herself. "Everyone was Hispanic or black, and EVERYONE wanted to be a star!"[29]

Throughout her first months in New York City, she literally lived from hand to mouth. She somehow knew that she was destined to go places—she just wasn't certain where those places were. "I wasn't worried about not getting anywhere as a dancer," she claims. "I knew I was a decent dancer. It was great."[2] She moved from one apartment to another, eating popcorn for sustenance because it was cheap and filling.

For money, Madonna found herself spinning around town in a veritable revolving door of menial positions. "I was working at all sorts of stupid jobs," she says. "I worked at Dunkin' Donuts, I worked at Burger King, I worked at an Amy's [Greek fast food restaurant]. I had a lot of jobs that lasted one day. I always talked back to people, and they'd fire me. I was a coat-check girl at the Russian Tea Room for a long time. I worked at a health club once for a week."[1]

Concerned for his daughter's well-being, Tony Ciccone paid Madonna a visit once she had gotten herself settled. At the time she was studying with the Ailey company, earning money by selling Dunkin' Donuts, and living alone in a rundown, fleabag walk-up apartment in the East Village on Fourth Street and Avenue B, one of the worst neighborhoods in New York.

When Mr. Ciccone came to visit, he was naturally appalled by his eldest daughter's living arrangements. "The place was crawling with cockroaches. There were winos in the hallway, and the entire place smelled like stale beer," she recalls.[5]

After several months in the Alvin Ailey scholarship program, Madonna won her much sought-after audition with the Pearl Lang company. Lang, a former Martha Graham dancer, had gone off on her own to emulate her slightly darker vision of modern dance. Madonna was disillusioned, however, and found Lang's style to be filled with "a lot of pain and angst."[29]

n, Madonna would go off on her rebellion trip, just to set herself
n the other dancers. She felt as if she had seen the world
compared to the other ballerinas who spent most of their lives in dance
class. "They came from really rich families and bored me," she says.[5]

Unlike the nurturing atmosphere of a progressive Michigan college
campus, New York City is the original asphalt jungle. The highs can
be glitteringly fabulous, but the emotional lows can be devastating.
Madonna soon found that the dance world wasn't exactly sitting around
waiting for the arrival of a hopeful waif in ripped-up safety-pinned
leotards.

Madonna's first few years in New York weren't easy. No money,
no friends, and little work can make the city intimidating. "I'd go to
Lincoln Center, sit by a fountain and just cry. I'd write in my little
journal and pray to have even one friend. I had been used to being the
big fish in the little pond and all of a sudden I was nobody. But never
once did it ever occur to me to go back. Never!"[28] The person she most
closely identified with was the character Holly Golightly, whom Audrey
Hepburn portrayed in *Breakfast at Tiffany's*.

Loneliness was not her biggest problem, however. Lack of money
was. No one who knew Madonna at this time was advised to write her
address and phone number in their phone book in ink, as she seemed
to move every month. She learned not to have too many belongings—
no more than she could carry to wherever it was that she would end up
next. Her lack of funds turned her into a virtual nomad during this era
of her life.

One of the few material possessions that she dragged around from
place to place was a photograph of her mother riding a horse as a young
girl. "It's a lovely picture. I stole it from my father when I left home."[20]
From place to place, she always carried that photograph with her. Today
the photo sits on her dresser in her Hollywood house. It was—and is—
her good luck charm.

It was during this same period that she first started taking her
clothes off for money, as a model. "I used to model a lot for an art
school—the Art Students League," she explains. "At that time I was
dancing, too, so I would dance all day, and go to these drawing classes
at night—just walk in and strip."[1]

She learned to have few qualms about having to resort to nude modeling. "You have to remove yourself from everyone looking at you," she reflectively rationalizes. "It's a job. But I knew that those people were not just looking at me esthetically."[1]

In late 1978 Madonna landed a gig posing for Bill Stone at his studio on West 27th Street. Looking at the photos in Stone's studio, Madonna was impressed to find that in the late 1930s he had photographed dancers from the Ballet Russe de Monte Carlo. Far from pornographic, his photos of nude women were inspired by classic paintings of Botticelli, Titian, and Modigliani.

"She was an accomplished dancer and was very helpful in improvising poses. I was thinking Matisse, the odalisques [female slaves], but she was posing herself, really," Stone distinctly recalls of the twenty-year-old Madonna. "I saw that she was special."[50] When she signed his model release, she wrote, "Madonna." When Stone asked her about a last name, she replied that Madonna would be just fine.

Always obsessed with how people perceived her, Madonna asked the veteran photographer what he thought of her potential as a star. He assured her that she had the bare essentials to possibly make it. Stone can't recall whether he paid her $25 or $50, but he remembers that she was astounded with the kind of money she received. She informed him that she was usually only paid $7 an hour and was pleased to receive more than she expected. Stone expressed interest in possibly photographing her again and inquired what the girl's address was. "Here and there," she replied.[50] Stone didn't see her again, but he never forgot how lovely she was.

The winter of 1978–1979 was typically cold in New York City, and Madonna was in need of money. On February 12 and 14 of 1979 she landed additional nude modeling jobs. This time around she arrived at the studio of Martin H. Schrieber, who taught a course for The New School in Greenwich Village. Calling herself "Madonna Louise," she posed for Schrieber's students, insisting that she be paid in cash, as she didn't have a bank account of her own in which to clear checks. "There was no hesitation on her part—'Here I am. It's no big deal'— that's the way she was. I was fascinated by her," Schreiber recalls.[51]

At the time, Madonna was dating a T-shirt designer named Norris Burroughs. Although they had a fun fling, they realized that neither was the love of their life. One night Norris threw a party to mix all his eclectic friends together. In the back of his head, Norris thought that Madonna might hit it off with a close friend of his named Dan Gilroy. Like most matchmakers, he found that the pairing he put together didn't exactly result in love at first sight, so he decided to give Cupid a bit of a shove.

It seems that Dan wasn't as enthralled with Madonna as Norris had hoped, so mid-party he queried Dan for his opinion of Ms. Ciccone. According to Dan, "She was wearing these clothes that looked like a clown outfit, [and] she seemed sort of draggy, like depressed or something."[52]

Later in the evening, the ever-confrontational Madonna looked into Gilroy's eyes and asked him if he were going to kiss her. From that point on things began to change, and a long-shot chance blossomed into romance. Only a few weeks later, Madonna moved into Dan's place. This wasn't just your run-of-the-mill apartment, as Dan lived with his brother Ed in an abandoned synagogue in the borough of Queens, in an area known as Corona. The Gilroys and Madonna slept in the basement, using the synagogue's meeting place as rehearsal space and recording studio.

Dan and Ed were struggling musicians and sometime comedians. They had a stand-up comedy act they called "The Bil and Gil Show" and a band that eventually became known as "Breakfast Club." It was Dan who was responsible for transforming Madonna from a dancer into a singer/musician. It was also Dan who was to become the first in Madonna's long line of "useful boyfriends." Without him, the whole Madonna phenomenon might never have occurred.

Dan introduced Madonna to the guitar, which may have marked the beginning of the end of her professional dancing career, which didn't seem to be taking off, at least not from a financial standpoint. She began to consider music as a new branch of her directionless fascination with stardom.

Gilroy distinctly remembers Madonna's frustration that she made more money doing nude modeling than anything else she did. She modeled strictly for money and would often complain about it or describe how some painters or photographers would make a pass at her.

Through the Art Students League, Madonna found that one modeling job led to another, and at one point she was getting a couple of jobs a week. Some of the photo sessions yielded shots that she was quite happy with—she even presented a collection of them to Dan and composed a poem to go along. The poem spoke about Chinese women, how some had bound feet and some had feet that were free. "Maybe it was her way of saying that she was free and liberated," Gilroy surmises.[53]

Madonna and Dan's relationship was just taking off when a major hiatus interrupted. Madonna was forever scouring the trade papers— *Show Business, Backstage,* and *Variety*—for the casting notices. One day in early 1979 an advertisement caught her eye.

"I saw this ad in the newspaper for this French singing star, Patrick Hernandez. He had this record called 'Born to Be Alive.' His record company [Columbia] was trying to put together an act to go on this world tour with him, and they wanted girls to sing backup vocals and dance. It was going to be this big gala performance. I thought this would be great, I'd be dancing and singing and travel around the world—I'd never been out of America. So, I went to the auditions, and after they were over they said they didn't want me for Patrick Hernandez, they wanted to bring me to Paris and make ME a star."[1]

When she explained what was mapped out for her to Dan, she couldn't believe that someone had finally noticed her. Figuring that this was her big break, Madonna packed her bags and headed off to Paris with producers Jean Claude Pallerin and Jean Van Lieu. The plan they laid out for her seemed like a dream come true. "They promised me anything. They said, 'Come to Paris, we'll give you everything you want. You'll live like a queen, we'll give you a vocal coach and you'll decide what direction you want to go in. I did live like a queen and they did give me anything I wanted. It was the only time I lived comfortably my entire life."[1]

Instead of promising her the moon and delivering nothing, they made good on all their financial and material promises. They flew her to Paris, where she worked with a vocal coach and a dance teacher. She lived in an apartment they provided and was chauffeured from place to place. In a short period of time, Madonna went from struggling in New York City to living in the lap of luxury in Paris. Her life was like a dream.

However, the dream began to turn sour. In spite of the money she earned, the food she ate, the liquor she drank, and the security of having a cockroach-free roof over her head, she found that she was merely window-dressing for the Hernandez entourage. Madonna was given everything but what she desired the most: the center spotlight.

"I missed my friends and I missed struggling," she explains. "I was used to really working hard and they wanted to spoil me and they wanted me to dress a certain way. So they dragged me to restaurants and no one would speak English to me. So once again I was playing the part of a rebel. I didn't want to do anything they wanted me to do. I gave my money away. I hung around with lowlifes, I rode around on motorcycles all the time. I did everything I could to be bad. I kept saying, 'When are you going to do something with me?' And, they were busy with Patrick. Everytime I complained they gave me money."[1]

While Patrick Hernandez ultimately turned out to be a one-hit wonder, disco was a huge international craze at the time, and the song "Born to Be Alive" was his entree to several top nightclub performances around the globe. Madonna accompanied the Hernandez troupe to Tunisia and to several hot spots in Europe, so the whole experience gave the naïve girl from Pontiac, Michigan, a taste of what the world had to offer.

Thousands of struggling would-be actresses, singers, and models would have just given up the struggle right there. Not Madonna. She wanted fame *and* power, and she was determined to have it on her own terms. For her rebellion she pierced her ears and put safety pins in the holes. She ran all over town with a pack of hooligan Vietnamese boys, on the backs of their motorcycles.

For Madonna it was a fabulous adventure, but it wasn't long before she grew tired of it. "I never signed a contract, so I wasn't obligated to stay there. So I waited to see what would happen, and meanwhile I was starting to write a lot—lyrics and stuff, but I didn't really have an idea of what direction I was going to go in musically. I didn't know how to play an instrument," she remembers.[1] She was beginning to feel like a squashed cabbage leaf. She wasn't happy playing Eliza Doolittle to anyone's Henry Higgins.

After six months, she suddenly announced to Pallerin and Van Lieu that she was going home for a brief visit. They purchased a plane ticket for her and chauffeured her to the airport. To avoid suspician, she simply left everything she had behind—and never returned.

While in Paris she stayed with Mr. and Mrs. Jean Claude Pallerin. Mrs. Pallerin recalls, "Madonna wanted only one thing—to be a star."[54]

Regularly, Madonna would receive letters from Dan Gilroy. "His letters were so funny," she recalls. "He really made me feel good . . . he was my saving grace."[29]

As soon as she got off the plane from Paris, Madonna headed back to Dan Gilroy and the synagogue. She was anxious to resume her affair with him, and she was determined to move full speed ahead toward becoming a musician, singer, actress—or all of the above.

In her absence, the brothers Gilroy had been forging ahead with their synagogue-based, experimental rock and roll band. Dan began teaching Madonna how to play a myriad of musical instruments. Retooling her dreams of stardom, Madonna began to fantasize about becoming a singer. Together, she and Dan and Ed, plus an ex-dancer named Angie Smit, worked at creating a group and a sound. Madonna fondly refers to this period of creative development as "my intensive musical training" and one of the happiest of her life. While doting on her, Dan Gilroy made Madonna feel special and loved.

Ultimately the group featured Angie on bass, Ed on guitar, with Madonna and Dan switching back and forth on the drums and vocals. While alternating roles in the band, eventually everyone tried everything in a futile effort to find any real musical success as a unit.

While the band was polishing its repertoire, Madonna got busy on the phone, trying to get the group some work. She would begin early in the morning, coffee in hand, calling everyone from the record stores to potential managers.

She had left town just six months ago as a wannabe dancer and part-time nude model; now Madonna was suddenly set on becoming a musician, singer, and songwriter. Gilroy recalls how hard she worked, practicing the drums up to five hours a day. "She was a dancer and she had a sense of the beat."[53]

Ambitious Madonna dove right in and took control of the group's future. She spotted Dan's band as a possible vehicle for her own aspirations. "I was just a lot more goal-oriented and commercial-minded than they were. I wanted to know everything they knew, because I knew I could make it work to my benefit," Madonna recalls.[29]

For immediate money, Madonna got back into modeling nude for various artists and photographers. One of her steadiest employers was Anthony Panzera, an artist and painter who also teaches art in Manhattan. He would regularly employ nude models for his classes, as well as for his own paintings. At the time he had his own studio in a loft on West 29th Street. It was in an area of town known as the flower district, due to the heavy concentration of plant and flower shops. From the summer of 1979 to the fall of 1980, Panzera employed Madonna as his model on an ongoing weekly basis, paying her the standard seven-dollars-per-hour rate. Their year of working together as artist and model yielded dozens of nude sketches and drawings, and one grand masterpiece.

"I did a whole series of drawings on her, and a painting," explains Panzera. "I teach figure drawing at Hunter College, and so I get models up there all the time, and at the time I also had my studio in New York. I had a small group that would meet every Thursday night, and then another group that came on Friday mornings. So, the man who was booking models for me—Robert Speller, a model booker for Parsons School of Design—sent Madonna to me. I liked her, we got along well, and we proceeded to work on these projects. She worked for me for about a year—almost every Friday."[55]

Panzera really enjoyed the work they did together. "The thing that impressed me most," he says, "was the fact that she was working very hard. She was involved with one or two little bands that she had going, and she would work hard at practicing. She would practice in the evenings, sometimes late at night, and she managed to get to work for me the next morning at nine and be just as energetic. She had a lot of energy, I thought."[55]

After he had sketched her for several weeks, Panzera was inspired to tackle a larger project. "I did one painting of her which took us a couple of months," he recalls. "It's a classic nude pose. It's based on a painting by the French nineteenth-century painter, Ingres. She has this turban on her head. I got the idea to do the painting from a series of drawings we did. I did a series of sibyl drawings—the five sibyls from the Sistine [Chapel] ceiling—because her face was so flexible. She'd take a pose, and she'd look completely different. The next time she'd change positions. So that suggested these sibyl drawings, and there were five of those."[55]

He explains, "The sibyls were prophets that were basically in the classical world—Greece or Italy. They are spread out on the Sistine ceiling—the sibyls and the prophets juxtapose each other. What made me think of them was a famous drawing called 'The Libyan Sibyl' by Michelangelo. It's kind of a back view of a figure holding up a book, and you see the face in profile, and that figure is wearing a turban. When we were playing around with these, I had this bolt of cloth that she was wearing around her waist, and around her head, it suggested this series of drawings."[55]

While she was posing as a sibyl, Madonna would talk to Anthony about her aspirations for Breakfast Club. He remembers that she pinned a lot of hopes on the band. "She invited me to a couple of little gigs," says Panzera. "There were some bars along Sixth Avenue that she worked at, and she basically was working hard at trying to put something together, to get a record out."[55]

As the months went on, Madonna felt more and more comfortable with Panzera—and in time, in their conversations, she would open up to him, talking honestly and directly about the path she wanted her life to take. "She would have been in a vulnerable state," he recalls of his ambitious young model. "One is vulnerable when one is sitting there stark naked. So it sounded more like her ambitions and her dreams of what she wanted to do with her life were in the forefront of her mind. I could sense that there was a real determination there."[55]

Stoked by her Parisian fling, and determined to leave no stone unturned in her desperate quest for artistic fame, Madonna continued scouring *Show Business, Backstage*, and *Variety* for casting calls. Three weeks after she returned to America she spotted one that looked interesting, and she promptly wrote a reply on a lined yellow legal pad.

This particular want ad had been placed in the newspaper by an aspiring young filmmaker by the name of Stephen Jon Lewicki. He had decided to take his Super-8 movie camera, round up an unpaid cast, and make an experimental avant-garde movie—on a shoestring budget. Ultimately it became the underground film entitled *A Certain Sacrifice*. Of his original plot concept and the resulting finished project Lewicki recalls, "I started off with the idea of human sacrifice, and worked back to Madonna!"[56] Sound bizarre? It was.

Describing the ad that he placed in the papers, Lewicki explains, "I do remember I was looking for a dark-haired woman, 'dominatrix-type.' I think I said it, I don't remember exactly, but I was at least hinting at that if I didn't say exactly 'dominatrix.' Plus, exotic dancers and miscellaneous other characters and a middle-aged man. Madonna sent me a letter and photographs."[56]

The letter, written in July of 1979 read in part:

Dear Stephen:

I was born and raised in Detroit, Michigan, where I began my career in petulance and precociousness. By the time I was in the fifth grade, I knew I either wanted to be a nun or a movie star. Nine months in a convent cured me of the first disease. During high school, I became slightly schizophrenic, but I couldn't choose between "class virgin" or the other kind. Both of them had their values as far as I could see. When I was fifteen I began taking ballet classes regularly, listening to Baroque music, and slowly but surely developed a great dislike of my classmates, teachers, and high school in general. There was one exception, and that was my drama class. For one hour every day, all the megalomaniacs and egotists would meet to compete for roles and argue about interpretation. I secretly adored when all eyes were on me, and I could practice being charming or sophisticated, so I would be prepared for the outside world ... [she goes on to explain college and her Paris adventure].

...I came back to New York. I've been here three weeks now working with my band, learning to play the drums, taking dance classes, and waiting for my 20th birthday ... is that all?

—MADONNA CICCONE
Height: 5' 4½"
Weight: 102
Hair: Brown
Eyes: Hazel
Birthdate: August 16, 1959[57]

She was truthful about being a megalomaniac and an egotist, but she conveniently fibbed about her age and birthdate—by one year. In the letter, Madonna enclosed three photographs of herself. Two of the photos were standard 3 × 5-inch color prints. One of these depicted Madonna in a pink-striped leotard with her arms raised as though she were doing a dance routine. Another was an 8 × 10 black and white full body shot of Madonna as an innocent twenty-year-old brunette with short-cropped brown hair. It was the second 3 × 5 color snapshot, however, that clinched the deal, hands down. The color shot was of Madonna sitting on the seat of a New York City public transport bus, applying bright red liquid lipstick with one of her fingers. The way her finger teasingly brushed across her pursed lips aroused Lewicki's curiosity. He found it sexually suggestive without being lewd.

He says, "The picture of her, where she's putting lipstick on on the bus, really grabbed my attention. I took one look at it—and I had seen literally two hundred trashy eight-by-tens, so-called 'professional' headshots—and they were, like, girls from New Jersey trying to be actresses, who, just by looking at the photographs, had absolutely no talent. Or, if they did, it was not apparent."[56]

While sorting through the package from Ciccone, Lewicki recalls, "I took one look at the picture of Madonna, and then I read the letter, which was a very revealing, very vulnerable kind of letter, and it was the most personable communication that I got from anybody. She gave me her life story in two pages, handwritten, which is pretty amazing! It just seemed like it was a fated kind of thing. She must have been pretty curious to have written a two-page letter that was that revealing."[56] Ironically, the mention of her birthday also piqued his interest in the would-be actress, as his birthday was also August 16th.

With that, he telephoned her and arranged for a meeting in Washington Square Park, which was to become one of the locations for the film. The aspiring actress he met that afternoon had never acted before, with the exception of having appeared in talent shows and high school plays back in Michigan. Yet, she had a snotty and self-confident attitude about who she was.

"Madonna thinks that everybody's impressed with her," Lewicki contends, recalling his first observations that day in 1979. "Her impression of the world is—'The world is impressed with me!' And that's how she views things. On one hand, I was impressed with her. I was looking for something very specific, and she was exactly what I was looking for, this kind of nasty, sexually charged—at the same time vulnerable—female. On one hand, it was kind of a fantasy that I had at the time. At the same time I immediately got the impression from Madonna that there was a lot more trouble to that than meets the eye."[56]

Lewicki immediately decided to cast her in the role of Bruna, the vengeful dominatrix. The movie was filmed in October of 1979, and again in November of 1981. Those two months, and the two-year gap that separated them, represent the periods when Lewicki had enough spare cash to invest in the film. Although he had the central plot down, the script was written as he went along.

Another aspiring actor, Jeremy Pattnosh, played the lead character, Dashiel. His role was that of a misfit who came from a hostile family and found it impossible to get along with anyone in the preppy Ivy League college he attended. Hitchhiking to New York City, frustrated, Dashiel wanders into Washington Square Park, where he meets and instantly falls in love with Bruna.

In her first frames in the film, Madonna is seen frolicking in a fountain in the park, looking as if she is giving the camera her impression of Martha Graham entering a wet T-shirt competition. Clad in a red T-shirt, her wet brown hair hangs in a stringy fashion, and in the sequence that unfolds, she and Pattnosh make out while the dirty New York City fountain water spills down on them.

The next scene, which is set in a seedy diner, introduces the viewer to the villain of the film, the bigoted Raymond Hall, played by Charles Kurtz. The scene, which establishes the obnoxious personality of Raymond Hall, seems to go on forever. Several scenes that follow feature much too much dialogue and far too little action.

The hour-long film's most interesting scene is some sort of bizarre theater rehearsal/sex orgy in which a man, a woman, and a drag queen physically seduce an innocent young girl. Guess who plays the innocent young girl? Madonna—naturally. In the course of the scene she bares her breasts and achieves multiple orgasms with her proclaimed "family of lovers." The scene itself mainly consists of a lot of groping and heavy breathing (which is far less sexual than Madonna's controversial 1990 "Justify My Love" video).

After her multiple-orgasm spectacular, we find Madonna trying to explain to Jeremy that she is in love with him. The dilemma this entails is having to explain her infatuation to her family of lovers.

"They idolize me . . . " Madonna confesses. ". . . I can't get out [of the group sex scene]." Madonna's best line in the whole film comes when she asks, "Do you think for once that any lover of mine could be tame? It's not possible!" She adds, explaining of her family of lovers, "They're like irritated hornets, and they want to sting!" It's a remarkably subtle scene, as Madonna plays a warm, vulnerable role with a degree of candid honesty. Odd to think that later in her film career, as the stakes grew higher, she often appeared on camera as more awkward and stiff.

As the plot progresses, the villain Raymond Hall maliciously derides Dashiel, causing Dashiel to lose his apartment. He is then reduced to residing on a park bench. In a confrontational scene in the scuzzy diner we find Madonna as Bruna, making out with Dashiel, while Raymond Hall argues with the waitress behind the counter. When Bruna excuses herself and goes into the diner's bathroom she is cornered and raped by Raymond. Crying and screaming hysterically, Bruna/Madonna emerges from the bathroom, her face smeared with theatrical blood. Dashiel vows with vengeance, "He will pay."

Enlisting the aid of Bruna's family of lovers, Bruna and Dashiel hijack a black Cadillac stretch limousine and proceed to track down Raymond Hall. Cornering Hall in the doorway of a sleezy porno theater, Madonna ad-libs the line "He's scummier than any scum!" Kidnapping Hall, the vigilantes proceed to the Brooklyn Bridge for the grand finale to the film: a human sacrifice musical number. While dismembering Raymond Hall, the family of lovers, Bruna, and Dashiel sing the rock and roll sacrifice song, "Raymond Hall Must Die Today."

According to Lewicki, Madonna's band partner from Breakfast Club, Angie Smit, was featured in the dismemberment sequence. "Angie came with Madonna," he recalls. "She played one of the sex slaves. Madonna and Angie had a really intense relationship, almost like sisters/ mother-daughter/lover or something. It was a very complicated relationship, very tight. They would walk together and chew gum at the same time! There was just a real closeness, intensity, about the relationship, and I don't know anything about what was going on. They were doing the Breakfast Club thing while I was doing this movie. As a matter of fact, I went to see Madonna a couple of times at different venues. That's when she was playing with Angie, and Dan Gilroy, and his brother Ed."[56]

The aspiring filmmaker says there was a nice sense of camaraderie on the set of the film, which was a big experiment for everyone involved. It was kind of like one of those Judy Garland–Mickey Rooney "I've got a barn, let's put on a show!" situations. "There was no attitude around the set," recalls Lewicki. "We just did this thing, got out the Super-8 camera and filmed it, and the batteries would go, and I wouldn't have any extra batteries, and Madonna would shout, 'Goddamn it, Stephen, can't you keep extra batteries!?!' "[56]

Through it all, Lewicki knew instinctively that he had struck gold when he signed Madonna for the female lead. He says, "She had energy; she had charisma. She's got these sparkling eyes. At the time she had this dark brunette hair that was very attractive. She was a very appealing, very sexual person. She works well on film, and I knew that instantly. It was just an immediate thing."[56]

Lewicki had an obvious crush on Madonna, but they behaved like friendly adversaries more than friends. He recalls with fondness an afternoon in Battery Park, eating blueberry yogurt out of Madonna's ear. "That woman has more sensuality in her ear than most women have anywhere on their bodies." Of her acting talent and their sparring friendship, he explains, "She was totally undeveloped, and I was totally undeveloped, so we kind of had this sort of pissy attitude toward each other. We'd kind of insult each other a little bit along the way."[56]

Stephen had enough money to shoot most of the movie in October of 1979, but midway into the filming, his bank account fell to the empty mark. The most important scene that was missing was the sequence in which Bruna is raped in the diner bathroom. Since none of the actors had been paid for their initial work on the film, the company just dispersed for the time being as Lewicki struggled to scrape together enough cash to finish his dream film project. This wasn't the end of Lewicki's interaction with Madonna, it was merely a pause in the friendship.

Meanwhile, back at the synagogue, work continued on the development of the band Breakfast Club and Madonna's music. Madonna knew from an early age that she wanted to perform, but never specifically in what form. That was quite evident during this developmental period. Increasingly, in this her second year since dropping out of college, her interests began to focus more and more on music.

Madonna continued to do occasional modeling, while Dan and Ed both held down day jobs. "They would go to work every day, and I would stay there. I lived like a hermit for a year, I didn't leave Queens. I'd play drums for four hours. They taught me basic chord progressions on piano. As soon as I learned to play guitar a little bit, songs came out of me. I don't know where they came from, it was like magic. I'd write a song every day. I said, 'Wow, I must be meant to do this.' I stopped taking dance classes."[1] Madonna claims that once she got into a songwriting mode, the music started pouring out of her like crazy.

She began to become obsessed with the idea of writing and performing her own songs. With what little musical knowledge she had, she found that she thirsted for more. As she understood more and more about music, she wrote more and more songs. "I played the first things that came out of me," she recalls.[28]

During the year that Madonna spent living with the Gilroys, it was back to her old ways of pinching pennies. Having sampled what it was like to be wined and dined in Paris didn't erase her basic survival instinct. "One time we were on our hands and knees, looking for loose change to buy a few potatoes," recalls Dan.[53] Living from hand to mouth never seemed to dampen her spirits, it only served to make her stronger.

The Gilroys, Madonna, and Angie rehearsed and rehearsed, and eventually, through their mutal contacts, landed a couple of scattered engagements. However, they couldn't seem to get constant work. The band members felt they were playing pretty well, but the gigs were few and far between. When they did have paying jobs, they had to split the money four ways, so it never amounted to much.

For a while, Madonna's relationship with Dan went along nicely. Dan recalls that they had fun together, and that Madonna loved to go out to the dance clubs. For Madonna, Dan represented boyfriend, lover, teacher, and mentor. However, like all of her relationships with "useful boyfriends," the relationship was not destined to last.

Within the structure of the group, Madonna's main competition came from Angie, who—by virtue of her blonde hair and her appearance—garnered a great deal of the on-stage attention. "When we would play our gigs," Dan explains, "Angie always dressed really sexy with see-through clothes, and she moved sensuously onstage."[53] Madonna took note of the attention Angie garnered with her blonde hair and sexy moves, eventually imitating her style.

Although Angie was a lousy bass player, more people stared at her from the audience than those who focused on Madonna. This began to piss her off, as she wanted to be the center of attention. One of Angie's most famous outfits consisted of strings of beads strung together like a section of chain-link fence. Madonna, still ensconced behind the drums, felt driven to do something to get more attention. To keep harmony in the group, Dan devised a plan. Madonna would play drums for most of the set, and then she would come out front and belt a couple of songs of her own. She wanted to sing more often, but the band vetoed this. So Madonna walked out the door, leaving Dan and the band behind her.

Madonna had gotten a taste of what it was like to sing lead vocals on the stage of a loud rock club, and something seemed to click. She knew exactly what she had to do—she had to start a band of her own. The only difference was that this time around, she had to be the un-disputed star.

Five

All my boyfriends have turned out to be very

Boy

helpful to my career, even if that's not the

Toy

only reason I stayed with them.[58] —*Madonna*

Knowing when to leave is an instinct Madonna learned to employ with masterful aplomb. It is an intuitive reflex that she would exercise again and again. Case in point: her relationship with Dan Gilroy. When the romance was over, and she had learned all she could from him, it was time to move on to bigger stakes.

"I missed her very much," recalls Gilroy.[29] But he knew that someone with her drive would eventually make it.

During this era of her life, as an unknown commodity in New York City, circa 1980–1981, she spent much of her time crashing on friends' sofas. "I lived off the good graces of other people," is how she described this particular period of literally sleeping around town.[59]

At one point she befriended the celebrated graffiti artist Keith Haring. His living room was one of the places in which Madonna occasionally took refuge. Andy Warhol reported in his infamous diary, "Keith said that when Madonna was staying at his apartment, sleeping on his couch, the *stories* he could write about the people she had sex with."[60]

She continued to keep her weekly appointments with Anthony Panzera, posing nude for him every Friday at his studio on West 29th Street. In his appointment book and on model release forms, he has records of Madonna's changing addresses and notations of the seven-dollars-per-hour rate for which she posed.

"At one point I was living in New York and eating out of garbage cans on the street," she recalls of this particular period when she was "squatting" in vacant buildings like a common baglady.[15] Surviving off the streets like a homeless waif only served to strengthen her determination to make her dreams come true. It was only months before that she was being wined and dined in Paris. As the winter of 1980 began, Madonna found herself searching for abandoned offices in which to huddle for warmth.

She found a commercial loft in the garment district that was normally used for offices or as a warehouse. "There was no hot water. There wasn't even a fucking shower!"[61] Although Gilroy and Madonna had broken up, she would often visit his loft for conversation and a hot shower.

If she was going to position herself as a singing star, she first had to put together a band. Utilizing her unabashed bisexual charm and her flirtatious communication skills, Madonna got on the phone and pulled together her own musical group. One of the first calls she placed was to Michigan—to her old boyfriend Steve Bray. Pleasantly surprised to hear from her, Steve quickly discovered that the phone call from Madonna wasn't to tell him that she missed him and loved him—it was because she needed something from him. Madonna wanted Bray to take musical control of the band. She recognized that she wasn't an experienced enough musician to do the job. Bray left for New York the following week.

There is a converted building in New York City's garment district, not far from Macy's in Herald Square, known as the Music Building. At the time it consisted of twelve floors of studios, filled with musicians—literally trying to get their acts together. Beside Madonna were a host of other bands including the System, the Dance, and Nervus Rex. During the day, the building was a spawning ground of musical creativity.

Ever-observant Madonna had a good eye for spotting who was going to ultimately accomplish something, and who was not. While she felt affection for and camaraderie with the members of the other bands, she says, in a quick-to-judge fashion, "I thought they were all lazy."[29]

Of the Music Building group, only Madonna and the System really accomplished anything major. The System scored with a late-eighties hit called "Don't Disturb This Groove," and Madonna of course became the ultimate female pop icon. However, at that time she was still eyeing wastebaskets for uneaten pizza crusts.

According to Bray, she stood out from the crowd even then. This was both good and bad for Madonna personally. "I think there was a lot of resentment of someone who's obviously got that special something," he says. "She had trouble making friends."[29]

Like Madonna's address, the name of her band was ever-changing. At one point they were known as "The Millionaires," and for a while they were called "Modern Dance." According to Ms. Ciccone, "I wanted just 'Madonna,' [but] Steve thought that was disgusting."[29] To avoid sacrilege, yet have her own personal moniker as the group's handle, she settled for "Emmy," which was a nickname Dan Gilroy had given her.

"She was playing really raucus rock and roll," remembers Bray, "really influenced by The Pretenders and The Police. She used to really belt."[29]

The Music Building was a comfortable place to be. It was such a hotbed of potential creative energy that Madonna enjoyed being there. Little did she suspect that she would soon be spending more time there than she had bargained for. With no money for rent, eventually Madonna took up residence in one of the rehearsal rooms. She would hang out until everyone else left for home, and she would find a warm corner to curl up in. One cold winter's night, while squatting in one of the building's loft spaces, she accidently set it on fire.

In order to keep warm, she had plugged in electric space heaters around the piece of carpet on which she slept. When she woke up in the middle of the night, she was surrounded by fire. In an effort to squelch the flames, she poured water on the burning space heaters, which made the situation worse. In order to save herself from certain demise, she grabbed a few essentials and headed for the Music Building, where she set up yet another bed.

While Madonna and Steve, and their new band, Emmy, were playing dates at avant-garde rock clubs, they were virtually living hand-to-mouth. "We shared our rehearsal loft with another band, so they practically paid the rent for us. . . . Steve and I slept between amplifiers. We budgeted what little money we had to about one dollar a day. . . . With our dollar we'd get some yogurt and peanuts. . . . When we'd run out of money, I'd pass by the garbage can in the lobby of the Music Building, and if it smelled really good . . . I'd open it up, and if I was lucky, there would be french fries that hadn't been eaten."[15]

What Madonna needed the most was a manager who believed in her talent. Someone to invest time and energy into the business side of things, so that Madonna could concentrate on the creative end of things. Enter: Camille Barbone.

"Madonna says she's stepped on a lot of bodies to get where she is. I'm one of those bodies," claims Camille,[62] who has asserted that their relationship was more than just that of client and manager. Camille claims she was used emotionally to benefit the singer's climb to the top of the music business.

Says Camille Barbone, "Madonna loves beautiful women, and she is into anyone sexually—male or female—who is beautiful."[37] She especially recalls the night she and Madonna went to see Tina Turner perform at The Ritz on East 11th Street. During Tina's performance Madonna stood transfixed next to the stage just staring at those famous legs.

Madonna would call all over town—to managers, agents, record companies, club owners—but no one would return the calls of the then unknown.

When she met Camille, however, Madonna decided to turn the tables. This time she was going to be in control of the situation. Camille, a shrewd professional with an eye for talent, was obviously impressed by the young girl from the moment she laid eyes on her, and Madonna played the situation for all it was worth.

"One day there was a knock at my office door, and it was Madonna," Camille distinctly remembers. "She wanted me to listen to her tape. . . . There was something about her that was sensational. . . . She needed money immediately. I gave her some. She wasn't shy about asking for more money after that."[63]

Once she met Camille, Madonna's days of searching the wastebaskets for uneaten french fries were over. The next thing she knew, Camille had signed her to a management contract and moved her to a spacious Upper West Side apartment.

"What struck me most . . . was her extraordinary beauty, her star quality, her sexuality, and her sense of dignity," recalls Barbone.[36] Madonna also knew how to use her looks to get what she wanted, and she flirted with Camille.

"Madonna has a really nice body and she's proud of it," says Barbone. "She sweats profusely while she is performing. . . . She'd rip off her clothes, throw me a towel and say, 'Towel me off.' "[64]

According to Camille, "Madonna and I share the same birthday, August 16th. . . . For her twenty-second and my thirtieth birthday we went to the beach and I made a lobster dinner . . . I told her what a big star she was going to be, how special she was and that I did love her very much. . . . We drove back to New York hugging."[64]

Things accelerated very quickly, and before long it was Madonna who was in a position of power. As she had done time and time again, she learned how to get someone else to do what she wanted. At first it was Camille who had rescued the seemingly helpless singer from the gutter, but before long it was Madonna who had the unsuspecting manager eating out of her hand.

"She seduced me psychologically," admits Camille. "After that, I put her first, which was my downfall."[63]

Professionally, Camille fired Madonna's "lousy" band, and tried to put the girl on the right track. As Madonna tells it, "I had a band called Emmy when I came across this manager who told me to forget all this adolescent band crap."[5] Camille hired first-rate studio musicians to accompany her, and she encouraged Madonna to write her own songs, but in the long run, the two had different ideas about the direction of Madonna's career. Things only became more and more complicated after that.

Part of their professional agreement involved several rules that Camille laid down. One of the first things she insisted upon was that Madonna not sleep with any of the members of the band. When Madonna had an affair with the band's drummer, Bob Riley, a lot of stress was put on the working relationship of the band. At first Madonna denied sleeping with Bob, then in a sudden turnabout she told Camille she wanted him fired—and replaced by Steve Bray. In an effort to retain her position of authority, Camille had the unpleasant task of canning Bob. After she fired him, the band was told that if they were to fool around with Madonna, they, too, would be canned.

At that point Madonna and her manager had a blowout fight over her behavior. It was at this point that Camille realized Madonna was out of control. "I knew I had created a monster who would turn on me."[63]

Madonna resents authority figures, and she loves to play mind games with them. Camille recalls another of Ms. Ciccone's sexual antics, involving a female friend. "A dancer called Janice would come to town and they would hang out together," says Barbone. "They used to sit in the back of my car and just kiss. Often before Madonna or Janice would go to bed with a man, they'd put him through a test. They would kiss each other in front of him."[62]

When Camille's teenage cousin, Peter, came to see one of Madonna's shows, another scene ensued. Madonna focused all of her attention on Peter, and he was fascinated. After the show, the two had a few minutes alone in her dressing room. When Camille returned, the two were kissing. To this day Peter hasn't forgiven his cousin for thwarting his one opportunity to sleep with Madonna.

Meanwhile, Madonna fell head over heels for a musician named Ken. When Madonna found out that Ken was seeing other women she threw a tantrum. Consulting Camille on everything from sex to contraceptives, she asked how she could get Ken to do what she wanted him to. Camille suggested he might not stray if she didn't openly flirt with so many other men. Madonna, needless to say, couldn't be bothered with her advice.

Spurned, Camille used to watch Madonna flirt with dozens of men, many of whom Madonna slept with. According to Camille, Madonna had standard ways to hook men like they were fish. "Do you want to stay after rehearsal and play a little music?" she would ask invitingly. After that she would ask, "Why don't you take me for a drink?" The final ploy would begin with, "You have great lips. Why don't you kiss me?"[62] Camille claims that Madonna's siren antics virtually always worked.

In spite of her flirtatious flings with countless men, the working relationship between Madonna and Camille went on for almost two years. Finally, stylistic differences split them apart. According to Madonna, "She wanted me to do Pat Benatar–like rock. I was trying for a more funky sound, black stuff."[5]

Madonna and Camille had vastly differing ideas about the future star's image. "We split not too amiably," Madonna recalls.[5] In one of their last arguments, Camille realized she would never be able to satisfy Madonna. Unfazed, Madonna replied, "I always want more. That's me. I'm a bitch and you are a bitch, but we work well together."[63]

Realizing that she had gotten onto the next step of her career via Camille, it was again time for Madonna to move on. At the time Madonna was heavily influenced by the music she heard on the radio, on the streets, and in the clubs—dance music. She wanted to create music that would be played in clubs and that people would want to dance to.

Right after her split with Camille, disillusioned, Madonna broke up the rock band they had assembled. She and Steve Bray stuck together, and she started writing songs in the "urban contemporary" genre, as personified at the time by the New York radio station WKTU.

Another consequence of the professional break with Camille meant that Madonna was back on her own for living quarters. She immediately headed down to the East Village, an area that is a strange dichotomy of seedy drug dens and slums and a young hip-hop urban arts and music scene. In addition to Keith Haring, Madonna befriended several other young creators of new wave art there, including the graffiti artist who calls himself Futura 2000 and a young gay graphic artist, Martin Burgoyne.

Her living situation continued to evolve and change—almost monthly. She ended up losing one East Village apartment when Futura 2000 spray-painted his name on the walls. At another point she moved into a tiny apartment adjacent to Martin Burgoyne's pad on the Lower East Side. When Madonna's apartment was vandalized by neighborhood kids, she fled to a building on East 13th Street, which was reportedly Abbie Hoffman's old digs. Two days later, Burgoyne's apartment was not only ransacked, it was strewn with voodoo symbols: chicken droppings and blood. He quickly fled for Madonna's place on 13th Street, where they helped each other struggle to survive.

In 1981 Madonna stumbled into two more paying gigs. The first was a job singing background vocals on a handful of dance songs that were being recorded by an aspiring German vocalist named Otto Von Wernherr. Madonna lent her vocals to three songs: "Wild Dancing," "Cosmic Climb," and "We Are the Gods." Her actual participation on the tracks was minimal, consisting of repetitive chorus lines behind Von Wernherr's mainly spoken, flat, and heavily accented vocals. Six years later the songs were remixed to bring Madonna's vocals farther out in the songs and released on Receiver Records, a London-based label. The disc containing the three songs (featuring two extended dance mixes) is now marketed as *MADONNA (& Otto Von Wernherr): In the Beginning.* Not only are the songs dreadful, but Madonna's vocals are shrill and off-key.

On the third song from the Von Wernherr sessions, Madonna exclaims the line "Oh, here come the gods!" with all the conviction she might put into the sentence "I've got to do the laundry." Clearly Madonna had jumped at the opportunity to get some additional experience in the recording studio. These recordings are a curious document of where she was vocally at this time in her musical education. Listening to these recordings, it is hard to believe that she ever landed a recording deal, let alone became the largest-selling female rock artist in the world!

The second gig to suddenly appear that year was due to the return of Stephen Lewicki. He had fallen into another sum of money and wanted to complete his film *A Certain Sacrifice.* Says Lewicki, "I called her up, and I said, 'Madonna, there's this other scene I want to shoot,' and she'd say, 'Oh, Stephen, isn't this done yet!?!' She would give me all this shit, and I would placate her on the phone for ten minutes, and then she'd finally agree to do it. Then, when she did it, she was very, very good."[56]

At this point Madonna could really use some cash, so she had a certain amount of negotiating power when he called. "The only person I paid was Madonna," explains Stephen. "I paid her one hundred dollars and that was when she finally agreed to do the last scene I wanted her to do, which was the rape scene, and a couple of other scenes that I wanted her to do. After she agreed to do it, she said, 'Well, I want a hundred dollars.' She needed the money to pay her rent, she told me."[56] Those final scenes were shot in November of 1981, and Stephen disappeared for several months while he edited the footage.

Stephen was also in touch with Angie Smit, Madonna's former Breakfast Club partner. He claims that after the additional footage for *A Certain Sacrifice* was shot, Madonna and Angie had a falling out. Angie had gotten involved with a group of people who were into drugs, and Madonna wasn't interested in dealing with substance abusers, or with Angie. Says Lewicki, "I remember Angie telling me that Madonna had just become a real bitch . . . just too much of an egotist, but there are two sides to that story. I met Angie's boyfriend, and he was a real asshole, so I can see Madonna's side of it."[56]

Having transplanted herself in the middle of the East Village, with its Puerto Rican street scene and new wave graffiti artist sensibility, Madonna began to develop one of the most important aspects of her initial fame: her look. During this period, Madonna began purchasing previously owned "antique" clothing—including garments that cost almost nothing—and then concoct one-of-a-kind outfits. With rags knotted in her hair and layers of junk jewelry, she created an identity and an image that would eventually be copied the world over.

Through an evolution in the combined elements, her style developed. "Adidas sneakers with different-color laces, nylon tracksuits in all bright colors, belts, leather caps and gloves with the fingers cut off," explains Madonna.[65]

After hanging out with artists like Futura 2000, Martin Burgoyne, Keith Haring, and Kano, Madonna began to get into painting graffiti on the decaying brick walls of the East Village as well. Using different colors of spray paint, Futura 2000 would paint his nickname on walls around the city. When Madonna got involved in the graffiti scene she decided that she had to have a title to spray on subway trains and walls, and so she became known as "Boy Toy" to her friends. "It's my tag name," she explained at the time. "Everybody had their name on a belt buckle."[65]

Madonna's silver belt buckle with the words BOY TOY spelled out in big letters became one of her unique and identifiable fashion accessories when she became famous. Explaining the reason why she became known as "Boy Toy," Madonna states with matter-of-fact obviousness, "I toyed with boys."[65] Although the mere idea of a sexy woman declaring that she was a "boy toy" would seem antifeminist, for Madonna it was clearly a play on words. She controlled every situation, and it was the boys who ultimately became her toys.

Camille remembers, "That pre-star Madonna used and manipulated a lot of men to get what she needed. Madonna is an absolutely sexual creature, who has men eating out of her hands."[36]

Madonna herself admits, "I used to borrow money from people—

I'd let some poor sucker take me out to dinner and then I'd go, 'Can I borrow a hundred dollars?' I was always borrowing twenty-five, fifty, a hundred dollars from people."[1]

The next objective to be obtained was a record deal. Free from Camille's influence, Madonna again enlisted the help of Steve Bray. The two of them pooled their resources and recorded three demo tapes of songs that they had written. The rough cuts were: "Ain't No Big Deal," "Everybody," and "Burning Up."

For a fun night on the town, Madonna and her friends would don their rags-as-riches outfits and hit the hot dance clubs. On Friday nights they'd go to the Roxy, a former roller-skating rink on West 18th Street that became an urban dance spot when roller-disco suddenly fell out of fashion. Other nights it was Danceteria, a four-story something-for-everyone club on West 21st Street. The first level had a dance floor with a small stage for a variety of live presentations. Sometimes the club would feature experimental rock theater pieces like Casino Evil, other nights it would showcase name performers like Nona Hendryx, and more often than not it would play host to unknown acts on their way to stardom, like Sade. The third floor had chairs, booths, and dozens of TV screens for chilling out and socializing, and the fourth floor was a multipurpose area used primarily for invitation-only private events.

However, it was the second floor that Madonna and company would usually frequent. It was a hot dance floor where the D.J. would program nonstop danceable rock and post-disco new wave music. It was a veritable see-and-be-seen, dance-your-ass-off "in" spot. It especially flourished when the flash-in-the-pan punk pad, The Mudd Club, began losing its downtown crowd.

Madonna would often hit the clubs with her girlfriends Debbie and Claudia, looking for some action. They would do all of the latest inner-city dance steps like the Smurf and the Webo (Spanish for "ball shaker"). Their graffiti-artist pal Kano painted each of the three girls' jackets. Emblazoned on the jackets were the words *Webo Gals*, which was what they had nicknamed themselves. Together, they made a cocky trio who were out for a good time. No one suspected that Madonna was about to turn a night of dancing into a brilliant business move.

On the second floor of Danceteria, the primary D.J. was a hot guy on the scene named Mark Kamins. Like so many of the dance floor

D.J.'s from this era—like Jellybean Benitez, Shep Pettibone, and Manny Parrish—Mark longed to go beyond spinning other people's records; he wanted to produce and remix records of his own.

Remixed recordings would become a huge segment of Madonna's career. Not only would she be able to sell millions of copies of her albums, with three- and four-minute versions of her songs, but by employing a creative remix producer, she could sell extended five- to ten-minute versions of those same songs on twelve-inch single discs as well.

When Madonna went out for a night of club-hopping, she carried with her a copy of her demo tapes. What she needed the most at this point was the interest of a D.J. who was in the know, who would test-drive her songs on the dance floor. Enter "useful boyfriend" number three: Mark Kamins.

When Madonna, Debbie, and Claudia hit the floor at Danceteria, they made sure that all eyes were upon them. "Going out dancing with my girlfriends in New York clubs, we would dress for provocation," Madonna recalls.[30]

From the very start, Mark Kamins couldn't help but notice her. She was one of the girls who stood out in the crowd. "Madonna was special. She had her own style—always with a little bellybutton showing, the net top, and the stockings. When she'd start dancing, there'd be twenty people getting up and dancing with her."[3]

Madonna knew exactly what she was up to when she caught Kamins's eye one particular night at Danceteria. "I was flirting with him!" she admits.[9] Equipped with a four-track copy of one of her recordings, she had to figure out a way for him to play it on the turntable. Knowing from experience what the crowd at Danceteria was into, she was confident that the song would get a great response. She knew that if Kamins played the song, and she and her troupe of Webo Girls went into their dance, they were certain to cause a commotion on the floor.

In her own inimitable fashion, she went up to the D.J. booth and began to work on Mark. Kamins took the bait, and the rest is history. He quickly became the next stepping stone on her trail to the top. It was Kamins who was to snag her a record deal.

"It was just a tape she was working on. That was 'Everybody,' and she brought it up to the booth, and I listened to it, played it, and got a great reaction," he recalls. "It was a great song and she had a great voice. And plus, I knew she wasn't signed [to a recording contract]. And, she had that quality about herself—so there was an aura that was surrounding her even at that stage."[66]

The song, "Everybody," was a simple repetitive cut set to a strong progressive dance beat. Set off by Madonna's high-pitched girlish vocals, the lyrics are all about entreating everybody within earshot to get up on their feet, to dance and sing, and do their own thing.

Needless to say, the crowd of dancers—led by Madonna and her friends—all went crazy when "Everybody" was played. It had a fresh sound to it, which immediately grabbed everybody's attention. Overwhelmed by the reaction, Mark Kamins and Madonna made a pact right then and there. If he could get her a record deal, he wanted to be the producer of her first album. She immediately agreed to his plan. After all, she had nothing to lose and everything to gain. A few days later Kamins and Madonna went into the studio and made a new recording of "Everybody," which was polished up enough to submit to a record label.

It was early 1982, and Mike Rosenblatt was the man in charge of finding new acts for Sire Records, which is a small "custom label" distributed by Warner Brothers. A friend of Mark's, Mike agreed to meet with him and Madonna and to take a listen to "Everybody" and the other demo tapes. Rosenblatt remembers the meeting and how he was instantly impressed with what he heard and what he saw: "She had her 'look' together, her image was all there, maybe a little more raggedy than today. She had a great tape, but what's more she had that intangible certain something."[67]

Seymour Stein, the president of Sire Records, was flat on his back in a hospital the week that Mike Rosenblatt met with Mark and Madonna. In fact, he was lying there, recovering from an attack of endocarditis, when Rosenblatt phoned him, raving about a hot new female singer he had just been introduced to. Although Stein was hospitalized, he was still conducting his day-to-day business on the phone. Rosenblatt arranged for a meeting between Seymour and Madonna that very day.

"From what I'd heard I wanted to meet her immediately. . . . I signed the contract there right in the hospital. . . . I was excited to meet Madonna."[3]

According to Stein, "When she walked into the room, she filled it with her exuberance and determination. It hit me right away. I could tell right then she had the drive to match her talent."[3] The record company president met Mark and Madonna dressed in a bathrobe he had brought from home.

The original deal that Madonna was signed to at Sire was not a guaranteed album deal. In fact, she was only signed to the dance division of Sire, contracted to do two twelve-inch dance singles, which could be edited down and pressed into 45s for potential pop radio play. If the two releases did well, she had a shot at more, and possibly an album.

Madonna was thrilled to have her foot in the door at a major record label. However, there were still obstacles to overcome before she actually landed an album deal. Madonna remembers doing most of the work necessary to land a record deal. Once the deal was done, she had to change the record company's perception that she was just another flash-in-the-pan girl singer. According to her, "Warner Brothers is a hierarchy of old men and it was a chauvinistic environment to be working in because I was treated like this sexy little girl. . . . It wouldn't have happened to Michael Jackson or Prince."[68]

With the go ahead from Seymour Stein, and money up front, Madonna and her producer Mark Kamins went into the recording studio to begin recording the first single. Not only was Madonna on trial, but Mark was as well.

"Seymour believed in me," says Kamins in regard to his chance at producing Madonna in the studio. "So he said, 'Okay, give it a shot,' 'Everybody' was actually a B-side. There was an A-side called 'Ain't No Big Deal.' 'Everybody' was supposed to be the B-side, but it came out so great!"[66]

What ended up happening was that Kamins produced a five-minute fifty-six-second twelve-inch single version of "Everybody," which was released with a nine-minute twenty-three-second "dub version" of the same song, which became the B-side. The Mark Kamins–produced recording of "Ain't No Big Deal" ended up scrapped, and he still has a remixed version of that song which has never been released. Sire Records released "Everybody" in April of 1982. Although it didn't become a pop hit, it almost instantly became a huge dance hit, garnering consistent play on the dance floors across the country.

"They put 'Everybody' out [as] the first single," explains Kamins.

"It went to Number Three on the dance charts. It was about [Number] 102 on the pop charts. That's when they went and picked a new producer!"[66] Mark was totally miffed, and things suddenly became complicated. Madonna envisioned herself going big places in a huge hurry, and she didn't feel that Kamins was the person to take her there. So, she dropped him like a hot potato.

Mark had gotten Madonna the record deal that he had promised to obtain for her, but instead of letting him produce the album as she had agreed to do, she canned him after the first single. That, however, wasn't the half of it. There were actually three different people fighting over the chance to produce Madonna's next single. The stakes included an even larger piece of the pie, because if the follow-up single became a success, the lucky producer would almost assuredly end up producing the whole album. Since "Everybody" had become a Top Ten dance hit and had sold respectably well, Sire was already openly talking about the album deal to follow as though it were fact.

What Madonna failed to tell Kamins was that she had also promised the album production assignment to Steve Bray. Needless to say, both Kamins and Bray found themselves in total shock when she blew them both off and chose one of the Warner Records house producers, Reggie Lucas, for the album honors.

According to her, "In my mind I thought, 'Okay, Mark can produce the album and Steve can play the instruments.'"[29]

Madonna didn't trust Steve enough with the album's production because of his inexperience. Although his feelings were hurt, Bray took it on the chin, and while he was disappointed, he didn't let it affect their friendship.

"The relationship's too old to have something like that stand in its way," Bray says in retrospect. "Exploited? Some people say that, but that's resentment of someone who's got the drive. It seems like you're leaving people behind or you're stepping on them, and the fact is that you're moving and they're not. She doesn't try to be that polite. She doesn't care if she ruffles someone's feathers."[9]

One of the interesting things about the first twelve-inch single released by Madonna was the marketing. Since the sound of "Everybody" was aimed at the "urban contemporary" crowd—which was mainly black and Puerto Rican—Madonna's identity as a white girl was masqueraded for the record-buying public. The picture sleeve for the initial dance single featured a colorful photo montage of inner-city black kids in New York street scenes. For all that the unsuspecting record buyer knew, "Madonna" could have been a band, a soloist, or even a studio group. In this way, if black radio stations started playing "Everybody" first, no one would know if Madonna was black or white.

Oddly enough, there was a video of "Everybody" produced by Sire Records, directed by Ed Steinberg, which almost no one has seen. To this day it remains in a vault somewhere at Warner Bros. Records, with only a few seconds of it surfacing in 1990 as part of an MTV documentary on Madonna. The video of "Everybody" was more of a home movie than the big budget production music videos eventually became. It was a simple live performance of Madonna and two dancers, filmed onstage at the black gay disco, Paradise Garage. "The Garage," as it was known in underground circles, was actually located in a converted garage at the corner of King and Varick streets in lower Manhattan.

MTV had just begun broadcasting in November of 1981, but Madonna did not have a big enough name in rock circles for them to even consider programming her. To MTV, she was just a one-shot dance artist.

The person responsible for getting Madonna introduced to all the right people at the dance clubs was an energetic and well-respected man named Bobby Shaw. At the time he was the national dance promoter for Warner Bros. Records. His job was to take acetate pressings of soon-to-be-released dance records around to the hot clubs and get the D.J.'s interested in playing his company's product.

Originally Shaw was introduced to Madonna by Mark Kamins and Mike Rosenblatt. Bobby immediately liked Madonna, and when he was promoting "Everybody" to the club D.J.'s, Madonna gladly accompanied him on his rounds, and he personally introduced her to the people who spin the records. That bit of extra promotion could make all the difference in the world as to whether a record got played or not, and if so—how often it got played.

Madonna was more than willing to go that extra mile to learn the business and do whatever it took to make sure that her record was heard. When Bobby was taking her around from club to club, she was always asking him questions about how the whole promotion end of the record business worked. "She's a smart girl," Shaw proclaims. "She's charismatic—that's what's really won her. She has the charisma, man—people want to see her. She has a mystique about her—people want to know. She works it—period!"[69]

After Bobby informed her that he was very friendly with the club D.J.'s, and that there were weekly gatherings in his office, she became a frequent visitor. These were the people who could make her career happen, and she was going to make sure they got to know her.

"Madonna used to come up to my office and hang out in my room," Bobby recalls. "On Fridays I used to have a lot of D.J.'s come and listen to records. We used to bring records of all different labels, and imports, and at that time—Warner Brothers' records, too. We used to sit around until seven or eight at night and listen to the records. She used to come over once in a while to hear what we were playing. She was 'hanging' with the D.J.'s, and she was wearing torn jeans."[69]

Shaw claims that he immediately thought Madonna had the makings of a star. "I always knew she was gonna be big. The potential was there, it was whether or not Warner Brothers got behind it," he recalls. "I just thought that everything that [she] needed to be—to be a star—was there: charisma, the voice, the personality, the stage presence. It was just all there. The prettiness—I mean she was a pretty girl. Something about her—it worked! All of the pieces of the puzzle were there. There were no blank spaces to be filled in later."[69]

What Madonna needed now in her career was to further ensconce herself in the circle of dance club D.J.'s. Again she used her naturally flirtatious ways, this time to snag one of the hottest club disc jockeys on the scene as her next boyfriend. Enter: John "Jellybean" Benitez. He was the star disc jockey on the dance floor at the hot Latino disco of the moment, The Funhouse, on West 26th Street. Spinning records in a D.J. booth shaped like the head of a giant clown, Jellybean really knew how to "rock the house." He could whip the crowd into a dancing frenzy by sequencing the records he played just right. Saturday nights at The Funhouse, with Jellybean at the helm, were HOT.

For Madonna, Jellybean was to become the ultimate "useful boyfriend." While on his arm, she was suddenly seen at all of the hot industry parties and was introduced to scores of people who could help her with her climb to the top.

"We met in my D.J. booth at The Funhouse," Jellybean vividly recalls. "Bobby Shaw, who was the dance promotion person for Warner Brothers, brought her by. I mean, most record companies from the New York market would bring by artists to Jellybean. And, when I met Madonna, I was attracted to her right away. We just sort of hit it off. . . . [We] sort of played games with each other. I thought she was just being friendly with me because she wanted her record played. And, she thought she didn't want to be nice to me because everybody was always nice to me to play their records. So we were just playing little cat-and-mouse games. So, that's what happened."[70] According to Jellybean, their initial meeting was in October or November of 1982.

During this same period, Madonna was still dating Ken on and off. However, she and Jellybean were destined to become steady lovers for almost a year and a half. In addition to his duties spinning records on the weekends at The Funhouse, Jellybean was also gaining a lot of respect in the business for remixing several dance versions of current hits. Among his two biggest remixes were Irene Cara's "What a Feeling (Theme from *Flashdance*)" and "Say Say Say" for Paul McCartney and Michael Jackson.

John's schedule was very hectic, but he began pursuing Madonna. "We were attracted to each other, but we were just playing with each other. I was immediately attracted to her. We exchanged numbers, and started talking to each other on the phone. I was going back and forth to L.A., so I would call from L.A. We kept trying to set up to meet, then make a plan, and ended up canceling it, because I had to be in the studio, and she had to go to Europe or something. We had a big scheduling problem," he recalls.[70]

Madonna met Jellybean after "Everybody" was released. He introduced her to many more of the D.J.'s spinning at clubs like The Garage, The Funhouse, and Studio 54. In the early days, their relationship was platonic. "A lot of people bring him tapes and I thought, 'I won't make him think that I'm playing up to him to help my career,'" she says.[68]

Madonna was not exactly swept off her feet by Jellybean. "I didn't like him right away," she recalls. "Like—tacky! He had really long hair and was walking around in really short shorts. I thought he was a girl at first. He has a really pretty face—feminine features. 'Jellybean'? Who's that? That doesn't have a sex. Then I ran into him again at a show at The Ritz. Vanity was playing with The Time. Then I knew he wasn't a girl. He started dragging me around everywhere, introducing me to all these industry people. I liked the way he held my hand. That changed my mind. He wasn't such a wimp anymore."[1]

When Reggie Lucas went into the recording studio with Madonna to begin work on the second single, he wanted to change her musical focus. Says Lucas, "I wanted to push her in a pop direction."[29]

The first two songs that Madonna cut with Reggie were her composition "Burning Up" as the A-side for her next twelve-inch single, and a song he had written, called "Physical Attraction" as the B-side. While both cuts had slamming bass lines to appease people on the dance floor, the sound was clearly more out of the rock/pop/dance bag, and had great radio crossover potential.

Madonna respected Reggie's decisions and got along well with him in the recording studio. "He's a good producer, very open and sensitive," she says.[14]

Released in March of 1983, "Burning Up"/"Physical Attraction" bolted up the dance charts to Number Three. With that, Sire/Warner knew that Madonna was on her way to the top, and they gave her and Reggie the green light to proceed with the production of the album.

Like her first twelve-inch single, the record was marketed with racially nebulous sleeve art. This time around the sleeve was designed and drawn by her artist friend Martin Burgoyne. The cover of the dance single of "Burning Up"/"Physical Attraction" features a grid of twenty postage stamp–sized portraits of Madonna in every color of the rainbow, including blue and green. On the back is a pointillist portrait of the singer, which further obscures her real skin color. From the look of it, she could easily be Puerto Rican or even mulatto.

During that era, Michael Jackson and Prince were the only black faces seen on MTV, and there was a huge controversy about it from the black sector of the music industry. Regardless, it was time for Madonna to expose her face to the public, and let the chips fall where they would.

It was a confusing situation that worked both for and against her. In some states, D.J.'s wouldn't play her music because they thought she was black, while other stations wouldn't give her air time because she would be taking time away from black artists.

When her second single began to take off in the clubs, Madonna and her dancers would lip sync to her recordings on Friday and Saturday nights in clubs from New York to Fort Lauderdale. This was a common way of breaking new dance records, with special live performances at clubs like Twelve West, Xenon, and Studio 54.

It was Bobby Shaw who was responsible for planning and booking Madonna's performances at the start of her recording career. "I was getting her all the club dates in the beginning," he recalls. "We did New York clubs a lot, and we did Fort Lauderdale and south Florida. I remember we played the Copa in Key West once on a rainy night. There must have been only twenty-five people there! We did three songs—'Burning Up,' 'Physical Attraction,' and 'Everybody.' It was great! It was me, Madonna, her two dancers—Erika and Bags. Her brother Christopher would come along sometimes. It was like a little family—'Dance and sing—get up and do your thing!' It was fun."[69]

This time around, Sire/Warner Bros. Records realized that stardom was potentially in the cards for Madonna, so they went all out and produced a beautiful video for "Burning Up." With direction by Steve Baron and camera work by King Bagot, this video was very much responsible for cementing the initial Madonna "look." One of the most notable accessories she is seen wearing are the little black rubber bracelets that she became famous for the world over. Warner hired a jewelry designer who called herself Maripol as the stylist for the shoot. The rubber bracelets were actually typewriter drive belts, which Madonna wore up and down her arms.

The video opens with a series of colorful close-ups: Madonna's eye, a bouquet of daisies, Madonna's red lips, a brilliant orange goldfish, Madonna's milky white throat, and finally Madonna spinning around like a whirling dervish. Interspersed throughout are scenes of Madonna in a short white dress, sitting in the middle of a street while singing the song about "Burning Up" with sexual desire.

Visually, one of the most impressive aspects of the video is the high contrast of the dramatic colors: Madonna's skin is a warm peach color; her lips are bright cherry red; the laser beams shooting through the screen are a bright green; and Madonna's newly bleached hair is yellow gold. The look of the video and its star is fantastic. Although the production was simple—compared to Madonna's more recent video offerings—"Burning Up" is one of her most appealing videos.

end of the action in the video, it looks like Madonna—
ing in the street in the middle of the night—is going to
ir driven by a handsome guy. However, at the end of the
na is driving the car—and she has gotten rid of the guy.
Leave it to Madonna to ditch the guy—and get to keep his car. This is
truly a case of art imitating life.

Although the song "Burning Up" didn't become a pop hit, the video
caused somewhat of a minor visual stir on MTV. It represented America's
first look at the girl who was destined to rival "Dynasty"'s Alexis as the
dominatrix of the airwaves.

According to Madonna, the handsome guy driving the car in the
"Burning Up" video is none other than her soon-to-be-ex-boyfriend Ken.
Madonna has described Ken as the man with whom she's had the longest
monogamous relationship. The word *monogamous* should be read as
ongoing, because Madonna slept around with other people during the
two and a half years she claims to so dearly cherish with Ken. "I've had
my heart broken, too," says the multimedia love goddess, "All my
boyfriends hurt me in their way."[15]

Explaining her love-them-and-leave-them tactics, Madonna says,
"All those men I stepped over to get to the top, every one of them would
take me back because they still love me and I still love them."[15]

Now that her album deal was locked into place, Madonna began
to feel more confidently in control. More than ever she was resolute
about when her affairs of the heart began—and ended. "Most of the
fights I have with boyfriends are over how I'm not paying enough attention
to them or I'm always off doing things for my career."[15]

Madonna never pulls any punches. Although she uses people for
her ultimate benefit, she rarely pretends that the rules of the game are
any more complicated than that. According to her, "I think most people
who meet me know that that's the kind of person I am. It comes down
to doing what you have to do for your career. I think most people who
are attracted to me understand that, and they just have to take that
under consideration."[9] As Tina Turner put it so eloquently: "What's love
got to do with it?"

"I think that a lot of people do feel exploited by her," says Jellybean.
"But then again, everyone's got so many expectations about a relationship
with her. She's very intense immediately with somebody, very friendly.

Perhaps people feel, 'This is what our relationship is about,' and then if there is any cooling of that, it's taken as a rejection."[70]

Although Mark Kamins was still smarting from being dumped from Madonna's debut album project, he says, "She's a star, and you get where you have to go. She's got a good heart . . . deep, deep down there." When asked if he felt any lasting animosity toward her, he replied, "No, none at all."[66]

Says Steve Bray, "She's extraordinarily talented, and a friend. But with her—being polite and ladylike gets left behind."[29]

Even Camille Barbone proclaims, "I don't hate her. I miss her."[63]

As 1982 ended, the door closed on Madonna's life as a struggling unknown with more drive than talent. She was at least finished with the struggling part.

Does she ever think back to those days of digging through wastebaskets for food? "I think about that a lot," says Madonna, looking back on her days as a street waif, living off the money, favors, and kindness of others. Withstanding the elements taught her to take what she could get, and how to climb, claw, and manipulate her way toward whatever it is that she ultimately wants. "I never had any money and I never had any help, and probably having to deal with all that and having to struggle to survive has made me as tough as I am."[61]

For Madonna, her era as a "Boy Toy" was far from over. Boys just continued to be more and more important in what they could do for her. She was soon to graduate from mere "Boy Toy" to full-fledged "Material Girl."

Six

I know exactly what

Like

I want. If that makes me

a

a bitch, okay![12] *—Madonna*

Virgin

N ew York City in the late seventies and early eighties, when
young Madonna Ciccone and a thousand other would-be stars
arrived in the city, was a hotbed of creative activity. For
anyone young, ambitious, and open, the environment was
permissive and exciting. For the first time in years, Manhattan was
"where it was at" in the music industry. It wasn't Detroit's Motown
sound, Philadelphia's inner-city soul, Nashville's country twang, or any
other city's music that was happening then. During this era, New York
seemed like the *only* place to be. Manhattan was where the new acts
were being discovered, signed, launched, and promoted, at places like
the Pyramid, CBGB's, the Mudd Club, Max's Kansas City, and
Danceteria. There were music industry parties at Studio 54, Flamingo,
Paradise Garage, Xenon, Magique, the Roxy, and several other clubs
around town, almost any night of the week. If you knew someone, and
you were on the A-list, you had it made. This was the permissive era
before AIDS, and *everyone* was doing *everything*. Sex and drugs and rock

and roll still ruled the day, and there was a sense of *anything goes* in the air.

Although she was still on the ground floor when the year 1983 began, Madonna was on her way to getting where she wanted to be. She had a record contract that called for delivery of her debut album, and she now had the added security of money coming in from Sire/Warner Brothers Records. She was dating Jellybean Benitez, and he was showing her what it was like to be in the big leagues. Before the year was up, she would finish her first million-selling album, film her first major movie role, hit the Top Twenty pop charts, and establish herself in the music business as the hottest newcomer on the horizon.

Objective number one at this make-it-or-break-it juncture was to make certain that the album she was working on would be a hit. Having two Top Ten dance singles was a definite feather in her cap, but Madonna had yet to crack the pop charts, the acknowledged jackpot in the music business.

When Madonna and Reggie Lucas returned to the studio, they had several songs they intended to record. Madonna had written a bright, optimistic song called "Lucky Star," plus two more compositions: "Think of Me" and "I Know It." Reggie, who had written the dance hit "Physical Attraction" for Madonna's second "12-inch" single, had another song he had written called "Borderline." In addition, they decided to rerecord "Ain't No Big Deal," which she had laid down with Mark Kamins at the beginning of her Sire recording contract. However, everyone agreed that "Ain't No Big Deal," which was written by Steve Bray, could be spiced up a bit. So, a new version of it was cut for Madonna's debut album, with Reggie producing.

At first, Madonna deferred to Reggie's opinion in the studio about how the songs should sound. But when Reggie's finished cuts started coming out overlaid with too many audio embellishments, she began to question some of his decisions. According to Madonna, the album strayed further and further from the original concept of her demo tapes. "I didn't know if I knew enough to speak out. It wasn't until my first album was three-quarters of the way done that I realized, 'Hey! I know a lot more about this than I'm allowing myself to speak out about.'"[13] Madonna preferred the tracks to be simpler, sparser, so working from the finished product backward, she was finally able to produce the effect she wanted.

Although Madonna was unsatisfied with the way "Lucky Star," "Burning Up," "Ain't No Big Deal," and "Physical Attraction" turned out, she was uncertain as to what to do with them. That's when she first consulted Jellybean about solving the problems. Since remixing hit records was his biggest claim to fame, it seemed logical to ask him for his advice and help.

In Reggie's mind, he had completed his work on the album, so he was already off on another assignment.

"They were putting out the next twelve-inch and they wanted me to mix it," recalls Jellybean. "So I went to dinner with her and Michael Rosenblatt—the A&R guy at Sire who signed her—and Bobby Shaw at Shun Lee in the East Fifties. That's where they asked me to mix 'Physical Attraction.'"[70]

"What I was doing was additional production, or co-producing," explains Benitez. "But I didn't have the power to say, 'I want co-production credit.' I was just doing it because I wanted the record to sound good. So, I went in and did all these new guitar parts on 'Lucky Star.' The guitars you hear on 'Burning Up' and 'Lucky Star'—on the album—are all new parts that Reggie Lucas didn't do. And, there are new vocal parts. Even though those songs were produced by him, those weren't *only* produced by him, because I went in and did all this additional production—and totally different mixes."[70]

Then there is the matter of the song "Ain't No Big Deal," of which there were three different versions. Everyone liked the song, but no one cared for the versions that Lucas or Kamins came up with. According to Jellybean, "We were gonna work on—not Reggie Lucas's version, not Mark Kamins's version—but the version that Steve Bray and Madonna did together as a demo originally. So, I was going to do all of these overdubs on that. But then, Steve Bray sold the song to an artist called Barracuda on Epic Records and they put out the song."[70]

Since "Ain't No Big Deal" was Steve Bray's composition, and Epic was releasing Barracuda's version, Warner Brothers didn't want to have Madonna release the song on her album. This was at the end of April 1983. Recalls Jellybean, "They're rushing to get this album out, and Madonna's like, 'Oh shit! I need a new song now!'"[70] That's where the song "Holiday" came into the picture.

Jellybean had yet to produce a song of his own from start to finish, and he was dying to be in the driver's seat for once. He had a demo tape of "Holiday," which had been written by Curtis Hudson and Lisa Stevens from the group Pure Energy, and he was convinced that it had the potential to become a huge hit. He had already offered it to two other performers, but he was rejected both times. "I offered it to the A&R guy at Arista Records for Phyllis Hyman," he recalls. "He thought it was okay, but it didn't blow his mind."[70] He then offered it to former Supreme Mary Wilson, but she was unimpressed with the song as well.

So when "Ain't No Big Deal" was bumped off Madonna's album, Jellybean suggested "Holiday" to her. "When Madonna heard it, she liked it right away. She didn't have much choice, she had to get her album done," he recalls. Next, he had to convince Warner Brothers: "I played it for them, and they liked it a lot, and gave me a week to produce it."[70] This was Jellybean's big break, and he was determined to put every ounce of energy he could into it. After Madonna cut her vocal parts, he spent four solid days in the recording studio tinkering with the song to try to make it into the hit he instinctively felt it could become.

"I worked like twenty hours a day to finish it," he recalls. "It was a desire on my part to really accomplish something."[70] Just to make sure he was on the right track, he would run down to The Funhouse to crank the song up full blast on the club's speakers. Finally it was finished, and the fate of the song was out of his hands.

After remixing and sequencing the album, it was time to sit down with the executives at Sire and Warner Bros., to decide if the album was up to everyone's expectations. Everyone loved the album, especially the cut "Lucky Star," with its resounding bass line and crisp guitar work. And Jellybean's "Holiday" was widely praised. Although it was an underdog cut, produced as filler, the song would ultimately make Jellybean an instant industry star alongside Madonna.

The album *Madonna* was released in July 1983, without the immediate benefit of a third single. Since Madonna was the current darling of the dance clubs, it was decided that the LP and special promotional single would be serviced to discotheque D.J.'s to see what they picked up on.

"The *Madonna* album came out," recalls Benitez, "and 'Lucky Star' was supposed to be the first single, and no one liked 'Holiday.' 'Yeah, it's okay, but "Lucky Star" is the smash.' In the back of my mind, I'm going, 'Well, I don't know—I think "Holiday" is a hit.' So, they put out a twelve-inch [D.J.'s-only] promo on 'Holiday' and 'Lucky Star.' 'Lucky Star' was the A-side, and 'Holiday' was the B-side."[70]

Startlingly, it was "Holiday" that grabbed everyone's attention. By October 1983 the album cut of "Holiday" was the Number One dance song in America, according to *Billboard*. That was it: Sire/Warner Bros. Records was forced into rush-releasing "Holiday" as Madonna's third single. Jellybean sees a secret network behind this success: "I knew as soon as D.J.'s saw 'John "Jellybean" Benitez' on the 'Holiday' side, that was *it*, because D.J.'s stick together."[70]

The week of October 29, 1983, "Holiday" entered *Billboard*'s "Hot 100" pop singles chart. By February 1984 the song peaked at Number 16. Mary Wilson, who had turned the song down, recalls, "I was driving down Sunset Boulevard in my car one day with the radio cranked up, and all of a sudden I hear this song called 'Holiday' come pouring out of the speakers. I couldn't believe that that was the same song I had turned down, and it became Madonna's first huge hit. I still kick myself to this day for having passed on it!"[71]

While she was still working on her debut album Madonna was without a manager. Says Jellybean, "When I first met Madonna, she didn't have a lawyer, or a manager, or an accountant, or a bank account."[70] These were all situations that had to be immediately remedied.

When she went manager shopping, Madonna started at the top. In the world of music and the whole new vista of music videos, the reigning star in 1983 was Michael Jackson. At the time he was managed by Freddy DeMann, who was part of the firm Weisner-DeMann Entertainment.

"One day, I forced myself into his office and began auditioning there and then—in front of him. He was quite dumbfounded by my nerve," Madonna recalls.[20]

After her impromptu audition, DeMann was suitably impressed. "She had that special magic that very few stars have."[24] Bingo! Madonna now had a manager.

When Madonna's debut album was released, Freddy DeMann was listed on the album credits as her manager. He was to become instrumental in making certain the record company put their big guns behind his new client. Piece by piece, Madonna's patchwork career quilt was becoming a well-oiled machine.

Several things had set Jellybean apart from other dance club D.J.'s. Besides spinning records at the hottest club where records were broken in, he was the only D.J. in town who had the vision to market himself to the public. One of the things he did was to hire a publicist to make his name a household word. The publicist he hired was David Salidor, who has worked with such acts as Run-DMC, Seduction, and Debbie Gibson.

According to Salidor, "As people got to know Jellybean's name, he suddenly found himself invited to all of the hot industry events. At several of the press activities that I accompanied him to, Madonna would be his date. From the beginning of my work with Jellybean, I would spend every Saturday night in the D.J. booth of The Funhouse staging photo opportunities and bringing down industry bigwigs to press the flesh. On any given Saturday night, there would be a string of celebrities networking with Jellybean, including Quincy Jones, Penny Marshall, Paul Simon, Bill Medley, Billy Joel, and Pat Benatar. It was there that I first met Madonna. My initial impression of her was that she was someone who was definitely going to succeed in this business, because of her perseverance and drive. She was going to make it, the only question was when. Here was someone who excelled at making a statement wherever she went, because of the way she dressed, the way she spoke, and the way she carried herself. She was totally original. No one else presented themselves quite the way she did."[72]

Salidor immediately spotted Madonna's aggressive side. She rarely made casual conversation, and there was an objective to every one of her questions. "Madonna was someone who was fixated on succeeding," David recalls. "None of us knew how she was going to do it—but there was no question that come hell or high water she was going to become a star. She was willing to go farther than anyone else to make it, and none of us who hung out with her realized just how far she would take it. From the start she would begin asking me how a publicist worked. She was especially eager to find out how a successful publicity campaign was mounted and executed. She later took the knowledge and applied it to her own career. I remember one night at Sigma Sound Studios, when John was remixing a song for the group the English Beat and Madonna was at his side. I had made arrangements to come down to take some publicity photos of John with the group to service the trades— *Cash Box* and *Billboard* magazines. Originally the photos were just going to be shots of John and the English Beat, but by the time we took the pictures—Madonna had also worked her way into the photos."[72] she obviously learned very quickly how to turn a casual evening into a publicity opportunity.

It wasn't long before Madonna's lifestyle started to change as well. "The first real money I ever got was $5,000 from Sire Records," she explains, "and the first expensive thing I bought was a Roland synthesizer."[15]

After the first five grand, she received money from the song publisher for the tracks she'd written on her first album—a thousand dollars for each song. With money in hand, she rented her first apartment in the East Village. As the money continued to roll in, she eventually moved to a much more expensive loft in the trendy neighborhood south of Houston Street known as SoHo.

With Freddy DeMann behind her, several new opportunities were presented to Madonna. One of the first doors opened into fresh territory was the one to the movies, and one of the first people she met in that arena was film producer Jon Peters. Their initial interview ultimately ended up snagging Madonna her first appearance in a major movie: *Vision Quest*. Although her role in the film was a musical performance without dialogue, she was able to cut her teeth in front of the cameras.

Jon Peters was looking for a real singer to play the role she landed in *Vision Quest*. "They wanted someone with a lot of style already," Madonna recalls.[17] According to her, "I just sing in it. I sing: I perform in a nightclub that the lead actor and actress come into. They dance a slow dance to a song. I have three songs, but I don't know what they're going to cut out of it."[1]

Madonna's part in *Vision Quest* was filmed in Spokane, Washington, in November 1983. She complained about the filming process: "It was very cold, lonely, and boring."[17] However, through Jon she was introduced to Peters's ex-girlfriend and business partner, Barbra Streisand. Madonna had dinner with Peters and Streisand in Los Angeles and recalls that Streisand genuinely cared about her as a person and a singer.

"I had this rag tied in my hair the way I do, and she wanted to know everything about the way I dressed, the jewelry I wore, the way I sang, about how I grew up in Detroit."[17]

The filming in Spokane ran right up to the week of Thanksgiving. Madonna recalls the awkward family reunion she had when she dragged Jellybean back to Rochester for a turkey dinner with the Ciccone clan. "I came home with black pants, a black T-shirt, no jewelry at all and my hair just sort of not combed—that's pretty conservative." Her father assessed her outfit, assuming it was a costume for the movie. He said, as Madonna recalls, " 'You always dress like that?' "[17]

On January 14, 1984, Madonna appeared on the world's most famous teenage TV dance party: "American Bandstand." Lip-syncing to her hit single, she performed "Holiday" and chatted with the show's famed host, Dick Clark. Although her "Burning Up" video had been aired on TV before this date, this live appearance represented her national television debut. After she finished performing the song, Clark asked her, "Now what do you really want to do when you grow up?" Without missing a beat, Madonna replied, "Rule the world."[73]

Since "Holiday" was also climbing the charts in England, Madonna flew to London that same month to do some promotional gigs and be interviewed by several British magazines including *No. 1*, *The Face*, and *Record Mirror*. She impatiently told British journalists, "I'm desperate to start my second LP, but because of 'Holiday,' I'll have to wait."[74] Indeed, since finishing off her first album, she had already gathered together a sizable amount of material for her next LP.

In early 1984, although she was beginning to make money, Madonna still felt basically unchanged. "I still ride the subway every day," she told one reporter. "People come up and say, 'You look just like Madonna,' and I'll go, 'Thank you.' Or, they'll say, 'Are you Madonna?' and I'll say, 'Yes.' Then they'll go, 'No you're not!' and I'll say, 'O.K., I'm not.' "[31] It would not be long before all that would change.

Along the way, Madonna performed at several clubs around New York to promote her recordings. In early 1984, Madonna was booked at Studio 54 for the birthday celebration of the fashionable uptown clothing store, Fiorucci. Also on the bill was Manny Parrish, who was promoting his album, *Man Parrish*.

The performances that evening were tightly scheduled. At midnight, Parrish was to descend from the ceiling and perform his song, and then at two A.M., Madonna was to jump off a portable balcony onto Fiorucci's enormous birthday cake and slide down to the floor, where she would perform. Both singers and their dancers were all clad in outrageous Fiorucci clothes. However, Madonna didn't like that particular setup. According to Parrish, "She was on a fucking rampage—as usual. She wanted to go on at midnight when the room was full, not later on. I was the headliner—so to speak—and she wasn't."[75]

Madonna's first ploy was to tell Parrish and his troupe that there had been a little change in plans. According to Parrish, "She told us that I wasn't going on at midnight, that she was, and that things were switched around. So everybody left the room and started walking around the club. She did this to fuck up my act, and the stage manager came in and said, 'Hey, you're going on in twenty minutes—where is everybody? What's going on?' I told him, 'Well, Madonna said we're going on second, and she's going on first.' And he said, 'WHAT?!?' and ran into her room and started screaming at her."[75]

When Plan A failed to work, Madonna came up with still another ploy: she'd hide Manny's group's stage clothes. "That fucking bitch stole my fucking jackets!" Manny recalls of his dilemma at midnight. "We had our costumes—we had graffiti jackets from Kansai, and we were getting ready to go on—and they were missing! So, we're looking around, and looking around, and looking around, and one of her dancers came in from outside, and said, 'Look, she'll kill me if she finds me in here, but your costumes are hidden behind the boiler—in the back over there.' Somebody hid them, and her dancer was implying that it was her. And, they were plastic, so I had to soak them in ice water to keep them from melting!"[75]

Several weeks later, Madonna and Manny Parrish again shared the bill at another nightclub. "I played at the Red Parrot, and she went on last," he recalls. "It was Sonic Force, and myself, and Madonna. Sonic went on at eleven P.M., I went on at one A.M., and she went on at three A.M. She complained afterward that we ruined the audience—that we wore them out and ruined them. She went onstage and said, 'Well, thanks for waiting around. If you have anything left in you, we're going to have a good time.' The audience didn't really respond to her, and she screamed at the people who organized the evening for putting her on last."[75]

Like so many people who met Madonna during this era, Manny distinctly remembers how abrasive she could be. "In the very beginning she was very determined—very snotty, with an attitude, and pushy," he recalls. Looking back on Madonna's backstage antics, Parrish laughs forgivingly. "The bitch! She had to do what she had to do to get herself through."[75]

In March 1984, "Borderline" was released as Madonna's next single, with an accompanying video, which represented her first work with director Mary Lambert. Unlike the "Burning Up" video, in which Madonna was dressed in a short white dress, this time around she was sporting an outfit that was to become identified as "the Madonna look." She wore mismatched layers of clothes and rags tied in her hair, like a fashionable street waif. Alternating between color and black and white sequences, the video tells a story.

Madonna is spotted dancing in the street with a bunch of inner-city kids. A professional photographer spots her, offers her his business card, and the next thing you know, Madonna is in his studio doing a photo shoot. She ends up torn between choosing the well-to-do photographer or her street ruffian boyfriend. In the end she goes back to the street boyfriend. Along the way we see several telling early Madonna trademarks, including shots of her spray painting several of the photographer's possessions, including his car, with graffiti.

The song "Borderline" became Madonna's first Top Ten pop hit. Things were jelling, and she became a bona fide New York celebrity. Madonna herself was amazed to watch the transformation that was taking place. When the video for "Borderline" was released, people began to recognize Madonna on the street. Her first two singles didn't have hit videos, so she was a voice without a face. She went from "unknown" to "immediately recognizable."

Suddenly Madonna didn't feel so comfortable riding around New York City on the subway. In one of her favorite East Village restaurants, a girl she had never met before came up to her table and started snapping pictures of her. Madonna nearly flipped out, but the fact of the matter was that she had crossed the "borderline" between anonymity and stardom.

ough she still liked to hang out at the Roxy and The Funhouse, couldn't do it quite so easily as an unknown patron. "Half the people I hung out with from the downtown area have totally snubbed me," she stated with amazement that spring. "They think that I'm selling out and stuff. If I go back to clubs they won't talk to me."[17]

While her record company was busy pulling hit singles from her debut album, Madonna returned to the studio to begin work on her second LP. Since the *Madonna* album was so successful, especially the new single, "Borderline," Reggie Lucas assumed that he would be called in to produce its successor. However, like so many men in Madonna's life, he was dumped from the Madonna camp.

One of Madonna's favorite albums in the past year had been David Bowie's smashing multi-platinum *Let's Dance*. It was produced by Nile Rodgers, one of the masterminds behind the successful seventies' funk-dance group, Chic.

In addition to being a member of Chic, and having gone on to produce hits for Diana Ross, Power Station, Duran Duran, Sister Sledge, and Debbie Harry, Nile is known in music business inner circles as a consummate professional. When the idea of hiring him to work with Madonna came up, several people warned him that she was a totally self-centered bitch who was a pain in the ass to work with. He had initial doubts in regard to getting involved with her.

"Everyone told me she was a terrible ogre, but I thought she was great," he recalls.[49] "She's a true professional—one of the best I've ever worked with."[76] He does however admit, "She's more temperamental than anyone I've ever worked with."[77]

Nile's musical approach was different than the one employed on the *Madonna* album. Instead of relying on a mechanical drum machine, like Mark Kamins, Jellybean, and Reggie Lucas did on the tracks they produced for her, Nile chose to utilize his former Chic bandmate, drummer Tony Thompson.

Says Nile, "It seemed really important for Madonna to have just a little more musical credibility—just a little more artistry. Because when you're dealing with songs that have the subject matter of Madonna's songs, critics tend to say that they're really weak."[78]

By giving her more musical integrity, the music on *Like a Virgin* definitely had more of an edge; it wasn't so much out of the mechanical Eurodisco arena. That would ultimately help create the across-the-board pop success the LP was met with when it was released.

Nile claims that Madonna, for the most part, has been misunderstood in the industry, and that part of this is due to misogynistic sexual politics. "Someone like Iggy Pop can get out there and be super-sexual and wild and that's great," he explains defensively. "But Madonna is a woman, so they say she's sleazy. And all the arrogance bit—she sticks to her guns, that's all."[14]

This is not to say that Madonna didn't throw a temper tantrum or two in the studio. "It was over some little thing," Rodgers recalls of one of their arguments at the Power Station recording studios. "I can't even recall what it was about now." Rodgers eventually walked out of the studio. Madonna followed a few minutes later. He recalls, "She came up to me and said, 'Does this mean you don't love me anymore?' "[76] He couldn't resist her charm. The anger was behind them.

Madonna remembers, "When we got into the second album, I had a lot more confidence in myself and I had a lot more to do with the way it came out soundwise."[13] Madonna and Nile's successful collaboration yielded a sound with which both parties were content.

According to Madonna, the sound on *Like a Virgin* was a musical progression. "It's much harder, much more aggressive than the first record," she stated when it was released. "The songs on that [first album] were pretty weak and I went to England during the recording, so I wasn't around for a lot of it—I wasn't in control."[31] On the new album Madonna chose all of the songs, with plans for each one to be a hit. She used six of her own songs and six written by other artists.

While Madonna and Nile were working on the *Like a Virgin* album at the Power Station, one of Madonna's idols, Diana Ross, stopped in to meet her. Ms. Ross had been recording in a studio in the same building. Nile and she were friends, so he introduced the two. "Her kids really like my stuff, so she brought a bottle of champagne and toasted my success. I was so flattered."[31]

The recording sessions for *Like a Virgin* were completed in April 1984; the entire package was in the can and ready to release. However, Sire Records was forced to shelf the project for six months—because

Madonna's first album was suddenly selling like hotcakes. To complicate matters, the record company was pleasantly forced to release another single in America.

Jellybean explains that a confusing situation arose, due to the fact that "Borderline" did not become a hit in England. According to him, Warner Brothers in Great Britain wanted to release "Lucky Star" as a single instead, so he was brought in to remix the song. "I thought that I could have done a more outrageous dance version—this was my chance to make 'Lucky Star' more danceable," he recalls. "So, I made it, and they made a video to my version for Europe. It was a big hit in Europe. Then 'Borderline' was a big hit in America, so they decided, 'Well, let's just give the ['Lucky Star'] video to MTV. Then, the video got on MTV and just exploded! They hadn't released a single of 'Lucky Star' over here yet, so they did. They had this all planned, and they never told Madonna. But, when she found out that 'Lucky Star' was coming out as a single, she was really *not happy*."[70]

By this point, the *Madonna* album had hit million-selling status in the United States, as well as having become a huge hit in the U.K., France, Canada, Australia, and South Africa. Instead of releasing *Like a Virgin* on the tail of "Borderline," as previously planned, the record company couldn't risk killing "Lucky Star." Jellybean says, "MTV started playing the 'Lucky Star' video, and then all of these radio stations got requests for 'Lucky Star.' So, the *Madonna* album already had 'Everybody' as a single, 'Physical Attraction,' and 'Burning Up,' then 'Holiday,' then 'Borderline,' [and] 'Lucky Star,' so she was sitting on that album for half a year!"[70]

"Lucky Star" ended up as the biggest single yet for Madonna. However, she knew that the *Like a Virgin* album—musically—was twice the artistic accomplishment of its predecessor. Unfortunately no one could hear it, because Warner Brothers wasn't going to do anything to detract from the sales of "Lucky Star."

Even by September 14, 1984, when Madonna was scheduled to perform the song "Like a Virgin" on the MTV Awards, the record was two months away from release, because "Lucky Star" was headed for the Top Ten—ultimately peaking at Number Four on the pop charts in October.

Broadcast live from Radio City Music Hall, the first annual MTV Awards put Madonna on the same stage as Tina Turner, Rod Stewart, Hall & Oates, Huey Lewis and the News, and ZZ Top. The appearance on the show served many purposes. Not only did Madonna get to introduce her upcoming release, "Like a Virgin," but she was also seen in the context of being a full-fledged rock-and-roller. Although she didn't win the award she was nominated for—Best Video by a New Artist, for "Borderline"—she gave the program's most controversial live performance.

Dressed in a tight-fitting white lace bustier and a skirt and veil composed of yards and yards of white tulle, as the curtain rose she was seen as the bride on top of a huge wedding cake. With her "Boy Toy" belt buckle on, accessorized in chains, strings of pearls, and dangling crucifixes, she was quite a sight. Her blonde-with-dark-brown-roots hair was matted and standing on end. It looked as if she had styled it with Crisco, then tied it in rags. From her right earlobe hung a metallic heart and small crucifix, and from the left earlobe hung a rhinestone-covered silver star. Her wrists were encircled in dozens of bracelets. Madonna was a fashion statement in action.

As she sang the song with a pouting look on her face, she descended from the cake and spun around, with the veil trailing behind her. During the song she removed the veil from her head and threw it to the floor. Then, in the middle of her prime-time debut, she proceeded to hump the floor on her hands and knees as if she were having sex with it. With her tulle skirts creeping up her thighs, revealing her garters and panties, she made an indelible impression. The song ended with Madonna on her back, sprawled on the stage floor.

Bette Midler, who was the show's hostess, returned to the podium and cracked, "Now that the burning question of Madonna's virginity has been answered, we are free to go on to even more GAPING questions— such as, how is a video made? We *know* Madonna's story!"[79]

In an interview a couple of weeks later, I prodded Madonna. "Everyone was talking about you on the MTV Awards."[1]

"That and my underpants," she said, finishing the sentence. "If I ever see those cameramen I will personally kill them. They unleashed cameramen on the stage. I had no idea they were going to be there.

When I rehearsed, there were two cameramen, one was center stage, and one was off on the side. When I did the actual show, there were six all over the place. A camera up my dress, a surprise for everyone."[1]

When I asked her if she saw herself doing a duet recording, Madonna thought for a moment and said, "He'd have to be a man and he'd have to be black—Prince! That would be cool. We're on the same label. Other than that, I'm not interested. There are not that many singers I'm really crazy about."[1]

The Madonna look was beginning to get as much press as her music. In the November 1984 issue of the monthly fashion bible *Harper's Bazaar*, Madonna was depicted in a four-page spread on hot new jewelry accessories. The photos were taken by none other than fashion-photography great Francesco Scavullo. At the sessions he dubbed the aggressive young songstress "baby Dietrich," for her photogenic flair. The jewelry that she modeled in *Harper's Bazaar* was a combination of costume pieces, with price tags in the $100-to-$200 range. But in her own day-to-day wear, Madonna's accessories were comprised of very inexpensive pieces of junk jewelry.

Almost immediately, Madonna was looked upon in the fashion industry as a trend-setter. For little girls especially, her look was much easier and cheaper to replicate than Cyndi Lauper's tie-dyed hair. Madonna's junk jewelry was an immediate hit. The little rubber bracelets—which were actually O-rings used as drive belts for typewriters—became the hottest selling and least expensive accessory to acquire. A store on Manhattan's Canal Street called Canal Rubber, mere blocks from Madonna's new SoHo loft space, saw a fast change in their clientele. Mingling with the beer-bellied mechanics who usually frequented the store on any given Saturday afternoon were hordes of scantily clad teenage girls. At twenty-five cents each, girls and guys could line their forearms with the "bracelets" by the dozen. It wasn't long before Canal Rubber had to stock them by the case.

The person who takes credit for coming up with the rubber bracelet craze is a jewelry designer known as Maripol (pronounced *Mary Paul*). A striking woman with a thick French accent and a look reminiscent of Lina Wertmuller, Maripol was one of Madonna's closest friends during this era. The two women met on the photo session for Madonna's first album. Maripol was invited by the photographer, as a fashion stylist. Maripol was also Madonna's fashion stylist for several key events, including the filming of the "Burning Up" video, the photo session for Madonna's second album cover, and the controversial MTV Awards telecast.

Madonna immediately made a strong impression on Maripol. According to the jewelry designer, "Madonna is a child-woman. She is fun and joyful, but she is also a femme fatale. She is vulnerable—but then she's not that vulnerable. She's not tough exactly—but she'll survive through anything. She's a natural star. She is born to stardom."[80]

Explaining their initial connection, Maripol recalls, "I met Madonna actually on the first album cover—and we came up with the idea of the rubber bracelets. It was an idea that I had, and now everyone is wearing the idea. But originally it was my idea. We met and we became friends. And, since I'm a stylist, she became very involved with me, and I helped her a lot. I did the costume for the MTV look—the MTV Awards. And, I did style the last album [cover photo] *Like a Virgin*. And, I don't know if you realized, but I kind of got the 'soft' feeling, because I thought it was interesting to have a wedding dress, and we did that. And so, we did the whole thing—from the bouquet, to the veil, to the hair."[80]

Said Maripol then, "Madonna is very faithful to my 'look,' and she wears my jewelry all of the time. I do make special things for her that I don't sell to the public—special items."[80]

With Madonna parading around town in her jewelry, the enterprising French woman put together the backing to start her own shop in Greenwich Village, Maripolitan. As Madonna's popularity flourished, Maripol's business blossomed. Her shop was filled with jewelry laden with irreverently placed religious symbols. According to Maripol, the crucifixes in her designs became a common bond between them. "We do collect rosaries together. Whenever I buy them, or I get them—I give her," she said. "I started to make crosses during the punk movement in 1979, which was by religious belief also. But, just because it was fun to wear it on the ears. It was a punk sign of rejecting religion.... It's kind of a little voodoo protection, whatever sign. With Madonna, it's perfect, because of the name she wears, and she really likes it right away. I guess she assimilated herself to that. The trend was set right after that, because everybody started doing it . . . a trend became a trademark."[80]

Finally, by November 1984 "Lucky Star" had cooled down on the charts to the point where the album, the single, and the "Like a Virgin" video could all be released into the marketplace without any conflict. The way the last ten months had gone for Madonna laid the perfect groundwork for the new product. The fact that MTV treated the new video with the importance due a movie premiere assisted the single and album sales in a flawless fashion.

The outrageously titillating fact that a sexy, self-confident girl with the name of "Madonna" could release a song entitled "Like a Virgin" piqued everyone's curiosity. The factor of Ms. Ciccone obviously being no virgin, and the added element that the whole product had a borderline tinge of sacrilege, only further promoted the package. The single was in the Top Forty in two weeks, and by Christmas it was in its six-week reign as the Number One single in America. Likewise, the album was Top Ten in two weeks, and Number One by January.

Madonna was immediately crowned the pop provocateur *extraordinaire*. Madonna was shocked by the reaction to the single, "Like a Virgin." What she had intended to be a harmless, upbeat song was perceived as something else. "Everyone interpreted it as 'I don't want to be a virgin anymore—fuck my brains out!' That's not what I want at all."[81]

Bette Midler's line about her was perhaps the most tongue-in-cheek and on-target of all: "Like a virgin, indeed!" she sniped. "The only thing Madonna will do like a virgin is have a baby in a stable!"[82]

The press immediately jumped on the situation, having fun with the puns that the ironic song sung by the "Boy Toy" represented. PRIMA DONNA MADONNA proclaimed *Us* magazine, with the subhead: "The lady didn't become a phenom by obeying the rules of Emily Post." "VIRGIN TERRITORY: How Madonna Straddles Innocence and Decadence," wrote *The New Republic*. And Britain's *19* magazine headlined its take on Madonna: VIRGIN ON THE RIDICULOUS!

Madonna was on the top of the world, and her romp was just beginning. But from the start, some of the press coverage was less benign.

It was asserted more than once that she had slept her way to the summit, using sex as a tool of trade. She was publicly incensed by the allegations.

"The fact of the matter is that you can use your beauty and use your charm and be flirtatious, and you can get people interested in you," she claimed while plotting how she was going to have the last laugh.[76] While beauty may buy you a ticket, it can't guarantee that the show will last. Ultimately, talent is all that matters. Although it took time for some people to figure out that Madonna was as much talent as she was beauty, her videos, records, and movies more than proved her skill.

The criticism only enhanced her tough-as-nails survival attitude. She's been called every name in the book, but she doesn't seem to care. "I'm tough, I'm ambitious, and I know exactly what I want—and if that makes me a bitch, that's okay."[12]

The video version of "Like a Virgin" represented a hallmark for Madonna; her video productions were to grow more and more elaborate as time went by. This time around she was seen as a hip chick in Venice, lolling, writhing, and undulating in a gondola in the Grand Canal. In intercut segments, she poses as a classic virginal bride, being laid down on the nuptial bed, obviously anticipating the loss of her "pure" status. One of her co-stars is a furry lion, whose role as anything more than an impressive feline is never quite established. But then, videos don't have to make any sense.

According to Madonna, the filming process was quite entertaining. "I had such a wonderful time there," she says of her on-location filming. "We just felt that Venice symbolized so many things—like virginity. And, I'm Madonna, and I'm Italian."[83]

They used a live lion in the video, teeth and all. Despite the fact that the lion tamer assured her the lion wouldn't bite, Madonna remembers the experience as a scary one. The lion didn't follow directions as well as Madonna had hoped. While she leaned against a pillar, the lion was supposed to walk past her right side. The lion tamer tried to lure the lion in that direction, but the next thing Madonna knew, the lion was nudging against her left leg. "I looked down and the lion was RIGHT THERE with his head in my crotch! So, I lifted my veil and had a stare-down with the lion!" The two stared at each other for nearly one minute, then the lion opened its mouth and roared. "I got so frightened my heart fell in my shoe," Madonna recalls. By the time the lion moved on,

Madonna was so shaken, she took a short break. She says, despite the scare, "I could really relate to the lion. I felt like in a past life I was a lion or a cat or something."[84]

Amid the tidal wave of Madonna excitement, Warner released an album filled with rare B-sides by some of its top artists, including Fleetwood Mac, Talking Heads, and the B-52's. Entitled *Revenge of the Killer B's,* the album also included one of the three existing versions of "Ain't No Big Deal"—the Reggie Lucas–produced rendition of the song. Although an interesting curiosity, had it been included on the original *Madonna* album it would definitely have had the distinction of being the weakest cut on the album. The *Killer B's* album went on to become a collector's item, totally eclipsed by the excitement created by the release of "Like a Virgin."

Madonna had been courting fame for the past three years, ever since she zeroed in on Mark Kamins at Danceteria and signed with Sire Records in 1982. In December 1984 she was the most talked about female in the record business. Her running mates on the record charts were sleek British pop/jazz singer Sade and kooky Brooklynite rocker Cyndi Lauper. However, the tarty "Like a Virgin" controversy pushed her even further up the scale of notoriety. With fame came changes.

One of the first new pressures was the fact that she was immediately recognizable on the streets of New York City, or—thanks to MTV— everywhere else in North America. Whether walking down the street or shopping in a store, Madonna realized people recognized her. She was often approached with questions like, "Are you really Madonna?" While shopping, fans would take note of what the star would buy. "It really bothered me," she says.[5]

The next occurrence of outward pressure was directed at her relationship with Jellybean. Earlier that year, while she was in England, she made an offhand comment that was a preview of the future. When an inquiring reporter asked her what it was like dating someone who was also entwined in the music business, she replied, "Very tiring. When you're working—and your private relationship is falling apart, it's hard to carry on. When you're getting on, you can't stop talking about the record business and then you wonder if you have anything else in common."[85]

After "Like a Virgin" was released, Jellybean watched Madonna's fame surpass his almost overnight. "It gets pretty crazy sometimes," he explained at the time. "People are constantly—not clawing her—but we go to a restaurant and we can't go anyplace where she has to sit idle for too long. If we go to a movie we have to get there just before they let people in—walk into the theater and get the worst seats. We can't go to Macy's shopping. Things like that, that I never thought about before, have to be considered now. We can't go to a restaurant where it's really bright. We can't just go to any club anymore, because we have to be careful of the type of people that go to the club."[70]

On November 7, 1984, there was a private party for Madonna at a popular video club called Private Eyes, on West 21st Street. It was a reception to kick off the release of her *Like a Virgin* album, and a chance for the press to mingle with Madonna. Her date for the evening was Jellybean, and the guests included Andy Warhol and designer Dianne Brill. However, when she arrived at the intimate high-tech club, she was almost immediately mobbed, so she had to be whisked up to a secluded balcony, where she could look down on the crowd and talk to her friends through the railings. Her new status was about to cut her off from dozens of people who were once considered close friends.

"I can't take the subway," she complained that autumn. "I did till a few months ago. Now it's really a pain in the ass. I take a cab everywhere, and I hate taking cabs. I ride my bike a lot, too. It's really hard when you go to restaurants and everyone stares. I don't want people staring at me. I want to eat! Or, standing in line at the grocery store, and people are looking to see what you're buying. Or, when you're in a store and everyone wants to see what you're buying. I just leave. It turns a lot of things off to me."[1]

According to Jellybean, "Right after the 'Borderline' video, people started noticing her a lot. I mean, people used to notice her a lot—just from walking down the street. And then, people would bother her. I really shouldn't say 'bother' her—but fans would come over all the time and want autographs and stuff. So, it was a learning experience for her, something she had to adjust to."[70]

That Christmas, Madonna and Jellybean decided to get away from the hassle of her newfound notoriety in New York City. They got on a jet and breezed off to the Virgin Islands to escape the craziness. They had an extremely relaxing holiday together—until they got on the plane to come home.

"We were coming back from our Christmas vacation in St. Martin," explains Jellybean. "On the plane, she didn't want to give any autographs at all; she was on vacation. And, I had to agree with her, it was like constantly, constantly, people hounding her—'Madonna! Madonna! Madonna!' She was in one of *those* moods. It was a really difficult plane flight, because people kept wanting to take pictures, and everybody's on vacation, so they wanted her autograph. So, I was like a security guard on the way back. These little girls kept coming over and trying to take a picture, and I kept blocking Madonna's face with a magazine. And this woman comes over and says she wanted an autograph, and it was the least that Madonna could do—because she was a pediatrician, and she works hard for her kids to buy Madonna records. It was like half of the plane was rooting for Madonna, and half of the plane was rooting for the other woman."[70]

As far as their love affair was concerned, in February 1985 Jellybean philosophized, "I think that the relationship will run its course, just like any other relationship. If it was meant to be, it will last. I'm a real strong believer in fate. I think that it was really good that we ended up meeting when we met—because we helped each other through some very difficult times."[70] It was wise of Jellybean to be so level-headed about his relationship, because he was about to become history as far as Madonna was concerned.

During this same period, Madonna was also waxing philosophical about her position on the planet. According to her, "My image—to people—I think, is that I'm this brazen, aggressive young woman who has an OK voice with some pretty exciting songs . . . and has the potential as an actress."[2] The acting potential was, at this time, more in Madonna's mind than in the world's image of her. But with her relentless drive— she was about to change all that.

Seven

I always said that I wanted

Desperately

to be famous. I just love the glamour

Seeking

and the attention.[12] *—Madonna*

Fame

I t is an acknowledged fact that Madonna has an attitude problem. Especially at the beginning of her career, Madonna behaved like a stuck-up bitch. There is a fine line between being ambitious and being downright pushy, and she often crossed it. According to her friends, if you ever provoke her, she'll treat you like you never existed, but if you can do something for her—she'll act like your best friend. Madonna rubbed a lot of people the wrong way right from the start. She can be charming if she chooses to be, but if she doesn't she can come across as cold and arrogant.

The minute she became famous, Madonna began making statements that caused people to question her motives and her sincerity. It wasn't just that she was perceived as having questionable morals; she seemed to go out of her way to look for conflicts to create. She quickly learned that the more outrageous her statements were, the more press she received.

Religious groups, especially members of the Catholic church, immediately bristled at the sight of all the crucifixes she wore—dangling from chains around her neck, her earlobes, and any number of other parts of her body. While she openly displayed several crucifixes as part of her fashion accessories, she was usually wearing them on top of outfits that would get her banned from any church, synagogue, or mosque. When asked about wearing the crucifixes, Madonna would reply, "Crucifixes are sexy because there's a naked man on them."[86] That statement was always good for maximum shock value.

She would elaborate, "When I was a little girl, we had crucifixes all over the house, as a reminder that Jesus Christ died on the cross for us."[15]

Since the song that really made her an international sensation was "Like a Virgin," another popular press query centered on the evident loss of her own virginity. How did she feel about losing it? According to her, "I didn't lose my virginity until I knew what I was doing."[15]

She claimed that the negative press she began to receive was unjust. She quickly learned to confront the press head on, accusing the press of sexist double standards. "Sexy boys never get bad press,"[15] she said, citing Prince as a specific example.

As everyone in show business knows, even bad press is good press. A good scandal can sell as much product as a favorable review, and Madonna was well aware of that. With her typically bratty attitude she clairvoyantly proclaimed, "1985 is going to be my year. You watch!"[87]

In the beginning of 1985, Madonna remained mistress of her own destiny. She had learned to rely on one of Warner Records' head publicists, Liz Rosenberg, to field the mounting requests for interviews. She had also hired crackerjack lawyer Paul Schindler to represent her business deals. Through her intelligent business acumen, Madonna wanted to communicate to the music industry that she wasn't just another blonde bimbo. "I am in control of myself," she said.[65]

Especially in the beginning of her career, she was a willful and abrasive girl, and she knew it. "I can be arrogant sometimes, but I never mean it intentionally," she claimed. "I always acted like a star long before I was one."[84]

Although Madonna's success in 1985 was a combination of brilliant timing and masterful strategies, several of the things that occurred were totally out of her control. Once she got the ball rolling, it was impossible to stop her fame from growing. By the time the avalanche of a year was over, anyone who didn't know Madonna must have lived under a rock.

Madonna's fame was magnified a thousand times larger than any new one-shot singer with a hit album and Number One song, mainly by the fact that as soon as she hit the top of the music charts, and became a fixture on MTV, she was also seen as a brilliant new movie star as well.

In the summer of 1984, when Madonna was signed to appear in the modestly budgeted feature film, *Desperately Seeking Susan,* no one could have predicted how successful the film was to become. A simple light-hearted screwball comedy, the movie was originally seen as a starring vehicle for promising young actress Rosanna Arquette.

With a 1930s-style plot involving amnesia, a case of mistaken identity, and a stolen Egyptian artifact, the script was fresh, light, and charming. Another interesting aspect to *Desperately Seeking Susan* was that it was very much a women's production. With the exception of executive producer Michael Peyser, the four key people involved in making the film were women: director Susan Seidelman, producers Sarah Pillsbury and Midge Sanford, and screenwriter Leora Barish.

The film was to become the first milestone for the acclaimed but relatively unproven director, Susan Seidelman. The film represented her first shot at big league movie-making and it was a gamble that has paid off. (She has directed such major features as *She-Devil* with Meryl Streep since then.) A graduate of New York University's film school, Seidelman had previously directed the popular low-budget cult film *Smithereens,* about a young woman's adventures in the East Village punk rock scene. When Susan first read the script for *Desperately Seeking Susan,* it immediately appealed to her.

It was Warner Brothers Pictures that originally had the script in development, and they were hoping to end up with Cher, Goldie Hawn, or Diane Keaton in the starring role. When producers Sanford and Pillsbury parted company with Warner, they took the project to Orion Pictures, and the ball suddenly started rolling.

According to Seidelman, "When Orion decided to do the movie, they knew that it was going to be this script, me as the director, and

Rosanna as the star."[88] Arquette's role of Roberta, a New Jersey housewife who longed for adventure, was in contrast to the title role of Susan.
Finding Susan was a pivotal point in the production casting.

"We were looking for somebody to play Susan," recalls Seidelman.
"I knew Madonna for a couple of years. She was beginning to get popular.
I kept seeing her face when I read the script, as Susan. She seemed
like an exciting choice. And, I think at first the producers and the studio
people were a little nervous."[88]

Producer Midge Sanford said they were looking for an unknown
actress with a wild side and a strong screen presence. When the idea
of using the aspiring "Lucky Star" singer was suggested, Sanford had
to admit, "Madonna has an incredible look and a very strong style."[48]

When co-producer Sarah Pillsbury met her, she found Madonna to
be a "punk Mae West" and "a total fantasy for both men and women."[7]
It was a gamble, but one they decided to bank on.

At this point, *Vision Quest* was mired down in a series of delays,
so no one had it as a reference point for Madonna's reliability. Initially
it was difficult for the producers to take Madonna seriously as a professional. "I think they were shocked when I showed up every morning
like clockwork," Madonna recalls.[24]

Seidelman had nothing but glowing things to say about Madonna's
performance on camera. "There was something about Madonna. I think
it's just kind of 'her.' She's got a sort of 'bad girl/good girl' quality that
I think is real interesting. She's a little tough, but not too tough. A little
'street,' but also, I think, really appealing. Earthy, in a way that I thought
was essential to the character. I didn't want to get an actress who was
going to try to put on clothes and sort of a make-believe street attitude.
I thought that Madonna had an authentic quality that would be really
good to try to capture on film. I was a little nervous myself, because
there was a lot of dialogue in the script, and I just didn't know how well
she'd do. But I had seen her in her videos. She's a performer. I think
that if she can perform on video, she can perform on film. Once she
had the confidence to allow herself to be uninhibited on the film, she's
wonderful. There's a presence."[88]

The film's unit publicist, Reid Rosefelt, echoed Seidelman's praises
of Madonna: "She was always there when she had to be there. I think
when people are talking about hiring somebody from the world of rock

and roll for a movie, they don't believe that they ever go to sleep, or they're always at parties, or something like that. But, that's not the case with Madonna. She was really dedicated, and a real pro all the way."[89]

The filming, which was done in September, October, and November of 1984, began before Madonna had appeared on the MTV Awards telecast, and before the whole "Like a Virgin" sensation exploded. The growth of Madonna's fame created an unexpected problem for the film: the possibility of alienating Rosanna. According to Susan Seidelman, Rosanna was hired as the movie's star. When the film began, Madonna was relatively unknown, but as filming progressed, so, too, did Madonna's fame. "I think Rosanna's fear was that it was going to turn into a Madonna vehicle," Susan recalled.[90]

Arquette was known largely for her acting on the small screen. Her roles up to that point included parts in the television movies *Executioner's Song* and *Harvest Home* with Bette Davis. Her movie work had included *S.O.B.*, a starring role in *Baby, It's You*, and Martin Scorcese's *After Hours*. She also had a curious rock and roll identity, having been the inspiration for the hit song by the group Toto: "Rosanna."

During the filming of *Desperately Seeking Susan*, Madonna and Rosanna reported to interviewers that they had become close friends. According to Madonna, "We're like sisters—we've got lots of miseries in common, and boyfriend problems."[91]

"I love her—she's my long-lost sister," Rosanna claimed with praise for Madonna.[91] "I have never met anyone who has such a focus."[92]

Although Madonna was nervous for the first few scenes, it wasn't long before she found her sea legs on the set. Everyone who knows Madonna agrees that in *Desperately Seeking Susan*, the singer isn't acting as much as she is being herself on film. The Madonna that you see on the screen in this movie is the real Madonna Ciccone, only slightly magnified.

One of the production aspects that was important for the believability of the part of Susan, and for Madonna's identification with her, was the costuming. "She's wearing a lot of her own stuff," says Rosefelt of Madonna's clothes in the film, "because 'Susan' has a lot of crucifixes on, and a lot of jewelry. In large part, these are Madonna's own clothes."[89]

Explaining how this came about, Rosefelt says, "Santo Loquasto was the designer of the costumes as well as the production designer for the whole film. He's worked with Woody Allen—he won an Oscar nomination for *Zelig* and a Tony Award for *The Cherry Orchard*. So, he's a very big guy in the design world. He knows what he's doing. His vision of the character was much more 'West Side'—old clothes and 'thrift shop,' which is not Madonna's look at all. He went up to Madonna's place and looked through her things, and I think there was kind of a give-and-take between what Santo wanted, and what Madonna wanted, and what the plot needed—what Susan Seidelman needed. I mean, there are certain clothes—there's a pair of boots which are very important to the plot. They're like glitter boots, and that's a very important part of the story of the film. And, I think that those might not be boots that Madonna would want to wear, but they looked very good on film. Certain things had to be worked out. It was a mutual discussion."[89]

Explains Madonna, "In the beginning, the costumes Santo had gotten for me were things—I never would have dressed that way. They were from vintage shops, like Cyndi Lauper dresses, like lots of layers of antique clothing. I hated it! Stiletto heels and stuff." When she saw what he had chosen for her, she very vocally protested. "So now," she said, amid production, "I wear a lot of my own accessories—I have rags tied in my hair, tights in my hair. I wear a pair of men's trousers. I didn't want to wear these fifties dresses, chiffon black dresses. I put together things, like one outfit will be my shirt, their skirt, my socks, their shoes. It's a combination."[1]

Explaining the character of Susan, Madonna illuminates, "I thought I shared a lot with Susan. She's a free spirit and she says and does what she wants. She's a clever con artist and she doesn't let you know when you're being conned."[87] That is Madonna to a T.

"Acting is just another kind of performing," claimed Madonna during the filming. "It's just an expression, it's just being honest with your audience."[87] After Madonna read the script for *Desperately Seeking Susan*, she was confident she would be able to pull off the part. Susan, like Madonna, was the character that everyone flocked to. She had few roots, but she had a strong sense of personal freedom.

Madonna claims that there were both similarities and differences between herself and the character she played on the screen. "She's exciting and unpredictable—irresponsible, vulnerable," she says on the shared characteristics list. "But, we're not exactly alike. She doesn't have any goal, it seems, except to complicate everyone's life. And I did. I want to be somebody. I have goals and directions. Susan doesn't have an occupation or any skills. She just appears and disappears. That gives her a real enigmatic feeling, a sense of fantasy. I think I have more of a definition about myself."[1]

According to Seidelman, Madonna was a charm to work with. "She is an incredibly disciplined person," she says. "During the shoot we'd often get home at 11 or 12 at night and have to be back on the set by 6 or 7 the next morning. Half the time the driver would pick Madonna up at her health club. She'd get up at 4:30 in the morning to work out first."[24]

Film acting requires a lot of patience, which was difficult for Madonna. One can often sit for six or seven hours before shooting a three-second scene. More than once, Madonna lost her composure altogether. According to her, "I'll be working on a scene and doing it the way I think it should be done. Then the director will tell me to try it a different way."[48] Criticism often angered Madonna. But thanks to a supportive cast, she was able to work through her bad moods.

Waiting around between takes was what pissed her off the most. "I would like to work the whole time I'm on the set. They get you in in the morning and you're all made up and you don't work till after lunch. Or you have one scene really early in the morning, and you don't work again till five, and you're just sitting there—you can't screw up your makeup or your costume. I'm a hyperactive person. I'm used to dancing eight hours a day, and now I'm sitting around eight hours a day."[1]

In her scenes as Susan, she always seemed either to be eating junk food or kissing one of the actors. "I'm making out in every other scene," she claimed. "I don't sing in the movie, but I eat Cheez Doodles a lot. I'm always stuffing my face in this movie—constantly! I spit a lot of it out. In the morning I do not want to eat gumdrops and Cheez Doodles. She's really a pig, you know. She eats all the time—always has something in her mouth, whether it's a cigarette, a drink."[1]

According to Madonna, her favorite scene is one in which she's in bed smoking a joint with a married man while his wife is out of the house. "I don't have any method of acting, but I just knew that scene was funny."[93]

Added pressures arose that threatened the filming schedule due to Madonna's mounting fame. When the production began in September, she was still relatively unknown. However, by November, when "Like a Virgin" began to hit the airwaves, she was an overnight celebrity. But there was an unwritten law on the set that *Desperately Seeking Susan* was not to become "the Madonna movie" and that it was not going to end up a vehicle for her recording career. It was an ensemble film, and everyone who appeared in it was to have equal importance in it. However, Madonna being who she was, and by the sheer coincidence of "Like a Virgin" just happening to take off when it did, the movie ended up with its own Madonna hit song: "Into the Groove."

One sequence of the movie needed a song with a strong dance beat, so the director, Susan Seidelman, asked Madonna whether she had something that might work. Madonna brought in a tape of "Into the Groove," which she and Steve Bray had made. They played it a few times and eventually the director, the producers, and Orion recognized that it perfectly suited the film's needs.

Although Madonna was for the most part dedicated and professional in her work on *Desperately Seeking Susan*, she still displayed her arrogant side from time to time. "She had attitude," recalls Reid Rosefelt. "She's cool, but there's also a kind of wink in it as well. I've worked with people like that before, and I wasn't surprised by it. And, I figured that if she acted like that, that she wasn't really serious. I think that some people can meet her for one meeting for a half-hour, and they can get the wrong idea. When we finished up publicity, Madonna gave me a poster, and she signed it, and it said: 'To Reid: You've been a real pain in the ass. Thanks a lot!—Madonna.' That sort of sums up the whole thing."[89]

In January 1985, before the release of *Vision Quest*, and before the release of *Desperately Seeking Susan*, Madonna had a full schedule ahead of her. "Like a Virgin" was still the Number One single in America, but it was time to prepare for the release of her next hit song, "Material Girl," by filming the accompanying video.

The resulting video was a concept piece for Madonna, one that would start off a career-long theme: her obsession with Marilyn Monroe. Madonna had always been fascinated by the legend of Marilyn, and it was her idea to mimic one of Monroe's most famous scenes, from the film *Gentlemen Prefer Blondes*.

"Well, my favorite scene in all of Monroe's movies is when she does that dance sequence for 'Diamonds Are a Girl's Best Friend.' And when it came time to do the video for the song, I said, I can just redo that whole scene and it'll be perfect," she claims.[94]

Gentlemen Prefer Blondes, based on a famous Anita Loos novel by the same name, was about a pair of gold diggers—girls out to snag a rich man—on a wild romp. "Material Girl," which was written by Peter Brown and Robert Rans, immediately struck a chord in Madonna. Pondering the stance that holds true for all gold diggers—herself included—Madonna explained, "I'm very career-oriented. You are attracted to people who are ambitious that way, too, like in the song 'Material Girl.' You are attracted to men who have material things because that's what pays the rent and buys you furs. That's the security. That lasts longer than emotion."[95]

With regard to the whole Marilyn connection, Madonna feels a link with Marilyn Monroe. "In those days, you were really a slave to the whole Hollywood machinery, and unless you had strength to pull yourself out of it, you were just trapped," she reflects.[81]

For the "Material Girl" video, Madonna again tapped the talents of director Mary Lambert. She was originally set to work with Jean-Paul Goude, Grace Jones's husband, but she didn't like his ideas for the song. She had worked with Mary on her "Borderline" and "Like a Virgin" videos. Lambert has since graduated to feature films, including the wildly outrageous *Pet Sematary*.

Just one year earlier, Mary had worked with Madonna on "Borderline." Since then, she felt that her whole strategy in a Madonna video had changed. For the first video, Lambert wanted Madonna's video persona to gibe with her off-screen personality, so that viewers would feel as if they knew her. After the first video, however, Madonna had reached star status, so Lambert felt free to let her play any image she chose for "Material Girl."

The conceptual work on the "Material Girl" video began just before Christmas 1984. Lambert had one concept of what the video should look like; she wrote up the scenario, storyboarded it, and presented it to

Madonna. However, Madonna was insistent on her "Diamonds Are a Girl's Best Friend" concept. Taking that idea, Lambert went back to the storyboard, and on New Year's Eve day, came up with a new concept in which to set the takeoff on the Monroe number. The pressure was on to produce the video almost immediately, so the whole production was a mad dash.

On New Year's Day the concept was approved, and preproduction began. "Madonna had two days during the entire month of January when she could shoot it," recalls Lambert.[96] With her newfound stardom, Madonna was booked to go to Tokyo and Hawaii shortly thereafter. Once the concept and the treatment were finalized, Lambert and her crew had to work fast.

The concept is that Madonna is an actress filming the musical number on a soundstage and behind the scenes she is being pursued by a handsome filmmaker, played by Keith Carradine. The musical number is intercut with the behind-the-scenes action.

The dress that Madonna wears in the video was an identical copy of the one Bill Travilla designed for Marilyn in Howard Hawks's 1953 *Gentlemen Prefer Blondes*. It is an ankle-length, pink satin shoulderless gown, worn with three-quarter-length evening gloves. Over the gloves she wears sparkling diamond bracelets, in addition to a diamond necklace and diamond earrings. Watching the Marilyn number back-to-back with Madonna's video, it is clear that "Material Girl" was done on a smaller budget, but on television the effect it creates is perfect.

According to the video's producer, Simon Fields, in her videos Madonna creates an air of beauty and charisma. Designer Bill Travilla claims that by mimicking Marilyn, Madonna is "searching for herself."[73] While in the original number, Monroe projects a bubbly joy along with the gold digger posture, Madonna gives off more of an air of cold calculation. The effect, however, is hysterically amusing, driving home the materialistic message of the song.

On January 10, while she was filming her "Material Girl" video at a breakneck pace, someone totally unexpected showed up on the soundstage in Los Angeles. It was actor Sean Penn, the sullen, brooding "Brat Pack" actor. He was friendly with director Mary Lambert, and she had invited him to stop by if he found the time. That chance meeting was to culminate in one of the most headline-grabbing unions of the entire decade.

Madonna was in the middle of one of her scenes and there before her eyes was Penn. She recalls, "I noticed this guy in a leather jacket and sunglasses kind of standing in the corner, looking at me. And I realized it was Sean Penn, and I immediately had this fantasy that we were going to meet and fall in love and get married."[26]

Witnesses remember that Madonna was cool with Penn on the set that day, acknowledging him simply with a brief hello. Penn stuck around for several hours, and Madonna ran into him again. According to her, "I was like, 'Oh, you're still here?' So I went outside to talk to him."[26] With the production people still swarming around, it was difficult for the two to have a conversation, but just before Penn left the set, Madonna gave him a rose. She had bought roses for all of the cast and crew members, and as an afterthought she presented him with one.

That was their less than dramatic first meeting. Later that evening, Sean went over to a friend's house and couldn't stop talking about Madonna. Holding a book of quotations in his hand, he would choose a selection about love and claim that it described her. When he wouldn't quit talking about her, the friend finally advised him: "Go get her!"[97]

From Los Angeles, Madonna flew to Hawaii to shoot a series of photo sessions that would yield a *Madonna 1986 Calendar*. The photos of her wallowing in the black sand of the volcanic beach at Kaanapali, Hawaii—in a Jean-Paul Gaultier backless outfit and a huge crucifix— have since been reproduced in several publications. The sessions marked her first solo work with the photographer Herb Ritts, who was known for his unique celebrity portraits on the covers of *Rolling Stone*, *Vanity Fair*, and *Esquire*. Madonna had met him only months before when he photographed her with Rosanna Arquette for *Desperately Seeking Susan*. They have worked together countless times since then.

Her next stop was Japan, for a promotional visit. Then she quickly returned to Los Angeles to appear on the January 28th American Music Awards telecast, where her date was Jellybean Benitez. Madonna was nominated for Favorite Female Pop Vocalist, but the award went to Cyndi Lauper. Also on the show, Madonna presented an award to Prince and his band, The Revolution. She and Prince chatted backstage, and

Madonna happily posed for the sea of photographers who swarmed around her. She was in her element—basking amid the glow of dozens of flashbulbs.

That night was to be Madonna's final date with Jellybean. Their relationship was now officially over. The former New York City dance diva was now the hottest new Hollywood arrival, and her dance card was soon filled.

Madonna had known for a while that the relationship wasn't going to last. "He's a Scorpio and we both want to be stars, so it's tough going all the way," she said.[84]

According to Jellybean, at the time he was still in love with her. However, he simply was not on her agenda for the future. He realized that her career came first. "She really wants it—that's the difference between her and a lot of other artists," he claims.[76]

After Jellybean flew back to New York, Madonna stayed behind. For the first time, Madonna was in Los Angeles with time on her hands, and she was soon intrigued by a whole new world full of people, places, and thrills to discover. In her eyes, suddenly New York City was looking comparatively gray and dirty.

Several days later, back in Manhattan, and unhappy about his breakup with Madonna, Jellybean sat in a posh restaurant on East 12th Street called the Gotham Bar & Grill and confided, "We had gone through changes just like any other couple—we'd break up for a week or two." Tracing his history with her, by the apartments she dwelled in, he reflected, "She went from Fourth Street, to 13th Street, to SoHo. We were living together in SoHo, until we started not getting along."[70]

Meanwhile, on the West Coast, the day after the American Music Awards, Prince contacted Madonna and offered her tickets to his upcoming concert at the Forum. She gladly accepted the invitation to attend one of the concert dates, which were three weeks away.

Among her activities in L.A. that month, Madonna had her first date with Sean Penn. The initial night they were together, Penn took her to a party at Warren Beatty's house. "I guess he wanted to show me off—I'm not sure."[98] Not only did she meet future love interest Warren Beatty, but she was also introduced to her future buddy Sandra Bernhard, as well as Mickey Rourke and several other members of the Hollywood glitterati. "He was introducing me to all his friends." she recalls.[99]

Also during that same visit to Los Angeles, Sean took Madonna on a sightseeing tour around town to all of the places he thought would interest her. Sean took Madonna to Marilyn Monroe's grave in the Westwood Cemetery. "Joe DiMaggio's rose was there," she sighed, at the sight of the regularly delivered flower, "he really loved her."[24]

At the time, she was impressed with Sean, but she wasn't exactly blown away by his charms: "I don't feel swept off my feet, but he is somebody whose work I have admired for a long time. He's wild, though."[24] The two had very much in common: both were temperamental, they were born one day apart, and, according to Madonna, he resembled her father.

Sean Penn already had a reputation for burning the candle at both ends. The son of director and actor Leo Penn and actress Eileen Ryan, he and his brothers Chris and Michael were encouraged to pursue careers in show business.

Hanging out with a group of BMW-driving young actors, Sean and his cohorts became the talk of Hollywood in the eighties, not only for the screen roles, but for their camaraderie. Soon they became dubbed the "Brat Pack," reminiscent of Frank Sinatra's "Rat Pack" in the fifties. Sinatra's clan included Dean Martin, Sammy Davis, Jr., and Peter Lawford; the Brat Pack included Penn and pals Timothy Hutton, Emilio Estevez, Tom Cruise, Rob Lowe, and Judd Nelson.

Growing up in affluence with other Hollywood brats, Penn was always a thrill-seeker, fascinated with guns and violence. He recalls one sick gag he staged as a school kid, involving a .22-caliber machine gun loaded with blanks and a movie studio "blood bag." The objective was to stage a drive-by machine-gun shooting, kidnap a school friend named Kelly, and scare him senseless. Sean and another friend, with ski masks over their faces, pretended to machine-gun their buddy Emilio. At the sound of the gunfire, Emilio clutched his chest, bursting the bag filled with stage blood, while terrified Kelly looked on. They then kidnapped Kelly at gunpoint, dragged him into a car, and drove him to a secluded wooded area.

Recalls Penn, "We stop and tell him to get out of the car, and we say, 'We're not going to hurt you, but we're gonna tie you to this tree, and then we're gonna take off.' This was the greatest ever—out of the back of the car we take this gasoline can—it's full of water—and my buddy lights a match. The guy starts screaming. I pour water on the guy, and my buddy flips a match at him! Then we tell him. Emilio arrives, and we have a little picnic." And what happened to Kelly? Says Sean, "That guy has never been the same since."[100]

Growing up in the movie capital of the universe, it wasn't long before Sean began to long to become an actor. Encouraged by his parents, he started going to auditions. With his beady, close-set eyes, long nose, and sneering mouth, he gravitated toward brooding bad boy roles. His mother once gave him an effective piece of advice about going to acting auditions: "When you go in, you have to picture them *not* sitting at a desk but sitting on a toilet." According to him, "It's amazing how that will make you feel strong."[100]

His professional acting debut came in a short-lived Broadway play called *Heartland,* which opened and closed in a matter of weeks. However, he was spotted on-stage by an agent who recommended him for his first movie role. He made his debut in the 1981 *Taps,* a film about anarchy in a boys' academy. Because of *Taps,* his career, and those of his co-stars—Timothy Hutton and Tom Cruise—were cemented. Penn next starred as a drugged-out high school jerk in the popular teenage comedy *Fast Times at Ridgemont High.* He became the answer to a director's prayer whenever a young, mean, misfit part appeared in a script. Roles in Louis Malle's comedy caper *Crackers* and Richard Benjamin's *Racing with the Moon* followed in 1984. According to Penn, his dream role is to one day portray the disillusioned sixties protest singer Phil Ochs on the screen.

In the early eighties Penn was engaged to marry Bruce Springsteen's younger sister, Pam, but the romance didn't last long enough to get to the altar. When he was filming *Racing with the Moon* he began a much-publicized romance with his co-star, Elizabeth McGovern. Around the time of their affair, Penn's volatile temper began to become a much-talked-about issue. A highly insecure and immature young man, Penn would explode at the mere thought that his current love interest would so much as look at another man. There was a famous incident on the set of *Racing with the Moon.* Elizabeth was in her makeup trailer, chatting with a male reporter, when Sean threw a fit—pounding on the trailer and rocking it. He was so insanely jealous that his only rational response was to cause an insane scene.

The reportedly stormy relationship lasted up until he became infatuated with Madonna. At one point there were discussions of marriage, but Penn's relationship with McGovern was eclipsed when the "Material Girl" arrived in town.

When Prince's concert dates at the Los Angeles Forum arrived, he sent around a limousine to pick up Madonna. When she arrived, she was besieged by autograph seekers and fans. She joined Prince onstage for his finale, and attended an after-concert party with him. Two days later, following the Grammy Awards, Madonna and Prince went out for Japanese food at a restaurant called Yamashiro, in the Hollywood hills, and made an appearance at a discotheque called Facade. On another occasion, they dined on sushi at an "in" eatery called Sushi on Sunset.

By now Madonna and Sean were seeing each other regularly, and according to the tabloids, on March 2, they had their first blowout fight—over her dating Prince. Penn reportedly stormed out of Madonna's apartment, after punching his fist through one of her doors.

Their antics continued in New York that spring, where Madonna had by now become a weekly staple in all of the gossip columns. The fourth estate had a ball when Sean and Madonna had one of their early scenes in a Manhattan eatery. While dining in a local restaurant, Madonna and Sean had an impromptu encounter with Elizabeth McGovern. She stopped to chat with her ex-beau, but soon the conversation became heated. Patrons were shocked when Madonna suddenly exploded into a tirade of expletives and stormed out of the restaurant.

While all of this intrigue was blossoming in Madonna's private life, her career seemed to have a life of its own. In the first half of 1985, Madonna virtually dominated the pop charts, with singles seemingly being released right and left. Right after "Like a Virgin" peaked, Sire Records released "Material Girl," with the Marilyn Monroe–inspired video debuting on MTV February 1. Meanwhile, *Vision Quest*, which had been filmed fifteen months before, was finally released on February 15. More important, the soundtrack album, featuring two of the three songs that Madonna had recorded for the movie—"Crazy for You" and "Gambler"—had been released by Geffen Records. Using movie clips of dramatic action, plus movie footage of Madonna performing the songs, MTV videos of both songs were prepared by Geffen and began showing up on the music video programs. To top it all off, *Desperately Seeking*

Susan was released on March 29, and along with it came another video comprised of movie clips, set to Madonna's song "Into the Groove." This meant five current Madonna videos were in rotation at once. To meet the demand for "Into the Groove," which was a bona fide hit on MTV, when the third single off the *Like a Virgin* album, "Angel," was released in April, "Into the Groove" became the dance hit B-side of the special twelve-inch single. Including MTV airplay, radio airplay, and dance club airplay, in the first six months of 1985, Madonna had six separate hit singles on the charts.

While Warner Brothers had control over their product, they couldn't prevent Geffen Records from doing all that they could to capitalize on Madonna's sudden popularity. The irony was that *Vision Quest*, which was bombing at the box office, was being distributed by another wing of the same company, Warner Brothers.

The *Los Angeles Times* reported that there were "enormous arguments" between top execs at Warner's record and film divisions "over the timing of the releases of Madonna singles," particularly in the case of "Crazy for You." Eddie Rosenblatt, president of Geffen Records, said then, "In retrospect, the concern may have been unwarranted."[101] There was plenty of room in the marketplace for two Madonna singles.

It was an accurate call: "Material Girl" peaked at Number Two and soon was surpassed by "Crazy for You," which became Madonna's second Number One hit. The week of May 11, 1985, both songs were in the Top Five on the charts. "Angel," which peaked at five, kept the Madonna phenomenon hot into summer. There was a planned video of the song "Angel," but that was killed, simply because there were too many Madonna videos on television, all vying for broadcast time.

Meanwhile, by February of 1985, Madonna's *Like a Virgin* album had been certified triple platinum in America, for sales in excess of three million copies. Her debut *Madonna* was at 2.5 million album sales domestically, and it was still in the Top Forty on the album charts.

During that same month, Madonna had three singles out that were produced by Jellybean Benitez. "Gambler" and "Crazy for You" had been recorded in late 1983, with Jellybean and Phil Ramone producing the cuts for *Vision Quest*, but when it came time to release the soundtrack album, Jellybean was called in to rerecord them without Ramone. In addition, Madonna wrote and sang background vocals on a song called

"Sidewalk Talk," which was the first single off Benitez's debut album, *Wotupski!?!* Based on Madonna's participation on the record, "Sidewalk Talk" became a Number One dance hit. Now, instead of club D.J.'s playing a record because Jellybean's name was on it as producer, they were playing it because Madonna wrote it.

According to Russ Thyret, Warner Bros. Records' head of marketing and promotion: "This is almost unprecedented, for one artist to have so much coming out from so many different places at the same time. We just want to do what's best for Madonna's long-term career."[101]

The confusing situation caused big problems for staff members at Warner and Sire, but the effect was an unprecedented blitz of product: six hit songs, five separate videos, and two films all hitting at once. What could happen to blanket the market further with Madonna product? Well, the Madonna concert tour, for instance, which was already under way at this point.

Six months previous, Middle America wasn't really aware of who this Madonna character was. Now, she suddenly had two movies playing at theaters across America. *Vision Quest*, which was a little weak in plot, ended up the least successful of the two.

Vision Quest is a teenage variation on the *Rocky* movies, this time centered around a high school wrestling team. The film stars Matthew Modine as an aspiring and determined young wrestler, who sets about the task of dropping his body weight to become eligible as a contender in a more competitive weight classification. He falls in love with a tough girl, Linda Fiorentino, and searches for his own identity. It is a basic coming-of-age film, and it had a rock soundtrack album. Sometimes, as in the case of *Footloose*, the album can be a bigger hit than the movie.

Madonna's one scene in the movie is in a club where Modine goes. She is the featured singer onstage. The ballad that she sings, "Crazy for You" became the most remembered aspect of the film. Although she is seen for only fleeting seconds performing the song in the movie, its placement in the film is a nice touch. Madonna's brief performance was listed in the credits merely as a "Special Appearance."

Since the beginning of November, when *Like a Virgin* was released, Madonna had taken a lot of flak from the press. They portrayed her as a fly-by-night singer with minimal vocal talent, a lot of ambition, and an ability to shock the public whenever she opened her mouth. In *People*,

Ralph Novak called her album "a tolerable bit of fluff," noting that "the lyrics on this album are on the primitive side. They might have been lifted off cave walls, full as they are of 'oohs,' 'ahs,' and 'shoo bee doo bees.'" Dennis Hunt wrote in the *Los Angeles Times:* "This disco star of the 80s really isn't a very good singer. She's great if you like a singer who sounds like Little Bo Peep, but with her bleating vibrato, it sometimes makes her sound like a sheep in pain. Her vocals also have an annoying little-girl quality." In *Us* magazine, Michael Musto theorized, "With her paper-thin, slightly nasal (but somehow sexy) voice, Madonna is the perfect vocalist for lighter-than-air songs. She's not what you'd call a heavyweight talent—her emotional range is far smaller than, say, Cyndi Lauper. But packaged by the right people, she manages to cram coyness and spunk into a dance beat."

Probably the biggest slam of all came from Gina Schock of the girl group, the Go-Go's. In 1984's year-end issue of *Rolling Stone*, Schock proclaimed, "People like her give people like us a hard way to go. She doesn't help anybody take women seriously. But you know what? I love the record."[102]

Madonna was definitely having the last laugh from all of the critical press. And now to top it all off, she was going to become a movie star.

When disparaging comments were made about her ability to make the transition from a singer into an actress, Madonna argued, "You can cross over—Judy Garland did it. I don't see how it's not possible. If Sissy Spacek can be a country singer, why can't I be an actress? I don't see it as being so diverse, especially with video becoming so strong."[103]

Desperately Seeking Susan, released on March 29, became the surprise hit of the season. Simply and unpretentiously filmed, it had a great ensemble cast and a script infused with a quirky sense of humor. It became an immediate comedy hit, and suddenly people were falling all over themselves with praise for the film—and for Madonna.

"As rotten a singer as Madonna is," wrote Rex Reed in the *New York Post*, "she's a kooky, swinging actress in a role that fits her like a sequin G-string." "A modish East Village comedy that features trampy self-parodistic Madonna in the title role . . . she has been type-cast, and fills the bill with delightful sluttishness," wrote David Ansen in *Newsweek*, while the *New York Times* simply dubbed *Desperately Seeking Susan* "the Madonna movie!"

The film did great box office business, and word of mouth was excellent. *Desperately Seeking Susan* was a huge hit, especially considering its modest budget. And although *Vision Quest* was a dud, Madonna escaped unscathed from the wreckage with a Number One hit. Even in the face of disaster, she was able to emerge triumphant.

Desperately Seeking Susan was basically an eighties' homage to the Preston Sturges films of the thirties and forties. In the film, Rosanna Arquette's character is a dull suburban housewife who gets hit on the head, develops amnesia, and somehow thinks that she is Madonna's character, Susan. The mistaken identity aspect is straight out of Shakespeare, and the visuals are straight out of the East Village.

"We don't actually meet until the end," Madonna explained of her relationship to Rosanna's character in the plot. "I find her and she's got all my stuff. She takes over, from about ten minutes into the movie. Everyone thinks she's me, because of a jacket of mine she gets from a thrift shop that I've traded for a pair of boots. In it is a key to the locker that holds all my personal worldly belongings. Rosanna gets amnesia after she gets the jacket, so when she wakes up she thinks she's me, and goes and gets that stuff and starts dressing like me. She's completely opposite of me, she doesn't smoke cigarettes, but she becomes me. In the end we meet up and become friends."[1]

When it was released, no one was more surprised by its success than Madonna. "I think it worked because it's a comedy that defies description."[93]

Hollywood was now taking Madonna seriously as an actress. She was being considered for a biographical film about notorious torch singer Libby Holman, who shot and killed her husband in a delicious scandal of the thirties.

Herb Ross was one of the first Hollywood directors to have a crack at putting Madonna in the movies. When he was casting the lead female role in *Footloose*, Madonna's name was submitted to him. Instead, he used Lori Singer. Said Ross, when *Desperately Seeking Susan* became the surprise hit of the spring 1985 season, "There is a definite buzz about her. It reminds me of what was happening to Barbra Streisand just before we did *Funny Girl*."[104]

Producer Ray Stark was one of the movie people standing in line for a chance to work with Madonna. According to him, "She really projects a feeling of truth and energy in her persona like the stars of the '40s."[104] According to Madonna, her favorite classic movie stars were Carole Lombard and Marilyn Monroe. Finally she was courting the chance to become a movie legend as well.

In early 1985, Madonna and her *Susan* co-star Rosanna Arquette did a series of photo shoots to promote the film. When Madonna was originally signed to appear in the film, she was just part of the supporting cast, but here she was getting above-the-title billing alongside Rosanna. After the smoke settled following the film's premiere, a couple of bitchy items surfaced from behind the scenes.

Jacquelyn Nicholson, in her gossip column in *Beverly Hills [213]* magazine, announced in catty fashion that there were several distinct personality problems on the set of *Desperately Seeking Susan*. Dispelling the "one big happy family" press releases, Nicholson claimed, "The only family the '*DSS*' gang even remotely resembled were, er, a lesser branch of the Borgias."[105]

Film reviewer David Edelstein likewise claimed that Madonna's moods on the set of the movie left a bad taste with the cast and crew.

Arquette had no compunction in complaining about the rush release the film received in order to jump on the Madonna bandwagon. Arquette understood why the studio decided to rush the film's release to take advantage of the hype Madonna was receiving, but she did say, "As an actress, I feel cheated."[106]

Furthermore, Susan Seidelman admitted, "It's no secret that Rosanna and I knocked heads a lot. She was hired to be the star, but her participation was clouded by Madonna's fast-rising star."[106] Seidelman claimed that Arquette's performance was affected by Madonna's presence. But she also recognized that most anyone would be shaken by such an upstaging.

Although Madonna has taken on several more acting roles since then, why is it that they have all paled in comparison to her portrayal of Susan in this flick? It's because she wasn't acting in this movie. The Madonna you see on the screen in *Desperately Seeking Susan is* Madonna.

All of a sudden Madonna was now the most newsworthy person in the universe. Since the media had virtually burned out Michael Jackson in 1984, the press was actively looking for a successor to the throne. They found the perfect new pop deity in Madonna. It was officially

Madonna's year for the blitz, and it was only April. In 1985 she was the cover story in *People* not once but four times! She also made the covers of *Time, TV Guide, Rolling Stone, Interview,* and, of course, the *National Enquirer* and *Star.* Madonna had wanted all eyes poised on her, and finally she had the attention she'd so desperately sought.

When, in March 1985, it was announced that Madonna would be mounting her debut concert tour, it instantly became the most talked about tour of the year. The previous October she had bitched at the mere mention of having to take her act on the road. "I have to admit I'm not really thrilled about it," she said. "If I go on tour it means I have to start auditioning all the musicians, sit for hours and hours and listen to a bunch of awful musicians, and then I have to get them to play all my songs right! And, I don't like traveling when I'm working."[1]

For Madonna, the road show, which was christened "The Virgin Tour," was the final piece of the puzzle to fall into place. When the tour became a huge success it confirmed that she could tackle five simultaneous arenas: records, music videos, video cassettes, movies, and live performances.

Likewise, from the very start, her concert tours have all become cleverly planned and plotted promotional events. Not only does a concert performance advertise her albums and singles, but by reproducing the choreography and look of her videos and her movies onstage, we find Madonna copying and parodying her favorite star of all: herself.

In October 1984, Madonna had predicted, "I'll probably do a major city American tour in the spring. Up to now, I've sung live to tape and used dancers. I'd combine dancing with it."[1]

By February 1985 she had already begun hiring and rehearsing a band. She wanted to hire the best musicians she could find. In December, Michael Jackson had just completed his much-touted "Victory Tour" with his brothers, so Madonna turned around and hired a band of red-hot musicians, including two members of the Jackson touring band: drummer Jonathan "Sugarfoot" Moffet and keyboardist Patrick Leonard. Both Moffet and Leonard were to become frequently recurring players in the Madonna camp. She also hired two male dancers, Lyndon B. Johnson and Mykal Perea, to visually augment her show and to sing background vocals.

While the Jacksons' tour was still under way, Freddy DeMann was already in contact with Source Point Design, Inc., planning the stage set that Madonna would need to bring her two albums and seven videos to life. DeMann consulted lighting designer Jim Chapman and his partner Robert Roth, who run Source Point and were responsible for the Jacksons' impressive stage set. According to Roth, "Madonna was a child of MTV. She was a visual product, and the images from her videos could be tied into a live show."[107] Working from that concept, the preliminary sketches were prepared.

When Madonna approved of the proposed designs, it was already mid-February and the first concert was set for the first week in April. However, when Madonna attended Prince's concert in Los Angeles, she was impressed by several of the auxiliary platforms in his stage set and the use of a central staircase. With only three weeks to go before the technical rehearsals began, Prince's designer Ian Knight was brought in to design and supervise the additions to Madonna's set that she decided she had to have. Whatever Madonna wanted, Madonna got.

Taking Madonna's own self-styled dancing moves—especially those employed in the "Lucky Star" video—Brad Jeffries choreographed and staged the show. Using Madonna's own fashion sense, and Maripol's jewelry, Marlene Stewart designed Madonna's three costumes.

Quickly establishing herself as a performer out of the "What will she wear?" echelon of stardom, Madonna consulted with designer Stewart to get exactly the look she wanted. After all, creating the Madonna look was every bit as crucial a part of making her into a show business legend as every other aspect of the show. She opened the concert in a sixties-style painted jacket with peace symbols and swirling paisleys, a mini-skirt, and purple lace leggings. Later in the show she changed into a black outfit, including a top with a crucifix cut into the chest, and a fringed vest. For "Like a Virgin," Madonna returned to the stage dressed in virginal white, with a crinoline skirt, bare midriff top with a crucifix cut into it, and a white sequined jacket.

In a matter of six months Madonna had gone from a hopeful singer with a couple of dance hits under her belt to the fastest-rising female singing star in the world. She had never been on a real concert tour in her life, and she certainly had never had to carry a seventy-minute stage show on her voice alone. Thanks to records and videos, Madonna was one of the hottest stars of 1985; she had become front page news largely due to her performances in videos, and now—thanks to *Desperately Seeking Susan*—on the silver screen. But the unanswered question remained: "Can she really sing?" Or, better yet: "Can she sing AND dance at the same time?" A couple of "track dates" at Paradise Garage and lip-syncing to a recording during a video session do not a concert performer make. Could she really deliver the goods?

When the Virgin Tour opened on April 10, 1985, in Seattle, Washington, all eyes were on Madonna. Much to everyone's surprise, she pulled it off with ease. Her voice was a little shrill at times, and her choreography was mainly an assemblage of classic sixties dances and spins. However, the fact remained: Madonna kicked ass onstage. On "Gambler" she rock-and-rolled in a league with the best of them. "Like a Virgin" and "Material Girl" were served up like musical theater. The show included all of Madonna's hits from "Holiday" to "Crazy for You." Naturally, there were some suggestive segments. When it came time to perform "Everybody," she brought out a large portable radio, commonly known as "a ghetto blaster" or "a box." Straddling the musical appliance, Madonna turned to the crowd and said, "Every lady has a box. But mine makes music."[108] Roll over Mae West.

During the finale of "Material Girl," Madonna picked each of the band members' pockets to amass a collection of baubles, bangles, and beads. She also tossed the crowd specially printed "Material Girl" stage money, with Madonna's picture in the center of the bill!

As she left the stage each night after "Material Girl," a paternal male voice was heard over the loudspeakers, shouting with disapproval, "Madonna, get down off that stage this instant," to which Madonna's reply was a prerecorded "Daddy, do I hafta?"[108] It was reminiscent of what Tony Ciccone would have liked to have said to his daughter when she was doing her Goldie Hawn go-go routine in elementary school years ago. When the show rolled into Detroit, the real Tony Ciccone made a guest appearance when he dragged Madonna into the wings while the prerecorded finale message played.

When the show toured America, the critics' reviews were mixed, but tickets sold out across the board. MADONNA SEDUCES SEATTLE glowed *Rolling Stone*; MADONNA ROCKS THE LAND claimed *Time* magazine; and IT'S MADONNA MAGIC! cheered the *New York Post*. However, *The Hollywood Reporter* blasted her, claiming, "Madonna came across more like a cross between Charo and Wayne Newton than a latter-day Gina Lollobrigida/Marilyn Monroe–type. But at least Charo can play her own guitar. Rumors that the Virgin could dance proved to be, for the most part, completely unfounded."[109]

Madonna's Virgin Tour wasn't necessarily aimed at the critics. The people who liked her were the young "wannabes" the tour was geared for.

"The people who loathed me didn't get it, and my success pissed them off. I think it would be kind of boring if everyone really just loved me a hundred percent."[26]

Madonna was really quite flattered by the dress-alike "wannabes" who came to the concert in lace gloves, crucifixes, torn leggings, and rags tied in their hair. Never were there so many pubescent smiles showing equal amounts of ruby red lipstick and brace-covered teeth as there were displayed on her tour that summer. It was like Halloween without the pumpkins and candy.

Quick to cash in on a trend, Madonna signed a merchandising deal with a clothing manufacturer called Entertainers Merchandise Management Corp. The manufacturer then marketed the official Boy Toy clothes under the name of Wazoo fashions. In turn, Wazoo distributed official Madonna clothes to department stores across the country, including Bullock's in California, Macy's in New York, and Merry-Go-Round stores in shopping malls across the land. Hot items that the Wazoo line featured included a knee-length roll-waistband skirt ($30), a "Boy Toy crop top" for displaying your navel ($26), and Madonna "Like a Virgin" T-shirts ($14).

When Madonna rolled into New York City, the Herald Square flagship store of the Macy's chain opened its "Madonna Department" in the heart of its junior fashion floor. You could also purchase Maripol's Catholic "voodoo" jewelry and listen to nonstop Madonna tunes in the official Madonna section of the store. According to Maripol, "Not everybody can afford gold or pearls, but everybody can buy a package of twelve rubber bracelets for five dollars!"[80]

Lisa Engler, who was the merchandise manager for Bullock's in Los Angeles, said at the time, "Whatever Madonna was wearing, they'd wear. She's that strong an influence."[110]

To really work the press, the Madonna department at Macy's held a Madonna look-alike contest on Thursday, June 6, the day she opened at Radio City Music Hall. Andy Warhol, who was the celebrity judge of the contest, commented that he was amazed by the amount of money the girls spent to mirror Madonna's fashions and makeup.

Unlike other concert acts, the crowd that Madonna's Virgin Tour drew was primarily teenage girls, dressed up like their idol. In fact, ticket sellers confirmed that the audiences at her shows were 60 percent female. According to Jerry Seltzer, executive vice president at Ticketmaster in Los Angeles, "The demand was unbelievable. We could've sold 100,000 tickets if we had them."[111]

It was Freddy DeMann's decision that Madonna would play at smaller venues across the country—like Radio City Music Hall in New York, and the Universal Amphitheatre in L.A. "This is Madonna's first tour," he said while tickets were selling like hotcakes, "and we wanted to start conservatively. If I had known what I know now, we'd have done three nights at the [Los Angeles] Forum!"[111]

There was an opening act on the Virgin Tour, but their inclusion on the bill was a mere formality, as they were totally eclipsed by Madonna's blinding presence. They were the Beastie Boys, and their set was barely tolerable enough to sit through.

If you're the headliner, the unofficial rock concert rule is never to have an opening act with more talent or more hits than you. Madonna personally took care of that situation when she called Russell Simmons, manager for the white rap trio, and inquired whether the Beastie Boys were interested in opening for her. Their songs about drinking beer and "getting laid" must have seemed like a great smoke screen of an opening act for her. They were moderately popular, but basically rude and musically untalented. After their set, the crowd would impatiently clamor for Her Virginness to hit the stage. Even if she dry-humped anything during her set—like she had on the MTV Awards telecast—she'd still come across as ultra-talented by comparison.

Needless to say, this was the Beasties' big break, and they jumped at the opportunity. Opening for Madonna was to be their biggest claim to fame as performers. Reviewing their act on the tour, *Time* called it "a forgettable 30 minutes by a raunchy rap band."[2] The group later produced a Number One album, 1987's *Licensed to Ill*. When they embarked on a tour to support the album, they were less than popular with parents across the land. Their troubles stemmed not only from their lewd lyrics but also from the twenty-foot-tall pink penis that was one of their stage props and for coercing young girls in the audience to bare their breasts.

From April 10 to June 8 the Virgin Tour wound its way from one excited venue to the next. Wasting no time, Madonna had gone directly from dance club and lip-sync video phenomenon to full-fledged rock star almost instantly. Thanks to her own aggressiveness, and the top notch manager she snagged, Madonna was officially rated as having attained "superstar" status.

On May 15, Madonna played the Pontiac, Michigan, Silverdome stadium. The massive complex is just off Featherstone Road, near the house she grew up in. Her father, her family, and even her grandmother came to see little Nonnie's triumphant return to her hometown.

In the middle of the song "Holiday," Madonna stopped to talk to her audience. That night at the Silverdome she received a thunderous round of applause and had to bury her eyes in her hands to hold back the tears. Facing the cheering crowd—literally in her old neighborhood—she said, "I was never elected the homecoming queen or anything, but I sure feel like one now."[108]

When 17,622 tickets went on sale for Madonna's three scheduled concert performances at Radio City Music Hall, they sold out in thirty-four minutes—setting a new house record. The demand for Madonna tickets in the Big Apple reached such proportions that two dates at the 18,000-seat Madison Square Garden had to be added to the tour, June 10 and 11. Madonna said from the stage at the Garden: "I used to look at the Garden and say, I wonder if I'll ever get in there?"[112] She had come a long way from those days.

To welcome her back to Manhattan, a massive party was held on June 11 at the Palladium. For $15, patrons could party with Madonna, or at least try to catch a glimpse of her. Only blocks away from the Palladium was the grimy East Village digs that she once called home. Her entire life had since changed dramatically. Instead of having people in the neighborhood chasing her for her late rent, they now chased her for autographs.

When she began her two-month concert tour, Sean Penn had been in the middle of production meetings regarding his forthcoming film, *At*

Close Range, co-starring Christopher Walken. When Madonna's tour opened in Seattle, Sean flew in from New York to catch her concert debut. When she played Detroit, Sean also flew in to see her show and to meet her parents for the first time.

An interesting note: When Madonna played Los Angeles, one of the people who attended her concert was Jellybean Benitez. The gossip columnists were quick to mention that he watched the show with fascination but made no attempts to visit his former girlfriend backstage.

The night before she opened at Radio City, Madonna attempted to hang out at the massive Palladium discotheque on Fourteenth Street incognito. It didn't quite work out. With a cap pulled down over her eyes, and in the company of nine male friends, she was still recognized by the paparazzi. When photographer Felice Quinto of the Associated Press attempted to take shots of Madonna, the singer's bodyguards threatened to break her cameras. Quinto managed to get a few shots in, which ran on the cover of the *New York Post* under the headline MADONNA'S DISCO FLAP. It was as though she had surpassed the mere moniker of "star" and ascended to the role of "media goddess." Suddenly Madonna's every move was considered front page news.

It was June 1985 and Madonna was the reigning queen of rock and roll. Her last six singles all hit the Top Ten, her *Like a Virgin* album had sold over 4.5 million copies in America and another 2.5 million abroad. Her first professional acting role in a major film yielded a certified box office hit. She was being discussed for her first starring vehicle. Besides a biopic on Libby Holman, another on fifties stripper Blaze Starr were both bantered about. And, to top it all off, she was being romantically pursued by a movie star. How much more perfect could life be?

For the past six months, America—and the rest of the world—had been bombarded by Madonna. Wherever you turned, you were confronted by Madonna's name, her likeness, or her voice. Madonna was suddenly the "It" girl of the eighties. Not only was this an accomplishment worthy of celebration, but Madonna called her own shots.

At first it seemed like Madonna controlled the media. She knew when to manipulate it and how to cause a stir. Her objective was to shock the press, and she never failed to deliver. She knew just how far to push comments for shock value, without offending *everyone*. She knew how to be scandalous in a titillating fashion, and her brashness somehow made her seem enticing. While she was an easy target for critics, she emerged unscathed. Caustic comments about her aggressive behavior and her less-than-virginal displays just seemed to roll off her.

In addition to the press coverage, move for move her career was proceeding brilliantly. She had so far triumphed in every arena she entered: records, videos, movies, and now live concerts. No one could deny that she was masterfully succeeding at the game of fame, that she had hit nothing but home runs so far. Little did she suspect, but she was about to be thrown her first couple of curve balls.

Eight

I used to go out with graffiti writers . . .

Causing

but I really lost the zest for writing my

a

name everywhere. Now I have suitors

Commotion

that do it for me.[19] —*Madonna*

Before her Virgin Tour even started, Madonna had already selected a condo in Los Angeles and planned to spend the majority of her time there. She still maintained her New York loft on Bleecker Street, but she was now ready to conquer Hollywood. The vast majority of the time she had spent in New York had been as a struggling unknown. But when Madonna arrived in Los Angeles, she was not only a star, she was also a much sought after fresh face in town.

Because of her recording successes she had become a red hot singing sensation. But with the added dimension of having scored a huge success in *Desperately Seeking Susan*, Hollywood welcomed her with open arms.

On her last couple of trips to Los Angeles she had scoped out real estate. She longed to live like a movie star. "I'd like to get a house in the hills: a real Hollywood house," she announced. "There's one that belonged to either Anna Pavlova or Isadora Duncan. I want that house! It's on top of a hill and it's very dramatic."[1]

She was also plotting her course in the movies. "Director-wise," she pondered at the time, "I'd love to work with [Francis Ford] Coppola, [Martin] Scorsese, Bob Fosse. Actor-wise, I'd like to work with Mel Gibson. He's a great actor and he's great looking, and he's normal. He doesn't seem like"—she paused and gave a look of disgust—"he's not like Matt Dillon! Mel Gibson is past that, he's not an arrogant snot-nosed brat."[1]

In addition to mapping out her next career move, romance was also on her mind. "I need love and I need to give love," she said.[94]

But was Madonna looking to "justify" her love, or was she simply seeking out her next "useful boyfriend"? From the very start of her affair with Sean Penn, the pair was a bizarre match. What did they have in common, with the exception of surly attitudes? Clearly, as an established hot young movie star, Penn had achieved the kind of stature that Madonna had in her sights for herself. In the past few months she had by far eclipsed Jellybean's fame. He was already being referred to in the press merely as Madonna's "ex-boyfriend." She was going places, and Sean Penn was clearly the type of person who could take her there. Having had a taste of cinematic fame via *Desperately Seeking Susan*, she longed to become a movie star. What better way to be greeted with open arms in Hollywood than on the arm of an established film star? The stage was set for her next career leap.

When Madonna completed the Madison Square Garden dates on her Virgin Tour, she almost immediately headed for Nashville to be at Sean Penn's side. He was in Tennessee for location filming on the movie *At Close Range*.

"Sean to me is the perfect American male, and that's all I can say. I'm inspired and shocked by him at the same time," she claimed at the time.[94] When she arrived in Nashville she was about to be "inspired and shocked."

Without the pressure of the tour on her mind, Madonna was primed and ready for romance. That week on location Sean asked her to marry him. He popped the question in Tennessee. "We were out in the middle of nowhere. . . . It was a Sunday morning and I was jumping up and down on the bed. . . . He got this look in his eye and I felt like I just knew what he was thinking. . . . I said, 'Whatever you're thinking, I'll say "yes" to.' That was his chance, so he popped it." Madonna later said, "Sean is my hero and my best friend."[13]

The week wasn't all champagne and roses for the dynamic duo, however. It was the same week Sean Penn engaged in his debut fistfight with members of the press. The big blowup occurred when Madonna and Sean were approached by a pair of photographers from Britain. When the photographers insisted on taking photos of the celebrity couple, Sean grabbed one of the photographic tools and "camera-whipped" the photographer and then assulted him with a rock. The press had a field day when Sean was brought up on assault charges by the Fleet Street lensmen, in addition to facing a million-dollar civil suit.

When all of the excitement was over, Madonna left Nashville and flew to Los Angeles, where she planned to kick up her heels and celebrate the wonderful year she was having. On Sunday, June 23, Madonna attended a beachside party at David Geffen's Malibu house. She was the center of attention at the party, and it was there that she made the grand announcement of her upcoming wedding. The following morning, syndicated columnist Suzy broke the news of Madonna and Sean's engagement to the world. The date was set for "sometime in August," pending the completion of the filming of *At Close Range*. Suzy also reported, "Sean and Madonna have plans to make a movie together, *Pipeline*, set in the Alaskan oil fields."

Just as the excitement of her wedding was sinking in, Madonna was hit with her first negative surprise of the year. On Sunday, July 7, Bob Guccione, the publisher of *Penthouse* magazine, announced that his publication was going to be publishing twelve pages of nude photographs of Madonna in the September issue. The photos were selected from sessions she had done in 1979 and 1980, when she was modeling for art classes in Greenwich Village.

The previous summer, it was *Penthouse* that caused a major scandal when they printed nude photos of the then-reigning Miss America, Vanessa Williams. Because of the stir those photos caused, Williams was forced to relinquish her crown. Guccione seemed to take great pleasure over the scandal his magazine caused; the Vanessa Williams issue ended up setting sales records for *Penthouse*. Guccione was confident that he had again struck gold with Madonna.

Many of the Madonna nudes appeared in Guccione's office around the same time. They came from many different sources, from the students and teachers she used to pose for, as well as from professionals. Guccione claimed that *Penthouse* had first choice and that they selected the best of the bunch. "She is completely nude, and the pictures are fully explicit," he bragged to the press.[113]

In a surprise move, just as word of *Penthouse*'s Madonna issue was hitting the Monday morning newspapers, a publishing coup was under way. The following day, *Playboy* announced that they, too, were going to feature Madonna on the cover of the September issue and in the buff in its interior. Furthermore, the September *Playboy*, which was originally scheduled to hit the newsstands on July 30, was going to be on sale in New York and Chicago the very next day—Wednesday, July 10!

Suddenly, the war of the girlie magazines went into full swing. Scooped by *Playboy*, it was strictly "stop the presses" time over at *Penthouse* headquarters. In an emergency move, *Penthouse* quickly rushed copies of its September issue from its warehouse in Des Moines, Iowa, to hit major city newsstands on a limited basis July 10, with the bulk arriving by July 16.

Anticipating the demand for the magazines, both publishers upped the print runs. At five million copies, *Penthouse*'s run was up 15 percent over their usual run, and the presses stood poised and ready in case a second printing was required. With an additional 350,000 to 500,000 copies of *Playboy* printed, the Hugh Hefner–published men's magazine was 7 to 10 percent above normal for its print run.

Playboy published its Madonna photo feature with an accompanying editorial dig aimed at competitor *Penthouse*. "Since we turned down those nude photos of Vanessa Williams, some people will ask why we're publishing these."[51] *Playboy* said they thought Vanessa Williams didn't know what she was getting into and they had no desire to ruin her career. In a very nice, polite, and gentlemanly way, *Playboy* was in essence saying: Miss America was framed by big, bad *Penthouse*, but Madonna is a slut, so—hey, what the hell!? Here she is in the nude.

Guccione was pissed off that *Playboy* had beaten him to the newsstands and blasted them publicly. "The *Playboy* photographs are rubbish. I bought all of the best ones," he argued.[114]

In its Madonna issue, first-on-the-newsstand *Playboy* used photos from two different photographers: Martin Schreiber and Lee Friedlander. In both sessions, Madonna was indeed nude, but instead of appearing sexy, she looked bored out of her mind. In *Penthouse*, the photos by Bill Stone were much more creative. Using a soft focus and a beautiful antique camelback sofa, several of the photos look like artistic shots from the turn of the century. The Friedlander sessions depicted Madonna as a "natural woman," with abundant dark brown underarm hair, while the other photos displayed Madonna's sexy armpits following a shave.

What was even more amusing than watching the pair of skin magazines battle it out at the newsstands, was Madonna's whole take on the situation. In response to the disclosure of the photos, Madonna's press agent Liz Rosenberg announced, "Madonna has acknowledged in interviews that she posed nude for art classes." Liz added, "I can tell you that she doesn't feel she's done anything to be ashamed of."[115]

In an effort to further publicize the whole escapade, Bob Guccione announced that *Penthouse* would go to great lengths if Madonna would pose nude for him. "I'd pay as high as a million dollars for an exclusive photo session with her," he claimed.[114] Not to be outdone by *Penthouse*, and eager to enter into the race to expose more of Madonna, another sexually oriented magazine, *High Society*, claimed that they would up the ante by offering Madonna $1.2 million for the same services. *Time* magazine labeled the whole episode a "navel battle of the newsstands."[116]

One of the best takes on the whole episode is a now famous front page of the ever-colorful *New York Post*, which, with a photo of Madonna, in inch-and-a-half-high letters brandished the headline, MADONNA ON NUDE PIX: SO WHAT! On the cover of its metro edition the *Post* offered an alternate headline, which read, MADONNA: "I'M NOT ASHAMED".[117]

To top it all off, on the Saturday following the newsstand arrival of the nude Madonna mags, the singer was scheduled to appear on the "let's feed Ethiopia" mega-concert of the century: "Live Aid." Here she was to perform for a satellite-broadcast, semi-dignified humanitarian charity while nude photos of her were on sale at the local 7-Eleven store.

Madonna herself was not the least bit amused. According to her, "I think when I first found out about it, the thing that annoyed me most wasn't so much that they were nude photographs but that I felt really out of control."[112]

With regard to the photos themselves, she explained, "When they were taken seven or eight years ago, they weren't meant for publication in *any* magazine. They were done by these guys who took pictures of nudes for exhibits and showings and stuff. At the time I wasn't a known person and it didn't really occur to me that I was setting myself up for scandal for years to come. . . . I consider the nude a work of art. I don't see pornography in Michelangelo, and I likened what I was doing to that. It was a good way to make money."[13]

Although she wished that things hadn't unfolded quite the way they had, she accepted the events. "I'm not ashamed of anything that I did."[13]

Two years after, the whole thing had blown over and Madonna was able to reflect on the trauma it had caused.

"When *Desperately Seeking Susan* came out, and I was going with a well-known actor, then I announced my marriage, *then* the *Playboy* and *Penthouse* pictures came out—everything sort of happened at once, one big explosion of publicity," she recalls. "*Penthouse* did something really nasty—they sent copies of the magazine to Sean."[81]

With huge all-star concerts in London and Philadelphia, the Live Aid concert, held on Saturday, July 13, 1985, was heralded as the grandest and most unified rock event ever staged. Crosby, Stills, Nash, and Young; Mick Jagger; Tina Turner; Hall and Oates; Paul McCartney; Bob Dylan; Ron Wood; Joan Baez; Keith Richards; the Beach Boys; the Four Tops; Sade; Bob Geldof and the Boomtown Rats; Teddy Pendergrass; Eric Clapton; and reunions by The Who and Black Sabbath highlighted the twenty-one-hour rock extravaganza to end all extravaganzas. And, sandwiched into the middle of it came a three song performance by Her Virginness herself.

The concert was her first public appearance since the photos appeared, and she was still smarting. "Part of me felt this big," she said as though she had shrunk with embarrassment. But Madonna wouldn't let the negative press get her down. She said, "I'm gonna get this dark cloud out from over my head."[112]

The concert was a mere six months after the all-star recording session that yielded the Number One hit "We Are the World." That fateful night in January, producer Quincy Jones had instructed a virtual who's who of the rock world to "Check your egos at the door." It was anticipated that Live Aid would be a selfless, attitude-less event as well, and 99 percent of it was—except for Madonna.

Calling her a "prima donna," *USA Today* reported that "the only artist who acted like a superstar was Madonna."[118] Breezing into the backstage area, and clutching Sean Penn's hand for dear life, Madonna was surrounded by a phalanx of over a dozen bodyguards. Several of the bodyguards held their hands in front of Madonna's face to obstruct picture-taking by the press photographers assembled there. It was a new ploy she had just learned from the obnoxious Penn.

Remaining difficult, Madonna switched dressing rooms twice so that the press couldn't find her. This was a decided change of pace for her. Up until her engagement to Penn she gladly posed at public events for anyone within lens distance.

Madonna ended up sharing a dressing room with the Beach Boys, Ashford & Simpson, and Eric Clapton. Several people found her to be stuck-up that afternoon, and she became the brunt of several jokes onstage and off, especially in light of her nude photo spreads.

Quipped Mike Love of the Beach Boys, who was one of Madonna's dressing room mates, "We were looking for her clothes, but we hear she doesn't wear too much."[118]

The ever-funny Bette Midler got the best dig in when she introduced Madonna onstage and called her "a woman who pulled herself up by the bra straps, and who has been known to let them down occasionally."[4]

"I ain't taking *shit* off today! You might hold it against me in ten years," were Madonna's opening words when she took the stage that evening.[119] Well, so much for Madonna acting like a lady on live television. No one expected a performer to use obscenities on the special, so there was no way that her comment could be bleeped from MTV's live broadcast. When Dick Clark ran his edited version of the highlights of the concert later that evening on network television, Madonna's expletives were deleted from the show.

Madonna sang three songs for Live Aid's global audience: "Into the Groove," "Holiday," and the world debut of "Love Makes the World Go Round." She wore a brocade jacket, lots of gold jewelry—including crucifixes and peace symbols—and oddly enough her hair was dyed a brownish shade of red. She later returned to the stage to sing harmony vocals with her new friend Alannah Currie, from the rock trio Thompson Twins, during the Twins' set.

Away from Sean's side for several minutes, Madonna posed for a staged photograph for the cover of *People* magazine—with her clothes on. She shared the cover with fellow rockers Turner, Jagger, Dylan, Wood, and Hall and Oates. Aside from that photo, she remained uncooperative to press and fans alike. When she was whisked through the backstage Green Room on her way to the stage, her entourage instructed all of the stage personnel and "techs" not to look at her as she walked by. At the simultaneous London event, royal Princess Diana couldn't have been more gracious toward her rock and roll countrymen. Who did Madonna think *she* was?

Regardless, Live Aid was one of the most dramatic humanitarian and logistic feats of the entire decade. Via satellite, it was viewed simultaneously by billions of people around the world and raised millions of dollars in relief money for the starving people of Ethiopia.

The following week, Madonna was in New York City, shopping for an apartment to share with Sean. However, co-op shopping isn't as easy as thumbing through the *New York Times* real estate section. A prospective buyer not only has to have the requisite amount of cash, but a resident-led co-op board has to approve of the sale as well. Similar to the DOGS AND ACTORS NOT WELCOME signs that hung in boarding house windows in Hollywood in the 1920s, Madonna quickly discovered that in some posh Manhattan co-ops rock stars were instant "undesirables."

On July 20 and 21, Madonna scoured the Upper East Side looking for suitable digs. She fell in love with a pair of connecting brownstones that had been converted into nine condo units in the $1.8 million range. The board of the building in question, 11–15 East 70th Street, was less than enthusiastic about the prospect of housing the "Material Girl" and her Brat Pack fiancé. In fact, the co-op board turned them down flat. When she was pressed for details, the building's sales director, Nancy Carter, claimed, "We have to keep our clientele very confidential."[120]

The co-op in question was owned by actor Bill Gerber and his wife, Arlyne Rothberg, who is a television and movie producer and Diane Keaton's manager. Madonna had her heart set on that particular apartment and thought it was a bargain. C'est la vie.

In addition to everything else that was going wrong, Stephen Lewicki had resurfaced with his completed version of Madonna's debut role in the dreadful Super-8 film *A Certain Sacrifice*. Between the nude photos and this breast-exposing film, Madonna's imperfect past seemed to be coming back to haunt her.

When the "Like a Virgin" single had begun climbing up the charts eight months earlier, Lewicki realized he had a potential gold mine on film. He fully intended to capitalize on Madonna's star status. He invited Madonna and Jellybean up to his West Side apartment for a screening of the completed film. According to Stephen, Madonna was not bothered by the film and even complimented the first-time filmmaker.

"As she was getting ready to leave she shook my hand at the door, and said, 'Well, Stephen, thanks and fuck you.' 'What's that supposed to mean?' I asked her. And, she replied, 'Well, you and I always had an antagonistic relationship, so I've decided to maintain that.'"[56]

When Lewicki announced that he was going to market and sell the film, Madonna alerted her lawyer, Paul Schindler. In turn Schindler attempted unsuccessfully to purchase the rights to the film for a paltry $10,000. Lewicki refused and furthermore produced a signed copy of the release form to which Madonna had affixed her signature. According to Lewicki's lawyer, Alvin Deutch, the said release "fully authorizes our client to use her name, photography, and likeness in the film and in connection with its advertising and promotion."[121] While Schindler couldn't stop the film from being marketed and sold, he attempted to stop Lewicki from advertising the film using Madonna's name. On Friday, August 2, 1985, Supreme Court Justice Ira Gammerman refused to block Lewicki from using Madonna's name in his ads. Gammerman claimed that Stephen "has the right to identify the artist who participated in the work."[122] With that, *A Certain Sacrifice* went on sale at video stores across the land.

Purchasing a copy of *A Certain Sacrifice* cannot exactly be likened to obtaining a rare print of Greta Garbo's silent film debut. In fact, it was purchased by hard-core Madonna devotees alone and was critically panned by the press. Still, Lewicki made a tidy amount of money from the film. A British magazine called *Hot Talk* reviewed Madonna's performance in *A Certain Sacrifice* by stating: "As in her other movies,

141

Madonna shows no sign of knowing how to act, walk, wear makeup, dress or, for that matter, how to get gang-raped properly. She doesn't even scream on key."

Defending her role in the film, Madonna told the press that it was something she had done a long time ago and that she wasn't ashamed of her part in the film, or the nudity.

The part of the summer she spent in Los Angeles, Madonna stayed in a $1,350-a-month, two-bedroom apartment she had rented in the hills, not far from the massive HOLLYWOOD sign. She felt quite at home there and quickly established her own day-to-day routines. For her own daily workout, she regularly attended aerobics classes at the prestigious Hollywood health club, The Sports Connection, on Santa Monica Boulevard. Located in the vicinity of several gay bars, it is often jokingly referred to as "The Sports Erection."

With several stars among its clientele, The Sports Connection is not the type of place for a star to act like a diva—or word will be all over town.

"She was 'The Material Bitch,' and that's how people would refer to her," says John McCormick, who managed the health food bar at the club. According to him, the staff found Madonna to be unfriendly, rude, and stuck-up. "We dealt with a lot of celebrities there, and some of them have bad reputations, and some of them are normal, and average, and just get along with everybody, and aren't necessarily pretentious. And there are those that have their moments, and they get a reputation."[123]

McCormick remembers regularly encountering Madonna in one of the exercise classes, held with several of his co-workers. "She used to take aerobics with us," he says, "and she used to stand in the middle of the aerobics room, with her arms straight out, and spin, and that was her space, and no one was to enter that. The aerobics room is a public domain—except, of course, her space. She had her space, and no one was to go into it, and she wasn't even Madonna then, she was still up and coming, but she knew who she was. She used to do this every class; that was her routine for exercise. I assume that she didn't want to be bothered, but there are other ways to achieve that. That was how she got ready for her classes. That was her space, and pity anyone who was near her.

"She was in great physical condition then," he recalls. "I don't think she ever showered there. She just came in and took the classes, and left. I don't think it was a major social event for her. She never really associated with anyone beyond that. It was that one little idiosyncrasy that everyone picked up on."[123]

McCormick fondly recalls meeting several other stars while working at the health bar, including Brooke Shields and Bruce Springsteen, and he found them to be warm and outgoing. He was also on staff when John Travolta, Jamie Lee Curtis, and Laraine Newman filmed the movie *Perfect* at The Sports Connection, and he remembers them as being friendly and down to earth. However, Madonna was another story. "She was a star in her own mind," he says. "Although, I have to say, she had a lot of success at that point. People knew who she was, there was no mistake about that, even though she changed her hair color from week to week."[123]

Meanwhile, the invitations to Sean and Madonna's nuptials went out in the mail to a select number of their family and friends. Everyone was still trying to figure out what the hell she found so appealing about the elusive, eccentric Penn. "I don't think she needed Sean in opportunistic ways. Movie people are already beating down her door," Susan Seidelman surmised. "It's got to be love."[124]

Madonna's longtime friend Martin Burgoyne thought Madonna's relationship with Sean was healthy. He said that their relationship was "fifty-fifty. She can learn from him, and he can learn from her."[97]

The bride-to-be publicly defended her choice. "We have so much in common. He's really smart and he knows a lot."[124] On several occasions she said she thought Sean resembled her father. "Maybe that's why I feel really close to Sean."[24]

While she was in New York in July, Madonna was the guest of honor at a traditional bridal shower, hostessed by her East Coast friends. Attending were Alannah Currie and Mariel Hemingway, in addition to half a dozen of Madonna's male friends—in full drag. The event was held at the apartment of Nancy Huang, who was Nile Rodgers's girlfriend.

Nothing was conventional about Sean and Madonna's wedding, beginning with the cryptic invitations. Printed on shocking-pink paper, they featured a sketch of a demonic-looking Sean and Madonna on one side, depicted as the man and woman with a pitchfork in Grant Wood's famed painting, *American Gothic*. The illustration, drawn by Sean's brother Michael, had many amusing details including a SEAN TOY belt buckle on Madonna.

The wedding date was set for Madonna's twenty-seventh birthday, and the day after was Sean's twenty-fifth birthday, so it was destined to be quite the double-Leo event in astrologer's terms. What was about to ensue, however, was to rival the best of Hollywood's disaster films of the seventies, complete with insane plot twists and star-studded casts.

Not only did everyone want to know what the bride was going to be wearing, but they also wanted to know where the hell the event was going to take place. This wild goose chase of a wedding was destined to go down in history books as one of the maddest marital events of the century.

The rumors were flying for weeks about details of the event. One press report claimed that Madonna was going to poke fun at her snow-white "Like a Virgin" wedding gown by wearing an all-black "widow's wedding gown." Because she had only known Sean for several months, there was also speculation as to whether or not Madonna was with child.

All the publicity she was getting from the wedding helped keep Madonna-mania running high on the record charts. The week of the wedding, her latest single, "Dress You Up" was in the Top Forty in America, on its way to Number Five. In England, where she was revered as well, Madonna had three songs in the Top Twenty: "Into the Groove" at Number One, "Holiday" at Number Two, and "Crazy for You" at Number Nineteen. "Into the Groove" was Number Seven in West Germany, and "Crazy for You" was Number Three in Australia, and the Japanese Madonna album *Into the Groove* was Number Ten in that country.

On Monday, August 13, Madonna and Sean were accompanied by a bodyguard as they arrived at the Los Angeles Civil Courthouse, where they took out a marriage license. They were waited on by clerk Gloria Guerra, who recalls, "Most of the time she tried to hide her face. She didn't want people to recognize her. It seemed like she wanted to leave very soon." Sally Chavez, another clerk at the courthouse added, "They were chuckling, that I did notice."[125]

Two days before the wedding, the future bride and groom were feted by their respective friends. Ten of Madonna's girlfriends gave her a bachelorette party. It was held at a sleazoid mud-wrestling emporium called the Tropicana, in Hollywood. To avoid being recognized, Madonna wore minimal makeup and put her hair up in a neat little bun. On the other side of town, Sean and the boys whooped it up in a private room upstairs at the rock club the Roxy, on Sunset Strip. Penn was joined by a host of his friends and family, including Harry Dean Stanton, Tom Cruise, David Keith, Robert Duvall, and screenwriter Cameron Crowe. The stag gathering was entertained by stripper Kitten (42-24-36) Natividad.

That week, details slowly leaked out to the press. Designer Marlene Stewart announced that Madonna's gown "is somewhat in the fairy-tale category."[126] Meanwhile, Wolfgang Puck, chef-proprietor-celebrity of the restaurant Spago, revealed clues about the menu he was creating for the wedding of the season. In addition to Madonna's favorite—Spago pizza and curried oysters, the buffet would also feature lobster ravioli, swordfish, baked potatoes stuffed with caviar and sour cream, hot and cold meats, and a vintage champagne. "It will be one of the most lavish spreads I have ever prepared," claimed Puck. "No expense has been spared to make it a party to remember."[127]

Not everyone invited was looking forward to the Hollywood hoopla. Madonna's maternal grandmother, seventy-three-year-old Elsie Fortin, announced prior to traveling to Los Angeles from Bay City, "I have second thoughts about going. Some days I feel like chickening out, especially when I think I've got to meet all those fancy Hollywood people."[126] She ended up relenting. Grandma Elsie was in for quite a show.

The night before the wedding, Sean and Madonna stayed at his parents' Malibu house so that they could be near the yet-to-be-revealed site of the next day's main event. The following day, at noon, the invited guests began to be informed as to the whereabouts of the wedding. It was to take place at the $6-million Malibu home of architect and real estate developer Kurt Unger, who was a family friend of the Penns.

According to British journalist Maggie Hall, "The whole thing was a promotional setup for Unger, because his house was up for sale. Unger was hoping that by staging the wedding there, it would be enough free advertising to sell the house. It wasn't. The day after the wedding, I went back to the house, knocked on the door, and was invited in. They were eager for a prospective buyer, and hoped that I was one, or knew of one."[128]

The house, which is located next door to Johnny Carson's Malibu digs, has a breathtaking view of the ocean from the seventy-five-foot cliff at the edge of the backyard. Located at a scenic bluff known as Point Dume. The safety railing that lined the cliffside was draped in white tulle the afternoon of the wedding, and billowing white canopies were set up in the yard surrounding the Olympic-sized swimming pool.

News of the locale of the wedding spread like a California brushfire, and it wasn't long before the media got wind of the site. Anticipating the outdoor event, the media had secured a half-dozen helicopters for the day and were prepared to do whatever it took to end up with exclusive photos of the matrimonial ceremony of the year.

At four o'clock in the afternoon, Madonna was in an upstairs room at Unger's ultramodern house laying out her trousseau when the press helicopters began buzzing overhead. The event had already acquired the earmarks of an all-day fiasco.

Security guards were positioned around the house, and they had already discovered one Italian photojournalist, wearing camouflage gear and combat makeup, crawling around in the bushes with his camera. Hot-tempered Sean decided that he would take matters into his own hands. Armed with what appeared to be a .45-caliber automatic pistol, Penn paced the grounds steaming with anger at the fact that the supposedly secret site of the wedding had been discovered. Dressed in a pair of black jeans, Sean crouched in the shrubery by the swimming pool, waiting for the next helicopter to buzz by. As it approached, Madonna leaned out of an upstairs window and vainly yelled at him not to do it.

Ignoring his fiancée, as one of the helicopters buzzed the property Sean leapt from his crouched position amid the foliage, aimed, and fired two shots at the intruding air vehicle.

"I'm not trying to hit it, I'm trying to scare it away," he shouted back at Madonna, with a menacing look in his eyes.[129] Pleased with his act of aggression, Sean had a sneer on his face as he turned and walked back inside the house.

After five o'clock, the 220 invited guests began to arrive. Since the legions of armed guards had blocked off the driveway to the Unger house, the guests had to park or be let off down the street, on Wildlife Road, and walk up the driveway. Several limousines pulled up to the Unger property and began letting out guests. Christopher Walken, Martin Sheen, Rosanna Arquette, Diane Keaton, Emilio Estevez, Carrie Fisher, Timothy Hutton, David Letterman, David Geffen, Candy Clark, and producer John Daly were among the rich and famous in attendance.

Cher arrived in an outrageous shag-cut purple wig and crucifix earrings, accompanied by her dates: short-time fiancé Josh Donen and longtime friend and *Mask* co-star Eric Stoltz. Andy Warhol, who was Martin Burgoyne's guest, arrived with fellow-artist Keith Haring. The pair walked up to the house with several gifts of artwork: painted, mounted copies of the *New York Post* front pages with the headlines about her nude photos. According to Warhol, "We rode in a limo out to Malibu, and when we saw helicopters in the distance, we knew we were at the wedding. Somebody had tipped the reporters off about where the wedding was, and about ten helicopters were hovering, it was like *Apocalypse Now!*"[60]

Sean's brother Chris came with his girlfriend, ice-skater Tai Babilonia, while Madonna's family flew in from points all over the countryside. Her father, stepmother, and grandmother were all present to witness the ceremony.

According to Maggie Hall, "In the street outside of the house there were hundreds of press members gathered to see the display of stars who walked up the long driveway. I was shocked when I saw Madonna's grandmother having to trudge up the driveway on foot, and she had a look of dismay on her face when she saw the crowd she had to pass through to get to her granddaughter's wedding. Imagine that—even her grandmother had to run the gauntlet of the press to get to the event. You'd think that Madonna would have been considerate enough to have at least sent a golf cart down the driveway for her granny!"[128]

Friends and family members were seated on white folding chairs set up around the swimming pool and in rows near the cliff. Seating was arranged so that the couple could have their hands joined in matrimony on a small triangle of land that jutted out toward the ocean. The best

man was *At Close Range* director Jamie Foley, and the maid of honor
was Madonna's sister Paula.

At seven P.M. the bride and groom appeared on the lawn as the
press helicopters circled overhead, fighting each other for the ultimate
shot of the event. The groom wore a black double-breasted Gianni Versace suit and looked dashing. Much to everyone's relief, the bride did
not wear black, except in her accessories.

Madonna's gown was a strapless white creation, low cut with a skirt
composed of several layers of billowing tulle. With it she wore a sash
of pink silk netting that had dried roses, pearls, and jewels encrusted
on it. As an eccentric touch, on her head Madonna wore a black bowler
hat, with a veil attached to it. Explained designer Marlene Stewart, "We
wanted a fifties feeling—something Grace Kelly might have worn."[97]

The ceremony, which only took five minutes, was performed by a
local judge, John Merrick. Unfortunately, no one could hear a thing that
was going on.

According to wedding guest John Daly, "They had a good, big kiss
when they were pronounced man and wife and then they went into the
house and up onto the balcony, where Madonna tossed her bouquet to
her sister Paula. Then Sean disappeared under Madonna's dress, which
got a big cheer from the crowd. He emerged with her garter, and threw
it backward. His brother, Chris, caught it."[129]

"That whole time was almost too much," Madonna recalls of the
event. "I mean, I didn't think I was going to be getting married with
thirteen helicopters flying over my head. It turned into a circus."[81]

One entire room of Unger's house was set aside for the wedding
gifts, which were elaborate. Christopher Walken gave the couple an
African sculpture; John Daly presented them with a silver tea service
from 1912; and Mo Ostin, chairman of the board of Warner Bros. Records, gave them a vintage jukebox, complete with two dozen of Madonna's
favorite singles.

When it came time to cut the five-tiered hazelnut wedding cake,
for the first time all day Madonna seemed unsure of herself. Standing
before the cake with a knife in her hands, she turned to purple-tressed
Cher and asked about cake-cutting protocol. Cher gave her a surprised
look, and later commented, "As if I know."[60]

Madonna then turned to other guests and inquired whether or not she should serve the cake on individual plates. In her own unconventional fashion, she was soon cutting up cake and passing it to people with her hands.

After serving up several handfuls of cake, Madonna and Sean prepared to feed each other pieces of cake. The pair ended up smearing cake and icing on each other's faces.

There was of course at least one mishap involving Sean and someone bearing a camera. Photographer Kip Rano had somehow gotten past security, and Sean spied his camera under his suit jacket.

"Suddenly he threw two punches at me, which I blocked. Then we were wrestling and fell to the floor. The security people pulled him off me and escorted me to the gate."[129] Rano's film was ripped out of his camera, and he was promptly expelled from the premises.

From that point on, the wedding became one big party, with dancing and carrying on, especially since the pressure was off, and the helicopters had gone home so that the photographers could go home and develop their aerial pictures of the ceremony.

Disc jockey Terrance Toy was among the soundmen at the event. When it came time for the couple's wedding dance, Toy programmed Sarah Vaughan's "I'm Crazy About the Boy." There was a ban on Madonna music at the wedding, but somehow "Lucky Star" and "Into the Groove" found their way onto the turntable. Quipped Terrance, "I didn't play 'Like a Virgin.'"[130]

At one point Madonna was having fun on the dance floor with a young man who was a dead ringer for Prince, and ever-jealous Sean shot several dirty looks at his new bride. But for the most part, even volatile Penn unwound and had a good time, when he wasn't beating up photographers. The reception lasted until four o'clock in the morning, at which point the bride and groom retired for the night, totally exhausted. Later that day they left for their next "top secret" destination: the honeymoon.

The place that the couple escaped to—*sans* helicopters—was the exclusive Highlands Inn, located in Carmel, California. Madonna checked into Suite 429, which is the honeymoon suite. At $225 per night, it came complete with wall-to-wall mirrors, a sunken bathtub, and a balcony private enough for nude sunbathing. Members of the room service staff were reportedly drawing straws for a chance to deliver something to the Penns' love pen. Madonna maintained her vegetarian diet, breakfasting on raspberries and cream. When the pair emerged from their suite, Madonna wore a brimmed hat and looked at the ground when she walked. One night the Inn opened their restaurant after hours so that the couple could dine in total privacy.

While the couple was enjoying their honeymoon, and the public was avidly reading the press reports about the *Apocalypse Now* ceremony that joined them, several people were already wondering how long this marriage would last. Madonna loved to flirt and had longed her entire life to become a star, to see her name in print, and to have her photo taken. Sean was withdrawn and insanely jealous, grew up in a Hollywood fishbowl, hated publicity, and kept himself busy beating up anyone he ran into who brandished a camera. It was a difficult match from the start.

"I have a theory that she just married into the Penn family to meld herself into Hollywood, and that Madonna just used him for his contacts," said one family friend who was at the Unger estate the day they wed.[128]

Even Madonna's old manager, Camille Barbone, put her two cents' worth in: "The relationship is stormy and violent. I don't think the marriage will last."[131]

According to Andy Warhol's infamous diary, Madonna was mad at him. Said the entry, dated September 4, Madonna complained to Martin Burgoyne, who in turn told Keith Haring, who then told Warhol. Apparently she was steamed that Andy and Keith had posed for *People* magazine's photographers when they arrived at her wedding. They were depicted as part of the publication's "Madonna Weds Sean" cover story that week. Warhol and Haring were photographed bearing mounted copies of *New York Post* front pages with headlines about Madonna's nude photos. Madonna might have been an expert at manipulating the media, but she could never hope to control it.

On September 19, Madonna and Sean were caught on film in New York—obstructing the photographer by holding their coats over their heads. Two days later, *sans* coats, Madonna and Sean were photographed shopping on Madison Avenue. Both sets of photos were immediately published in the daily newspapers.

On October 1, *A Certain Sacrifice* hit the video stores. Throughout that same month, the press was reporting that Sean and Madonna were already fighting. There was one story circulating that they were going to make an appearance at a peace rally together, and when Sean refused to go as planned, Madonna left their apartment in a door-slamming huff. There were also several reports that she had gained eleven pounds since her marriage, and talk was rampant that she was several months pregnant.

On the 17th of October, Sean appeared in court in Nashville to answer the charges against him for assaulting the pair of British photographers in June. He pleaded no contest, and ended up with a $100 fine and a suspended 180-day jail sentence.

At the Nashville airport Sean spotted a journalist with a camera. "I wish I had AIDS so I could shoot you. I wouldn't do it fast, but slow, from the toes up," he told him.[132]

In early November, Madonna was in New York to host the 1985–1986 season opening show of "Saturday Night Live." It was a great showcase for her comedic talents, and would be a great personal success for her.

Delivering her opening monologue, Madonna appeared in a blue hooded jogging suit, sunglasses, and a fur boa. She introduced herself, then said, "I'd like to clear up a few things about my wedding." With that she proceeded to explain that the wedding was not supposed to be a secret, as she held up a mock full-page ad in the Los Angeles Times headlined, MADONNA'S WEDDING TODAY—EVERYBODY INVITED . . . B.Y.O.B.[133]

She went on to say she realized most of the audience couldn't attend, so she brought some home movies to watch. With that she began narrating a film lampooning her insane wedding, complete with an actor playing Sean. It was hysterical. The Super-8 camera first shows Madonna dressed as a bride and then is aimed at "Sean," who instantly puts his hand up to block the camera. Madonna introduces her family as the camera pans across a group of gaudily dressed Italians, and all of the women—including the grandmother—are clad in crucifixes, bare midriff tops, brassieres over their clothing, rags tied in their hair, ruby red lipstick, and drawn-on beauty marks. The camera next hits a girl dressed as Cyndi Lauper—a la the cover of her album She's So Unusual. When the camera hits Sean's family, they all—including the grandmother—hold up their hands to block it. When it comes time to show the ceremony in this mock home movie, the action cuts to footage of an Air Force helicopter maneuver. In Madonna's narration, she says, "Everybody had a great time until the press got there." Conducting the ceremony is Don Novello as Father Guido Sarducci, but Madonna can't hear a word he is saying, and keeps yelling, "What did you say?" According to her, Sean decides to "turn the other cheek" and she has to take matters into her own hands.[133] With that, she pulls out a bazooka and shoots down the helicopter from the *New York Post*.

Returning from the "home movie," Madonna announced the other guest stars appearing on the show and neatly squelched a running rumor. She said, "I'm not pregnant, and we'll be right back."[133]

In the first live skit, Madonna portrays her idol Marilyn Monroe in a reenactment of the actress's final hours. The skit is entitled "The National Inquirer Theatre." In it Madonna plays Marilyn, costumed in a replica of *The Seven-Year Itch* dress that blew up when Monroe stood on a breezy subway grating. In this version, Marilyn's maid (Joan Cusack) is vacuuming the room, and the vacuum cleaner blows up the dress to cause the same effect. Randy Quaid, who was a regular performer on the show that season, portrayed President John F. Kennedy.

Madonna's other comic skits included one called "Pinklisting," in which she plays a Joan Collins–like soap opera star who has to kiss an actor she suspects is gay. Another skit found her singing a cha-cha version of the A-Ha song "Take on Me," as Marika, the star of a Spanish-language variety show called "El Espectacular de Marika."

Later in the show she portrays a frustrated Princess Diana, visiting the White House. Jon Lovitz plays her bored husband, Prince Charles. In drag as Nancy Reagan, actor Terry Sweeney is a riot portraying the former first lady as a bitchy dipsomaniac. As the skit proceeds, Madonna's Princess Di throws herself at Randy Quaid's stupefied version of President Reagan, as though looking for a father figure.

In her final bit, Madonna is seen as a menaced Tippi Hedrin–like character in a skit called "The Limits of the Imagination." It is a car phone variation of *Sorry Wrong Number*, and Madonna looks fabulous and Kim Novak-ish with her hair in a French twist.

An excellent showcase for Madonna, the show demonstrated that she did indeed have a great sense of comic timing and could pull off a demanding acting assignment. Some of the skits were less than brilliant in the way they unfolded, and it appeared that the writers didn't know how to end the Marika skit. However, that was not Madonna's problem. Her job was to draw ratings and to kick the season off with a bang. This she did.

Not once, but twice during the broadcast of "Saturday Night Live" that night, they ran advertisements for Madonna's new video cassette, *The Virgin Tour—Live,* which was due to be released November 11. What better way to publicize it?

Having returned to Manhattan, Madonna found herself walking down the same streets she used to walk down when she was a moneyless unknown. However, thanks to the incredible events of the past year, this time around she was hobnobbing in the most elite circles.

On November 14, the Thursday after she hosted "Saturday Night Live," Madonna was invited to a chic little get-together at Yoko Ono's apartment at the Dakota. Yoko was throwing a bash for Bob Dylan, and she had everyone take off their shoes when they arrived. Madonna complied, but claimed that since she didn't have socks on, she'd feel more comfortable taking off her top than removing her shoes. The guest list included David Bowie and Andy Warhol—who had a hole in his sock. According to Warhol, "She said she was so relieved her husband Sean wasn't with her, so she could really have fun."[60]

There was definitely trouble in paradise.

On November 29, in an attempt to erase some of the bad publicity that they had both been receiving, Madonna and Sean visited the Cornell Medical Center at New York Hospital to distribute Christmas presents to kids who wouldn't be traveling home for the holidays. Upon the Penns' insistence, there was no press—or photographers—allowed.

That fall it came time to return to the recording studio to begin work on her next album. Instead of looking to an outside producer, Madonna decided to co-produce the album herself. All the songs slated for the album were co-written by her, with the exception of "Papa Don't Preach," which was written by Brian Elliot, with "additional lyrics by Madonna." She recorded four cuts with Steve Bray, five cuts with Pat Leonard, and one cut with both of them. Nine of the ten songs ultimately made the album.

She also contacted several of the musicians that she had used before and trusted. One was keyboardist Fred Zarr. When she first landed a recording deal with Sire, Mark Kamins brought Fred into the sessions to play keyboard on the song "Everybody." Zarr vividly recalls the first time he ever laid eyes on Madonna. "When she walked into the room, I could feel the energy," he claims. "I looked up when she walked into the room. I just felt her walking in. I'll never forget that first time, meeting her."[134]

After she dismissed Kamins from the project, she wanted to continue to work with Fred on the album's additional cuts. Says Zarr, "Madonna liked working with me, and she introduced me to Reggie and wanted me to be used. All the songs that he produced I worked on. I did some of the keyboards, not all of them, on each song that he did. I remain friendly with Reggie to this day, as a result of Madonna's introducing us."[134]

Fred remembers that Reggie and Madonna didn't have the same strong rapport: "He really didn't get along too well with Madonna. They had some personality differences."[134] Zarr had known and worked with Jellybean Benitez for several years, so when it came time to record "Holiday," he was brought in on that session as well.

After the first album was completed and released, Madonna maintained contact with Fred Zarr. "We had tried to write [songs together] once; she had come to the house. She's been here two times, I guess. Then when she did 'Like a Virgin,' and she was working at the Power Station with Nile Rodgers, I was working with somebody else, and I ran into her. A couple of years later, she called me up one day and said, 'Fred! It's Madonna! I want you to come do some "Zarrisms."'' So, I got to do 'Papa Don't Preach,' 'True Blue,' and 'Jimmy Jimmy.' I was also on 'Spotlight,' which wasn't put on that album, it was on a later album. It was originally going on that album."[134]

Madonna produced four songs with Steve Bray at the recording studio that Bray had constructed in his Brooklyn apartment. "I did the intro to 'Papa Don't Preach,' which I wasn't credited with, unfortunately," says Zarr. "What happened was, I was at Steve Bray's studio—he produced it with her, and he had an Emulator II synthesizer. At the time it was brand-new; I had never heard it before, or played it before. It had a string sound that was incredible, and, as we were working on the string part—that 'da ta da da da' part—and they were rewinding the tape, I was doodling around, as I always do, and I came up with this intro. Madonna really liked it. I was just playing. Madonna said, 'I like that! What is that?' So, we put it on the beginning of the song. But, that was actually my intro—it's classic—it's the signature of the song. I'll never forget hearing her a few years after that in concert, and as soon as the audience heard the first two notes, they went nuts. Every time you heard that on the radio, you just knew—there it is. I'm proud of that."[134]

All four of the songs co-produced with Bray for the *True Blue* album were totally different in style and approach. "True Blue" was obviously a love song about the devotion that Madonna was trying to express to Sean. "Jimmy Jimmy" was a frivolous but fun pop song out of the Motown-ish "Jimmy Mack"/"Nathan Jones" mold. "Spotlight" was a typical Madonna look-at-me dance number, and "Papa Don't Preach" was a brilliant statement song about teenage pregnancy.

Fred confesses, "I never was crazy about that song 'Jimmy Jimmy.' I didn't like 'True Blue' either. Who knew it was going to be the title cut!"[134]

Zarr says working with Madonna was much more exciting and creative than recording sessions he has done with other artists. "It was really interesting working with her, because she always knew what she wanted, and she's real demanding. She used to just let me kind of do my thing, and then she'd say, 'Oh, I like that,' or 'I don't like that.' But, she'd just run the tape and let me play a lot. It was really Madonna who liked that intro the most on 'Papa Don't Preach.' It was her idea to actually do it, because there was no intro on the tune before."[134]

The songs that Madonna recorded on the West Coast with Pat Leonard co-producing had their own unique flavor as well. "White Heat," which was dedicated to actor James Cagney (the star of the movie of the same name), was a tribute to 1930s gangster movies. However, in this song, it is love that is the valued object of desire instead of money derived from bootlegging liquor. "La Isla Bonita" is a seductive Caribbean flavored tune that Madonna's character Marika might have sung. "Love Makes the World Go Round" is her salute to the peace songs of the sixties, similar to The Beatles' "All You Need Is Love." For high drama, Madonna and Pat came up with the stunning song "Live to Tell," which was the theme song for Sean's still forthcoming film *At Close Range*. The final song on the album, "Where's the Party?" was produced by Madonna with Leonard and Bray together. It was to become the album's "get down, get funky, get loose" dance tune.

Regarding Madonna's working relationship with Pat and Steve, Fred Zarr observed that they perfectly complemented each other. According to him, "Madonna is smart, and she doesn't think that she can do it all herself, but she is a driving force. She has talented people around her who she can work with, that she feels comfortable with. Steve is really good to work with. I enjoyed working with him. He's very talented, and they've made a good team. I think they work real well together. And, Madonna is very smart. She finds people who she can work with, like Steve and Pat Leonard. She knows a good thing."[134]

It was a calculated risk taking on the responsibility of co-producing her own album, with two people who were for the most part unproven as producers. However, Madonna's sense of direction and musical intuition proved successful. According to Zarr, Madonna seemed much more relaxed and confident on the sessions for this particular album than she had been in the beginning of her career. Her discomfort on her first two albums had caused her to argue with Reggie Lucas and to "give attitude" with Nile Rodgers.

"I know that during the *Like a Virgin* album, a lot of people thought she was pretty nasty," says Fred Zarr. "My relationship with her was one that started when she didn't even have enough money to get home from the studio. I used to drop her off at home. She didn't have enough money to take a cab. I liked her then, when she was broke, and we got along then, so I think I have that kind of perception about her. I just know her for who she is. She's been to my house, and I took her for a ride on my motorcycle, and we got along real well. She was very direct as far as, 'I don't want that.' If I played something, and I really liked it, and she said, 'I don't want that,' she didn't want that, and it wasn't going in, and that was it. She was very direct. It wasn't insulting, I mean, it was her record. A lot of people think she's bitchy. In the relationship I had with her, I didn't find that."[134]

It was a mutually beneficial relationship. "I like to think that I helped," Fred states with honesty. "It changed my life, you could say. It changed my life in that, after working with her, I got so many calls to do keyboard work that I got real busy. It was really a turning point in my career, so I thank her for that."[134]

Fred Zarr's work with Madonna occurred in October and November of 1985, at a time when there was a lot of activity in and around the Madonna camp. Sean had just been sentenced in Nashville for beating up cameramen, and several days later Zarr decided to bring his camera to Steve Bray's to snap a couple of shots of Madonna.

Fred Zarr recalls his own camera conflict with Sean Penn. "He came to pick her up from the studio a few times," says Zarr of Penn. "I met him when I was working over at Steve's studio. Sean would come to pick her up, and he was real quiet. I had brought my camera, because I realized that I had never taken a picture of Madonna, and I had worked with her all this time. And so, he showed up, and he was telling the story about how he was in *People* magazine because he had just punched somebody recently who took his picture. So I asked him, 'Is it OK if I get a picture of Madonna?' I don't know why I asked him. And Madonna said, 'You don't have to ask him! You can take a picture.'"[134]

Zarr took two photographs of Madonna that day at the studio—without being punched out by Sean. "She was getting ready to do this movie, *Shanghai Surprise*, where she was a missionary. So, she was kind of dressing strange. She was wearing glasses and had her hair up in a bun. She hadn't started the movie yet, but she was starting to get into the frame of mind of not being the 'wild Madonna,' and trying to get into this part. So she looked kind of funny that day. And she said, 'You're not going to show this to anybody are you?'" Fred recalls.[134]

The idea of Madonna portraying a missionary in the forthcoming movie *Shanghai Surprise* was in direct contrast to the image she had been projecting throughout the tumultuous year of 1985. Ever since "Like a Virgin" had hit the charts, she had been taking the heat as a bad influence on the youth of America. Right-wing groups from across the land were kicking up a stink about her image, her costumes, her nude photos, and the fact that teenagers worshiped the ground she wallowed on.

Kandy Stroud wrote an editorial in *Newsweek* that was titled "Stop Pornographic Rock." In addition to lambasting Madonna's song "Like a Virgin," Stroud also carried a torch against Prince's song "Darling Nikki," which is about a girl masturbating with a rolled up magazine in a hotel lobby. Also indicted were Sheena Easton's "Sugar Walls" (an obvious ode to her genitals written by Prince), W.A.S.P.'s sadomasochistic "The Torture Never Stops," and Frankie Goes to Hollywood's orgasmic "Relax."

Said Stroud, " 'Feels so good inside,' squeals Madonna on her triple-platinum album, *Like a Virgin*. Rock's latest 'It' girl hardly touts virginal innocence, as one can gather from her gyrations and undulations on Friday-night video shows."[135]

Other moralistic critics took a more dramatic stance. According to Margaret Scott of the California right-wing group United Parents Under God: "Our youngsters are being exploited and manipulated by Madonna. She takes a public-be-damned attitude to morals. Yet the kids worship her. She should be banned to save our children from ruin!"[136]

Madonna was quick to defend herself. "I think it's the kids' parents who don't understand, and they're frightened," she claimed. "Most of the lyrics in my songs have double entendres or lots of different meanings, so if you're thinking in a purely sexual way—I'm not using any offensive words or profanity at all."[137]

She defensively elaborated, "I'm definitely against violence in videos. But, I don't think that the MTV videos have any more violence than things people see all day long. So if you don't want your child exposed to violence, you shouldn't let them watch TV at all."[137]

And to think, at this point in her career she was just warming up. The so-called Moral Majority had no idea what kind of tricks were up Madonna's sleeve!

Nine

The

The most offensive people

on the entire planet![138]

Poison

—New York Daily News on

Penns

Madonna and Sean, circa 1986.

The year 1986 brought mixed blessings for Madonna. It seemed as though everything she was involved in with Sean turned out to be an incredible disaster—personally and professionally. At the same time, everything she touched as a solo project blossomed beautifully.

On the negative side of things came the horrendous Sean and Madonna movie *Shanghai Surprise*, the experimental theatrical production *Goose and Tomtom*, and the public hatred of Sean's childish outbursts toward the press.

When the idea of doing *Shanghai Surprise* came up, it sounded like a great joint project. According to Madonna, "We didn't actually plan on working on the film together."[139] She had just finished recording her *True Blue* album, and Sean was between projects. The original script was submitted to her, and she read it and liked it. Since Penn had more experience in film than she did, she asked him to give it a quick read. He ended up liking the male role, and the concept of working together seemed like a natural career progression.

It was going to be produced by HandMade Films, a company with ex-Beatle George Harrison as one of the owners. HandMade had been responsible for several box office hits, including *Time Bandits, A Private Function, Privates on Parade,* and *The Life of Brian.* With George Harrison as one of the executive producers, a production company with a strong track record, and a potentially amusing script, the Penns agreed to star in *Shanghai Surprise.*

The trouble began the first week in January 1986, as Sean and Madonna left Los Angeles and headed to the Far East to begin filming. They spent a week in Hong Kong, and everything went smoothly. They drew little attention as they traveled to the nearby island of Cheung Chau by boat and dined at a local restaurant. Madonna was able to do her jogging in the morning in the parking lot of their hotel, and it looked as if their stay was going to be uncomplicated.

The Penns arrived in the Orient in the middle of the night. Because of the long flight across time zones, they found their mental clocks were turned upside down, and neither of them was ready for sleep. "We ended up just walking around in the streets on this steel-cold morning," recalls Madonna.[112] As dawn broke, the couple wound their way through the twisting streets; they found themselves fascinated with the signs of life: people doing tai chi, readying shops to open, or scurrying toward their homes with cabbage and meat to feed their families.

Madonna was immediately struck with her virtual anonymity. She noted that people stared at her merely because she had blonde hair, but then went on about their business. The concept of her celebrity status never crossed their minds. Unfortunately, it was not a phenomenon that lasted long.

The following week, as production went into full swing, the Penns traveled forty miles west to the Portuguese port of Macao, and that's where the fireworks began. Accompanied by two assistants and a bodyguard, on January 16 Sean and Madonna were ambushed by a press photographer as they returned to their suite on the eighteenth floor of the luxurious Orient Hotel. The photographer was Leonel Borralho, owner of two newspapers in Macao, who was determined to scoop everyone else by getting the first exclusive photos of the couple since their arrival.

As they neared their suite, Borralho leaped out from behind a service door and began shooting. With that Sean and the bodyguard attacked the surprised lensman. According to reports, Sean and the bodyguard proceeded to "punch out" sixty-one-year-old Leonel, but in reality it was more of a scuffle than a pummeling session.

Borralho recalls of Sean's actions, "He was like a madman. He was screaming at his bodyguard, 'I want that film. Don't let him get away. I want that camera.'" Sean grabbed the photographer's arm, and the bodyguard attempted to remove his camera, which hung from a strap around his neck. Borralho struggled and refused to surrender the camera. Penn and the bodyguard demanded that he give it up. Realizing the consequences that could arise from physically seizing the camera, Sean offered to barter with Borralho. If the journalist gave up the roll of film in the camera, Sean swore that he would be granted an exclusive interview with Madonna. "I decided to agree to this, because I knew there was no chance for me," Borralho remembers.[140]

Borralho gave up his film and threatened that if he didn't get a call that night regarding the promised interview with Madonna, he was going to press charges. When no phone call was made, the police were brought into it. Penn and his bodyguard were summoned to the local police headquarters, and they were questioned for two and a half hours. To top off the affair, the photographer and newspaper owner filed a $1 million lawsuit against Sean.

According to Paul Campbell, an editor at the *Hong Kong Standard*, Sean had opened quite a can of worms by attacking the photographer: "Macao is a small place, and apart from owning two newspapers, [Borralho] also has a lot of local influence."[140] As a former legislative member Borralho was not going to let the case drop until he raked the Penns over the coals in print.

Madonna and Sean's living conditions on the set were apparently less than luxurious. "There were big black rats underneath our trailers," says Madonna with disgust. "I kept saying, 'I can't wait till I can look back on this, I can't wait!'"[112] For the duo, the film turned into one massive survival test. Madonna was especially vexed by the ordeal. She realized that the entire nightmare experience was not only going to put her acting talents to a test, but it was also going to add undue stress to her marriage. As the shooting began, Madonna found herself doubting her own capacities. Instead of concentrating on her screen portrayal, she spent more and more mental energy assessing her own insecurities. She kept telling herself that if she failed as an actress in this film, it could also signal the end of her marriage to Sean.

As the filming progressed, so did the problems. Two days following the Borralho fiasco, reporters and photographers in hot pursuit of the Penns embarked on a wild chase scene, causing a huge traffic jam. Trapped in their car in the jam, Madonna was cheered by the mob of pedestrians that surrounded their vehicle.

Meanwhile, the international press was having a field day reporting the daily scores from the media war in the Far East. So far the score was: Photographers - 2; Sean - 0.

Paula Yates, the wife of Live Aid organizer Bob Geldof and hostess of the popular British television show "The Tube," traveled to Hong Kong to film a documentary on Sean and Madonna. Madonna had gladly consented to the interview by Paula, but Sean flatly refused to allow his wife to cooperate with the press in any way. "She didn't pose any problems at all, but Sean laid down the law," recalls Geoff Wonfor, Paula's producer. "He decided he just didn't want her to talk."[141] After every scene, Sean led Madonna back to her trailer and forbade the journalists to talk to her.

It wasn't long before the planned documentary was sabotaged by Sean. "Every time he saw us take our cameras out to film what was going on he screamed and yelled and demanded that all the footage be scrapped," said Wonfor of Penn's daily tantrums.[141] One morning, while Sean and Madonna were filming a scene in a boat a quarter-mile out in the bay, Wonfor had his cameramen shoot some long shots of the couple that could be used without their approval. However, even that seemingly harmless footage was scrapped at Sean's insistence.

Madonna later revealed that in addition to Sean's bouts with the press, the entire experience was one long ordeal. She found herself in a foreign country in cold winter weather walking around in cotton blouses, as though it was summer. There were also communication problems on the set, she was constantly getting sick from the food, and it was such hard work, she couldn't believe that she had willingly consented to this project to begin with. "It was very grueling, and there was a lot of tension on the set between the director and all the actors. It was just endless tension," she complained.[22]

In an effort to call a truce between the press and the Penns, the film's unit publicist, Chris Nixon, suggested that the pair should host a media photo session. That way, the press would get all the shots they needed, and there wouldn't be a need for the surprise confrontations. As soon as he had made his suggestion, Nixon was immediately fired, at Sean's insistence.

The situation between the Penns and the press was beginning to distress the executives at HandMade Films, and they began to worry about their $15.5 million investment. As part of an emergency mission, George Harrison flew to Hong Kong, where he reportedly gave Madonna and Sean a stern lecture about their behavior and told them about the stories that were appearing in the papers in London.

When Madonna was later asked if George had imparted any acting advice, she replied that he had given her more advice on how to deal with the press than how to make movies.

Somehow the location filming was finished within the scheduled six-week stay in Hong Kong and nearby Macao. Filming was scheduled to resume in London. On February 20, Sean and Madonna landed in Germany to attend West Berlin's International Film Festival. When they arrived at the airport, Madonna wore dark glasses, and Sean pulled his jacket up over his head. The resulting photos, which ran in that afternoon's *New York Post*, look like Madonna is out on the town with the Elephant Man.

The following day, when the Penns arrived in London, they were mobbed by members of the press. To make for further bad press, Madonna's Mercedes limousine ran over the foot of one of the photographers. Apparently he had been sprawled across the hood of the vehicle only seconds before. Regardless, war had been declared between the Fleet Street journalists and "the Poison Penns," as they were dubbed.

Madonna recalls of the experience, "When we got to England, it was like the Third World War!"[22] While interior shots were filmed in a studio in London, news reports of press photographers wresting with Sean Penn and/or bodyguards were arriving on a daily basis.

Finally, something had to be done to calm down the volatile atmosphere on the set. In an unprecedented move, George Harrison stepped forward to call a cease fire between the press and the Penns. On March 6, Madonna and George appeared at a press conference to answer the questions of the fourth estate.

One of the most glaring questions was the obvious "Where's Sean?" Defensively, George replied, "He's busy, working."[142] "I don't think he's into talking to press," Harrison continued in his olive branch of a press conference.[138] "I happen to like Sean very much. Apart from all the bullshit that's been said, he's actually a human being and he's very nice, and he's a very talented actor."[139] According to George, all of the sensationalism came simply because he happened to be married to Madonna.

It was a nice try on George's part, but Sean's absence from the press conference spoke louder than words. That day in London, Madonna recemented her relationship with the British press, but it was just the beginning of Sean's media scuffles.

When Madonna was asked if she was one of George Harrison's fans, she replied, "I wasn't a Beatle maniac. I think I didn't really appreciate their songs till I was much older. But he's a great boss. Very understanding and very sympathetic."[139]

In reality she was more concerned with her work on screen than she was with Sean's murky moods. With regard to her acting, she claimed that the most difficult part for her was the point in the script in which her character goes through a transformation and becomes more liberated. Another hard part, she complained, was the beginning of the movie, where her character, Gloria Tatlock, is quite repressed and so opposite of her own temperament. To portray innocence on camera was a real stretch for Madonna, and she realized she had gotten herself in over her head.

She was, however, able to illuminate the reasons why she wanted to portray a repressed character on the screen: "You have to think about the political climate in the U.S. at that time," she said of the film's 1938 setting. "Rather than stay home and raise children, I wanted to do something exciting with my life—so I go to Shanghai to be a missionary."[139]

When the press started to get personal with their questions, George jumped into the fray on her behalf. "Do you fight with Sean?" one reporter asked Madonna. Answered Harrison, "Do you row with your wife?"[142]

Although he was a tonic for frazzled nerves that day at the press conference, Harrison was a bit put off that Sean and Madonna had acted so poorly off screen.

"The Beatles always handled the press brilliantly, and we had far more press than any pop star today," George said, a year after *Shanghai Surprise* had come and gone. "We also had a sense of humor about it," he said with reference to press relations and giving interviews.[143] In his eyes, Madonna and Sean took it all too seriously.

In January, while Sean and Madonna had been in China filming *Shanghai Surprise*, her lawyers had finalized negotiations to secure an apartment on Central Park West. It cost an estimated $850,000. The lease, however, was not in both of their names—it was in hers alone. Her lawyers were careful to keep all of Madonna's belongings in her name, a practice which also fit the prenuptial agreement they had signed before they were married.

With the new co-op, the couple was officially bicoastal. In April 1986, with their work on *Shanghai Surprise* completed, the Penns were back in Los Angeles and basically walking on thin ice as far as the press was concerned. It was this month that a split seems to have occurred—one that found Madonna soaring and Sean sinking. Their next moves were perceived as crucial in determining how they were going to be treated in public.

Also that month the first single, "Live to Tell," off Madonna's soon to be released third album, hit the airwaves. Like "Crazy for You" a year before, "Live to Tell" was a sensitive and powerful ballad. She delivered it with sincerity and emotion, and it was an instant smash. It was the theme song for Sean's movie *At Close Range*, and that film's director, Jamie Foley, directed the stark and striking Madonna video. Without wild jewelry or a revealing outfit, her look had changed. Her hair was blonde and styled along the lines of the 1930s character she had just played in *Shanghai Surprise*.

While Madonna was proving her versatility with "Live to Tell," Sean kept busy causing conflicts. He went out of his way to comment candidly about the helicopter film crews that took photos of his wedding last summer. "I would have been very excited to see one of those helicopters burn and the bodies inside melt," he claimed. "Those were non-people to me!"[144]

On April 12, Sean and Madonna went to a Los Angeles club called Helena's. Also there that evening was songwriter David Wolinski, an old friend of Madonna's. When David spotted Madonna in the club, he walked over to say hello and kissed her on the cheek. Seeing this, Sean went into a rage and savagely began beating and kicking David with his fists, his feet, and a chair that he grabbed. The club's proprietress, Helena Kallianiotes, and Madonna had to drag Sean kicking and screaming outside.

Madonna was totally freaked out. This wasn't some aggressive journalist jumping out from behind a door, this was a friend of hers. Wolinski pressed charges against Sean. Penn in turn was fined $1,000 and got off with a year's probation.

Suddenly everyone was taking sides in the great "How long will this marriage last?" debate. Even Camille Barbone managed to put her two cents' worth in. "I don't think having a husband who throws tantrums and bricks is going to seem all that endearing much longer," said Madonna's former manager. "She is going to realize he is not a rebel, just a child."[140]

On June 6, Sean again blew up in public. This time, however, his anger was aimed at his wife. The pair was out on the town in New York with friends, and they couldn't seem to agree on anything. According to the gossip columns, the pair dined in Little Italy and then went uptown to the East Village to the trendy little underground dance club Pyramid. Martin Burgoyne had gotten a job as a disc jockey there, and Madonna and Sean stopped in to visit with him. Once they arrived, they got into a heated argument. At one point Sean grabbed Madonna and shoved her up against a wall. They quickly exited the club and hopped into separate cabs.

On June 30, Madonna's third album, *True Blue*, was released, along with her latest single, "Papa Don't Preach." Her new songs and a new video all received glowing reviews. Especially talked about was Madonna's new look: short-cropped blonde hair, fifties-style peg-legged pants, sleek, form-fitting tops, and no jewelry. Her new look was a combination of Marilyn Monroe, Jean Seberg, and Kim Novak. Gone was the assemblage of crucifixes and hair rags. In its place was a new gamine Madonna for 1986.

"I see my new look as very innocent and feminine and unadorned," Madonna proclaimed. "It makes me feel good. Growing up, I admired the kind of beautiful glamorous women—from Brigitte Bardot to Grace Kelly—who [don't] seem to be around much anymore. I think it's time for that kind of glamour to come back."[30]

The press really picked up on Madonna's fresh-looking makeover. Of this acting foray, *Vanity Fair* said that she looked like "a knocked-up blue-collar Italian Jean Seberg in the 'Papa Don't Preach' video."

As far as her wardrobe went, this represented a new era for her. "I wanted to change my clothes," she said. "Obviously, if you spend a couple of years wearing lots of layers of clothes and tons of jewelry and it just takes you forever to get dressed and your hair is long and crazy, then you get the urge to take it all off and strip yourself down and cut your hair all off just for a relief."[145]

Not everyone could do such an about-face with their looks and not lose their audience. However, Madonna pulled it off—as she would time and time again. Although her fans loved it, not everyone was ecstatic, especially her old fashion stylist cohort, Maripol. A year before, Maripol's rubber and metal religious symbol jewelry was a huge seller. As the summer of 1986 rolled around, it signaled the end of Maripol's shop on Bleecker Street and bankruptcy for her company. According to one of her acquaintances, "Maripol had it made until Madonna instantly changed her image. In her loft on Broadway, Maripol still has cases and cases of 'Lucky Star' jewelry she thought she was going to market—stars and rubber crosses. Madonna simply took off ahead of Maripol, and basically said, 'Hey, tough!' "[128]

Critics and fans alike praised the music on *True Blue*. Madonna admitted that it was her most personal album to date, and it encompassed a lot of her own thoughts and viewpoints. According to her, "Most people think there's something secret or magical to being a singer or writing a song. But you can do whatever you want. You have to throw out all the rules and all the advice everyone gives you about how to make it . . . and follow your own vision if you have one."[146]

She claimed that these new stances worked, because they were just different extensions of the same Madonna the world was crazy about on her previous albums. "Listen to a song like 'Like a Virgin,' and then listen to 'Live to Tell,'" she said. "There's a different mood in each one. They're the same person, but it's just my desire to focus on something different because of the mood I'm in."[11]

One of her personal favorite cuts on the album was "Jimmy Jimmy," which was about the late actor James Dean. "I used to fantasize that we grew up in the same neighborhood and that he moved away and became a big star."[30] Sort of the way that her former classmates at Rochester Adams High School must have looked at her by then.

The song "Papa Don't Preach" had a life all its own, and the song's message and plot were brilliantly brought alive in the video that was directed by Jamie Foley. The song's story is set in a working-class community on Staten Island. In the video, Madonna is seen as a teenager who is in her first months of pregnancy and is determined to keep her baby. She is first seen in a tight-fitting pair of jeans and a striped boat-neck sweater walking down the sidewalk with a determined gait. When she reaches her house, images of her past are flashing in her mind. Flashbacks tell the story of her life as an only child with only her father to raise her. While the song plays, Madonna convinces her father that this shouldn't compromise their love for each other. Danny Aiello portrays the father, and Alex McArthur is the strapping young boyfriend that Papa doesn't approve of.

In several scenes, Madonna is seen wearing a black T-shirt with the words ITALIANS DO IT BETTER emblazoned on it. Although Madonna's character is pregnant in the plot of the song, she herself is sleek and trim.

The story's action is intercut with footage of a black-bustier-clad Madonna. Dancing against a fade-to-black background, she appears to be the story's victorious narrator. With her blonde hair, red lips, and alabaster skin, she is strikingly glamorous.

Recalling his casting call for the video, Alex McArthur says, "I was out in the garage working on my Harley. I answered the phone, and a voice said, 'Hi, this is Madonna. I would like you to be in my next video.'"[147] Madonna had spotted him in a small role in the film *Desert Hearts* and decided to track him down herself.

When Madonna first heard the song, she was already weighing it for its controversial value. According to her, " 'Papa Don't Preach' is a message song that everyone is going to take the wrong way. Immediately they're going to say I am advising every young girl to go out and get pregnant. When I first heard the song I thought it was silly. But then I thought, 'Wait a minute, this song is really about a girl who is making a decision in her life.' "[30]

When several pro-life groups jumped on the bandwagon, praising the song's message, the misinterpretation was taken to a whole new level. Madonna claimed that she certainly didn't mean to pin an antiabortion message on the video. "I had no ambitions for this to be adopted by any special interest groups. I don't have any banner to wave. I just wanted to make this girl a sympathetic character," she explained.[28]

Since the videos Madonna makes are meant to bring her songs to life, she says she retains a much stronger control over their production than she can in the roles she lands in other people's movies. According to her, "I can never be JUST in front of the camera."[7]

By the end of August, both "Papa Don't Preach" and the album *True Blue* were Number One in America and in several countries abroad. Again the name "Madonna" was on everyone's lips.

Amid all this summer activity, Madonna received some tragic news: her old friend, artist Martin Burgoyne had AIDS. The first week in August she was in all the New York gossip columns—spotted on Columbus Avenue buying books "for a sick friend."[148] It was Martin, who had remained one of her few close friends from her salad days. He had gone down to Florida where he was spending time with his family. In the next couple of months Madonna would do all that she could to help and support him.

While *Shanghai Surprise* was still being prepared for release, Madonna and Sean embarked on their next acting venture. It was a David Rabe play called *Goose and Tomtom*, and it was a pet project of Sean's. It was about two criminals and a gun moll. Cast as one of the criminals, it was Sean who came up with the idea of Madonna playing the gun moll.

The last week in August, the play was staged as a work-in-progress and played four performances for an invitation-only audience. Among the friends and celebrities who caught one of Sean and Madonna's only scripted live performance together were Warren Beatty, Tom Cruise,

Tatum O'Neal, John McEnroe, Liza Minnelli, Griffin Dunne, Andy Warhol, Martin Burgoyne, Keith Haring, Cher, and Melanie Griffith. Although no press members were knowingly invited, the *Wall Street Journal* reviewed it, calling the play an "inarticulate and incomprehensible meditation on human grubbiness."

The word on the street was that the play was a complete disaster, and that Madonna and Sean's combined onstage presence couldn't save the production from obscurity. The show was never presented beyond those four "in rehearsal" nights, played in front of an audience of their friends.

Throughout the entire two-hour play, Madonna chewed gum and acted like Judy Holliday in *Born Yesterday*. The costume designer was Kevin Dornan, who was formerly the fashion editor of Andy Warhol's *Interview* magazine. Madonna made several beautiful costume changes, Sean wore fuschia-colored socks and shoes, and the overall look of the play was decidedly abstract. When asked if Sean and Madonna were getting along, Dornan claimed that they were crazy about each other.

Although the play was awful, several people enjoyed Madonna's performance in it. According to Griffin Dunne, "She seemed to be very inside herself. When she came out with a cigarette that needed to be lit—all you were concerned about was who was going to light it."[7]

On a warm Friday night, August 29, amid the brief nonpublic run of the play, came Sean Penn's next battle with the paparazzi. It seemed like a routine photo opportunity for the media. Sean and Madonna left Lincoln Center, walked to a local restaurant, and strolled home to their new apartment. Waiting for them in front of their building was a group of half a dozen well-known press photographers, including the renowned paparazzo Ron Gallella. When the cameramen began shooting photos, Sean flew into a rage, which erupted into a midnight fistfight with two press members, Anthony Savignano and Vinnie Zuffante.

The ensuing fight was a natural for instant worldwide coverage—and received it in spades. With six press photographers present, everyone from the *New York Post* to the *Star*, *Us*, and *People* magazine ran splashy stories on Sean's latest atrocity. Especially popular were one of Ron's shots of Sean spitting at Anthony; Vinnie's photos of Sean and Madonna hiding behind a "doggie bag" of leftovers, and Geoffrey Croft's photos of Sean struggling with Anthony, whom he had gotten in a headlock. It became the paparazzi photo opportunity of the year.

As one of the top paparazzi in the business, Vinnie Zuffante had been shooting the stars for years. From New York to Los Angeles to Cannes, he had traveled all over the world to take pictures of Madonna. From the very beginning of Madonna's relationship with Sean in 1985, Zuffante had followed the couple. Madonna knew who Vinnie was by sight, and whenever she asked him not to take a photo, he would obligingly wait until she was ready. On certain occasions, he would wait up to five hours for her okay to snap the one exclusive pose of the evening. Up until this point, Vinnie had what he considered to be a good working relationship with Madonna.

Sean, on the other hand, was an adversary from as far back as he could remember. According to Vinnie, "I remember Sean Penn when he was in New York doing a show called *Slab Boys*. He was going out at the time with Bruce Springsteen's sister, and he didn't like being photographed then—he never liked it. So he made the mistake of going into this business and not liking it. And then, marrying her, the most popular woman in the world—he just didn't have common sense about it."[149]

Vinnie vividly remembers that particular evening on New York's Upper West Side when Sean went berserk. "We were outside their apartment. They were doing a play at Lincoln Center, *Goose and Tomtom*, and they were on their way back from it. So we were shooting pictures of them walking up the street. After the performance they went to The Gingerman for dinner, and they had a bag full of food, and they're walking with the bag in front of their faces so they can't be photographed. And, they were laughing, thinking it was funny and stuff like that. They had smiles on their faces."[149]

Suddenly, and without warning, the look on Sean's face changed. When the six photographers reached the doorway, they turned the corner, and stepped into the entranceway. That was all the provocation Sean needed. They were no longer on the sidewalk, and he felt as if he were justified in resorting to violence. "We stepped into the courtyard by accident, and they misunderstood what we were doing," explains Vinnie. "Ron Gallella and Anthony stepped into the courtyard, and that's when Sean went crazy."[149]

He recalls that the fight between Anthony and Sean was more of a
shoving match than a fistfight. "No one ever really got a hit on anybody,
because—it was a 'hug' more, and they were trying to hit, no one could
get in any punches. At one point Anthony got Sean over to the banister,
and could have thrown him over the banister—down about fifteen feet.
But then he realized, 'Oh shit! I might kill him!' So they got away from
that, and the doorman was there with a broom, hitting us. There was
one Puerto Rican kid that was walking by, just ran into the courtyard,
and was starting to pull Sean away—trying to break up the fight. Sean
was more angry that he couldn't hit the photographer than anything
else."[149]

The next thing he knew, Vinnie was being dragged into the fracas.
"I wasn't in the courtyard yet," he recalls. "Madonna started yelling at
me to stop taking pictures. Up to that point, I was sort of like friends
with them. I wouldn't photograph when they asked me not to. Madonna
said, 'Stop them!' I said, 'I can't stop him, look at him, he's a madman.
Why don't you go inside, and they'll stop photographing you getting
angry.' So she started going inside, and then Sean turned around and
pulled me into the courtyard. The first thing he said was, 'And you,'
and then he hit me. I said, 'What the hell are you doing that for?' And
then he said, 'You're just as bad as they are.' And I said, 'If that's what
you think—just wait—I'm gonna be.' From that day on I went on a
streak to get them back. The only reason that I was in the courtyard
was because Madonna said, 'Try to break them up,' and I said, 'You're
crazy, I can't.' And she said, 'Stop taking pictures.' I said, 'I can't—
this is news!'"[149]

Vinnie maintains that Madonna is, was, and will always be in love
with all the media attention. "I know what she is really like, and she
is a publicity whore," claims Zuffante.[149]

His rationale is that if a celebrity is out in a public place, they are
fair game for press photographers, whether what they're doing is newsworthy at the time or not. Sean and Madonna could have resorted to
different tactics if they didn't want to be photographed together. "They
could have taken a cab or a limo," he maintains. "I can understand that
they had their privacy and all of that, but when they're walking down a
public street, they don't have their privacy, and they should know that.
Even though they were only going a block and a half—hop in a damn

cab and take it home. Let Madonna walk in first. Let Sean pay the cab, and then have Sean walk in, and no one would get the picture. They knew that we were down by the [apartment] house, waiting. They saw us walking up toward them, they were walking toward us, and then we backed up the street, walking toward the house. Madonna is not going to go out of her way for us. She will not change her routine, she will not do anything, because we're there. And, if that is going to be the attitude she has, she is going to keep getting what she is getting."[149]

Madonna claims she enjoys the exposure, but she is not in love with the photographers' attitudes. "The thing that annoys me more than anything about the paparazzi is that they really feel that they have put you where you are," she complains. "They really think that because you're a celebrity, you owe them all the pictures they can get."[13]

What she objects to the most is that the paparazzi seem to appear at the most bizarre times. She could be leaving a workout at an exercise club, shopping for clothes, or riding her bike down the street, and all of a sudden someone with a camera leaps out from behind a bush or a wall. These instances nearly give her a heart attack on the spot.

"It's not fun," Madonna said when she was questioned about what she thought of Sean's public fights with photographers. "But I've been dealing with the media since the very beginning of my career, and Sean never really had to. I wanted it, and I was sort of ready to deal with it, and he wasn't."[26]

The very next night, the Penns went to Sardi's after their show was over, and a group of fans and photographers clamoring for Madonna had gathered outside. In another of his endearing moves, Sean stuck his head out the second-floor window and spit on the crowd gathered below.

Unfortunately, that month's negative media blitz on "the Poison Penns" was just beginning. It was Friday, August 29, the same day as the New York paparazzi fiasco that the star couple's next major disaster occurred: the premiere of *Shanghai Surprise*.

Even before the film opened, it had failure stamped all over it. The fact that there were no prerelease press screenings was clue number one. MGM-UA, the American distributor, was justifiably terrified of what the critics were going to do when they got a peek at this debacle.

To hold the major media critics at bay, the film opened at four hundred cinemas in medium-sized cities across America. The film was kept off New York and Los Angeles screens until three weeks later. Then, on September 19, those two cities were among the second wave of four hundred theaters screening *Shanghai Surprise*. The longer they could hold off the New York and L.A. critics, the better.

Unfortunately, the reviews from the heartland set the tone. In the *Cleveland Plain Dealer*, reviewer Roxanne T. Mueller called the film "awesome in its awfulness." Douglas D. Armstrong wrote in the *Milwaukee Journal* that Madonna "acts and emotes with all the conviction of a guest in a sketch on a Bob Hope special."

When September 19 arrived, the real bloodbath began. "Madonna's first flop," is how *Rolling Stone* bannered their take on the film. "Shockingly amateurish," is how Fred Schruers described it in *Us*. It was Janet Maslin's review in the *New York Times* that really hit the coffin nail on the head: "The nicest thing about *Shanghai Surprise*, the widely publicized washout starring Madonna and Sean Penn, is that you can watch it in near-total privacy," is how Maslin's review began. And she was dead right. You could shoot a cannon through any of the theaters screening this film and not hit a soul. When *Variety* announced that the average box office take at the theaters screening this movie was $1,000 a week, it was time for HandMade Films to cut their losses. According to James Greenberg in the same publication, "I've rarely seen a worse opening."

Although she was stiff and unconvincing in most of the film, Madonna was singled out for blame in less instances than Sean. Claimed Maslin, "Mr. Penn, ever since his hilarious performance as a stoned surfer in *Fast Times at Ridgemont High*, has been greatly overrated."

Richard Corliss, writing in *Time* magazine, was perhaps the kindest to the stars. Although he claimed—of the film—that MGM "has dropkicked it into the marketplace like a turkey carcass," he illuminated the bigger picture as far as Sean and Madonna were concerned. According to him, "Neither glows like the incandescent movie stars they can and will be."

Shanghai Surprise disappeared from theaters almost instantly. It was ironic, because the week the film debuted, Madonna had the Number One album and single in the country. What became clear was that her fans wanted to see her behaving outrageously—and singing.

Shanghai Surprise is one of the most excruciating cinematic experiences ever created. It is dull, moronic, stiff, slow, unmotivated, and just plain boring. Madonna is totally out of her element, and every scene looks as though they filmed the dress rehearsal instead of the real performance. Sean is totally unbelievable as he does his best to play his character as though he were Indiana Jones. Madonna as a prim missionary was the Hollywood miscasting foray of the decade.

Shanghai Surprise didn't work on any level. It wasn't funny enough to be a comedy, it wasn't dramatic enough to be a drama, and there wasn't enough action to make it an adventure film. Twice the stars get themselves into deadly dilemmas and in the very next scene are shown miraculously rescued. The poor viewer never gets a clue how they escaped. Perhaps a Madonna song in the movie could have added some spark to the proceedings. As it was, George Harrison—who has an embarrassed cameo as a nightclub performer—provided all the film's music. If this was any other music star's first starring film project, he or she would probably be banned from working in the movies again. As a singer-becoming-an-actor, Madonna's performance in *Shanghai Surprise* is so awful that it makes Elvis Presley seem like Sir Laurence Olivier in comparison.

How could Madonna be so electrifying in the five-minute video of "Papa Don't Preach," and so embarrassing in *Shanghai Surprise?* After the dust settled, and this disaster film disappeared without a trace, the real stories began to surface.

"The truth is, we had just gotten married," Madonna revealed. "Sean wasn't supposed to do the film. He didn't want to do the film. But he also didn't want to spend four months away from me."[93]

She was looking for a role that would offer her a contrast. After *Desperately Seeking Susan,* people would claim that she was really playing herself. This made her want to play an opposite character to convince everyone that she really could act. That became a real trap for her.

"A hellish nightmare," is how she remembers the filming of *Shanghai Surprise.* "The director turned out not to know what he was doing, we were on a ship without a captain, and we were so miserable while we were working that I'm sure it shows."[26] Assessing the blame, Madonna was quick to point her finger at the director. "The director, Jim Goddard, wanted to shoot it fast without any production values. It was like a bad music video,"[93] she explained. "We wanted to do a movie that was about a love story, not about an adventure. Unfortunately, it was edited as if it was an adventure, and it's not. They left out all the important stuff about the relationship."[22] Still, she maintains that the film was an excellent learning experience for her.

Then, of course, there were Sean's temper tantrums that Madonna had to deal with as well. "Some of the tensions were on the set, some were because of the paparazzi," she says. "Sean's whole image was sort of blown up into this impossible person out of control."[26]

Although the release of *Shanghai Surprise* was comparable to the *Titanic* when it bumped into that iceberg, Madonna at this point was proving to be unsinkable. She was already making plans for her next movie role.

One of the most interesting ideas then being batted around Hollywood was getting Madonna to play the coveted role of Eva Peron in the proposed screen adaptation of the Broadway biographical musical, *Evita*. It was a fascinating casting idea. The role was someone Madonna could believably portray: a poor girl from South America who dates all of the right guys until one day—married to a political leader—she finds herself the glamorous first lady of Argentina. It seemed ideal, after all— the concept of useful boyfriends was one with which Madonna could surely identify. At that time, the film rights to *Evita* were in the hands of producer Robert Stigwood and negotiations were well under way.

Madonna had several meetings with Robert Stigwood, and while she was in China she read tons of literature on Evita Peron. Madonna envisioned the project as a classic American movie musical, while Stigwood insisted that it be filmed as the operetta it was written as. Ultimately, they locked horns at this initial stage of the project. While it didn't work out, this was to be merely the first round in the ongoing Madonna/*Evita* saga.

Exactly what was it that Madonna saw herself doing in future films? She had been offered several scripts—in spite of what the word-of-mouth reports about *Shanghai Surprise* foretold. When Mary Lambert was signed to direct *Siesta*, Madonna was considered for the lead in the film. However, she passed and Ellen Barkin starred in it instead. "I loved the script of *Siesta*, but I couldn't deal with all the nudity in it," she claimed. "I'm at a stage in my career where any kind of nudity would be an incredible distraction within a given movie."[7]

She was looking for a role that was sexy and not erotic, filled with action but nonviolent, featuring music but not a musical. "I think it's really difficult for Americans to express passion and desire in movies," she contemplated. "Something bad always has to happen—violence—or the relationship doesn't last. I will not be attracted to making violent films. I'm attracted to roles where women are strong, and aren't victimized. Everything I do has to be some kind of celebration of life."[7]

The films she liked most were the classic screwball comedies of the thirties like *Mr. and Mrs. Smith,* with Carole Lombard and Robert Montgomery. Katharine Hepburn and Cary Grant's 1938 classic *Bringing Up Baby* was another film that Madonna mentioned on her list of favorites. "I just love those films where the woman gets away with murder, but her weapon is laughter, and you end up falling in love with her."[7]

Working along those lines, talk was widespread about Madonna starring in a remake of *The Blue Angel,* the 1930 German film that made Marlene Dietrich a star. Filmed in simultaneous German and English versions, Dietrich became the toast of two continents when this cinema classic was released. It was all about "naughty" Lola, the trampy showgirl who seduces a school professor. Diane Keaton, who had a development deal at Fox, reportedly worked with producer Joe Kelly at enticing Madonna to play the title role. Robert De Niro was discussed as the ideal actor for the male lead. Although a great idea, it never quite panned out.

Meanwhile, in June 1986, before the resounding thud of *Shanghai Surprise* graced movie screens, another remarkable thing happened. Madonna was approached by Universal about starting her own production company, with her own office based on the lot. She aptly entitled her production company "Siren" and hired a staff to assist her in finding film properties. According to Carol Lees, Vice President, Acquisitions and Development, for Siren Productions, Madonna oversees the whole operation. "She's got her hands in everything," says Lees. "She's in a special position, she has a little bit of clout because of the success of her music."[26]

With her crew at Siren, Madonna was considering several different properties. There was talk about a remake of *Dead End Street,* originally directed by Israeli cinematographer Yaki Yosha. It is the story of a documentary filmmaker who finds his life turned upside down when he falls madly in love with a prostitute. The way it was discussed, Sean

Penn would play the filmmaker; his father, Leo Penn, would direct; and Madonna would naturally portray the lady of the night. Another remake under consideration was of the 1962 French film *Cleo from 5 to 7*. Directed by Agnes Varda, the film chronicles two hours in the life of an aspiring singer in New York City. Also discussed was a romance thriller called *Angel Flight*, which would co-star French actor Jean-Hugues Anglade.

That summer there was also talk about Madonna taking the female lead in *Blind Date*, with Blake Edwards directing, but negotiations broke down when Madonna found out that Bruce Willis had been signed as the male lead. About the same time, Jamie Foley approached her with a script for a comedy called *Slammer*, which ultimately became *Who's That Girl?* When Foley proposed *Slammer*, she thought that the opportunity was going to somehow be her reward for being selective.

While the script wasn't perfect, it was promising. She liked it, but realized it needed a lot of work. They ultimately went through several writers and several revisions until it was just the way they envisioned it.

After his work on the "Papa Don't Preach" video that everyone liked so much, Madonna knew that she had at last found a director she could work with. "Jamie Foley is a genius!" Madonna proclaimed. Echoing the "mutual admiration," Foley complimented Madonna by gushing glowingly, "There's always been this twinkle in her eye, only now it's in wide-screen Technicolor, and her sexuality is an undercurrent to her playfulness."[7]

If they could just capture this on film, they'd be all set.

In September of 1986 preproduction began on *Slammer*. It sounded like a potential winner. In it Madonna would portray the role of Nikki Finn, a wrongly incarcerated con artist who has a penchant for turning everyone's life upside down. Unlike her last foray this role was at least believable casting.

Before filming started, Madonna had a lot on her mind. Not only was she concerned about her film career, but she was also intently monitoring Martin Burgoyne's health. On August 30 he had given his ticket to *Goose and Tomtom* to Andy Warhol and had made plans to join his friends backstage after the show. He had seen the production earlier that week but now felt he was just too weak to sit still for its two-hour duration. After the show that evening, Martin arrived backstage to find Andy and Liza Minnelli among the well-wishers. People who hadn't seen him in recent weeks were aghast to see the sores that dotted his face. Someone had sent Madonna a large piece of Kron chocolate shaped like a leg as a "break a leg" gift. People were concerned as they watched Madonna taking a bite of the leg-shaped confection, giving Martin a bite, and then resuming eating it herself, but she was bravely oblivious. She knew that she couldn't contract Martin's disease from biting the same piece of chocolate, and she wasn't about to make him feel ill at ease.

Martin's friends did what they could to help him. Andy Warhol promised to do a portrait of Martin, so that he would have something of value to sell if he needed more money for his medical bills. On September 4, 1986, there was a benefit for Burgoyne at the Pyramid on Avenue A. At different points in the evening Warhol and Madonna came and gave their support. How odd to think that in six months both Andy and Martin would both be dead.

On October 13, Sean and Madonna were on the cover of the *National Enquirer*, which featured the headline: MADONNA'S FORMER ROOMMATE HAS AIDS—SEAN IS TERRIFIED & FURIOUS. "It's What's Really Ripping Their Marriage Apart." It was horrifying for Martin to read an article about himself in the *Enquirer* announcing to the world that he was dying. Friends consoled him on the phone all day.

On November 10, there was an AIDS benefit in the women's department at Barney's clothing store. It featured celebrity models in denim jackets that had been hand-painted by well-known artists. Madonna was on hand to model a jacket that had been painted by Martin. The money raised went to St. Vincent's Hospital, and, in addition to Madonna, models included Debbie Harry, Peter Allen, Paloma Picasso, Fran Lebowitz, and Paulina Porizkova. Other artists whose painted jackets graced the show included Andy Warhol and Robert Rauschenberg.

Less than three weeks later, Martin Burgoyne died. He passed away in his new apartment in Greenwich Village—the apartment that the benefit at Pyramid had enabled him to rent. On December 2, Madonna presided over a wake held in Martin's honor. From that day on, Madonna has done all that she can to raise money for AIDS research and become an active soldier in the battle against the disease.

Meanwhile, in the *Slammer* camp, casting was completed, and by October principal filming had begun. In the male lead, Griffin Dunne was signed to play Loudon Trout. Dunne had been a big hit in *American Werewolf in London*, and when he saw Madonna in *Goose and Tomtom*, he felt that their chemistry would be strong on screen. Sir John Mills was added to the cast as Montgomery Bell, a millionaire chum of Madonna's character, and Coati Mundi (a/k/a Andy Hernandez) was cast as Raoul, the film's villain.

The plot centers around Madonna's character of Nikki Finn and begins the day she is released from jail. It seems that she has been framed for a crime that she didn't commit. Playing a Cary Grant–like Loudon Trout, Dunne is instructed by his future father-in-law to pick up Ms. Finn as she leaves the jailhouse and to escort her to the nearest bus station. However, instead of being able to execute the seemingly simple task, he becomes embroiled in Nikki's life-endangering scheme to clear her name. Alternately torn between completing the assignment of getting Nikki out of town and getting ready for his upcoming wedding, thanks to Nikki all of Loudon's plans go awry. What follows is a madcap, plot-twisting romp through the streets of Manhattan. Nikki's old adversary, Raoul, is in hot pursuit of her, because she is in possession of a safe deposit box key that he wants. She and Loudon end up comically undermining his efforts. Loudon has his heart set on marrying into a wealthy family, but Nikki Finn's antics soon put him out of favor with his fiancée and her family. By the end of this slapstick film, Loudon's would-be father-in-law is unmasked as the real villain, and Loudon discovers that he has fallen head-over-heels in love with Nikki.

Coati Mundi and Madonna had known each other for years in New York. Coati was one of the original members of the group Kid Creole & the Coconuts when they met. In 1983, along with James Brown, George Clinton, Lou Reed, Nona Hendryx, Peter Wolf, and John Oates of Hall and Oates, Coati and Madonna were members of an artists' panel at the 1983 New Music Seminar, an annual music industry convention. They became friendly then and found their paths constantly crossing. Madonna and Jellybean Benitez came to a couple of Coati's performances in New York clubs, and they ran into each other at parties. They were also both signed to Sire Records, so they had several things in common.

When casting began on *Slammer*, in a single day Coati heard about the role of Raoul from three different sources: his agent, an executive at Warner Brothers, and an actor friend. They all told him how he fit the type they were looking for. Since he had just played a villain on the hit TV show "Miami Vice," everyone who knew him thought he'd be perfect in this film.

He auditioned for the casting director, who asked him to audition for director Jamie Foley, who liked Coati's morning audition so much, he had him return that same evening for a "call-back" audition. A month passed and Coati didn't hear a thing from the film's producers; then the call came and he was suddenly slated to be Madonna's co-star.

"At the first cast rehearsal we just had a reading at the Mayflower Hotel," says Coati. "And Madonna, she came up to me and she said, 'Look, I knew you were auditioning for it, but I didn't want to pull anything.' She wanted me to get it on my own—she didn't want to use her influence."[150]

Coati recalls that the atmosphere on the set was very friendly. He got along well with Foley, and he was most impressed with Madonna. "On the set, we got along great. What was flipping me out was that she's—as you probably know—a hard worker. She doesn't rest. She's got a bit of that perfectionist thing in her. She was doing the movie, and the soundtrack album for the movie, and also planning her tour at the same time. She's doing all this stuff, plus she's got the lead in the film!"[150]

According to Coati, "The film actually started filming in October of '86, up to about February of '87. So, it was kind of a Warner Brothers family kind of thing, because Madonna's on Warner Brothers/Sire Records, I was on Sire Records. We had known each other from the early eighties, so she made me feel comfortable. Most people are kind of intimidated by her, because they think that she's this big star—and she is, but I had known her for a long time and I felt very comfortable with her. We were always greeting each other, and hanging out, and dancing on the set all of the time. I had my radio turned on, and we would dance occasionally."[150]

The filming of *Slammer/Who's That Girl?* took place in New York and in Los Angeles. The first sequence to be filmed was one in which

Madonna poses as Griffin Dunne's fiancée at an approval interview in front of a co-op board. The scene also includes Coati Mundi and another of the film's co-stars—a live cougar.

"All of the scenes with the cougar are great," says Coati, who adds that the scenes with his feline co-star were among his favorites. "I did all of my own scenes with the cougar, so there's a point in the movie where I'm holding Madonna around the throat with the knife, and the cougar is supposed to get the knife out of my hand. So, the way they do that is, I hold a piece of raw meat in my hands, and then the cougar goes after the raw meat—and then, going after the raw meat, it looks like he knocks the knife out of my hand. I'm supposed to keep my hand on a certain level, up. So he goes up for the meat with his paws. He's declawed, but the first thing he does is go for the meat with the paws. When he hits my hand, I'm supposed to let it go, but the meat is attached to the knife. So he goes for the meat. So we rehearsed it a couple of times, and it came out okay."[150]

It was a different story, however, when the cameras started rolling. "So I've got both my arms around Madonna, with the knife, and I'm waiting for the director to say 'Action.' The handlers have let the cougar go before the director said action. Being the actor, I'm waiting for action. But the cougar doesn't know the word *action*. So, here I have the cor- poration—the star—in my arms, I've got a knife to her throat, and the cougar is going for the knife. And then they start yelling, 'Drop the knife!' If the cougar had jumped up on her, there goes the corporation, there goes the movie, there goes me. And Madonna wasn't fazed at all by it," he says.[150]

In another sequence, Nikki Finn is in the process of abducting Coati Mundi's character. The Cadillac limousine that they are driving in is on the twelfth story of a parking structure. When the car crashes through the guardrail, it teeter-totters on the edge of the concrete build- ing. (The scene was actually shot fifteen feet off of the ground in a Los Angeles soundstage; the backgrounds were filled in later.) In an on- screen ballet, Coati, Madonna, and two of their co-stars had to do a balancing act on the hood and trunk of the car. According to Coati, the sequence was actually choreographed, by Errol Flynn's old fencing in- structor, and was the most physically challenging one to film.

Toward the end of the movie, Madonna and Coati are seen running into a room after a mad chase sequence. Recalls Coati, "She said, 'Lookit, when we go in there, we're supposed to be out of breath, so let's do some push-ups.' She said, 'I'll bet you I can do more push-ups than you.' I said, 'O.K., let's go for it!' So we started doing push-ups. We never did find out who did more, because it was time to do the scene before anybody gave up. We were huffing and puffing when we walked in."[150]

One of the things about Madonna that surprised Coati was his discovery of her rapport with children. "During the filming," he recalls, "I noticed on the set that she was sitting real comfortable with kids because the whole crew would bring their kids to meet her and get autographs and everything. And she would just keep them around and play with them and everything like that. And I even brought my nephews to meet her, and she was cool about it. She has no problem with that."[150]

The real "touch of class" casting coup that occurred during the filming of *Slammer* was the addition of Sir John Mills, as Montgomery Bell. Mills plays a millionaire who has a microcosm of a rain forest in his rooftop apartment. The first day that Mills showed up on the set, he came clad in jeans, sneakers, and a T-shirt with the National Theatre emblem on it. Sir John, who is known for his roles in such great movies as *Ryan's Daughter*, *Tunes of Glory*, and *Great Expectations*, reportedly went out and bought a copy of Madonna's *True Blue* album to acquaint himself with his co-star.

Jamie Foley had nothing but glowing things to say about Madonna— on screen and off. "The form is big enough," he claimed, "she was made for wide-screen Technicolor. And she is precociously talented. Every time I would say, 'Action!' what she would do made me giggle with excitement. She's very instinctual, what comes out is unencumbered by analysis."[26]

Griffin Dunne found Madonna's screen acting technique to be just the opposite of his. "We work very differently—which worked well for our characters," he said. "She likes her first take best. I think my best is around the fourth. She always says, 'You got it,' and she was driving me crazy, just the way her character would. I mean, she's a very noisy girl."[7]

One of the most important aspects of the film was the soundtrack album. Not only was it planned to be an outlet for Madonna to record several new songs, she also appointed herself the film's musical director. According to Coati Mundi, it was the soundtrack album that was responsible for the movie's title changing from *Slammer* to *Who's That Girl?* "She couldn't come up with a word to rhyme with 'Slammer,' so she simply changed the name of the movie to *Who's That Girl?* and wrote the song to go with it."[150]

Since Coati was signed to Sire Records, he was in a good position to get one of his own songs used on the soundtrack. "All along, Madonna's friend and publicist Liz Rosenberg had mentioned that there was going to be a soundtrack album, and she encouraged me to see about trying to get a song on it, and she mentioned it to Madonna. So one day during shooting, Madonna told me, 'Listen, we're having a soundtrack album, and see if you can come up with a song.' I said, 'Yeah, yeah!' I was thinking about it. I wanted to talk to the music supervisor, and see how I could go about doing it.' And she said, 'You're talking to him.' "[150]

Coati remembers that "Basically she said, 'You gotta earn the spot on the album. Just because I know you, I've got to like the song.' In other words, she's not just gonna put it on—it's not gonna be a nepotism deal. Of course—I never get it easy! I said, 'O.K. Fine.' "[150]

Coati didn't have any of his musical instruments or recording equipment in Los Angeles, so on breaks between his scenes he would fly back to New York and lay down new tracks. This happened three times. One day on the set Madonna asked him where the song was. He explained to her that he didn't have a completed song, he just had the musical tracks with the background vocals. When she pressed him to let her hear the song, he convinced her that they were useless without the lead vocals, and why didn't he perform it live for her? She thought for a moment, agreed, and an appointment for the musical audition was made.

It was nighttime, and Coati arrived on the set during one of Madonna's breaks, as arranged. However, when he got there she claimed to be too tired to think about it at that moment.

"But I said, 'Listen, I made this appointment, come on—let's do it.' She said, 'All right Coati, let's go.' I dressed up to the hilt, like I was performing in a stadium. And I went there, and I brought the cassette, just her and me, we went into her trailer, and she said, 'O.K., I'll be the soundman here.' And she gets her cassette player and I typed out the lyrics, and I gave her the lyric sheet. We're in the trailer, and she's sitting there watching me, and she starts the tape, and the music comes on, and I start performing—like I'm trying to get into heaven for Saint Peter. Like if you don't do a good show, you won't get into heaven. I did my whole routine for one person—my jumping up, my dancing, my expressions, my singing, everything. I'm doing the whole live thing, and dancing up a storm, like going crazy. And she's loving it and laughing and enjoying it. Mind you, we're in a trailer, and this trailer is bouncing up and down. I don't know what people were thinking outside.[150]

"Even though I know her, I performed for Madonna 'the professional,' 'the business person.' It was an audition to have that song in there. I wanted to put my best foot forward. I didn't just want to give her the cassette, I really wanted to show her what the song is all about. So she was laughing and enjoying it, and she said, 'Oh, I love it!' Then she said, 'Wait right here.' And then she went and got Griffin Dunne and Jamie Foley, the director. And she brought them into the trailer and she said, 'Now do it for them, the way you did it for me.' So—I did an encore performance. I did the whole thing all over again, and the director is laughing and smiling, and said, 'I love it, I love it!'"[150] A couple of days later the song was accepted, and Coati's "El Coco Loco (So So Bad)" became officially part of the soundtrack album.

According to Coati Mundi, Sean Penn never visited Madonna on the set during the filming. "I saw him at the cast party," he says of Penn. "As far as the movie was concerned, he came to the cast party. That was in L.A. And at the cast party I was showing him how to dance, because Madonna was dancing the whole night. I practically danced the whole night with Madonna, and one point I'm dancing with Madonna *and* Sean. He came and joined us on the floor, and I said, 'Oh, let me show you a few moves,' and stuff like that. I started showing him how to dance, so we had a nice time."[150]

Concerning whether there were any of the famous Sean Penn violence episodes at the party, Coati states, "For the most part it wasn't a dark thing, as people tend to think when they think of Sean and Madonna. It was cool and fun, and then Madonna was gracious at the cast party with everybody, and she danced, so it wasn't this character."[150]

Madonna had high hopes for this movie and anticipated that its modern-day blend of slapstick antics, thirties screwball comedy, and music would be the right formula for success. "I think it's a good film," she explained. "I could have done others, but I like my character in this one."[93]

In November 1986, "True Blue," the title song from Madonna's third album, peaked on the American record charts at Number Three. A unique situation occurred with the video for that song. MTV sponsored a competition called the "Make My Video Contest." Two winners, Angel Garcia and Cliff Guest, were selected in the viewer response contest to star in a video for American release to accompany the music of Madonna singing "True Blue." Garcia and Guest were filmed in atmospheric black and white in a fifties setting of soda shops and pajama parties. In Europe, however, there was a full production video starring Madonna. In her colorful rendition of "True Blue," she is seen singing and dancing with three backup singer girlfriends. Again in a fifties mode, the video takes place on a soundstage with a blue "no seam" background. The stylized sets include a diner counter with stools and a white Thunderbird convertible. In it Madonna looks sleek in black ankle-length tights and a skirt. The outfit looks like something Patti Page would have worn in the fifties. Madonna's blonde hair was swept back and lacquered down, Elvis Presley–style. Dancing the synchronized choreography, Madonna is cute, fresh, and appealing.

Her next video was the exact opposite of cute and fresh. The song was "Open Your Heart," and the video presentation was sexy, steamy, and suggestive. Playing the role of an exotic dancer in a peep show, Madonna wanted to turn heads, and when this debuted in December 1986, it did just that.

The "Open Your Heart" video was directed by well-known video director Jean-Baptiste Mondino. It was not only Madonna's first overtly sexual video, it was also her first video to feature homosexual images.

In the plot of the video, a young boy (actor Felix Howard) is seen trying to sneak into the "girlie show" arcade where Madonna is performing. Inside the arcade are several booths with windows looking onto a center stage. When coins are inserted in a slot in a booth, the curtain rises to view the sex show onstage. The first shade to go up reveals a pair of identical pretty boy sailors locked in an embrace, staring intently at the show.

Madonna's exotic stripper is then seen performing with a wooden chair prop, borrowing from Dietrich's *Blue Angel* and Liza Minnelli's similar number in *Cabaret*. In her opening shot Madonna is seen in short black hair, wearing a one-piece bathing suit outfit with black high-heel shoes. Over each of her nipples she wears gold-sequined "pasties," with black tassels dangling from them. In her first seconds on screen she leans back in the chair and yanks the black wig off her head to reveal her own platinum blonde locks. Madonna proceeds to sing and dance to the song, while the viewer gets intermittent shots of the viewers in the booth. Naturally one of them turns out to be the underage boy, who is most fascinated by the sight of Madonna rolling around on the floor singing "Open Your Heart."

At the end of the video, Madonna emerges from the arcade in her street clothes—a man's suit, white shirt, tie, and hat. She plants a kiss on the young boy's lips, and they dance off into the evening.

The song became Madonna's third Number One single from the *True Blue* album. Also debuting on the charts in November 1986 was a single by handsome model-turned-singer Nick Kamen. He had become famous in a British television commercial for a brand of blue jeans. In the ad he walks into a laundromat, takes off his jeans, and stands there in his boxer shorts while the pants are in the washer. Madonna met him, was impressed with his James Dean–like good looks, and decided to produce his first single. The single, "Every Time You Break My Heart," was written and produced by Madonna with Steve Bray. Released on Sire Records, the record didn't do too much on the charts, but it made a big stir in the gossip columns.

Although Madonna had written in the liner notes of *True Blue* that "This album is dedicated to my husband, the coolest guy in the universe," the year 1987 was nothing but stormy weather for the couple. In March, while her next Top Ten single, "La Isla Bonita," was hitting the charts, stories that Madonna was having an affair with Nick Kamen were being reported in the tabloids.

That same month, two more of Madonna's men were radioactive on the music charts: Steve Bray and Dan Gilroy. The previous year Bray and Gilroy had joined forces and re-formed Breakfast Club. The new edition included Steve, Dan, Ed Gilroy, and Gary Burke. Burke had been in Madonna's short-lived early eighties band, Emmy.

This new version of Breakfast Club was signed to MCA Records and released a self-titled album and a hit single called "Right on Track."

The album, which featured original songs and a great version of the 1967 hit "Expressway to Your Heart," did well on the charts, and the video received good exposure on MTV.

That spring, while Madonna was reportedly having an affair with Kamen, Sean was busy filming his latest movie, *Colors*. Madonna insisted that her relationship with Kamen was strictly professional, in spite of his hunky good looks. When Penn was spotted in the West Beach Cafe in Venice, California, with two friends, an unidentified guy and girl, photographer Cesare Bonazza waited outside to snap photos of the trio. An argument ensued, and Bonazza claimed that Sean pulled a gun on him and threatened him.

According to Bonazza, "He [Sean] said, 'Give me the fucking camera! Give me the fucking thing!' The guy was crazy, lunatic."[144] Fearing for his life, the photographer backed off at the sight of the gun. Although he didn't take any more shots once he spotted the weapon, he sold his photos of Sean spitting at him to the tabloids.

On April 2, 1987, the stakes proved a little higher. While on the set of *Colors*, Sean spotted Jeffrey Klein, one of the extras, with a camera, taking his picture. Penn went into a rage and went over and socked the guy. Klein pressed charges, which violated Sean's one-year probation on charges of slugging David Wolinski the previous April 12.

To compound things, on May 25 Sean was arrested for running a red light in L.A. His 1983 Chevrolet Impala was clocked at 55 mph in a 35 mph zone. He failed a sobriety test, registering a blood alcohol content of .011. On June 23, pleading no contest, Sean was sentenced to sixty days in jail. In addition, he was to be on probation for an additional two years. In the ten-minute hearing in Municipal Court, Sean was also ordered to undergo counseling. According to Deputy City Attorney Alice Hand, "Given his history as we know it, through the media and the two incidents, it seemed warranted."[151] There were no grounds on which Sean could appeal the sentence, but it was anticipated that he would end up with time off for good behavior—as long as he didn't encounter anyone in jail with a camera.

He ended up serving five days, beginning July 7, then was released to fly to Germany to film scenes for *Judgment in Berlin*. He returned to serve twenty-eight more days of the sentence, and he was indeed given the rest of the sentence off for good behavior. His time was served at a tiny jail in the California mountains, the Mono County Jail. While he was there, the unkindest blows came from the headlines of the tabloids, particularly the *National Enquirer*. Their cover stories included JAILED SEAN PENN TURNS INTO A WIMP (August 25, 1987) and AIDS TERROR FOR JAILED SEAN PENN—HE HIDES IN CELL TO AVOID CONS WITH THE DEADLY DISEASE (September 22, 1987). Even notorious biographer Kitty Kelley got in one of her digs when she told *USA Today*, "This is not Hollywood eccentric. It is rude, obnoxious. He [Sean] is starting to make Frank Sinatra look semi-human."[152]

Meanwhile, Madonna's career was soaring even higher. In April her latest single, "La Isla Bonita," which peaked at Number Four, became her twelfth consecutive Top Ten single. The video that she did to accompany it was rich in religious symbolism and Spanish atmosphere. Madonna is seen in two intercut sequences. In one she is in a New York City apartment, dressed in a white slip, lighting candles at a living room altar, reminiscing about "La Isla Bonita." In the memory sequence she is seen in an apartment filled with lit candles. In it she wears a bright red flamenco dress, looking as if she is ready for a night onstage in Barcelona. In the end sequence she is in the red flamenco dress on the streets of Manhattan.

With Sean in the slammer, and Madonna about to release the film that was originally entitled *Slammer*, their lives couldn't have been more different. What was happening during the summer of 1987 would pull them even farther apart. Sean hated the publicity and attention he was receiving, while Madonna clearly wanted more. Speaking about himself, Sean admitted up front, "I like to drink and I like to brawl."[152] Madonna had other things on her mind. Without hesitation she proclaimed, "I don't want people to forget my name. I want everyone to know it. I want everything there is in life and love. I want to reach everyone."[28]

Madonna was about to get her wish.

I've always known this was going to happen to

Who's

me. . . . My success was something

That

that was meant to be.[153] *—Madonna*

Girl?

lthough she found Sean's behavior upsetting, Madonna had
her hands full with her own career. She had worked too hard
to get where she was to let her husband's surly behavior get
in her way. This was going to be the summer she first utilized
her multimedia blitz technique to its maximum potential. In the summer
of 1987, Madonna was ubiquitous. She mounted a massive summer
concert tour, dubbed the "Who's That Girl? Tour"; released the soundtrack album, *Who's That Girl?*; and launched the *Who's That Girl?* movie.
There was also a new music video for the song "Who's That Girl?" and
ultimately a concert video entitled "Ciao Italia." Just in case anyone
didn't know who "that girl" was, they only had to consult the cover of
any number of magazines to find out it was Madonna!

In fact, when Madonna appeared on the cover of the July 1987
Cosmopolitan, she was the first celebrity "Cosmo girl" since Elizabeth
Taylor in 1969. According to *Cosmopolitan*'s progressive editor-in-chief,
Helen Gurley Brown, she was perfect Cosmo girl material because she

190

started with nothing and she's very frank. In the cover story, Madonna told *Cosmopolitan* readers that she was really quite a down-to-earth girl. "I like washing dishes," she claimed. "I have this cleaning impulse sometimes. I think I got it from my mother."[26]

Although that statement makes it sound as if Madonna's home life with Sean was charming and homey, in reality they were going through some of their rockiest times. Madonna's publicist Liz Rosenberg denied that divorce was in the air, but admitted at the time, "All I can say is Madonna and Sean are definitely having problems, and they are taking time to work things out."[154]

Madonna's Who's That Girl? concert tour presented new challenges. She didn't just want to do a rock tour, she wanted to make it into a true spectacle. "I swore after my last tour I wasn't going to do another," she said. "That whole living-out-of-a-suitcase business. I don't know how Bruce Springsteen does it—I could never go out for a year. I told my manager the only way I would do the tour is if I could make it interesting for myself."[81]

According to Liz Rosenberg, "Madonna's idea was to do a Broadway show—in a stadium."[155] To accomplish this she assembled a cast, which included Chris Finch, a previously unknown thirteen-year-old boy who was hired to expand upon the role of the kid in the "Open Your Heart" video. She then hired three backup singers, including Niki Harris, and two additional male dancers, including Shabba Doo (a/k/a Adolfo Quinones).

Marlene Stewart designed Madonna's stage costumes around ideas the singer herself had. Shabba Doo, who had appeared in several break-dancing movies, including *Breakin'*, choreographed the show. And Madonna's girlfriend, Debi M. (Mazur), did the hair and makeup. Debi, who has since gone on to an acting career of her own, is the one who is responsible for Madonna's look at this time, right down to the shape of her lipstick line and the drawn-on beauty mark.

"There's obviously been a transition in terms of her look," Marlene Stewart explained at that time.[155] "She has drastically changed her style, and this tour is great, because it is a compilation of all of her personas."[156]

The plan was to have Madonna evolve to a new phase of her image. It was a conscious effort to break with the past. "What's really important is that she doesn't wear any jewelry at all on this tour," Stewart pointed out. Since "jewelry used to be her statement," they instead concentrated more on her face and silhouette."[156]

Madonna was deeply involved in every aspect of the show, including the images that were projected on the screen behind her, the pacing of the show, and the costumes. The images were controversial, the pacing was nonstop, and the costumes were extreme.

The show began with Chris Finch playing the role of the little boy trying to sneak into the peep show. However, this time around Madonna was behind a scrim with her chair, pasties, and nipple tassels. Projecting a huge silhouette, the band hit the first chords of "Open Your Heart." When it came time to sing "True Blue," Madonna changed into a flouncy fifties-style dress in blue, with the backup singers behind her, as she had done in the European video of that same song.

Singing "Papa Don't Preach," she added a black leather jacket to the same outfit, as several images of authority figures were projected on the huge screen behind her. These included Ronald Reagan and the Pope. The final image projected on the screen were the words SAFE SEX in huge letters.

For "White Heat," which was done complete with the James Cagney monologue from the movie of the same name, it was a gangster theme. Dancing with an identically dressed Shabba Doo, Madonna wore a fedora and gold lamé jacket. As part of the intricate choreography, both Madonna and Shabba grabbed at their crotches—a public action previously reserved for vulgar men. There is no question that Madonna has balls—so she may as well pretend to rearrange them onstage.

The costumes Madonna wore during this tour were designed for quick changes. She kept the basic "Open Your Heart" bodysuit on at all times and just switched her tops, pants, or skirts. When she went into "Causing a Commotion," a gold lamé jacket was added to the bodysuit—with the black tassels still dangling from the pasties. Her most bizarre costume change happened in a replica of a British cast-iron phone booth that was brought onstage. Emerging from it, Madonna looked like Edith Prickly, the nerdy Andrea Martin character from "SCTV." She wore rhinestone harlequin glasses, a fuchsia Mad Hatter's hat, and a billowy pink hoopskirt laden with trinkets like fuzzy dashboard dice, cloth flowers, kewpie dolls, and even a plastic lobster. Marlene

Stewart explained it as being "solidly encrusted with material objects—toy watches, ashtrays, coins, paper money, plastic fruit."[156]

While wearing that get-up, Madonna did a medley of three of her sexiest songs about seduction—"Dress You Up," "Material Girl," and "Like a Virgin"—parodying the overtly sexy image that she usually projected. When she bent over to "moon" the audience, her lifted skirt revealed panties with the word *KISS* in big letters on her ass. Dancing with two male dancers, at one point the trio goose-stepped with an upraised left arm—Nazi-style.

For the number "Into the Groove," Madonna wore another jacket decorated with colorful items, including a large letter *U* on one side, a Campbell's soup can on the other side, and the word *DANCE* on the back, so when she spun around, it formed a pictograph sentence: "U Can Dance." For "La Isla Bonita," Madonna changed to a layered red skirt and bolero jacket.

Being able to change her costumes onstage made for a seamless ninety-minute show of nonstop Madonna music. She danced up a storm, sold out arenas, and created a commotion wherever in the world she took the show.

Unencumbered by the presence of Sean or the pretense of a phobia against publicity, Madonna soared on this tour. It must have felt like a massive weight was taken off her shoulders not to have him around all of the time. Mounting the show was hard work, but it turned out to be a roaring success for her.

Originally, the group Club Nouveau, who appear on the *Who's That Girl?* soundtrack, were set as her opening act. A week before the tour began, the group backed out, and were replaced by Level 42. According to Jay King, Club Nouveau member and manager, "Madonna is big enough that she doesn't need us and we're big enough that we don't need her."[157] Jay King might have considered the two million people they would have played to had they remained on the tour. It is thinking like his that has kept his group a mere footnote in the music world. With the exception of their hit revival of Bill Withers's "Lean on Me," their career has been a case of Club *Who?*

The tour opened on June 14 in Japan at Osaka Stadium. It played there on Sunday and Monday nights, and then moved east for three nights at Tokyo's Korakuen Stadium, June 20–22. All five dates sold out almost immediately, and scalpers were commanding up to $700 per ticket. The only real mishap that occurred in Japan was a torrential rainstorm that made it necessary to cancel the opening night concert in Tokyo. Several of the 35,000 people who stood in the rain waiting for the show to start refused to leave the stadium and a riot nearly broke out. Unfortunately there was no leeway to reschedule the canceled date.

Madonna was fascinated by the devotion of her Japanese fans. Witnessing over three hundred people camped outside her hotel all night for a glimpse at Her Virginness, she waxed philosophical. "I think I stand for a lot of things in their minds," said Madonna. "You know, a lot of kinds of stereotypes, like the whole sex goddess image and the blonde thing."[81]

The North American leg of the tour was a nineteen-city, seven-week jaunt. The first date in the states was June 27 at Miami's Orange Bowl. The ticket sales, at $1 million gross, set a new record for a female artist at that venue. The last date in the United States was on August 9 at the Meadowlands—Giant Stadium—in East Rutherford, New Jersey. The tour also encompassed two Canadian cities, Montreal and Quebec.

On July 13, Madonna headlined at Madison Square Garden in New York City and donated the proceeds to AIDS research. According to record company president David Geffen, when he was planning a benefit at Madison Square Garden Madonna volunteered her whole show. She not only provided them with her lights, her set, and her musicians, but she also donated all the merchandising profits from the programs and the posters. Says Geffen, "The woman is not only a consummate professional, she's also got a big heart."[99]

Madonna stated, "I want to do anything I can to promote AIDS education, awareness, prevention—whatever. I think because I am a celebrity, a public person, I have a responsibility to be a spokesperson. Next to Hitler, AIDS is the worst thing to happen in the twentieth century. The sad thing is that it makes people even more bigoted. It gives people a reason to vent their true feelings about homosexuality."[99]

By making such a gesture, Madonna became the first American pop star to take such a stance. Up to this point, with the exception of Elizabeth Taylor, most public figures had avoided any such association with the fight against AIDS. As Madonna lost more and more friends to the disease, her resolve to stand up and do something about it only became stronger. When it came time to sing "Live to Tell," Madonna dedicated the song to the memory of her friend Martin Burgoyne.

There was also an informational pamphlet about AIDS prevention in comic book format, distributed at the concert. A note in the comic book, in handwritten script, said: "Read this booklet, then give it to your best friend. It just might save his or her life. It just might save your own. Love, Madonna."[158]

When he wasn't in jail, Sean made appearances at a couple of Madonna's concerts along the way. He was in Miami when she opened the tour, and came to Madonna's AIDS benefit at Madison Square Garden. According to Chris Finch, "Sean's a great guy. We played tennis in Miami, and when we were in New York we went lingerie shopping for Madonna. We got her underwear with, like leopard patterns."[159]

At the end of the song "Like a Virgin," Madonna leaned down and planted a kiss on Chris's virginal mouth. When the tour played his hometown of Anaheim, California, he recalls, "She knew all my friends were going to be there so she kissed me longer than usual. I lost my place and couldn't remember the next steps in the number."[159]

When asked what he thought of Madonna, Finch replied, "She's real nice, energetic, a workaholic. She works so hard you have to stop her sometimes. She gives 135 percent for every show. She expects everybody else to give that much."[160]

After the North American leg of the Who's That Girl? tour, Madonna headed for Europe, where she appeared in England, Germany, the Netherlands, France, and Italy. Not since the days of Marilyn Monroe had a blonde American performer caused such a stir. Throughout Europe, the image of Madonna was unavoidable. She was ubiquitous, on the covers of magazines, newspapers, and on billboards.

In France, Madonna's Paris concert was scheduled to be held in the suburb of Sceaux. Fearing that the concert would draw an unruly crowd, the local mayor threatened to cancel it only days before the singer's arrival. French Premier and mayor of Paris, Jacques Chirac, stepped in and saved the "holiday." Chirac's twenty-four-year-old daughter Claude, a dyed-in-the-wool Madonna fan, had begged her father to intercede. A contender for the 1988 presidential election in France, Chirac spotted a campaign-conscious move when he saw one. Not only did he make certain that Madonna's concert didn't get canceled, he also dropped the V.A.T. (Value Added Tax) on records, tapes, and CDs from 33 percent to 18.5 percent. He announced both moves at a press conference with Madonna.

Chirac won favor, at least with young voters. Daughter Claude was able to get "Into the Groove" at her idol's concert, and Madonna received even more publicity for her Paris dates. In fact, with 110,000 fans gathered to see her, the show broke attendance records. Onstage that night, August 29, Madonna proclaimed, "Causing a commotion—that's how I felt when I went to see Jacques Chirac!"[161]

In Torino, Italy, near Florence, Madonna closed the Who's That Girl? concert tour before 65,000 cheering fans. Onstage she showed off several of the Italian phrases she had memorized to use in her family homeland: *"Siete gia caldi?"* [Are you hot?] and *"Lo sono fiera di essere Italiana!"* [I'm proud to be Italian!][162]

Prior to the show, Madonna met with her Italian cousin Amelia, her husband, and two children, Annalisa and Giuseppe. Madonna's great-aunt Bambina didn't attend the concert because she was too frail to travel from Pacentro, the town Madonna's grandparents came from. But several Pacentro city councilmen came to deliver a parchment decree to the singer making her an honorary citizen of that village.

"Of course I'd like to see her and hug her," said Bambina. "After all, it is an honor to have such a famous relation." When pressed to comment on Madonna's unlike-a-virgin behavior, her great-aunt commented, "In my times we didn't behave like that."[162]

The final concert was taped by ID-TV Amsterdam as a live TV special, and that footage was edited into the American video cassette, "Ciao Italia." It was a fitting way to cap off Madonna's triumphant tour of three continents.

Amid all the hoopla for Madonna's Who's That Girl? concert tour came the premiere of the *Who's That Girl?* movie. Wedged in between an August 5 concert in Richfield, Ohio, and an August 7 concert in Pontiac, Michigan, Madonna flew to New York to appear at the premiere of the film. The evening of August 6, a crowd estimated at over ten thousand came for a glimpse of Madonna on a stage set up in the middle of Times Square. The irony came the next day at noon, when a few blocks up Seventh Avenue, at the 1,151-seat Ziegfeld Theater on West

*I*n her first decade of
fame, Madonna has
become one of the most
photographed women of
the twentieth century.
(*PHOTO: Ron Delaney/
Star File*)

𝕸adonna as a cheerleader at Rochester Adams High School.
In the top photo she is the second from the left. In the bottom photo, she's
the girl in the upper row, far right. (*PHOTOS: Mark Bego Archives*)

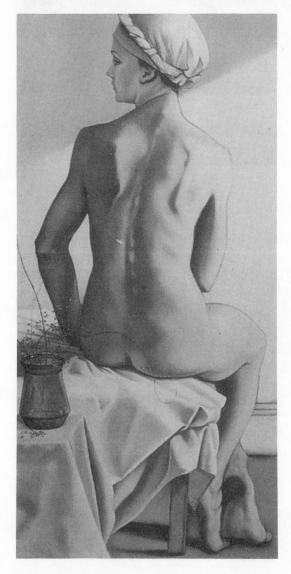

$\mathcal{M}$adonna in her high school yearbook as a sophomore, a junior, and a senior. (*PHOTOS: Mark Bego Archives*)

$\mathcal{W}$hen Madonna first moved to New York City, she posed nude for several artists, including Anthony Panzera; this painting is entitled *Madonna of the Bittersweet*. (*PHOTO: Anthony Panzera*)

$\mathcal{M}$aking her less-than-spectacular film debut in *A Certain Sacrifice*.

(*PHOTO: Charles Daguerre Alvare/Mark Bego Archives*)

$\mathcal{S}$imulating fellatio with a gas pump during the filming of *A Certain*

Sacrifice. (*PHOTO: Charles Daguerre Alvare/Mark Bego Archives*)

$\mathscr{P}$erforming in London in October 1983 (left). (*PHOTO: Pictorial Press/Star File*)

$\mathscr{O}$ne of Madonna's early concerts, on the rooftop of Danceteria in New York City (below). (*PHOTOS: Bob Gruen*)

𝒯rom the very start, there was something unique and alluring about

Madonna. (*PHOTO: Kate Simon/Star File*)

$\mathcal{M}$adonna belting out "Gambler" in the film *Vision Quest*. (*PHOTO: Warner Brothers/Mark Bego Archives*)

$\mathcal{W}$ith Grace Jones at a party at Private Eyes in 1985 (above left).

(*PHOTO: Robin Platzer*)

$\mathcal{M}$adonna in her "more is more" fashion phase (above right).

(*PHOTO: Roger Glazer*)

$\mathcal{L}$ooking slutty and singing the song "Like a Virgin" made Madonna

an overnight sensation—writhing in a gondola in Venice for

the video. (*PHOTO: Larry Williams/Mark Bego Archives*)

$\mathcal{S}$porting a "just rolled out of bed" look gave her the
reputation of a common tart and helped make her into an instant star.

(*PHOTO: Steven Meisel/Mark Bego Archives*)

$\mathcal{M}$adonna on the set of *Desperately Seeking Susan* with director Susan Seidelman. (*PHOTO: Andy Schwartz for Orion Pictures/Mark Bego Archives*)

$\mathcal{M}$adonna and her boyfriend at the time, Jellybean Benitez, and his publicist David Salidor. (*PHOTO: Kevin McCarrol/Salidor Collection*)

*M*adonna chatting with author Mark Bego between scenes on the set of *Desperately Seeking Susan*. (*PHOTO: Roger Glazer*)

*P*ortraying the title role of Susan made Madonna into an overnight film star. (*PHOTO: Roger Glazer*)

At the first
annual MTV
Awards telecast
she caused a
commotion in
her "virginal"
wedding dress.
(*PHOTO: Robin*
Platzer)

*W*ith lookalike Rosanna Arquette, posing for the poster for *Desperately Seeking Susan.* (*PHOTO: Herb Ritts for Orion Pictures/ Mark Bego Archives*)

*I*n the Maripol-styled outfit for the *Like a Virgin* album cover. (*PHOTO: Steven Meisel/Mark Bego Archives*)

A scene from *Desperately Seeking Susan* with co-star Robert Joy, in Battery Park. (*PHOTO: Andy Schwartz for Orion Pictures/ Mark Bego Archives*)

*M*adonna insisted on doing her own costumes for her portrayal of the eccentric Susan. (*PHOTO: Andy Schwartz for Orion Pictures/ Mark Bego Archives*)

The question remains, "Was Madonna really acting in *Desperately Seeking Susan*, or was she just being her bratty self?" (*PHOTO: Andy Schwartz for Orion Pictures/Bruce Baron Collection*)

Her 1985 Virgin Tour inspired fashion "wannabes" with "Material Girl" attitude. (*PHOTO: Bob Gruen/Star File*)

Celebrating the closing night of the Virgin Tour at the Palladium in New
York City. (*PHOTO: Vinnie Zuffante/Star File*)

$\mathcal{G}$etting into the groove at the Live Aid concert in Philadelphia.

(*PHOTO: Chuck Pulin/Star File*)

Two spoiled stars: Sean and Madonna backstage at the Live Aid concert. (*PHOTO: Vinnie Zuffante/Star File*)

With rock-and-roll royalty at the Live Aid festivities: (clockwise from upper left) Keith Richards, Daryl Hall, John Oates, Ron Wood, Bob Dylan, Madonna, Mick Jagger, and Tina Turner. (*PHOTO: Ken Regan/Camera 5*)

*W*ith Sean in the horrendous *Shanghai Surprise*. Madonna's performance was as stiff as cement. (*PHOTO: Vestron Video/Balz Photos*)

*M*adonna and ex-Beatle George Harrison attempting to patch things up with the London media by staging a press conference at the Kensington Garden Hotel. (*PHOTO: Pictorial Press/Star File*)

$\mathcal{F}$ilming the video
"Papa Don't Preach"
on Staten Island.
(*PHOTO: Vinnie*
Zuffante/Star File)

*S*ean and Madonna's union was plagued by his temper tantrums. "The Poison Penns" battle with press photographers outside their Central Park West apartment building. (*PHOTO: Vinnie Zuffante/Star File*)

*M*adonna's media blitz in 1987 included the stage show dubbed the Who's That Girl? tour. With Chris Finch (above), and sporting "Catwoman" shades and a boa (below). (*PHOTO: Vinnie Zuffante/Star File*)

℮lectrifying an audience in her nipple-tasseled "Open Your Heart"

costume. (*PHOTO: Paul Natkin / StarFile*)

ℬicycling with her personal trainer Rob Parr. Madonna's physical regimen is what keeps her energy at such a high level. (*PHOTO: Bob Scott/Star File*)

𝒜s Nikki Finn in *Who's That Girl?*, with the film's comic antagonist, Coati

Mundi. (*PHOTO: Coati Mundi Collection*)

With Griffin Dunne and Murray the cougar, Madonna racked up her second consecutive box office bomb. (*PHOTO: Warner Brothers Pictures/Balz Photos*)

In *Speed-the-Plow* on Broadway, with Joe Mantegna (left) and Ron Silver (right). (*PHOTO: Vinnie Zuffante/Star File*)

*G*irls just wanna have fun! Sandra Bernhard and Madonna

shocked and titillated fans by intimating that they were lesbian lovers.

(*PHOTO: Bob Gruen/Star File*)

With breastplates, Madonna strikes a pose in her 1990 Blonde Ambition

tour. It served as a backdrop for her first true hit film, the documentary

Truth or Dare. (*PHOTO: Bob Leafe/Star File*)

$\mathcal{M}$adonna and Warren Beatty arrive at the Washington, D.C., premiere of *Dick Tracy*, June 1990. (*PHOTO: Vinnie Zuffante/Star File*)

$\mathcal{T}$he lesbian kiss seen 'round the world, in the controversial video of "Justify My Love." (*PHOTO: Vinnie Zuffante/Star File*)

𝔐adonna proved herself a brilliant show woman in her 1990 concert tour.

(*PHOTOS: Vinnie Zuffante/Star File*)

𝒜s Marie Antoinette, Madonna performs "Vogue" at a special benefit for AIDS Project L.A. (*PHOTO: Vinnie Zuffante/Star File*)

𝒥n 1990, Madonna saluted dancing legend Martha Graham (second from right) with Kathleen Turner (left) and Calvin Klein (right). Madonna hopes to bring Graham's life story to the screen. (*PHOTO: Robin Platzer*)

$\mathcal{L}$ong before America had
Elvis Presley stamps, the
people of Grenada were
licking the backs of their
very own Madonna stamps.
(*PHOTO: Brett Lee/Star File*)

$\mathcal{A}$t the premiere of *Truth or Dare* in New York City,
with director Alek Keshishian (left) and brother Christopher Ciccone (right).
(*PHOTO: Robin Platzer*)

53rd Street, fewer than sixty people gathered in the air conditioning to see the movie.

Before the concert tour had played its last date in Europe, the film *Who's That Girl?* was already dead in the water. What business the critics didn't suffocate, word of mouth sufficiently killed off.

"A tired screwball comedy . . . *Who's That Girl?* may not sink as fast as last summer's *Shanghai Surprise*, but it eventually sinks almost as far," claimed *USA Today*. "A rattling failure," deadpanned the *Los Angeles Times*. "All of the noise and color of a carnival—but none of the thrills," wrote *MacLean's* in Canada. "*Who's That Girl?* bombs," bannered *Rolling Stone*. The only good review was from Vincent Canby in the *New York Times* who claimed, "Madonna is sexy and funny—a very engaging comedian. Griffin Dunne gives his most stylishly comic performance." Unfortunately, the audience who buys Madonna records generally doesn't consult the *New York Times* when making their movie choices.

Next to *Shanghai Surprise*, *Who's That Girl?* is a masterpiece, even if it is a flawed masterpiece. Immediately working against it is the nasal-sounding Brooklyn accent that Madonna affects for her role as Nikki Finn, a bleached blonde on parole. She sounds and dresses like an imitation Cyndi Lauper. Nonetheless, Madonna looks much more comfortable in this role than she did as a missionary in China.

There are some genuinely funny moments in the film, such as when Griffin Dunne asks Madonna with a straight face, "Are you the Antichrist?" When Dunne's fiancée (actress Haviland Morris) asks her muscle-bound bodyguard, "Is it possible for you to be any dumber?" his deadpan reply is, "I don't see how." And, Madonna has her moments, delivering lines like, "You've got to see me spend money to really appreciate me."

From a nineties perspective, having witnessed Madonna's transformation into an outspoken gay rights activist, it is interesting to note that there are several obviously gay characters portrayed in this film who are presented in a positive, matter-of-fact fashion—from the macho female prison guard to the persnickety salesman in Cartier. Two running male characters, police detectives Bellson (Robert Swan) and Doyle (Drew Pillsbury) spend the film bantering back and forth while chasing Madonna's Nikki Finn. In the end of the film, they end up comically falling in love and consummating their discovery with a dramatic mouth-to-mouth kiss.

Even more ironic about the failure of the film was the fact that in August, Madonna's latest single, the theme song "Who's That Girl?" hit Number One in America. Furthermore, the soundtrack album was a Top Ten million-seller, and the second single from the movie, "Causing a Commotion," hit Number Two in October and hovered there for three weeks.

With all of that promotion, what went wrong? Madonna was undisputedly the most popular female singer in the world, she sold out concert tickets from Tokyo to Torino, yet she couldn't get herself arrested at the box office.

Who's That Girl? not only followed one of the worst movies ever made—*Shanghai Surprise*—but it joined the ranks of several rock star vehicles that had recently bombed at the box office. Prince's *Under the Cherry Moon,* David Bowie's *Labyrinth,* and Sting's *The Bride* had recently proven that record sales and movie ticket sales are two different animals.

Even Madonna's co-stars were surprised by the film's failure. Coati Mundi tried to explain why it failed: "Probably one of the reasons is that Madonna has this thing about wanting to be an actress, and people really don't want to see her as an actress. One of the things is the public expecting to see this sort of street character, like *Desperately Seeking Susan,* and then see her performing a few songs. She was trying to do a stretch, and it probably wasn't accepted, and there were probably other problems—maybe the script wasn't as funny as people at first thought. God knows—I really don't know why. When you have big stars, people expect big things. And all it was was a little light-hearted comedy, nothing profound. You can't compare it to the big movies of the forties. It's a whole different thing, just a light-hearted comedy. If it wasn't Madonna, if it was somebody else, the axe wouldn't have fallen so hard."[150]

Just to prove that you can never predict what an audience will think of a film, *Who's That Girl?* went on to become something of a hit outside America. Madonna said, "I've been around the world and made a fairly large impression—and many of my ideas go over much better in Europe and Japan than they do in America. *Who's That Girl?*—the film—is doing really well in Europe and I'm getting great reviews. I think the movie did badly in America because I upstaged it with my tour."[34]

Since Sean was doing time in jail for much of the time that Madonna was out promoting her concert tour and new movie, she was frequently asked about her husband by the press: Has he learned his lesson? Why does he react so violently to the press? And what is she doing with him?

"I can never speak for Sean," said Madonna with regard to his fear of the media. "He will always deal with the press in his own way. For myself, I have accommodated the press a great deal."[81]

Citing their differences, she admitted that she courted and invited controversy, while Sean had a different attitude. His concept of being a serious actor had nothing to do with seeking publicity. Several times during this era Madonna expressed her sense of exasperation to the press. She was getting weary of Sean's disputes with them, and she was also becoming tired of seeing him provoked. It was to become a true "no win" situation, and the frustration was beginning to get to her.

In November 1987 Madonna had two new releases in the record stores. Her fourth non-soundtrack album, *You Can Dance*, was a compilation of extended dance remixes of six of her up-tempo songs, including "Holiday" and "Into the Groove." Also on the album was the song "Spotlight," which had been recorded during the *True Blue* sessions.

Some interesting people from Madonna's past and future worked on this album. Jellybean is represented in his mixes of "Holiday," but he was also brought in to do some additional production on "Spotlight." Shep Pettibone, who had remixed Madonna's single of "True Blue" when it was released earlier that year, worked on remixing "Into the Groove" and "Where's the Party?". Pettibone was later to become one of Madonna's most harmoniously successful collaborative producers.

Madonna was also one of the featured performers on the all-star rock-and-roll Christmas album, *A Very Special Christmas*. It has gone on to become one of the most successful Christmas albums ever released. Keith Haring did the cover art, and the stars featured on the album included the Eurythmics, the Pointer Sisters, Sting, Stevie Nicks, Run-DMC, Bruce Springsteen, U2, and several others. Madonna is heard on the album in an updated version of the fifties Eartha Kitt hit "Santa Baby." It's kind of a holiday version of "Material Girl"/"Diamonds Are a Girl's Best Friend," with Madonna giving Santa her list of what she wants for Christmas. The proceeds from the album went toward funding the Special Olympics.

When *Forbes* magazine tallied a list of the forty top-earning show business personalities for the year, Madonna ranked seventh. At an estimated 1987 gross income of $26 million, she had become the top-earning female in the entertainment world. Unscathed by the failure of her last two movies, she was the reigning queen of pop stars.

Now if only her personal life would go as smoothly. As the holidays rolled around, things were less than jolly at the Penn house. This became quite evident on Friday, December 4, when Madonna filed for divorce in Santa Monica Superior Court. Via her attorney, Michael K. Inglis, she petitioned for the restoration of her maiden name and asked that the couple's property be distributed as per the prenuptial agreement. The divorce papers were filed on the grounds of "irreconcilable differences."[163]

Madonna had reportedly warned Sean in July that if he didn't pull himself together, she was going to divorce him. They parted company in Chicago on July 31, and that night she performed in concert at Soldier's Field. When Sean returned to California to finish off his jail sentence, it was in a more rugged setting: Los Angeles County Central Jail. On September 17, when Sean was released—his punishment lessened for good behavior—Madonna was optimistic that it was going to be a turning point in their relationship. "I think Sean will emerge from jail as a better person, and as an even greater actor."[164] Sean had spent a total of 33 days of his 60-day sentence in jail.

In October, Madonna consulted with realtors about finding a new house—for herself. As quickly as she began her quest for a new abode away from Sean, she changed her mind and canceled the search.

On November 1, Madonna attended an AIDS benefit concert in Los Angeles, and Sean accompanied her, in spite of the fact that he is uncomfortable around gay people. There was a backstage flare-up when Madonna started talking with a male exotic dancer.

On November 15, Madonna was in New York to discuss the possibility of starring in *Evita*, with Oliver Stone directing. Gossip columnist Liz Smith reported that when Sean, who was in California, didn't get in touch with Madonna for four days before Thanksgiving, she became very perturbed. According to Liz, he showed up at the couple's New York apartment, expecting a grand turkey dinner. Publicists for Madonna and Sean claim that Penn's disappearance did not happen. Regardless of whether Madonna served Sean turkey or not, the fact remains that she served him with papers a week later.

On Thanksgiving Day, Sean headed for the airport and flew back to L.A. The following night, Vinnie Zuffante was hanging out with Billy Idol at the bar of Helena's. When Sean spotted Vinnie, he insisted that Helena evict him from the premises. Although Vinnie didn't have his camera with him, Helena complied. Later that evening, Sean went to the men's room and, after seeing the long line, stepped outside and peed on the side of the club.

In a surprise move, Madonna suddenly called off the divorce proceedings, less than two weeks after she had filed the papers. On December 16 there was a request for the court to disregard the previous petition.

With regard to the ongoing saga of the yet-to-be produced film version of *Evita*, when Madonna met with proposed director Oliver Stone, they did not get along at all well. She also pissed off the show's composer, Andrew Lloyd Webber.

"I didn't audition, I was asked to do it," she explains. "Because there were so many questions unanswered for me and there were too many cooks in the kitchen between Oliver Stone and Andrew Lloyd Webber and Robert Stigwood—who are all fabulous misogynists, I might add—I decided against it."[99]

Before the year 1987 closed, it was announced that Madonna was going to join the cast in a film based on Damon Runyon's *Bloodhounds of Broadway*. Already in the ensemble cast were Jennifer Grey, Randy Quaid, and Matt Dillon. Madonna began filming almost immediately, completing her part by the third week in January. Produced for PBS's American Playhouse, *Bloodhounds* was the first of three films in a row that Madonna would appear in as one of the stars, not the headliner. It was a wise move. As she had so painfully learned, if you have the starring role and something goes wrong, you end up with all the blame.

The film was done on a tight budget, but the project intrigued her. According to director Howard Brookner, "Everyone's dressing rooms were separated by shower curtains. There was Madonna, Matt Dillon, Randy Quaid, Jennifer Grey, and Rutger Hauer, all separated by shower curtains with their names scrawled on in Magic Marker."[165]

Madonna's role in *Bloodhounds of Broadway* was that of Hortense Hathaway, a 1920s nightclub showgirl in Newark, New Jersey. Damon Runyon, who is best known for having written "Guys and Dolls" and "The Big Street," had a flair for capturing the spirit of that era. With such an interesting cast, the project seemed to have a lot of potential.

Aside from the demands of the script, there was an added complication: the film's director, Howard Brookner, was dying of AIDS. "I knew something was wrong halfway through the movie, but I wasn't going to press him," Madonna explained.[166] When he pressed her to tell him all the gory details about Martin Burgoyne's death she became suspicious about his health.

Twice in January 1988, Sean caught prowlers breaking into the Malibu estate. On the 7th, Steven Stillbower, a thirty-two-year-old Anaheim resident, ran his truck through the gates on the Penns' property, and Penn made a citizen's arrest. On the 20th, Sean again went into action when he and Madonna discovered five people on their property. While Madonna telephoned deputy sheriffs from inside the house, Sean called the Malibu Police Station from inside his car. One of the prowlers tried to punch Penn, and Sean grabbed the nearest object, a bottle of salad dressing, and bashed him with it. The police then arrived and took over.

The year 1988 was one in which Madonna concentrated on her acting career. She didn't release any new music in the entire year, but she was writing new songs for her next album. It was going to shape up to be a year in which she would surround herself with new people, and she was open to new experiences. With this in mind, in January it was announced that Madonna had been awarded the role of Karen in David Mamet's new play, *Speed-the-Plow*. For the next six weeks she was in rehearsal for the play, which was scheduled to open at Lincoln Center's 298-seat Mitzi Newhouse Theater.

Actress Elizabeth Perkins had originally been cast in the part, but she suddenly dropped out of the project. When Madonna found out about it, she telephoned the play's director, Gregory Mosher, and asked if she could audition. Madonna was a big fan of Mamet's film *House of Games*, which had starred Joe Mantegna and Lindsay Crouse. With Mantegna and Ron Silver as the male leads of the new play, Madonna really longed for this part.

Madonna was so impressed with *House of Games* that in September 1987 she wrote Mamet a letter of praise. She claimed that was the first movie she had seen in a long time that stimulated her. She didn't feel that it had been written for the masses, and that it was intellectually exciting.

Joe and Ron didn't audition for Mosher, but Madonna was another story. According to the director, he needed to see for himself if she could sparkle onstage without the colored lights and costumes. He was pleasantly surprised. Says Mosher, "Madonna's strength just astonishes you when she walks in the room."[167]

"I pursued it like a motherfucker," Madonna recalls of her struggle to land the role. "I was at lunch with some people and one of them was a director [Mike Nichols], and he mentioned that David Mamet had written a new play. I was a fan of his, so I just started bugging my agents and people I knew."[61]

When she finally landed the audition, she was astonished at the way the director put her through her paces. Both Mamet and Mosher had her deliver multiple readings before they made their decision. She would read for them in one room, and then they would take their into another setting to see how her acting stood up. Madonna later complained that the duo put her "through the ringer" before they made a decision, but she remained calm and determined.[61] Finally they made their decision, and Madonna was Broadway bound.

According to Mantegna, "Madonna didn't 'Bogart' her way into the role. A lot of high-powered actresses also auditioned."[168] In fact, thirty other actresses auditioned for the part of Karen.

Sean, meanwhile, was busy in California with a stage production of a play he had written in jail. *The Kindness of Women* was presented twice at a sixty-seat theater in Santa Monica called The Pink. Sean also directed the play, which was viewed by several of his friends including Harry Dean Stanton and writer Charles Bukowski. It ultimately went no further than *Goose and Tomtom* did. Sean's next movie, *Casualties of War*, was set to begin production that spring. *Colors* opened that spring, and ironically the role he played in it was that of a police officer.

The play *Speed-the-Plow* is about two high-powered Hollywood film producers and a temporary secretary who changes their vision. The play centers on Bobby Gould (Mantegna), who has just gotten a huge promotion to the post of head of production at one of the movie studios. When he is visited by his friend Charlie Fox (Silver), Fox tries to call in a favor by railroading through a "green light" on a movie he wants to produce. When Gould's new temp secretary, Karen (Madonna), arrives at the office, Fox bets Gould $500 he can't get her into bed. When Karen gets wind of the two scripts Gould is juggling—a slick, meaningless one and an artistically and politically correct one—she gets into the act. By the end of the play, Karen, who was to be played like a pawn, ends up in a position of power.

As a theatrical experience, *Speed-the-Plow* is an excessively talky one to sit through. With so much dialogue, Madonna didn't fully grasp what her role was all about, until she found herself in the middle of the rehearsals.

With a bit of disillusionment, Madonna looked back on the production and explained, "It was a real mind-fuck of a script. Brilliant, but confusing. My part ended up being a plot manipulation. But at first I saw her as an angel of mercy who was coming down to save everybody. Little did I know that David Mamet and Greg Mosher and everybody else involved saw me as a vixen, a dark, evil spirit. That didn't dawn on me till halfway through rehearsals, when David kept changing my lines to make me more and more a bitch, a ruthless, conniving little witch. So in the middle of this process I was devastated that my idea of the character wasn't what she was at all. That was a really upsetting experience."[99]

The inclusion of Madonna in the cast elevated the entire production to a new level. In March it was announced that instead of opening at the end of the month at the intimate theater at Lincoln Center, *Speed-the-Plow* was going straight to Broadway, where it would open at the Royale Theater. Previews were scheduled for April 6, and the play's premiere was slated for May 3.

According to Ron Silver, "Joey [Mantegna] and I weren't mesmerized initially, because we weren't part of her constituency, and we weren't really familiar with 'Her Icon-ness.' It was only afterward that we realized the magnitude of her celebrity."[169]

However, Ron was fascinated by the kind of audiences that Madonna's name on the theater marquee drew. Madonna fans who had never seen a Broadway show were suddenly showing up to see "Her Iconness." According to Silver, "There were people coming for disparate reasons, and it was interesting to gather them all together under the tent."[169]

Mantegna was a bit blasé at Madonna's mention: "We have different heroes and bases of reference, but our roots are similar, and on a lot of levels, I relate to her. I feel as comfortable as I could possibly be with someone fifteen years younger."[170]

"She was early to every rehearsal, and the only time she ever got mad was when I ended a rehearsal early. She came and stuck her neck out, and she did a great job," Gregory Mosher said.[74] "She is an honest-to-God actress. She's got a clarity and transparency."[171]

When the show was still in rehearsal, Madonna had high hopes for her portrayal of Karen. "She's a sympathetic, misunderstood heroine who speaks the truth at any risk."[172] That was certainly a common thread that she could identify with.

Prior to opening night, Madonna admits that she was scared shitless of what was going to happen. With two widely acknowledged film bombs behind her, and word on the street that *Bloodhounds of Broadway* was going to be embarrassment number three, she knew the stakes were great.

The first night *Speed-the-Plow* was performed in front of a public audience, Madonna sent all of the cast and crew members flowers to wish them luck. "Not just the actors, but the dressers, the guys on the crew, the stage doorman," recalls Mosher.[74]

When the play officially opened on May 3, the critics were finally able to get a look at it for the first time. At the opening night party at Tavern on the Green, Madonna glowed triumphantly at the experience. "It was like good sex!" she exclaimed for the press. "It's great writing, and I have two great actors to work with."[173] Sean was not present for his wife's Broadway debut because he was in Thailand filming *Casualties of War*.

The next morning the reviews appeared, and they were decidedly mixed—especially as far as Madonna was concerned. Mosher's direction called for Madonna to keep the audience guessing. According to him,

"The audience is meant to go out asking one another—Is she an angel? Is she a whore?"[174] Unfortunately, there were other gnawing questions left unanswered, the most frequently asked being: Can Madonna act?

To acknowledge this query, the New York *Daily News* headlined their review of the show, NO, SHE CAN'T ACT. Clive Barnes in the *New York Post* claimed, "Madonna tries hard in a Judy Holliday role, but sounds more as if she were auditioning than acting, and the audition is scarcely for the big time. There is a genuine, reticent charm here, but it is not yet ready to light the lamps on Broadway." Frank Rich in the *New York Times* praised both men, and only lightly criticized Madonna: "Madonna serves Mr. Mamet's play much as she did the Susan Seidelman film *Desperately Seeking Susan*, with intelligent, scrupulously disciplined comic acting. She delivers the shocking transitions essential to the action and needs only more confidence to relax a bit and fully command her speaking voice." Dennis Cunningham, the reviewer for CBS-TV, disagreed. "Her ineptitude is scandalously thorough," he said, then publicly blasted Rich for accepting her performance: "Frank has taken leave of his senses. He should apologize to every actor he has ever given a bad review to."[174]

When it came time for the Tony Awards, Madonna wasn't even nominated, but Ron Silver ended up winning the Tony for Best Actor in a Dramatic Role. To add glitz to the telecast, Madonna was one of the presenters. With her dark brown hair—the color she wore for *Speed-the-Plow*—and a dress covered in cloth flowers, Madonna basked in all the attention and flashbulbs.

Madonna's fans didn't care about the bad reviews, they wanted to see the pop star in the flesh, and up close. Tickets for *Speed-the-Plow* were consistently sold out for the entire run of the play through the end of summer.

She knew she was in over her head, but Madonna was determined to display another side of herself. To have completed a run on Broadway, regardless of the reviews, had to show her off as being serious about becoming an actress. She was dead set on being seen as something more than a pop star. "I knew I was up against a lot," she recalls. "I'm from a world they have no respect for. It was a really good experience for me to prove myself in that context."[98]

Since the character of Karen was that of a victim, it turned out to be an excruciating personal experience. "It was devastating to do that night after night," she claims. "I saw her as an angel, an innocent. They wanted her to be a cunt."[98]

The other aspect that drove her crazy was the sheer confinement of the role. There was no room for ad-libbing, or stepping out of character, and there was also the routine of doing and saying precisely the same thing night after night. "Sometimes it feels like being in jail," she explained during the run of the play. "It's the monotony of one thing. It's having to do the same thing every night."[61]

Every night after the show, a throng of Madonna fans would encircle the backstage exit of the theater. They would be holding their cameras, plus Madonna photos and record albums that they wanted autographed by their favorite star. She would sign one or two and then be whisked into her waiting limousine by her bodyguards. But this was the most accessible she had been in ages.

In retrospect, Ron Silver claims that he is thankful about all the hoopla that was generated by Madonna's appearance in the play. If it were not for Madonna's name on the marquee, ticket sales might not have been great enough for the play to move to a Broadway theater, and Silver might never have gotten the notoriety that ultimately brought him the coveted Tony award.

"I felt very privileged," says Silver, whose career has soared since winning the Tony. "I think she's a lot smarter than people give her credit for. I think she can be a very good actress and I like her very much."[175]

While in New York, Madonna began to start a new life away from Sean, who was busy with his own career. In his absence, Madonna surrounded herself with a new circle of supportive friends, including Jennifer Grey and Sandra Bernhard.

Stand-up comedienne Sandra Bernhard had long been a cult favorite in comedy circles and had made an impressive movie debut in the 1983 film, *The King of Comedy*. In this particular summer of 1988 she was appearing in her one-woman show in the Village called *Without You I'm Nothing*. Jennifer Grey, the daughter of Joel Grey of *Cabaret* fame, was also riding a crest of success of her own, having just starred in the 1987 box office smash *Dirty Dancing*, with Patrick Swayze. The threesome made quite a high-profile unit, hanging out together as a trio, or accompanied by a circle of mutual girlfriends. While Sean Penn's young actor clique was known in Hollywood as "The Brat Pack," Madonna, Sandra, and Jennifer demurely referred to themselves as "The Snatch Batch."[99]

The Sandra Bernhard connection was one of the most talked about and most fascinating relationships in Madonna's career. The media attention that was drawn to this odd couple raised several questions: Are they just friends? Are they having sex with each other? Or are they just fucking with everyone's head?

Sandra Bernhard recalls when she first met Madonna, three years before: "I met her up at Warren Beatty's one night. It was kind of an uneasy situation. Nobody was really getting along, and Madonna was very quiet, kind of taking it all in."[176]

In the intervening three years, Sandra had added a section about Madonna—as pop icon—to her comedy act. In the context of the skit, Sandra begged Madonna to phone her up and be her friend. One of her on-stage ad-libs would include her pleading, "Be my friend, come live with me, Madonna. Push me over the borderline, Madonna. Fuck up my head, Madonna."[177] Little did she know, but that was exactly what was to happen. In 1988 both Sandra and Madonna were performing extended runs in their shows, Madonna in *Speed-the-Plow* and Sandra in her one-woman show *Without You I'm Nothing*.

"Afterward, I'd run into her here and there at parties and stuff, but we didn't really communicate," says Bernhard. "Then our shows were opening the same time in New York and I sent her an invitation. She came on Easter Sunday, and came backstage, and was so nice. She was so sweet, so excited, and then I went to see her show, and we just started hanging out. It seemed like the right thing at the right time."[176]

Both Jennifer and Sandra were on hand on opening night of *Speed-the-Plow*. It wasn't long before the press began trailing the trio and reporting all sorts of antics, including dressing identically. A couple of Madonna's evenings with Sandra found the duo staging belching contests at high-profile Manhattan restaurants. When Madonna's old graffiti-painting buddy, Futura 2000, opened an art exhibit at a local eatery, Madonna, Sandra, and Jennifer were on hand. "Her insanity is refreshing," explains Madonna of Bernhard.[178]

Bernhard recalls that their fast friendship was almost immediately misinterpreted. "Although the New York newspapers like to write about us terrorizing the town and stuff like that," she says, "actually neither one of us is as wild as we were made out to be."[179]

When Sean returned to the country, his reunion with Madonna picked up where it left off: he was a total pain in the ass to her and almost immediately reports of his caustic behavior spread through the press like a brushfire. On June 27, Madonna and Sean trekked down to Atlantic City to attend the Leon Spinks–Mike Tyson fight. Among the notables present were Jack Nicholson, Warren Beatty, Donald Trump, Jesse Jackson, and Richard Pryor. When the ringside celebrities were announced on the loudspeakers, the mention of Madonna's name drew a huge round of applause. When they announced Sean's name it was met with a mixture of cheers and extended booing.

When spectators roamed by with cameras or pieces of paper for the duo to autograph, Penn went into a tirade of acidic remarks: "Fuck off!" "Get that mother-fucking camera away from me." "You mother-fucking asshole, don't take my goddamn picture!" "I ain't here to give a fucking autograph, dipshit, I'm here to watch the fight. Why don't you watch it?"[180]

On Sunday, July 3, Madonna and Sean were in New York City, walking down Columbus Avenue near 70th Street. *New York Post* photographer Paul Adao was in his car when he spotted the superstar couple, and he began shooting photos through his windshield. Sean spotted Adao's camera and immediately threw one of his fits.

Recalls Adao, "He left Madonna and kicked my car. When I saw him coming I shut the windows and locked the doors."[181] After Sean kicked $800 worth of dents into the photographer's car door, Adao summoned a cop. The officer made Sean follow him to the local precinct, where he was ordered to appear in Manhattan Criminal Court later that month.

On July 28, at his Criminal Court appearance, Sean was once again surrounded by press photographers. Adao agreed to drop his charges against the actor if Penn paid for the damages to his car. Adao's boss, *New York Post* photo editor Harry Siskind publicly proclaimed that if Sean ever accosted another press photographer, he would make certain that Adao would be on hand to testify against Penn. It seemed that wherever Sean went, trouble soon followed.

Meanwhile, Madonna was becoming increasingly more disenchanted with her marriage. She had more fun with Sandra Bernhard than she did with her husband. Comparing the two relationships, in retrospect Madonna said, "I'd say that my friendship with Sandra was just beginning as my relationship with Sean was dying."[99]

On July 4, Madonna was accompanied by both Sandra Bernhard and Sean Penn to a Fourth of July party hosted by artist Peter Max. He chartered an 82-foot yacht and took his guests on a cruise in the Hudson River. Also aboard were Liza Minnelli and her husband, Mark Gero, Paul Sorvino, Melanie Griffith, and Jerry Stiller and Anne Meara. When the boat passed by the Statue of Liberty, actor Sorvino led the group in a singalong version of "America the Beautiful." Madonna and Sandra then went into their rendition of the theme song from "Gilligan's Island."

Later that month came the most talked about television event of the summer. Sandra Bernhard was booked to appear on "Late Night with David Letterman" and decided that she would turn it into a raucous impromptu event by bringing Madonna along with her. No one was more surprised than David Letterman.

Sandra wore a pair of cutoff bluejeans, a white T-shirt, white socks, and klutzy-looking black shoes. When Letterman questioned Sandra about her much-reported friendship with Madonna, he produced a copy of the *Star*, and inquired, "Let's talk about you, and your new good friend, Madonna. Is there any truth to this nonsense?"[182]

Sandra proceeded to read the headline of a story from the publication's June 28 issue: IT'S ALL-GIRLS NIGHT AS MADONNA LEADS TERRIBLE TRIO ON LATE-NIGHT LULUS.[183] When Letterman asked her to explain what she and Madonna did when they went out, she replied that they go out and drink tequila and party. Teasingly, she announced, "As a matter of fact she happens to be here tonight."[182]

When Madonna made her surprise appearance from backstage, she was dressed identically to Sandra—right down to the klutzy black shoes. What transpired was nearly ten minutes of nonstop bantering and inside jokes. When the subject of *Speed-the-Plow* came up, Bernhard exclaimed, "She hates it!" and Madonna screamed, "I want out!"[182]

After chatting about what Madonna was up to, Letterman turned the line of questioning to her friendship with Bernhard and Grey. "We carouse," explained Madonna.[182]

The controversy swung into full gear when the pair of girls on the loose claimed that they frequented the notorious lesbian nightclub the Cubby Hole. Sandra then blurted out that, on separate occasions, she had slept with both Madonna and Sean, and found Madonna to be the more pleasurable partner of the two. Although the performance was meant to be in jest, when the press got hold of the story, everyone began speculating as to whether or not Madonna was having a sexual affair with Sandra.

Throughout her career, there has been public talk and speculation about Bernhard's sexual orientation. After this television appearance with Madonna, wherever Sandra went, innuendo followed. As part of the media mind-fuck, Bernhard has proceeded to make conflicting statements about whether or not she is in fact gay.

After their controversial appearance on Letterman's show, Sandra explained that particular evening by claiming, "That was never something that was planned or that was intentional at all. We never said, 'Let's go out and be lesbians.' It was really like 'Let's just be girlfriends—silly, juvenile girlfriends.' The whole lesbian thing being read into it was just stupid, ridiculous."[176]

Explaining how the impromptu Madonna appearance on "Late Night" came to be, Bernhard said, "Because we thought it would be fun."[179]

Madonna was later to illuminate the burning question as to whether or not the duo indeed frequented the Greenwich Village lesbian hotspot. "I've never been to the Cubby Hole," she says. "That's the joke of it. My brother lives around the corner [from there], and I've walked by it with him, and I sort of go, 'Oh, yeah—look, there's a lesbian club.' Sandra and I were just fucking with people."[99]

Regarding speculation about an affair between her and Jennifer Grey, Madonna says, "That came out of me and Sandra Bernhard. Then it became a question of whatever female I had a close relationship with who is an outspoken girl—which Jennifer is—then I must be sleeping with her."[99]

When the press wasn't talking about Madonna's supposed affairs with women, including Sandra and Jennifer, and men, including John F. Kennedy, Jr., they were talking about her clothes. The dress that Madonna wore in the European "True Blue" video was given to MTV for a traveling display called "MTV's Museum of Unnatural History." The powder blue rhinestone-spangled dress was part of the display when the exhibit of rock and roll memorabilia rolled into Novi, Michigan, at the Twelve Oaks Mall. The dress vanished on July 15 from its Plexiglas display case and was recovered from a growth of bushes three days later. Apparently the perp, nineteen-year-old Krista Maria O'Sada, had stolen the dress on a dare from her friends. Once the robbery was completed successfully, the girl feared getting caught with it and ditched it in the bushes. That same week, it was found by another group of teenagers, and returned to the police.

When the end of the summer came, so did Madonna's run in *Speed-the-Plow*. The role of Karen was taken over by an unknown actress named Felicity Huffman. The minute that Madonna, Mantegna, and Silver left the cast, ticket sales for the play dropped off. Several weeks later it closed.

In retrospect, Madonna concedes that the show wasn't an especially fun experience, but it served a purpose. "If you asked, 'Would you ever do it again?' I'd have to say, 'Definitely,'" she claims.[61] However, the next time around, she wants to be the one in creative control.

On September 11, Madonna was one of the celebrity runners in a charity event called "The Race Against Time." According to her promo statement for this, "You can save a child from starvation. All you need is a pair of running shoes."[184] The event, which was to benefit the charity known as Care, called for simultaneous runs in fifteen cities across America. Madonna was the symbolic 1,000,001st participant to pledge her time.

The next entry on her pressing schedule called for recording a new album, for release the following year. Recorded in Los Angeles that fall, it was to be her most personalized work to date.

Since the summer of 1988 had been one of long separations for Madonna and Sean, during the coming months they planned to spend as much time as they could together. Sean accepted a role in the Los Angeles cast of David Rabe's hit play *Hurly-Burly*. He wanted to be near his wife while she worked on her album. However, instead of rekindling the flames of their love, the whole marriage ended up exploding in their faces—and onto the front pages of every major publication.

At this point Madonna had just about reached the end of her rope with Sean and his excessive drinking. When *Hurly-Burly* was in rehearsal, she would show up to pick him up and drive him home—to make certain he wouldn't go out and get drunk.

Meanwhile, Madonna had been cavorting about Hollywood with her new best friend Sandra Bernhard. In the middle of the *Hurly-Burly* opening night party in Century City, Sean and Madonna had a huge fight over her controversial friendship with Sandra. Several witnesses claim that when Madonna showed up at the party with her so-called "gal pal" Sandra, Sean screamed at her, "You cunt, how could you do this to me?"[185]

She had also been seeing a lot of Warren Beatty, who was openly courting her to play a role in his upcoming film version of the adventures of comic strip hero *Dick Tracy*. Madonna and Warren were seen having intimate dinners together at a Los Angeles restaurant called Sushi Cove, not far from Warren's estate. Occasionally they would dine alone, and on other evenings Sandra would accompany them.

Madonna and Sean argued almost nonstop after Thanksgiving and all through the holiday season. After one big blowout, Sean moved out of the couple's Malibu house to stay with his parents, four miles away. There, Sean would get drunk and call Madonna. During his late-night phone calls, Sean would hurl obscenities at her and make drunken threats. She was so sick of his liquor-ridden tirades that she got into the habit of leaving the answering machine on. Fearing for her safety, Madonna's friends, including Sandra Bernhard, would come over and spend the night with her.

Several people had access to the couple's private phone number and could dial in to hear the hate-filled messages Sean had left for Madonna. Recalls one source, "He left one message for her toward the end—'You can continue to suck the big dick of Hollywood if you want to, but you can count me out!' "[186]

If the uncontested tabloid reports are to be believed, on the night of December 28, a drunk and irrational Sean frightened Madonna to death when he burst into their house and began to scream charges at her about her relationships with Beatty and Bernhard. Sean reportedly overpowered Madonna, tied her up, gagged her, and left her alone in the house for up to nine hours, unable to move. When the inebriated

Penn returned later, she persuaded him to untie her by promising him a romantic night of reconciliation. When he undid the knots, she ran to her car and phoned the police. She immediately filed an assault charge against Sean. Concerned about her own safety, she fled the house and went to stay with her manager, Freddy DeMann.

The *Star* reported of Sean's actions: "He climbed the wall, broke into the house, found Madonna there alone, tied her up and scared her." The article went on to say, "Penn bound and gagged his wife, hog-tying her to an armchair with twine, then started yelling at her and slapping her."[187]

Sean's attack and alleged physical abuse was confirmed by records at the Malibu Police Station. According to Detective John Flaherty, "a possible assault had been attempted."[188] Although Madonna has been quite forthcoming about all of the seamy details of her life since then, she has never confirmed or denied any of the pieced-together accounts of that outlandish evening. Days later, in a lame attempt to gloss over accounts of the attack, Penn's publicist John West issued a red herring of a statement which read: "Sean and Madonna are separated. They plan to divorce and it's amicable."[189]

On January 5, 1989, in a Los Angeles court, Madonna again filed divorce papers on the grounds of irreconcilable differences.[189] All the paperwork was complete and ready to sign, as Madonna's lawyers had prepared the necessary documents a year before.

Because of Sean's previous arrests and the terms of his probation, Madonna had him in a compromising position. If she didn't withdraw the assault charges, Sean faced a possible ninety days in jail. She dropped the charges on January 10, but only after he signed the divorce papers she presented him with. In the settlement, he retained the couple's Malibu house, and she kept the New York apartment. She had already secured a new house for herself in the Hollywood hills, which she took possession of two weeks later.

Once all the documents had been signed, on January 10 the assault charges were dropped, according to Al Albergate, spokesman for Deputy District Attorney Lauren Weiss. "Madonna asked that there be no criminal charges pressed," Albergate confirmed. "There is no other evidence with which to base a criminal charge so there won't be a criminal charge filed."[188]

Was Madonna "trussed up like a turkey," as gossip columnist Liz Smith and several other sources claim? "I am absolutely convinced that these reports were accurate," claims Jerry George, one of the editors of the *National Enquirer*, who worked on the story and consulted with the Malibu Police Department.[190] Madonna claimed that the tabloids were all "extremely inaccurate, as they usually are. They're always making shit up. I've completely reconciled myself to that fact."[16] She, however, would not disclose the exact details of that evening, although police records show she claimed that she was both detained against her will by Sean that night, and that he had been guilty of "assault." Whether or not the "trussed turkey" theory is 100 percent accurate, it has become part of the accepted legend of Madonna's breakup with Sean.

Oddly enough, according to Madonna, to this day Sean remains the one true love of her life. She simply couldn't stand the pressure that marriage to him caused. Sean's out-of-control drinking problems and irrational hot temper, teamed with her naturally flirtatious and gregarious ways, finally spelled the dramatic end of the Poison Penns.

Madonna originally had high hopes for their marriage, but for once in her life things didn't turn out the way she had planned. Never one to miss a beat, within weeks of her divorce she turned around and launched a string of hot projects that were to leave Sean and all memories of their stormy marriage in the dust.

Eleven

I wouldn't have turned out

Everyone

the way I was if I didn't have

Must

all those old-fashioned values

Stand

to rebel against.[191] —Madonna

Alone

N o sooner had the press coverage about her divorce and her evening tied to a chair subsided, than the buzz about Madonna's new album, *Like a Prayer*, began. With the exception of four songs on the *Who's That Girl?* soundtrack, plus the cuts "Santa Baby" and "Spotlight," it had been three years since Madonna released a full album of new material. A lengthy hiatus like that can be a difficult hurdle to overcome for most female artists. The public is very fickle, and it was a year in which the latest albums from Diana Ross, Cyndi Lauper, and Aretha Franklin all died on the charts. However, with incredible ease, Madonna simply reinvented herself, milked the media for all it was worth, and triumphed again.

Her divorce from Sean Penn came at just the right time. His movie career of late had relegated him to the role of "Mr. Madonna," and the public was sick and tired of hearing about his childish, unprofessional antics. He had become a painful weight around her neck, but the publicity from their *Star Wars*–like breakup created the perfect launching pad for her newest projects. Freed from the negative force field that Sean created, Madonna was ready to soar to new heights. She emerged with a new look, a new sound, a new image, and, to put it bluntly, she kicked ass.

For the new album, Madonna looked within herself and drew upon her own life and emotional experiences. Whenever Madonna releases a new album, it is a major media event, but this one seemed to top them all in controversy and coverage. When it was released, the *Like a Prayer* album was not the giddy nonstop dance fest that one had come to expect from Madonna. Instead, it was a multi-textured, elaborate, and deeply personal work. With all the songs composed by Madonna herself, at least half the material was revealingly autobiographical. In fact, Madonna's whole family played heavily in the picture. She reconciled the death of her mother with the poignant ballad, "Promise to Try." She confronted her still-unresolved relationship with her dad in the song "Oh Father," and she sang about her brothers and sisters on the hot dance number "Keep It Together." To tie it all up with a bow, Madonna inscribed in the liner notes: "This album is dedicated to my mother, who taught me how to pray."[192]

Since her last album, Madonna had turned thirty. Although it was not a widely publicized event, it represented a turning point in how she perceived herself. Of her thirtieth birthday, Madonna said, "I wouldn't say it was traumatic. It's like, 'Oh shucks, I can't be twenty anymore.' It seems like when you're twenty there's more of an opportunity for you to behave childishly and get away with it. When you're thirty, you have to really grow up and get responsible."[74]

The emotions this milestone stirred up were based on memories of her mother: "When I turned thirty, which was the age my mother was when she died, I just flipped because I kept thinking I'm now outliving my mother," she said.[99]

A lot of the somberness of *Like a Prayer* stemmed directly out of what was going on around her while she was composing the diary-like lyrics. At the time she was in New York doing *Speed-the-Plow*, the inspirations and introspective moods of the play stirred up her feelings of frustration and despair. She was in a marriage that wasn't working, she was trapped in a play that she had grown to hate.

A lot of these fears that Madonna sings about on *Like a Prayer* were those of "little Nonnie," the confused Catholic girl she was as a child. Her ambivalence about the role the church played in her life became an underlying issue confronted in her writing. "The theme of Catholicism runs rampant through my album," she explained. "It's me struggling with the mystery and magic that surrounds it."[193]

Perhaps the most true to life song on the album is "Till Death Do Us Part." It focuses on her disastrous marriage to self-destructive Sean. "Like most of the songs on my album, it's very much drawn from my life, factually speaking, but it's fictionalized, too."[16] At the time she was very mixed up emotionally about her divorce. On one hand, she loved Sean. On the other hand, their marriage was impossible to deal with. Assessing the blame, Madonna claimed that it was outside pressure that broke them up.

When she was recording this fourth album, Madonna again turned to Patrick Leonard and Steve Bray as co-writers and co-producers. However, the most surprising inclusion on this album's team was a new collaborator: Prince. Together they came up with a swirling bilingual love song.

Ever since their brief meeting in 1985, Madonna and Prince had remained friends. Several times they spoke of writing together. At one point in 1988 the pair even considered writing a musical together. Madonna flew up to his recording studio in Minneapolis, and she and Prince kicked around several ideas to get a feel for working together. They worked on several different songs, but none were ever completed. Several days later, Madonna's schedule demanded that she leave Minnesota, but the pair vowed to keep in contact.

Time passed, and other things occupied her mind, like her Broadway debut in *Speed-the-Plow*. But while she was in that show, Prince came to New York to see her perform. When he came backstage, he handed her a rough mix of one of the songs that they had worked on the year before. It was called "Love Song," and when she heard the tape, she immediately loved what he had done with the song. Although they both wanted to find the time to get together to collaborate, the pair ended up sending tapes back and forth until the project was completed. The finished product, the Madonna/Prince duet, "Love Song," is one of the highlights of the *Like a Prayer* album.

Much of the music on the *Like a Prayer* album is reminiscent of styles and specific songs of the sixties. "Dear Jessie" sounds like something from *Sgt. Pepper's Lonely Hearts Club Band*. The bizarre "Act of Contrition," with its backward voice tracks, sounds as if it was inspired by John Lennon and Yoko Ono's audio experiments on the Beatles' *White Album*. And "Promise to Try" sounds like something that depressed folk singer Janis Ian might come up with.

Madonna's songs up until this album tended to be a reflection of her current life and experiences. This album has more to do with her musical influences. The songs "Keep It Together" and "Express Yourself," for instance, are her tributes to the group Sly and the Family Stone. "Oh Father" is her ode to Simon and Garfunkel, who she loved to listen to when she was growing up. In fact, the overall emotional context of the album is drawn from what she went through when she was growing up.

The song that most reflected the Madonna everyone had come to know and be shocked by was "Express Yourself." According to her, "The message of the song is that people should always say what it is they want."[193]

It is January of 1989, and the highly popular Madonna has recorded a new album that is a mixture of personalized ballads and celebratory dance tunes. So where's the controversy? She wrote a song about her divorce, the death of her mom, and the fact that she still doesn't see eye-to-eye with her dad. Big deal. Where's the scandal? Here's where the plot begins to thicken.

In the past five years the two top soda pop manufacturers, Coca-Cola and Pepsi-Cola, had learned that an effective way to reach the youth of America and the rest of the world was to sign sizzling hot recording stars to do television commercials publicizing the cola of their choice. It had worked brilliantly with Michael Jackson and Whitney Houston—why shouldn't it work with Madonna? Madonna's hit songs and videos had been about love, devotion, and searching for the latest party. She ought to make an excellent spokesperson to reach teenage consumers. So ran the thoughts of executives at Pepsi-Cola when they began pursuing Madonna for their 1989 celebrity commercials.

In December 1988, Coca-Cola announced that it had signed George Michael to sell its pop to the public, and the gears started to turn. On January 25, 1989, following eight months of negotiations, Pepsi announced that they had signed Madonna to a year-long endorsement contract, for which they would pay Her Virginness $5 million. In return, Madonna would appear in a series of television commercials and Pepsi would sponsor the singer's next concert tour, tentatively slated for later that year.

Pepsi was undaunted by Madonna's image in the tabloids. "Her appeal is in her music and her acting. That's where people's interests are," announced Pepsi spokesman Tod MacKenzie.[194]

The truly unique aspect of Pepsi's deal with Madonna was its sheer marketing brilliance. The plan was clever, tasteful, and right on target, to begin with. When controversy emerged it only placed a huge magnifying glass over the whole campaign. The by-product was a hundred times more publicity than they could have ever hoped for.

As originally outlined, Pepsi's projected plan went something like this: 1. January 25, Madonna signs her contract, and the next morning the deal becomes front page news in *USA Today*. 2. February 22, Pepsi unveils a commercial on the Grammy Awards telecast announcing the forthcoming March 2 debut of Madonna's Pepsi commercial. The upcoming event is heralded as the satellite premiere of the song "Like a Prayer." 3. A 30-second version of the commercial will air through the summer. 4. March 3, MTV debuts Madonna's own music video version of "Like a Prayer," getting a month-long exclusive on the clip. 5. March 21, the "Like a Prayer" video and singles hit the stores—and both become instant hits. 6. Madonna tapes a second commercial for Pepsi, which announces her upcoming tour. 7. Madonna goes on tour, which features Pepsi logos on everything. 8. Everyone makes a fortune.

What happened in reality is even crazier yet. Madonna had already met with Pepsi representatives to come up with the concept for the commercial. As planned, Pepsi paid her over $5 million for use of the song in the commercial, and production began immediately.

The director that Pepsi hired to execute the tightly scheduled video/commercial presentation was Joe Pytka, who had masterminded the landmark Michael Jackson ads for the company. According to Pytka, when he first drove to Madonna's Hollywood hills house to discuss the commercial, she had no idea that she was expected to perform in it. "Michael Jackson had always used a special sound system for his singing, so I asked Madonna where hers was. She said, 'What singing?' "[195]

Joe claims that she was also startled when he asked her to dance in the ad. But he felt that dancing was important for the ad because it's one of the main things that the public associates with Madonna. When Joe hired an outside choreographer, and Madonna saw the steps he was teaching the other dancers, she immediately insisted on doing her own dance.

Unlike Michael Jackson and Whitney Houston, Madonna refused to insert the word *Pepsi* in her song for the commercial. "I wouldn't put Pepsi in any of my songs—Pepsi is Pepsi, and I'm me," she explained. "I do consider it a challenge to make a commercial that has some sort of artistic value."[16]

When the Grammy Awards telecast rolled around, the planned "teaser" ad ran. In the ad, an Australian Aborigine is seen trekking for miles across the outback to get to a television in time to see the world debut of the forthcoming Madonna Pepsi commercial.

A commercial for a commercial? You bet. When you're dealing with Madonna, the first thing you have to do is throw out all the rules.

On March 2, as planned, Madonna's Pepsi ad ran on the Number One TV program in America, "The Cosby Show." It worked smoothly with the sitcom's wholesome family image. Elaborately produced, the ad presented Madonna in a sentimental setting that somehow successfully mixed Catholic Church imagery and Pepsi-Cola into the same two-minute clip.

The commercial, entitled "Make a Wish," opens on Madonna, lounging in her den, watching a black and white home movie of her eighth birthday party. She is wearing a shoulderless pants suit, several crucifixes around her neck, and is holding a can of Pepsi-Cola in her left hand. Her hair is shoulder-length, dark brown, with a large white streak in it. Suddenly the images change, and it is the actress playing eight-year-old Madonna who is watching the screen, and it is adult

Madonna in black and white up on the wide-screen projection TV. The little girl watches the image up on the screen—a vision of what one day she will become.

On the video screen, adult Madonna is shown dancing in the streets, while eight-year-old Madonna and thirty-year-old Madonna examine each other's worlds. The little girl is shown touring the house that she will one day grow up to live in, and the adult Madonna tours her past—including a trip back to a Catholic schoolgirl's classroom. At one point she is seen dancing in the school hallway while a class of uniformed eight-year-olds walk to class. It is an image of Madonna being at thirty what she only dreamed of becoming when she was eight.

While the gospel sound of the song "Like a Prayer" plays, Madonna dances up the aisle of a black church and joins the choir. Cutting back to the present, the time-traveling little girl walks into her adult bedroom only to find the same doll that she received for her eighth birthday. In that split-second, the little girl realizes that both she and the doll have a wondrous future ahead of them.

Suddenly the time travel is over for both of them, and the eight-year-old is back on the screen—holding a glass spiral-twist Pepsi bottle from the sixties, and thirty-year-old Madonna looks on in approval with her eighties can of Pepsi in her hand. Both images toast each other with a Pepsi, and the adult Madonna says to her childhood image on the screen, "Make a wish." With that, the little girl blows out the candles on the birthday cake, and the Pepsi logo comes up on the screen with the words *A Generation Ahead* below it.

It was a clever spot. However, it was only to be broadcast once.

When the commercial ran that night in March, it was shown in forty countries around the world, giving it an estimated viewership of 250 million people. Not only was it the first time a hit record had debuted in an advertisement, but it was the first time a TV commercial had been given a special around-the-world satellite premiere.

So far, everything was going according to plan. However, the very next day, when Madonna's own version of "Like a Prayer" made its "heavy rotation" debut on MTV, all hell broke loose.

In Madonna's video she witnesses a murder, runs into a church in a brown slip, kisses a statue of a saint, makes love with a black man on a church pew, dances in front of burning crosses, sings with a church choir, and shows bleeding stigmata on both palms as though she had survived a crucifixion. Only Madonna could pull this video off—it is stormy, mysterious, tragic, violent, dark, and exciting.

Prior to its airing, Madonna explained the difference between the Pepsi ad and her own video presentation: "The treatment for the video is a lot more controversial. It's probably going to touch a lot of nerves in a lot of people. And the treatment for the commercial is . . . I mean, it's a commercial. It's very, very sweet. It's very sentimental."[11]

Madonna knew that she wanted to shake people up with her own "Like a Prayer" video, especially since the G-rated version was going to be highly visible on network television.

When it had come to choosing a director to bring her vision to life, Madonna decided that Mary Lambert would be the right visionary to do the job. She explains, "Mary Lambert got involved as the director, and she came up with a story that incorporated more of the religious symbolism I originally wrote into the song."[11] According to Madonna, it was Mary who made the video so cohesive.

Although gospel recording star Andre Crouch and his choir were used on the recording of "Like a Prayer," when he heard that the video was going to entail burning crosses and potentially sacrilegious images, he wasn't interested in being involved. Instead, actors and singers auditioned to appear in the video, including members of the Friendly Friendship Baptist Church Choir in L.A. Actor and singer Bobby Glenn was a member of the choir who was used in the music video of "Like a Prayer." A background singer for Diana Ross since the seventies, Glenn auditioned for the part in a cattle call.

"I got the job," Glenn recalls. "Madonna wasn't at the audition. But what they did was they took different groups in and then they videoed it, and they showed her videos of the different groups, and I learned later that she saw me on one of the videos and wanted me to do it. Then we went down for the rehearsal. The rehearsal was at Solar [Studios] in Hollywood, and that was the very first rehearsal that we had with Madonna. That was really the only rehearsal."[196]

After all the things Bobby Glenn had heard about Madonna, he was surprised by how down to earth she was in reality. "One of the things that I was really astonished about was that she came to the rehearsal driving herself—with no security or anything, driving one of her cars herself, a black Mercedes convertible. She was very, very nice, and very comical—she's a very comical person. She knows what she wants and she has the attitude—'I'll do what I want to do.' And she doesn't care what the comments are. I didn't know at that time that this was going to be one of the videos that had a lot of controversy behind it. Neither did I know what the concept of the video was. When I saw the lyrics of the song and everything, I said, 'Oh this is great! She's going to do a gospel video, and a gospel song on her album!' I didn't really know until after it was shot."[196]

When the troupe was taking a break amid their only rehearsal session, Bobby approached Madonna. "The first rehearsal was really nice, and spiritual," he claims, "and, after it was over, I got a chance to chat with her, and to introduce myself, and she knew I was with Diana, and we began to talk about Diana. She said, 'Tell Diana I said "hello,"' and 'We don't get a chance to get together anymore since she married that rich man [shipping tycoon Arne Ness].' And I said, 'Well, you're rich, too!' And she said, 'That's right!' I found her to be very comical."[196]

The actual filming of the choir scene was done in a thirteen-hour day at a soundstage on Melrose. The video choir members worked with choreographer Vince Paterson, Mary Lambert, and Madonna all day on the scene which was about one-eighth of the final five-and-a-half-minute presentation. "She has a boldness about her," says Glenn in retrospect. "If she feels she wants to do something—she does it. She's got a lot of boldness, and I found her overall to be a very exciting person to work with."[196] The real excitement, however, began when the public got a look at the finished product.

By this point in her career, Madonna realized that the more scandalous the project, the more successful it would be. She was clearly begging for either the KKK or the "moral majority" to kick up a fuss. In a way she got more than she bargained for. It was only a matter of days before the controversy erupted onto the front page of every major newspaper. It was inevitable that Madonna's video was bound to stir up some sort of negative reaction from one right wing religious group or another. Reverend Donald Wildmond of the fanatical American Family Association, a self-righteous Christian group, threatened to have his *AFA Journal*'s 380,000 subscribers boycott Pepsi until the company bowed to his demands. From his home base in Tupelo, Mississippi, Wildmond demanded that Pepsi nullify their deal with Madonna because their commercial is "putting Madonna up as a clean, wholesome role model," while her video is busily "ridiculing Christianity."[197] Wildmond had just cut his teeth on a boycott of Martin Scorsese's film *The Last Temptation of Christ*, and he was primed and ready for a holy war with a soda pop company.

Stymied Pepsi spokesman Tod MacKenzie tried to deflect the negative press. "Why isn't he going after the video?" he asked with bewilderment. "Why has he targeted really an innocent, wholesome commercial people have responded favorably to?"[197] Oddly enough, the Pepsi executives didn't think to ask for a view of Madonna's video prior to its airplay on MTV. According to MacKenzie, "We have no right."[197]

Pepsi immediately put a hold on further broadcasting of the Madonna commercial until they could see which way the cards were going to fall. Next, a Catholic bishop from Texas, Rene Gracido, jumped into the fray and labeled Madonna's video offensive. Hot-headed Gracido not only called for a boycott of Pepsi but of its other holdings as well— including multimillion-dollar fast-food restaurants Taco Bell, Pizza Hut, and Kentucky Fried Chicken.

To put the frosting on the cake, Catholic groups in Italy started to protest. When a statement from the Pope was released by the Vatican that banned Madonna from appearing in Italy, Pepsi finally had to make a decision.

Fearing a situation that could lose the company a fortune, Pepsi bowed to Wildmond's and Gracido's pressure, and agreed to discontinue broadcasting Madonna's ad and to drop their sponsorship of her next concert tour. Furthermore, Madonna was allowed to retain her entire $5 million advance.

For once, even Madonna was surprised. "When I think of controversy, I never really think people are going to be half as shocked as they are at what I do. I really couldn't believe how out of control the whole Pepsi thing got."[18]

In the meantime, March 21 rolled around, and two million copies of the *Like a Prayer* album hit the stores. With flames fanned high by the controversy that the video, Pepsi, the self-righteous religious leaders, and the press had created, in three weeks *Like a Prayer* was the Number

One single and album in America, and it went on to top the charts in over thirty different countries around the globe. If there was anyone left in the world who didn't know who Madonna was up until that point, they certainly knew who she was now.

Her album was an assault of sights, sounds—AND smells. Each album, cassette, and CD was all doused with a splash of patchouli oil. According to one representative from Warner Records, "She wanted to create a flavor of the sixties and the church. She wanted to create a sensual feeling you could hear and smell."[198]

Not only was the album derivative of the musical styles of the sixties, but the cover photo was a takeoff on one of the most famous album jackets of that era. A close-up of Madonna's crotch and hands, it was a direct copy of the Rolling Stones' controversial 1971 album, *Sticky Fingers*, which had a close-up of Mick Jagger's crotch on its cover. In the Madonna version, the first button of the beltless jeans is undone, and her navel and exposed belly comprise the background her logo is emblazoned on.

Also aimed at the groin—in a favorable way—each copy of *Like a Prayer* came with an informative insert outlining, in frank terms, AIDS prevention facts. Never before, or since, has a recording artist turned up their nose at controversy for such a worthy cause. The insert urged the practice of "safe sex," spoke of using condoms, and listed an 800 number that could be called for further information. It ended with the message: "AIDS Is No Party!"[192]

Explaining the AIDS insert in *Like a Prayer*, Madonna stated in her uniquely eloquent fashion: "I'm saying I have a pussy and I'm dealing with my sexuality and you can deal with yours if you want to. I'm encouraging that. But I'm not saying, 'Go around and fuck randomly.' You can have sex, but you have to practice safe sex. There's no way around it. I think it's horrible that everyone thinks, 'Oh, my God! AIDS! Now we all have to sleep alone and never have anything to do with anybody.' Use your imagination. Be creative."[99]

In addition to the crotch-level-view on the front of the album, Madonna was depicted full body on the back. She had again turned around and adopted a new look. This time around it was very sixties, with dark stringy hair, well-worn bluejeans, several rings on her fingers, a string of colored beads and glass gemstones hanging around her waist, and a garnet-encrusted crucifix around her neck.

As she had done on the *True Blue* album, for photos Madonna turned to Herb Ritts to capture her with his camera. "We're on the same wave-length. She trusts me, and I try to come up with the best for her. She changes, I change. It's a true image that evolves," claims Ritts.[199] "Madonna has a specialness that comes from within. She's always changing and purifying her personal and professional image."[200]

The Madonna media blitz was on, and suddenly you couldn't turn anywhere without seeing her image or hearing her new music for 1989. The reviews for *Like a Prayer* were especially complimentary, and suddenly she was seen as having much more depth than her original dance diva image hinted at.

Rolling Stone referred to the album as "Madonna's True Confessions," calling it "as close to art as pop music gets. 'Like a Prayer' is proof not only that Madonna should be taken seriously as an artist but that hers is one of the most compelling voices of the eighties." The *New York Times* called it "Madonna's convincing bid for recognition as a serious rock artist," and contended that she "has never looked more beautiful or sung with more feeling." Several reviewers suddenly took her more seriously, including *USA Today*, which reported, "Madonna's voice will never be technically brilliant, but she summons so much emotional intensity on *Like a Prayer* that the calculated come-on in 1984's *Like a Virgin* sounds like a disembodied chirp."

While the Pepsi video controversy was brewing, Madonna reveled in the media attention. Since her divorce from Sean, she had been keeping company with her friends—especially Warren Beatty, Sandra Bernhard, or even the combo of Sandra and Warren.

The star electricity of Madonna and Warren Beatty provided enough wattage to light up a small town. And Hollywood is exactly that—a small town, where news travels fast. Not only was the pair making plans for their upcoming collaboration on *Dick Tracy*, but romance was in the air.

As much an ideal press release as it was an affair, the union of Madonna and Warren seemed almost plotted. But romancing his leading ladies has been a career-long legend for Beatty. His past loves include Joan Collins, Natalie Wood, Leslie Caron, Michelle Phillips, Julie Christie, Diane Keaton, and Isabelle Adjani. Madonna called him "Old Man," and he nicknamed her "Buzzbomb."

Simultaneous with the whole tempest in a soda pop bottle, Madonna had some more serious matters on her mind. Both Christopher Flynn, her dance instructor from her childhood, and Howard Brookner, the director of *Bloodhounds of Broadway*, were dying of AIDS. In both instances she was there for her friends.

On Sunday, February 26, Madonna was the star attraction at a benefit for AIDS Project L.A., which was held at the Shrine Auditorium Expo Hall. It was a fund-raising "Dance-A-Thon," and Christopher Flynn was one of the organizers. The dancing partners she brought were Sandra Bernhard, her background singer Niki Harris, and her *Who's That Girl?* co-star Coati Mundi. "They're here to make sure that I don't perform too many nasty dance moves that Christopher Flynn is responsible for teaching me," announced Madonna from the stage.[201]

Flynn, who also spoke to the crowd that evening, thanked his star pupil. He announced that she was among the first people he turned to when he was diagnosed. With that, Flynn commanded that as her oldest living disco partner, he claimed the first dance. Madonna and her friends danced for over an hour nonstop, and the event went on late into the night. The Dance-A-Thon raised $400,000 for AIDS Project L.A.

Coati Mundi says that Madonna coming that evening had meant an awful lot to Christopher Flynn. "He was a real nice guy," recalls Coati. "He was really touched that Madonna came through for him. He just loved her, and he really was overcome with emotion to see Madonna."[150]

That same year, when *Bloodhounds of Broadway* director Howard Brookner was hospitalized and dying of AIDS in New York, his friend, writer Brad Gooch, watched Madonna frequently visit. She not only visited Howard, but talked with all the other patients on the AIDS ward at St. Vincent's Hospital.

Madonna's actions continued to impress the people around her. She has proved again and again that she not only devotes her money

but her time as well. Time and again she puts her money where he
mouth is.

Another charitable event that she got involved in that spring was
"Bungle in the Jungle." It benefited an organization called Companions
of Arts and Nature, whose mission is to save the rain forest. The tickets
for the May 24th concert, starring Madonna, Sandra Bernhard, the Del
Fuegos, the Jungle Brothers, Ann Magnuson, Malcolm McLaren, Rob
Wasserman, and Bob Weir were $25 to $100. For an additional $250
you could attend a special reception; for $500 you could attend the
dinner.

Held at the Brooklyn Academy of Music, the evening's program
was basically a variety show hosted by Madonna and artist Kenny Scharf,
with special guests like the B-52's and Keith Haring. The most-talked-
about performance of the evening came from Madonna and Sandra.
Together they performed their own version of Sonny and Cher's "I Got
You Babe." Dressed identically in cutoff jeans covered with flowers and
patches and glittering bikini tops, the pair hugged and groped each other
while singing ad-libbed lines like "You don't need a dick."[202]

Confronting the controversy of their relationship, Madonna proclaimed, "Don't believe those stories you hear about us." "BELIEVE
them!" insisted Bernhard. That night, at the hip Vietnamese restaurant
Indochine, in front of 330 guests—including Billy Joel, Calvin Klein,
and Iman—Sandra made further pronouncements. "Madonna and I have
a heart-and-soul friendship," she explained. "What do you care more
about, the rain forest or our sexuality?"[203]

The controversy continued to brew. Only a month before, Sandra
appeared in London at the annual Prince's Trust Concert. In front of a
sold-out crowd that included Prince Charles and Princess Diana, Sandra
performed her rendition of Billy Paul's hit song "Me & Mrs. Jones (We've
Got a Thing Goin' On)," which she dedicated to Madonna.[204] The *London
Standard* newspaper referred to her performance as "a lesbian version"
of the song. When the program aired on television, the song was deleted
from the telecast.

Regardless of the details of the friendship between the two women,
they were having a great time in each other's company. Sandra wasn't
in awe of Madonna's superstar status, and they both felt as though they

hair down with each other. In October, when butch-
in country singer k.d. Lang was presented in concert at
eater in Los Angeles, Madonna, Sandra, and Jennifer
and to cheer her on. When the trio went backstage to
meet the mannishly tailored girl whose voice is likened to that of Patsy
Cline, Madonna posed for press photographers and shared her lipstick
with k.d. For Madonna it was just another night out with the girls, but
for the press it was another event to inspire sexual conjecture about
Madonna and Sandra.

When the speculation about their relationship created too much
heat for Sandra, that fall she announced, "We're friends and that's it.
. . . The press can't just be happy that two cool girls like us are tight
buddies—like no competition, no bitchiness, except that mock stuff we
put on, kind of like Martin and Lewis. By the way—did anyone ever
accuse Dean and Jerry of getting it on?"[205]

The ongoing rumor that they were lovers gained more attention
than any denial would. When she was promoting her *Truth or Dare*
film in 1991, Madonna addressed the issue. She neither denied or
admitted to an affair with Sandra; however, she just magnified the
confusion.

"Whether I slept with her or not is irrelevant," said Madonna. "I'm
perfectly willing to have people think that I did. You know, I do not
want to protest too much. I don't care. If it makes people feel better to
think that I slept with her, then they can think it. And if it makes them
feel safer to think that I didn't, than that's fine, too. You know, I'd
almost rather they thought that I did. Just so they could know that here
was this girl that everyone was buying records of, and she was eating
someone's pussy. So there."[206]

While production on *Dick Tracy* progressed, Madonna released
three more hit singles: "Express Yourself," "Cherish, " and "Oh Father."
Only the last failed to reach the Top Ten. At a reported $1 million in
production costs, the "Express Yourself" video had the distinction of
being the most expensive promotional rock video ever produced.

Directed by David Fincher, "Express Yourself" is one of the sleek-
est, sexiest, and most fascinating of Madonna's videos. Shamelessly
stealing from the look and plot of the classic 1926 fantasy film *Metropolis*,
it shows Madonna living in a high-rise tower, while the poor—and

incredibly muscular—toil below ground in a damp world of machines. The blonde, sexy Madonna—in her man's suit and monocle—decides to go slumming.

Doing an exotic dance in which she flashes her breasts and grabs her crotch, Madonna visits the underground area. In another scene, which doesn't seem to relate, Madonna is seen with a collar around her neck, chained to a bed. As though hearing Madonna's mating call, one of the underground hunks comes up to Madonna's tower to find her naked and waiting. In the scenes in between Madonna is seen slinking across the floor of her apartment like a cat. Dressed in a sexy black slip she laps milk from a dish on the floor, then pours the milk down herself so that it can be lapped off her body. The stud who she summons from the depths of the working-class quarters is male model Cameron. The video debuted to much acclaim by her eager fans in May 1989.

The video for "Cherish," which premiered in August, was directed by Madonna's friend and photographer, Herb Ritts. Shot in black and white, it depicts Madonna in a short dirty-blonde haircut rollicking on the beach, in the waves. In the lightly plotted video, Madonna falls in love with a half-fish merman and plays on the beach with a merchild.

Her next single and video in America was for "Oh Father." Also shot in black and white, this autobiographical adaptation of Madonna's childhood brings a haunting song to life. An actress plays childhood Madonna, rollicking in the snow, carefree, while her mother dies. In a snowstorm on a hillside in a soundstage, Madonna sings the song as the narrator of the flashback. The graveyard scenes, and shots of her mother's corpse with her mouth visibly sewn shut, were a bit macabre.

Explaining the source of the painful imagery in this video, Madonna says, "I have not resolved my Electra Complex. The end of the 'Oh Father' video, where I'm dancing on my mother's grave, is an attempt to embrace and accept my mother's death."[99]

In England, the song "Dear Jesse" was pulled from the *Like a Prayer* album as a single. It was accompanied by a cartoon video that depicted the pink elephants and pink lemonade of which the whimsical song's lyrics speak.

While these songs were playing on the Top Ten music charts of the world, Madonna was busily working on her next film role, that of Breathless Mahoney in *Dick Tracy*. Playing the role of the gun moll– chanteuse was so perfectly suited to her that she accepted union scale pay for the job—a paltry $1,440 a week. It was a bit of a comedown, but for the privilege of joining the cast of a film that would co-star her with Warren Beatty, Al Pacino, Dustin Hoffman, and James Caan, it was a bargain.

Speaking of films, whatever happened to *Bloodhounds of Broadway*? After Howard Brookner died of AIDS in mid-1989, it ended up being screened on a limited basis that fall and was quietly released as a video cassette that winter, when the producers, American Playhouse, couldn't find a distributor.

Although it had a stylish look and had an interesting cast, the film is quite dull to watch. Based on four of Damon Runyon's stories, there wasn't enough combined action on the screen to keep the film going. It was a shame, because the low-budget film had several strong perfor- mances. Madonna's portrayal of the gold-digging Hortense Hathaway was her most subdued and focused film role up till then. However, Madonna and the rest of the talented cast soon sink in the quicksand of a plodding story that never really inspires much interest.

Without the benefit of a premiere, reviews, or a theatrical screen run, at least Madonna escaped the undue bad publicity she surely would have gleaned. In the film, Madonna is seen performing three songs with Jennifer Grey, including "Big Bucks" and "I Surrender, Dear." In one scene Madonna turns to Randy Quaid after one of her nightclub musical scenes and asks, "Was I terrible?" No, she wasn't, but she should have thought out her participation in this film a little further before accepting it. The film is dedicated to Howard Brookner's memory, and he is seen in a cameo as Daffy Jack.

As 1989 ended, it was time for the media to survey the hits, the trends, and the newsmakers of the eighties. Needless to say, Madonna's name was on everyone's list. She was one of *People* magazine's "20 Who Defined the Decade." She was one of *Time*'s ten "Faces of the Decade." However, her greatest honor came when *Musician* magazine crowned her the "Artist of the Decade."

One of Madonna's most amusing honors came from writer Ann Powers in the *San Francisco Weekly*, who saluted her by announcing,

"What other major female pop star has the guts to date a woman in public (k.d. Lang sure doesn't, nor does [Tracy] Chapman)."[207]

Madonna provided the decade with seventeen Top Ten hits, had its most outrageous celebrity wedding and its most headline-grabbing divorce. She startled the public by dating both another woman and Warren Beatty. She was the queen of the nouveau art of the music video, and her ever-changing fashions set trends. Madonna was the most outlandish, the most written about woman of the entire decade. And she had already begun plotting her next multimedia assault.

Twelve

Whose side are you on?

Leave

—Warren Beatty as Dick Tracy

'Em

The side I'm always on—mine.[208]

Breathless

—Madonna as Breathless Mahoney

With the exception of *Desperately Seeking Susan*, the movie roles that Madonna chose to play in the eighties represent a hodge-podge of ill-chosen vehicles that ran the gamut from bad to worse. With *Shanghai Surprise, Who's That Girl?*, and *Bloodhounds of Broadway*, she had been searching for a wide-screen role that would not only give her the acting experience she desperately sought, but illuminate her strong points and enhance the persona the public adored on record and video. Totaled up, her on-the-job training cost producers millions of dollars, and the end results were less than what one would expect in an average summer stock theater production.

It is fascinating to look at her strongest videos—"Like a Prayer," "Papa Don't Preach," "Open Your Heart," and "Express Yourself"—

because each one of these proves that she can indeed act, project, and emote on camera. Yet the minute she opens her mouth to deliver straight dialogue on film, she falls flat on her face. How ironic that she seems to be facing the same dilemma that several silent film stars faced when talking pictures took over the movie business in 1929—an inability to deliver simple dialogue convincingly on screen.

When she worked with Griffin Dunne on *Who's That Girl?*, he was amazed that Madonna would insist that her first take was the best one, and that she would often refuse to repeat a scene. By accepting a role in a film directed by Warren Beatty—a director obsessed with filming every scene twenty to thirty times—she found herself in a position where someone else was in control, someone who was destined to draw out of her a believable screen performance regardless of the cost.

It was fortunate for her that the role of Breathless Mahoney was that of a comic strip vamp. She had only to keep in mind the role of Jessica Rabbit in *Who Framed Roger Rabbit?* and she would be all set.

The idea of doing a movie adaptation of the comic strip *Dick Tracy* had been kicking around for quite some time. It was a role that Warren Beatty had been linked with in the late seventies, and along the line a host of directors—including Martin Scorsese, Walter Hill, John Landis, and Bob Fosse—had bandied it about. Warren acquired the rights to the film in 1985 and began shopping it around to the studios. In 1988, when word of the upcoming production of *Batman* was on everyone's lips, Disney Pictures gave Beatty the green light to produce it on a $25 million budget. He not only decided to produce and star in the film, but to direct as well.

In the summer of 1988 Warren assembled a trio of film artisans, all recognized in their fields: production designer Richard Sylbert, costumer Milena Canonero, and cameraman Vittorio Storaro. Their first meeting to discuss the project was held at Warren's house high in the Hollywood hills. Tossing around ideas, Sylbert suggested two possible stars to play the role of the gold-digging Breathless Mahoney—Melanie Griffith and Madonna.

"Everybody said I would be perfect for the role," Madonna recalls of the buzz around Hollywood when the production was announced. "I waited and waited for Warren to call me. He never did. Finally, I decided to be pushy and called him. It took him a year to make up his mind."[209]

One of the first things they discussed was Madonna's disastrous box office track record. He told her that she had made a lot of stupid choices in movie roles.

Beatty, too, was trying to forget his disastrous last picture, *Ishtar*. It could play as a double feature with *Shanghai Surprise* and be billed as "A Night of Cinematic Torture." Both Madonna and Beatty were in a position where they could use a box office hit.

Finally Warren decided to give Madonna the part. With his Casanova reputation for igniting off-camera affairs with his leading ladies, the mere idea of working with suave and handsome Beatty was an intoxicating offer for Madonna. It was no wonder that she fell for him like a ton of bricks.

Madonna knew what she liked, and Warren knew what he wanted. According to her, "Warren insisted that I get fatter. He wanted to pour me into my dresses. I gained ten pounds. So much depends on the look. It's so stylized. I had to bleach my hair blonde again, pluck my eyebrows. It was traumatic to get the hair right. Hair is the most important thing to Warren. He would walk around me like a vulture, making me feel like the ugliest thing in the world. And the dresses! We were at Western Costume, and he'd say, 'Tighter, tighter, cut it down lower.' I felt like a mannequin, a slab of beef. I was treated that way on the set—the lust factor."[209]

While the actual comic strip character of Breathless Mahoney looked like 1940s actress Veronica Lake—of the shoulder-length peek-a-boo hair—Madonna's look was a unique incarnation of the vamp. Says costumer Canonero, "At the beginning of the movie, Breathless is wild, rebellious, untamable, a panther and a man-eater. In our story, she mellows down, acquiring a sort of purity like a moonbeam. That's what I tried to do with her clothes. My favorite is her blue dress with the moon and the stars. It's got everything—dreaming, sex, and dreams that don't come true."[210]

Her costumes were indeed form-fitting, and in many instances they were exceedingly low-cut—so low-cut that a couple of her dresses nearly had to be glued to her breasts. In one of Madonna's nightclub sequences, every time she raised her arms above her head, her breasts popped out of her dress. This was a matter that even had experts pondering the weighty issue of what glue to use. John Caglione, Jr., one of the many makeup men on the movie, said, "Look, Madonna must have the most valuable bust in the business. I'll bet each one of those honeys is worth six, maybe seven million. What if she has an allergic reaction to the glue?"[211] Finally, some adjustments were made to the dress, and the idea of glue was abandoned.

Another important aspect of having Madonna in the film was Beatty's decision to have her sing in it as well. The juxtaposition of having Madonna sing three Stephen Sondheim songs was one of the cleverest touches. Warren felt that the combination of Madonna with Sondheim was not only unexpected but it brought a fresh dimension to both of them.

When Madonna first received Sondheim's songs she wasn't used to his sense of rhyme and his wordy lyrics. "They're quite difficult," she announced before recording them.[11] The Sondheim songs captured the 1930s era the film was set in and were especially believable for both characters, Madonna and Breathless.

When filming began in February 1989, one-take Madonna had to comply with Warren's obsessive attention for details. One of her scenes as Breathless performing at the Club Ritz had to be shot over and over to get the right movement when she turns around and kisses her own shoulder. Another scene with take after take was one in which Al Pacino as Big Boy Caprice is rehearsing Breathless and the club chorines in a late-night session.

From the very beginning, the idea of Madonna and Warren Beatty having an affair sounded like a press release made in heaven. This was definitely the height of Madonna's "useful boyfriend" penchant. Since Sean Penn was now out of the picture, she clearly needed to align herself with an even more successful man. Throughout the year that they were an item, the whole affair was a gossip columnist's dream. "Madonna and Warren" sightings were published almost weekly, with Liz Smith, Suzy, and Cindy Adams all scrambling to "scoop" each other: Madonna and Warren spotted dining on lemon tagliarini at Hollywood's chic Columbia Bar & Grill; Madonna and Warren seen dancing at The Daisy in Beverly Hills; and on and on.

However, as famous as Warren Beatty is for having affairs with his leading ladies, Madonna is equally famous for living her entire life in front of a camera. Warren probably had no idea what he was ultimately bargaining for. One of the most telling scenes in Madonna's autobiographical *Truth or Dare* is the one in which Warren questions her obsession with living every moment on video. This clearly irritated him. Madonna's making public every detail of her affair with Warren reached a new height when she was asked by one interviewer about the size of Warren's penis. "I haven't measured it," she replied candidly, "but it's a perfectly wonderful size."[206]

The funniest thing about the whole Madonna and Warren affair was its rapid demise immediately after *Dick Tracy* was released. It was almost as if it was just a convenient fling for both of them. However, throughout 1989 they were almost inseparable. Madonna had just dumped the childishly volatile Sean, so what she needed in her life was a real man. For the time being, Warren Beatty perfectly filled the bill as her knight in shining armor.

The romance was also a great distraction from her career, because the whole Pepsi scandal was exploding while she was in production with *Dick Tracy*. In March 1991, when she launched her *Like a Prayer* album at a gala party Warner Records threw for her, Beatty was among the well-wishers on hand. Fame loves fame, and there is nothing like a superstar couple to magnify and intensify both stars' incandescence. The spotlight that was fixed on Madonna was just growing brighter and brighter and she loved it.

"I learned a lot working with Warren Beatty, who really knows the business," claimed Madonna. She was also confident about the on-camera results: "It's the biggest role I've had in terms of what I was asked to do, and how important my character is."[212]

Months before the June 1990 release of *Dick Tracy*, Walt Disney Pictures began plotting the $10 million campaign to publicize the film. Disney chairman Jeffrey Katzenberg was busy waging a war of the faxes with his friend Don Simpson, producer of *Days of Thunder*. Simpson sent Katzenberg a fax that read, "Wherever you go, you won't escape the *Thunder*." Katzenberg grabbed a pen and faxed back the reply, "Wait till you see how big my *Dick* is!"[23]

Media manipulator extraordinaire Madonna was already busy mounting her own multimedia assault to coincide with the release of *Dick Tracy*. The Pepsi-sponsored concert tour of 1989 had been aborted, and a more elaborately plotted tour was aimed at the summer of 1990.

The first year of the nineties was truly the summer of Madonna. Her sound, her image, her likeness were everywhere.

When *Batman* became the summer hit film of 1989, it was accompanied by two separate soundtrack albums. The biggest seller was the *Batman* album by Prince, which was composed of music he had written and recorded for that film, plus several cuts inspired by it that never found their way into the actual movie. The original score album, which was the instrumental and orchestral soundtrack, was composed and recorded by Danny Elfman.

The soundtrack of Beatty's *Dick Tracy* upped the ante with three separate album releases. Since Madonna was involved in the project, Sire Records president Seymour Stein was brought in as a music consultant. Warren's idea was to fill the soundtrack of his film with songs and music that were fresh and new, yet sounded as if they were from the 1930s. Stein turned to singer/songwriter Andy Paley to begin writing, producing, and supervising the recording of over a dozen songs that would evoke the era.

Paley consulted with Beatty, who described the kind of songs he envisioned. Paley immediately went to work and submitted the songs to Warren and Madonna. The song that most impressed Madonna was one called "Now I'm Following You." Madonna ended up recording it as a duet with Warren Beatty. Unfortunately, the song isn't heard in the film, because Warren felt that it would be uncharacteristic for the stoic Dick Tracy to suddenly burst into song. The version that made it into the film is the version recorded by Paley himself.

The songs that Paley wrote and/or supervised the writing of were recorded with an all-star cast. Paley chose several of his all-time favorite singers, including Brenda Lee, Darlene Love, Jerry Lee Lewis, and LaVern Baker, and gave them each a cut on the soundtrack album. He also turned to several contemporary artists, including k.d. Lang, Take 6, August (Kid Creole) Darnell, Al Jarreau, and rapper Ice-T, and took them into the studio. All of Paley's songs ended up on the *Dick Tracy* album, although only half of them actually ended up in the film.

For the orchestral album, Warren tapped *Batman* composer Danny Elfman to score the *Dick Tracy* action scenes and incidental music. This music is found on the album *Dick Tracy: The Original Score*.

Meanwhile, Madonna came up with her own album called *I'm*

Breathless. It included the three songs that Stephen Sondheim wrote for her character, which appeared in the film, in addition to two of Andy Paley's songs: "Now I'm Following You" and "I'm Going Bananas." She then wrote five songs with Pat Leonard that were based on the characters and ambiance that the film inspired. "He's a Man" was written as though sung by Breathless and dedicated to Tracy, and "Hanky Panky" was an outgrowth of a line Madonna delivers to Beatty in the film: "You don't know whether to hit me or kiss me."[208] The song is about being sexually aroused by having one's behind spanked.

The very idea of sexually explicit Madonna doing a film for squeaky-clean Walt Disney Pictures is something of a stretch of the imagination. Although the character of Breathless Mahoney absolutely exudes sex, Madonna found herself battling the Disney censors. They managed to talk her out of a couple of explicit S&M lyrics in the song "Hanky Panky," although she did manage to get a couple of "dick" jokes into her ad-libbed version of the song "Now I'm Following You (Part II)"— which did not appear in the movie.

The biggest song from Madonna's *I'm Breathless* album is one which not only did not appear in the movie, but had nothing at all to do with *Dick Tracy*. That song was "Vogue."

While Madonna was still pulling singles off her *Like a Prayer* album, she was working with dance remix producer Shep Pettibone. Shep had remixed "Into the Groove" for Madonna's *You Can Dance* album, and in the fall of 1989 the pair made their first stab at collaborating. While they were originally trying to come up with a B-side for one of her singles, what they ended up with was Madonna's next Number One international hit. Explaining the unexpected success of "Vogue," Pettibone recalls that he and Madonna were just trying to create a fun dance record. However, when the record company executives heard it they recognized that it was a Number One smash record and insisted that it become Madonna's next single release.

With lyrics mentioning Greta Garbo, Jean Harlow, and Bette Davis, the song qualified for the 1930s theme of the *Dick Tracy* project, which is how it ended up being the instant smash that launched the *I'm Breathless* album.

Vogueing is sometimes misconstrued as a mere dance floor move, characterized by lightning-fast arm movements around the face. It is in actuality the result of a whole New York City fantasy trip. In the mid-eighties groups of predominantly black and Hispanic drag queens got together for vogueing balls or events in which they would simulate the actions of runway models. The hand motions and spins were meant to mimic the demonstrative poses of high-fashion models, such as those on the cover of *Vogue* magazine—hence the name.

Groups of voguers compete with each other for the top prizes at vogueing events. They copy the pretentiousness of real-life fashion "houses," as in the "House of Chanel," the "House of Cassini." The drag versions would be outlandish things like the "House of Extravaganza," and the "House of Swatch." The whole vogueing phenomenon was ultimately captured on film in the hit documentary *Paris Is Burning*.

Although it was more of an uptown New York "in"-joke than anything else, Madonna took vogueing and its whole "strike a pose" attitude to the masses. When the single was Number One in America, only a tiny segment of the record-buying public realized that Madonna was giving a nod to a bunch of drag queens in Harlem. As usual, she had the last laugh when the single shot to the top of the charts.

With an album in the works, and her role in *Dick Tracy* finished, Madonna was on to the next layer of her marketing scheme for 1990: the concert tour. The tour had been in the planning stages since September 1989. This time around Madonna was determined to go all the way with sets, costumes, and outrageousness.

In January 1990 she placed a two-by-four-inch classified ad in the Auditions section of *Daily Variety*. Headlined MADONNA WORLD TOUR 1990, the casting call read: "Open Audition for FIERCE Male Dancers who know the meaning of TROOP STYLE, BEAT BOY and VOGUE. Wimps and Wanna-Be's need not apply."[213]

Two of her dancers, Jose Guitierez and Luis Camacho, she discovered on an evening nightclubbing in New York. "I went to the Sound Factory with my girlfriend Debi M. because I wanted to go dancing," Madonna explains. "At the time I was trying to visualize things for my show, and I was hanging around a lot of clubs—watching different styles, looking for dancers."[206]

They spotted a group of dancers who were part of the vogueing group House of Extravaganza. She immediately found herself blown away by the dancers, especially two of them: Luis and Jose. She approached them and set up an audition. When they really let loose at the audition, she hired Luis and Jose on the spot for her upcoming concert tour.

At this point, Madonna's friend Karole Armitage was set to choreograph the show. Present at the dancer's auditions at Landmark Studios in Hollywood were Madonna, Armitage, and Shabba Doo, who had choreographed her last tour. Madonna wore strategically torn jeans' and a black top, and she snacked on vegetarian health food chips.

The dancers auditioned in groups of ten, and they danced to a hot remixed dance version of "Keep It Together." She shouted at one group of dancers, "Sexy, we want to see sexy!" When one of the dancers showed up with a bandanna and a cap, Madonna shouted, "Get that stuff off and take that bandanna off. That shit went out in the sixties. I don't care what Axl Rose is doing!"[214]

Not long after the rest of the dancers were cast, Madonna had a change of heart about using Armitage as her choreographer, and replaced her with Vincent Paterson. Apparently Karole's vision of the show's choreography conflicted with Madonna's. According to Armitage, there was no room for her own thoughts and ideas, so Madonna fired her.

When contacted for the job, Paterson claims, "Madonna told me to break every rule I could think of, and then when I was done to make up some new ones and break them." With that they began staging the show. According to him, "This is Madonna's every fantasy come true. It's one hallucination after another—a combination of rock and roll, theater, and Broadway. It's a real mixed animal."[215]

She gave similar rule-breaking instructions to the tour's costume designer, Jean-Paul Gaultier. "We all have feminine and masculine aspects to our personalities, it's a reflection of reality," claims Gaultier of his perception of life and its effect on his fashions. Madonna sketched out some of her ideas herself, and sent them to Gaultier in Paris. "A tough outer shell at times protects hidden vulnerability," Jean-Paul said, explaining the costumes with the sensational metallic cone breasts he devised for the tour.[216]

In addition to Gaultier's revolutionary costumes, Madonna's friend Marlene Stewart was also responsible for costumes used on the tour—particularly the marabou-trimmed dance hall outfits used in the "Hanky Panky" number, and the bathrobes used for "Material Girl." Since this show was to have several settings and themes, Madonna felt that she needed some contrasting looks for the show.

Madonna's younger brother, Christopher Ciccone, served as the production's art director. Together they came up with the concepts behind the sets. Sending sketches back and forth from New York and Los Angeles, they collaborated. "We disagreed on a lot of things, but she trusts me," he explains. "The audience looks at what she might be sitting on, or rubbing up against, or where her hand might be. The set enhances her."[217]

The hairstyle that Madonna sported for the Japanese and most of the American leg of the tour was reminiscent of the one worn by actress Barbara Eden when she starred in the sixties TV show "I Dream of Jeannie." Her hair was pulled up into a topknot and a hairpiece crown of braids was affixed with bobby pins. From that crown of braids, a two-foot-long blonde switch descended down her back. It took a long time to devise a way of securing the hairpieces to Madonna's head so that the cascading ponytail wouldn't go flying into the first row of the audience when she danced. The exotic nouveau/retro style was created for Madonna by Joanne Gair and Sharon Gault of the Cloutier Agency. It took forty-five minutes each night to put together.

All the elements of the show pivoted around Madonna herself. She had already imposed her musical sensibilities on the world; she had created fashion trends again and again; now she wanted to change the way the world looked at human sexuality. According to choreographer Paterson, "She wanted to make statements about sexuality, cross-sexuality, the church, and the like. But the biggest thing we tried to do is change the shape of concerts."[218]

If she was indeed going to spend the summer as the cross-sexual multimedia goddess, then Madonna also wanted to reshape and tone up herself. While in rehearsal for the tour, and during the tour, Madonna employed her longtime physical trainer, Rob Parr, whom she has worked with since February 1987. By the time the tour kicked off in May 1990, she was toned up and in the best physical shape of her entire career.

"This transformation is not an overnight thing," Parr explained when the tour hit Los Angeles. "Madonna realized how important her health and fitness are to her performances. She knows how she wants to look and she works hard at it. Our workouts are very focused."[219]

On tour Parr and Madonna go through a two-and-a-half to three-hour workout that begins with an hour-long running session, followed by a half-hour session on a Lifecycle or a Versaclimber, a mountain-climbing device. Next comes a cool-down of running on stairs. The workout also includes sit-ups for a flat stomach and some pike-position lifts. The last fifteen minutes is spent stretching for muscle tone.

With her show shaping up, and her projects set to be released in a progressive order, the onslaught of Madonna's media blitz began. In March 1990, the single of "Vogue" was released. The week of May 19 it became her eighth Number One single, making her the solo female singer with the most chart-toppers in music history. That same week, the Australian single with "Keep It Together" as the A-side and "Vogue" as the B-side was Number One in that country.

Simultaneously, MTV began playing Madonna's "Vogue" video. Shot in black and white, it co-starred the seven dancers and two female background singers who were going to tour with her that summer. Madonna looks like a cross between Jean Harlow, Lana Turner, and Marilyn Monroe in the incredibly made-up and lit close-up shots. With her troupe, the video proved a glamorous outing before the camera for Madonna.

The following week, on May 22, the *I'm Breathless* album hit the stores, and based in part on the single "Vogue," sold like hotcakes. On June 15, the stakes heated up even further with the national release of *Dick Tracy*. Suddenly Madonna was everywhere again. Madonna and Warren were not only on the cover of every major entertainment and news magazine, they were also in toy stores—thanks to Breathless and Tracy dolls, stickers, buttons, and comic books.

Amid all this activity and brilliantly marketed cross-pollinating products, the "Blonde Ambition" tour had begun in Tokyo on April 13. While in Japan Madonna played nine sold-out dates in three cities.

Madonna was really proud of this show, and she flew her old dance teacher Christopher Flynn over to Japan so he could see her show in full production. Flynn then returned to Los Angeles, where on April 22 he presided over the second annual AIDS "Dance-A-Thon," while his star pupil continued her tour.

On the third date at Chiba Marine Stadium, near Tokyo, it poured rain. Officials urged Madonna to cancel the show, but when she got a look at the audience of thirty thousand people—willing to weather the rain to see her show—she decided to carry on as planned. The newspaper *Sports Nippon* called her the "Goddess of the '90s." With her cone-breasted costumes and vogueing dancers, she was a huge hit in Japan.

On May 1, Madonna appeared on a highly publicized episode of the "Arsenio Hall" TV show. In the beginning of the show, instead of Arsenio making the rounds of his studio audience shaking hands and waving, Madonna barreled past him and uncharacteristically wandered through the applauding crowd with an enthusiastic smile on her face. She was there to announce the opening of her North American concert dates and to stir up some controversy.

Dressed in a tailored white suit, she discussed Warren, "Vogue," *Dick Tracy*, Sandra, and the things she does for "shock value." Around her neck she wore a thick gold chain, and from it dangled a large $ which ultimately represented what she was destined to cultivate in bushel baskets that summer.

She was relaxed, candid, and, as usual, outspoken. In the song "Vogue," Madonna sings that Rita Hayworth "gives good face." When Arsenio asked her the meaning of that phrase, a nonplussed Madonna replied, "Well, it's not exactly like giving good head."[220]

He also asked her about the song "Hanky Panky" from the forthcoming *I'm Breathless* album. "It's about a girl who likes a good spanky," she explained in a titillating fashion.[220] According to her, she personally likes to get spanked only so it stings. They also discussed other body parts—especially breasts. Both Arsenio and Madonna expressed their opinions about LaToya Jackson's obvious breast implants. This sparked a conversation about the Jean-Paul Gaultier superhuman cone breasts she wore in the "Vogue" video, and how she has her male dancers wearing them in her concert.

Arsenio couldn't wait to delve into the subject of Madonna's affair with the notorious bachelor Warren Beatty. When he pointed out that Joan Collins once described Beatty as "insatiable," Madonna let him know that when he was with her, he indeed was "satiable."

Just to let Hall know that he wasn't the only one on the set who could zing embarrassing questions at one of his guests, Madonna pulled a similar stunt. When Arsenio got too personal with his Warren questions, Madonna asked him how it felt to have Paula Abdul dump him for John Stamos.

Digging deeper into personal controversies, they also bantered back and forth about the same-sex rumors about both of them. When he began pressuring her about Sandra Bernhard, Madonna inquired bluntly about Arsenio's friendship with Eddie Murphy, which erupted into a verbal match that had both of them giggling. Describing her table-turning ploys, Madonna announced at one point, "I knew you were getting in the direction of getting into my shit, so I thought I'd turn it around."[220]

It was a provocative interview, and ultimately no real bombshells or revelations were expounded upon, but it was certainly one of the most lively interviews she had given. It was much more interesting than the interview she gave to Kurt Loder of MTV, which was dubbed "Breakfast with Madonna." Taped early in the morning of April 14 in Tokyo, Loder is too polite an interviewer to be controversial, and toward the end of it Madonna looked as if she wanted to get hold of a pair of toothpicks to prop her eyelids open.

What the general public wasn't aware of at the time was that Madonna was simultaneously concocting the most in-depth look at her life and her celebrityhood ever released. She had employed the services of cinematographer-director Alek Keshishian, who had begun capturing every move Madonna made on this tour, beginning in Tokyo. It would ultimately become the 1991 documentary film *Truth or Dare*.

Meanwhile, on May 4, Madonna kicked off the North American leg of her Blonde Ambition concert tour in Houston. It was the most talked about, most highly praised, and most exotic/erotic concert event of the summer. Its content and concept were exciting from the opening notes of the first number.

Blonde Ambition as a show was provocative in its look, its sound, its "express yourself" message, and its dare-to-be-different themes. The sets, the props, and the star were unlike anything that had come before in a rock and roll arena.

If you were not seated in the audience for one of the Blonde Ambition shows during the summer of 1990, this is how the show unfolded: The eighteen-song, 105-minute concert opens with a mechanical set that simulates the underground world of *Metropolis*, as seen in Madonna's

"Express Yourself" video. Huge gears turn and a central staircase slowly rises from the floor of the stage while seven male dancers position themselves like workers in the mechanized fantasy world.

Slowly, from the center of the stage, Madonna rises on a platform that lands her at the top of the staircase, where she begins the "dance and sing" chorus from "Everybody." Suddenly the percussive music of "Express Yourself" erupts. Madonna is wearing the tailored Gaultier suit that the pair devised. It is tightly molded to her body, with huge slits from the shoulder that expose the pointy cone-breasted costume underneath. Around her neck is a monocle on a chain, and from underneath the front of the jacket, two garter straps dangle downward. She is joined onstage by her two background singers Niki Harris and Donna Delory in similar suits, *sans* breast slits.

When Madonna strips away her jacket, she reveals the armorlike garment that caused the most commotion on this tour, the pointy breasted, one-piece bathing suit outfit (constructed of a satiny material, it is mischaracterized in many descriptions as metal; its shininess only makes it look that way). Doing push-ups over dancer Slam (Sallim Gauwloos), Madonna lets the audience know that she is the liberated strong figure, and that the men are slaves in emotional shackles.

While dancer Oliver Crumes dances in a spangled see-through top on an upper platform, Madonna sings and dances with her *Blue Angel*–inspired chair while singing "Open Your Heart." For the next number, Madonna is rejoined by the girls and, with a jacket to modify her pointy breasted outfit, they perform "Causing a Commotion." The crotch-thrusting choreography continues the Madonna-as-dominatrix theme, as she boxes, wrestles, and is victorious over the girls. "What is this shit? I'm the fucking boss around here," Madonna shouts at the girls when they begin to dance out of step with her moves.[221] The number is a tightly choreographed song with a women's wrestling theme. At one point she hurls the girls to the ground and mockingly kicks them in the stomach—reminiscent of the way Bette Davis kicked Joan Crawford around in *Whatever Happened to Baby Jane?*

Dancing her ass off, Madonna swings into "Where's the Party?" utilizing the same stage set, where she is joined by her dancers. While the dancers continue onstage, she rushes backstage for a costume change.

When she returns onstage, her entrance is from underneath the stage. Slowly a set rises up with Madonna on a red velvet bed. On either side of the bed are two male dancers with Egyptian slave caps on their heads and pointy, velvet brassieres on their chests. Madonna likewise is dressed in one of the Gaultier pointy-breast costumes. On this set she performs a Middle Eastern sounding slowed-down version of "Like a Virgin." Writhing around on the bed, toward the end of the number, Madonna begins stroking her thighs and ends up simulating masturbation.

After humping the bed in a frenetic orgasm, the Catholic guilt aspect comes into play. A backdrop rises to expose a wall of church votive candles, Madonna says the one word, "God?" and suddenly the music for "Like a Prayer" begins. The bed disappears, and suddenly she is in church. In the light of the flickering votive candles, Madonna's dancers change her outfit to a long, black, hooded cloak. With her troupe all clad in black, she dances and sings her way through a stylized revival meeting number.

↪ Left alone on the stage, Madonna spins around while a stained-glass "rose" window depicting a saint with a halo and a confessional kneeling platform descend to the stage. There she performs "Live to Tell" and dances with Carlton Wilborn. Rejoined by four more members of her male dancing troupe, she performs "Papa Don't Preach."

After that song a curtain drops, and Madonna makes her next stage entrance from below the stage as well. Rising up this time, she is atop a black grand piano, as Breathless Mahoney. Singing "Sooner or Later" while Kevin Kendricks plays keyboards, she has gone from sinner to vamp. For this number she is wearing a slitted black Gaultier jacket, from which her breasts protrude. Underneath the black jacket with a floor-length tail she is wearing a pointy lime-green spangled and striped one-piece bathing suit—shaped creation.

Removing the black jacket, she teases the audience with her naughty, kinky "Hanky Panky." Rejoined by Donna and Niki, she turns the song into a burlesque number. During the song, Slam, dressed in a yellow Burberry raincoat and yellow fedora, wanders on-stage as Dick Tracy. The girls vamp with him as they finish the number. Amid Madonna's on-stage patter with Slam/Dick, he pulls out a phonograph record, and she hands it to her keyboard player and asks him to play it for

her. With that, Madonna and Slam pantomime the Warren Beatty–
Madonna duet version of "Now I'm Following You." This is the biggest
section of the show not featuring live vocals, and it is set up in such an
obvious way that it is clear that Madonna does not sing live. The other
spots where non-live vocals are used were in moments of set transitions
and costume changes.

The number ends with a chorus line of nine Dick Tracys in yellow
raincoats and hats finishing up the song (including the five aforemen-
tioned dancers plus Gabriel Trupin and Kevin A. Stea). While the Tracy
kick line continues, Madonna rushes offstage for her next costume
change. The Tracy number obviously plugs the movie, Madonna's next
record, and the millions of dollars in *Dick Tracy* merchandise flooding
the marketplace that summer.

Madonna's next number lampoons her glamorous image. Together
with Donna and Niki, Madonna is seen in bathrobes and hair curlers
singing "Material Girl." The girls strip off the robes and curler-covered
wigs and descend the lighted staircases that sweep down at either side
of the stage. From underneath the stage, three of her dancers as mermen
with tails appear, and Madonna sings "Cherish," in a re-creation of the
video of the same name.

Dressed in marabou-fringed costumes, Madonna and her girls go
into a very streetlike sex-talk sequence. When three male dancers in
black leather jackets strut onstage, Madonna, Donna, and Niki say in
unison, "You wanna fuck us?" To the audience Madonna then says,
"You never really get to know a guy until you ask him to wear a rubber."
She continues her unabashed condom-sense talk: "Hey, you, don't be
silly, put a rubber on your willy."[221] With that they launch into "Into
the Groove."

The black and white "Vogue" dance is excellently done, with a
very Bob Fosse feeling to it. Madonna and her nine backup performers
work it to death, dressed in skintight bicycle pants, tank tops, and form-
fitting leggings. Madonna's black longline bra is the torpedo-titted fantasy
to end them all.

"Vogue" really brings down the house every night, and after it is
over, the cast takes a deep bow. This is the pre-encore ending of the
show, and it is met with thunderous applause. It is on this number that
it becomes really evident that you aren't watching a star and her players,

you are witnessing a family, a team, a close unit. It shows Madonna off as the captain of this team, but you can see that she is also a team player.

The curtain falls, and several seconds later it rises and the spotlight hits Madonna in a black and white polka dot bellbottomed outfit. She prances around the stage singing "Holiday" and is soon joined by her singers and dancers. They playfully dance the Bus Stop and sing an extensive version of "Holiday" together.

The troupe then leaves the stage to prepare for the last number. Dressed in *Clockwork Orange*–inspired black outfits—British bowler hats and roller-derby knee and elbow guards—Madonna and her troupe return and dance with chairs, similar to Liza Minnelli's showstopper in *Cabaret.* Madonna begins the finale with Sly and the Family Stone's "Family Affair." The acrobatic number segues into "Keep it Together." With a strap-on headset microphone, Madonna and her family of dancers deliver a number that the best show on Broadway could contain. "The family that plays together, stays together," she announces from the stage.[221]

At the time of the concert tour, it hadn't been announced that the entire troupe was going to be exposed on film. A year later, when the concert film/home movie *Truth or Dare,* was released, the world got an inside view of how closely intertwined Madonna and her troupe really were.

Along the way there were several mishaps and traumatic moments. When the tour rolled into Toronto, the local authorities received several phone calls from concerned parents and civic leaders that Madonna's act was too "obscene" for the general public. When it was suggested that she might tone down her masturbation scene for the show at Toronto's Skydome, her manager, Freddy DeMann, was among those who urged her to consider doing a tamer version of the show for the Canadian audiences. Madonna's comment to him was, "Freddy, I ain't changing my fucking act!"[222] And, she didn't.

The largest commotion came when Madonna took the show to Europe in July. Catholic leaders in Italy released statements calling her show "blasphemous." When the troupe arrived in Rome on July 9, Madonna found that the second night of her concert performance there had been canceled for poor ticket sales—stemming from the Catholic protests. She held a press conference to voice her opinion, claiming that she was not promoting a way of life, that her show merely mirrored life as it happened. Addressing the television cameras in Rome in a pair of sunglasses, Madonna proclaimed, "If you are sure I'm a sinner, then let he who has not sinned cast the first stone."[222]

On August 5, playing before a screaming, cheering, enthusiastic audience in the beautiful French seaside resort city of Nice, Madonna concluded her Blonde Ambition tour with a huge bang. The concert was presented to American audiences via HBO's cable network. Even from across the Atlantic Ocean, Madonna managed to zing it to her critics in America. Referring to Roseanne Barr's attention-getting rendition of "The Star Spangled Banner" earlier that week in the United States, which Barr had finished by grabbing her crotch, Madonna got on-stage in Nice and commented to an audience of millions, "Speaking of grabbing crotches—Roseanne Barr, baby, thumbs up! So, I say to America—get a fucking sense of humor. Spend your time worrying about . . . how many girls Warren Beatty has slept with. Now, that's important!"[223]

The telecast was a huge hit in America. When the TV ratings were announced, the special received a 21.5 rating and a 31 share of the viewing audience. Madonna's special beat out all network competition, becoming the highest rated non-sports event ever to be broadcast on the Home Box Office network.

Needless to say, not a single four-letter word nor a suggestive crotch-fondling gesture was eliminated for the cable television audience that night. In fact, there was a lot of prebroadcast publicity advising "parental discretion" before allowing children to watch Madonna and her noto-riously foul mouth. The only thing that had changed in her act was her hairstyle. The "I Dream of Jeannie" topknot and ponytail had been dropped in Europe for a short curly blonde hairdo.

Madonna's devoting such a large segment of her show to the *Dick Tracy* phenomenon was its most openly self-promoting cross-pollinating part—especially since she had her seven male dancers dressed as her current beau Warren Beatty dressed as Dick Tracy.

"Disney didn't come to me and ask me to help market the movie," she explained during the tour. "But I know I have a much bigger following than Warren does and a lot of my audience isn't even aware of who he is."[224]

With so many projects hitting the marketplace all at once, Madonna was gleaning favorable reviews right and left, regardless of what religious groups had to say. With regard to her show, the press—for her artistry and growth as a performer—was unanimously glowing. "The Blonde Ambition tour is a nifty summation of the spectacle that is Madonna . . . entertaining and provocative!" wrote Keith Cahoon in *Rolling Stone.* Edna Gundersen in *USA Today* called it an "extravagant collection of videos-come-to-life." And Robert Hilburn in the *Los Angeles Times* claimed, "the singer-actress-dancer doesn't simply rest on celebrity . . . there is an uplifting edge to her performance . . . her energy and accomplishments stand as symbols of the ability of one to make the most of one's opportunities and talents."

The next Madonna product to blast into the marketplace was the *I'm Breathless* album. This especially impressed critics who once thought of Madonna as a wonderful promoter but a spotty musician. Greg Sandow in *Entertainment Weekly* referred to *I'm Breathless* as "this naughty and triumphant album . . . with Madonna riding the crest of her fame, basking in the glow of an album ten times more accomplished than any record she has made before." Anne Ayers in *USA Today* called Madonna's latest incarnation on this album that of "a bright 'n' brassy Broadway Baby" and saluted her "lyrics that paint larger-than-life cartoon characters" amid "sophisticated pop, as compelling as the scenes unfolding in a Broadway hit." And, proclaiming the album as one of 1990's "ten best," *People* magazine called it a "soft, fluid, generously entertaining album."

Amazingly, Madonna had gone neck-and-neck with Stephen Sondheim, and they both emerged victorious. By singing his songs, Madonna had gained a sort of musical respectability that her previous songs had failed to generate, and by writing songs for her Sondheim had reached an audience who was previously unaware of the acknowledged master songwriter of Broadway.

Although the album—which sold millions of copies—only made it to Number Two in *Billboard,* it was an undisputed hit where it really counted: at the cash register. *Pulse!,* Tower Records' in-house magazine, tallied *I'm Breathless* as having hit the Number One spot the week it entered their charts. (Note: The only thing that blocked the album from Number One in *Billboard* was the summer-long reign of M.C. Hammer's *Please Hammer Don't Hurt 'Em.*)

Last but not least in this cross-pollinating promotional cavalcade of Madonna products came the film *Dick Tracy*. On one hand, it didn't do nearly as well at the box office as *Batman* had the summer before. But in terms of artistic success, cinematic brilliance, and in presenting Madonna as an actress, it was a huge success.

What impressed audiences and critics more than anything was the look of *Dick Tracy*. The art direction was nothing short of brilliant. Everything was done in colors more vibrant than those found in a box of crayons. The reds outcrimsoned them all, the yellow rivaled the ripest lemon, the green made the lushest rain forest look pale. Likewise, the performances were all over the top. Beatty as the stoic detective was more upright than even the Sunday funnies portrayed him. The villains were every bit as comically portrayed as their creator Chester Gould had drawn them. And, as Breathless Mahoney, the vamp who is torn between good and evil, Madonna was more seductively presented, more glamorously photographed, and more acid-witted than ever before. Her look exuded pure sex, and out of her mouth came one-liners that would have made Mae West proud.

On TV's "Good Morning America," Joel Siegel claimed, "This is Madonna's best work ever—she redefines the phrase 'blonde bombshell' for a whole new generation." In the *New York Times* Vincent Canby wrote, "Madonna does right by the songs, two of which, 'More' and 'Sooner or Later' are vintage Sondheim. They, in turn, give her the kind of class she's never shown on screen before." Mike Clark of *USA Today* claimed that "Madonna (Breathless Mahoney) steals *Dick Tracy* from lead Warren Beatty." Meanwhile, Siskel and Ebert, the TV critics, both gave the film "two thumbs up."

The film did have its detractors. In *Rolling Stone,* Peter Travers's review was headlined "A 'Dick' with No Kick." Calling the stylish film "a great big beautiful bore," he still questioned Madonna's abilities. "It's still hard to tell if Madonna is an actress, but she is a definite presence," he pondered, yet admitted, "Madonna exudes enough come-on carnality to singe the screen." David Denby in *New York* magazine was less kind when he said, "The movie is only about style, and that's why Madonna gets by. She's an element in the design . . . she's an awful actress, but she's adequate as a masochistic, two-dimensional floozy."

When the film opened it was an instant box office smash. It hit

Number One the first week it was released, becoming the largest-grossing opening in the history of Walt Disney Pictures. The press hype had caused an avalanche of curious moviegoers to rush to their local cinema to see what all the commotion was about. Although *Dick Tracy* held first place spot at the box office the next week, it did not go on to become as big as *Batman* had the previous summer.

Regardless, Madonna was at last seen as a viable Hollywood commodity. *Dick Tracy* successfully restored Hollywood confidence in Warren Beatty and Madonna. For Madonna especially, it rescued her from three disastrous films in a row. Warren had drawn a fabulous performance from her, and she was now batting a thousand. She had a hit album, a hit movie, a sell-out concert tour, a scorching Number One single and video with "Vogue." That summer, there was nowhere you could look or be without encountering the sight, the music, or the likeness of Madonna—and that's just the way she wanted it.

On September 4, Madonna's nonstop domination of the media hit a new peak when she performed on the seventh annual MTV Awards telecast. Six years previous, she had used the yearly telecast to establish her stardom. This time around she used the show to lampoon herself and again it worked brilliantly.

Taking a cue from the look of eighteenth-century French aristocracy and the recent success of the film *Dangerous Liaisons*, Madonna and her savvy Blonde Ambition troupe presented a fresh interpretation of "Vogue." Wearing a towering white wig, Madonna presented an uproarious version of the song with herself as the French queen Marie Antoinette, and her troupe as her naughty courtiers. Madonna was brilliantly *in vogue*, right down to the hand-held fans, push-up boobs, cinched waist, and the sedan chair.

She had mimicked Marilyn Monroe, glorified Jean Harlow, personified Breathless Mahoney, and portrayed Marie Antoinette. Now it was time for Madonna to raise the curtain on her personal life, and raise it she did. She was about to invite her legions of fans backstage, behind the scenes, and into bed with her. In her next film she was about to portray her most outrageous role yet—that of Madonna.

Thirteen

It's a great feeling to be powerful. I've been

Truth

striving for it all my life. I think it's just

or

a quest of every human being—Power.[23] *—Madonna*

Dare

When Madonna's romance with Warren Beatty lasted about as long as it took to make and open *Dick Tracy*, people began to suspect that it was more of a publicity stunt than a love affair. Referring to Beatty's long-running reputation as Hollywood's primo Lothario, Madonna publicly called him "pussy man."[206] Theirs was the symbiotic romance of the season. He brought her the movie role of her career and a respectability in Hollywood that had been previously unobtainable. She in turn introduced him to young audiences who weren't even born when he made his scorching 1961 film debut in *Splendor in the Grass*.

By the time summer ended, and the hype of *Dick Tracy* had subsided, Warren and Madonna were an item of the past. He went back to dating Isabelle Adjani, and she found a new boy toy to justify her love. It had been rumored that Warren and Madonna were going to follow *Dick Tracy* with another co-starring feature, a comedy called *Blessing in Disguise*, but it never got off the ground. Soon afterward

Warren met Annette Bening, became a father-to-be, and the rest is history.

Madonna's new main squeeze was twentysomething aspiring actor and model Tony Ward. She had met him at a birthday party for Herb Ritts, and was immediately attracted to him. He turned out to be the perfect partner for her—at least for the time being. When she attended the premiere of the film *Goodfellas*, she flew him to New York with her. Several days later newspapers in London were announcing that handsome Tony once posed nude for the gay skin magazine *In Touch for Men*. The tabloids wasted no time running the nude photos, paralleling Madonna's nude sessions in *Playboy* and *Penthouse*.

"It didn't bother me," claimed Madonna. "He had these pictures done when he was really young and needed money. The same thing happened to me. I finally felt like, 'God, somebody can understand how I felt.' "[206]

With *I'm Breathless, Dick Tracy*, and the Blonde Ambition tour over, it was time for Madonna to move on to the next phase. Aiming directly at the Christmas 1990 season, Madonna was already preparing a batch of cleverly packaged "stocking stuffers" for the holidays. There had been talk of doing a greatest hits package of her recordings, and with an amassed wealth of hit songs and hit videos, two simultaneous packages were already in the preparatory stages. Both were entitled *The Immaculate Collection*.

For the album, Madonna wanted to give her fans a new incentive to run out and buy the greatest hits album, so she recorded two fresh cuts to set off the package. The new songs were entitled "Justify My Love" and "Rescue Me." Walt Disney Pictures had managed to make her tone down her songs from *I'm Breathless*, and the Vatican and the Toronto police had attempted to censor her that summer, so she was determined to go for broke with her latest project.

The song "Justify My Love" was written by Lenny Kravitz, with additional lyrics by Madonna. (After the song came out, Prince protegée Ingrid Chavez surfaced, pissed off at Kravitz and claiming an uncredited contribution to the lyrics.) An odd, smokey, plodding talk song, Madonna's vocal on the song sounds like a monologue she would deliver while making love. The song oozed sex, and naturally when it came time to do a video for the song, it, too, had to emulate the ambiance of seduction.

Checked into the Royal Monceau Hotel in Paris for two and a half days with director Jean-Baptiste Mondino, photographer Patrick Demarchelier, Tony Ward, and an assortment of sexually charged performers, Madonna filmed the video for "Justify My Love." The finished product had censors swooning, tongues wagging, and created a new tidal wave of controversy and publicity.

In November 1990, when the finished video was submitted to MTV for a pre-broadcast screening, the music video network that had contributed so mightily to Madonna's success refused to air it. Madonna was appalled that the network would decline the video merely because it contained homosexuality, lesbianism, voyeurism, cross-dressing, and semi-nude bodies. According to her, she felt that MTV was hypocritical in its policies. When she did her "Oh Father" video and showed a corpse of a woman—meant to be her mother—with her lips sewn shut, MTV swore they wouldn't broadcast it. Likewise, when Madonna filmed her video of "Express Yourself," MTV told her that they wouldn't show it because of the slave collar and chain around her neck. They ultimately broadcast both videos unedited.

This time around, MTV found the whole video unsuitable for their audience, composed largely of young teenagers. This really pissed off Madonna. She argued, "Why is it that people are willing to go to a movie and watch someone get blown to bits for no reason, and nobody wants to see two girls kissing or two men snuggling?"[225]

In the video, in crisp black and white, Madonna is seen walking down a hotel hallway, dressed in an overcoat, carrying a suitcase, and holding her hand to her forehead as if she has a headache. Through the half-open doorways of the hotel rooms there are glimpses of people in sexually suggestive poses: a woman dressed for an S&M sex act, a man seated on a bed and gyrating his pelvis as if he's getting a blow job.

When Tony Ward emerges from a doorway out of focus in the distance, Madonna starts singing about wanting and needing someone to "Justify My Love." As though in heat, she pulls open her coat and drops to her knees, revealing that she is wearing garters, stockings, a black teddy, and little else. There is a nifty close-up of her fondling the inside of her thighs while groveling at Tony's feet in the hotel hallway.

More sex scenes in open doorways come into view: a man and a woman in black leather, a woman exposing her breasts in a skintight bustier and tugging at her nipples, and a man in a black bodysuit wearing gloves with long claws. Meanwhile, in Madonna's room, she and Tony are disrobing, and as he prepares to mount her, she pushes him away. In the next scene we see a woman in short hair and heavy eye makeup on top of Madonna, passionately kissing her. While this is happening, Tony kneels by the side of the bed, obviously getting into watching the lesbian action.

As the song progresses, the viewer is also treated to scenes of female couples drawing mustaches on each other, male couples in drag fondling each other, and Madonna watching as Tony—who is tied to a chair—gets worked over by a dominatrix who is wearing only suspenders as her top. It's a five minute cavalcade of sex, sex, sex. When the steamy video ends, Madonna is seen fleeing from the hotel room with her suitcase. She giggles to herself and bites one of her fingers in disbelief. Having had her love justified, she has obviously gotten rid of her headache!

One of the most talked about aspects of the "Justify My Love" video was the question of who was the French girl kissing Madonna? It was twenty-four-year-old model Amanda Cazalet. Cazalet said of Madonna, "She knew exactly what she wanted. She has this inner power that's incredible." Regarding the titillating finished product, the androgynous-looking Cazalet proclaimed, "After seeing it, the first thing you want to do is make love."[226]

Describing the video shoot, director Mondino explained, "It's very real—that's what's so shocking about it." Regarding the lesbian kiss, he asked in disbelief, "With AIDS, shouldn't we celebrate kissing as a beautiful thing?"[227]

Watching the video was a turn-on. No matter what your sexual orientation, there is sure to be something to push your buttons. Looking like a naughty French film from the sixties, "Justify My Love" was simply a new high point in Madonna's ability to turn moves made for shock value into a scandalously successful hit.

What is even more brilliant than her intuitive sexual power, is Madonna's business sense. The minute MTV turned down "Justify My Love" for airing, wheels were set in motion to market the five-minute clip as the first ever video single. It was quickly packaged and released to the stores. Usually, if a video cassette sells 50,000 units, it is certified platinum and considered a hit. The initial orders for "Justify My Love" were so great that Warner/Reprise Video had to rush-release 250,000 copies before Christmas. The week before Christmas of 1990, *Video Insider* magazine ranked Madonna's "Immaculate Collection" video as Number One, and "Justify My Love" as Number Two. Again, she had taken a potentially disastrous scandal and turned it in her favor.

Addressing the controversy head on, on December 3, 1990, Madonna appeared on the late-night news program, "Nightline." There was an ongoing recession in America and a war brewing in the Middle East, but those things paled next to the scandal of Madonna's latest video. Whatever Madonna did suddenly eclipsed tawdry and mundane things like current world affairs.

The "Nightline" appearance was a brilliant coup for the television program, especially when it was announced that the video would be screened in its entirety. Interviewed by Forrest Sawyer, Madonna looked sternly serious when she argued about how she had been wronged by MTV's censors. With regard to the censors' contradictions, she pointed out that her nipples were visible through her diaphanous dress in the "Vogue" video, yet MTV had no problem with that. Now that she was writhing in heat, though fully dressed, they made a stink about it.

She admitted that half of her knew she was heading for censorship trouble, and half of her felt that she was again going to get away with it. When Sawyer pointed out that it was going to become a win-win situation for Madonna, the songstress admitted that it had indeed turned out to be profitable for her. "Yeah, lucky me!" she laughed.[228]

The night that Madonna was on "Nightline" was by far the highest-rated episode of the news program that entire year. It outranked the August 24 telecast about the Iraqi troops who had surrounded the U.S. Embassy and the January 19 show centering around the arrest of Washington, D.C., Mayor Marion Barry.

Other shows that broadcast edited or excerpted versions of the "Justify My Love" video also experienced record-breaking ratings. "Saturday Night Live" broadcast ninety seconds of the video in the "Wayne's World" segment, making it the highest-rated episode of the show that season. CNN's "Showbiz Today" had the greatest number of viewers they had all week on the day they showed a highly publicized 112 seconds' worth of the video.

The controversy stirred up by the "Justify My Love" video almost instantly thrust the single to the Number One spot in America. Madonna's *Immaculate Collection* album sold briskly and lodged itself in the Number Two spot on the charts for several weeks, with white rapper Vanilla Ice's *To the Extreme* locked in for a long run in the top spot. Madonna's album also spawned another Top Ten single with "Rescue Me."

When she released a special five-cut remix CD of "Justify My Love," Madonna pushed the envelope even further with spicier versions of the song. On the six-minute, thirty-second "Hip Hop Mix" of the song, Madonna ends with the words "Fuck me." And, on "The Beast Within Mix," she reads passages of the Bible that sound as if she is delivering a Satanic service. Jewish leaders were up in arms over a Biblical passage she quotes that refers to "the Synagogue of Satan," claiming that this was the same passage that the Nazis based several hate crimes upon. With this controversy, Madonna was truly breaking down prejudice barriers—she had already pissed off the Catholic church and conservative Christian groups, now another religion could get in on the fun.

During the fall of 1990, Madonna's every move was covered in the media. In October, she and Tony attended a Martha Graham tribute in New York City. Master choreographer Graham, at age 97, was in fragile health, and when she became ill that winter Madonna assumed the payment of a reported $150,000 of her medical bills. When Martha Graham died later that winter, it was announced that Madonna would portray the revolutionary dancer in a film about her life.

At the time, Madonna had gotten collagen injections in her lips, and, for several weeks it looked as if she had been socked in the mouth. The photo of her as a biker girl in leather, a cigarette hanging from her temporarily thickened lips, also appeared on the cover of the "Justify My Love" video cassette. The collagen injections, which temporarily thicken the lips, had been all the rage ever since thin-lipped Barbara Hershey had sported them in the 1989 film *Beaches*. Madonna's thick lip phase lasted about as long as any one of her ever-changing hair colors, and within weeks they had returned to their normal size.

Madonna also showed up on television that fall wearing only an American flag. The TV spot was a commercial for a movement called "Rock the Vote." With two of her dancers, Madonna did a takeoff on her song "Vogue," rapping, "Dr. King, Malcolm X, freedom of speec is as good as sex." She was urging people to register to vote in the upcoming November elections. Her message ended with a wink, as she threw open the flag that was wrapped around her, and in her red bikini announced, "If you don't vote you're going to get a spanky."[229]

The spot was very cleverly done and controversial as only Madonna could pull off. The ironic thing was that Madonna herself neither voted or ever registered to vote in the 1990 elections.

Business world bible *Forbes* magazine put Madonna on its October 1, 1990 cover, and in its headline, questioningly proclaimed her: "America's Smartest Business Woman?" The magazine estimated her gross for the year at $39 million and called her "a rarity among entertainers: a star who runs her own business."[230] The following month *Us* magazine devoted an issue to "The Heavy 100: The Most Powerful People in Entertainment." Madonna was ranked as Number One, above Michael Jackson, Bruce Springsteen, U2, and Prince. The article refered to her as a "consistently bankable superstar" and "a shrewd business-woman."[231]

In December there was a court battle over Madonna's shrubbery. It seems that when she moved into her new house off Sunset Strip she didn't read a rider requiring her to maintain the trees and bushes around her property in accordance with strict guidelines. The owner of the property up the hill from her was having his view of the ocean blocked by several cypress trees and other foliage that Madonna had added. She sent her brother Christopher to appear in court for her. Her neighbor, Donald Robinson, attempted to sue for $1 million in damages. That petition was rejected by Superior Court Judge Sally Disco, but Madonna was ordered to trim her hedges.

In January 1991, Madonna and Tony flew to New York so she could work on her new film: Woody Allen's *Shadows and Fog*. Co-starring with Mia Farrow, John Malkovich, and Allen himself, Madonna plays a circus performer in the 1920s. Shot entirely in black and white, the comedy features Madonna with still another look: a curly top brunette.

Two months later there were rumblings about trouble on the set, and rumors that Woody hated Madonna's acting in the film so intensely that he was planning to cut all her scenes. In a statement released to

proclaimed, "It's a total fabrication. Not a frame of her
or has that ever been contemplated. She's first-rate in

d to working with Woody, Madonna found him to be an
elusive character. Arriving on the set she was amazed at the small amount
of specific directions Allen gave her. She found that his directing technique calls for each actor to bring some kind of instinct to a character.
While she was put off by this style at first, she found that it exerted a
strong subliminal control to the situation.

According to her, Allen's casting the right people in the right roles
is part of his genius. "This is what he does that is so great, is that he
casts you perfectly. Basically I think he hires people to sort of exude
what they already exude. It's not a question of trying to be somebody
else," she claims.[233]

The fact that Woody Allen had asked her to appear in one of his
movies was an offer she couldn't refuse, even if it proved to be a semi-
traumatic experience for her. "To me, the whole process of being a
brushstroke in someone else's painting is a little difficult," she explained.
"I'm used to being in charge of everything. So on this movie it's hard
for me to shut up and do my job and, well, O.K., I have this stupid
little part and I have to sit around on the set and wait all day and then
say a few lines and blah, blah, blah."[234]

It is hard to imagine quiet and methodical Woody Allen working
with a take-control broad like Madonna. She admits that just sitting still
and doing what she is told to do is a bitter pill for her to swallow.
However, if she is going to actually become the respected actress she
would like to be thought of as, she will have to begin to alter her ways.

"I'll never learn patience," she proclaims. "But I've learned, watching Woody, how a real artist works. Woody is a master of getting things
out of people in a really gentle way. He's not a tyrant, and that's good
for me to learn because I can be something of a tyrant, in a working
situation. Well, in a living situation, too."[234]

The second week in March, the April 1991 issue of *Vanity Fair*
magazine hit the newsstands, with Madonna on the cover as Marilyn
Monroe. With Madonna striking ten of Monroe's most famous poses,
photographer Steven Meisel and stylist Marina Schiano worked lighting

and makeup miracles to transform the former Material Girl into a sex goddess of the fifties. For the cover shot she wore a revealing low-cut Bob Mackie gown that made her look sensational, and more voluptuous.

If the teaming of Madonna and Woody Allen seems a bit bizarre, then the mere idea of Madonna collaborating with Michael Jackson sounds like a "Twilight Zone" episode! Yet, on March 16, 1991, Madonna was seen at a chic Los Angeles restaurant called the Ivy with none other than "Wacko Jacko." An immediate alert went out for the paparazzi photo opportunity of the week.

"We're at the Ivy, and Madonna and Michael Jackson are there together. It was me and Greg Deguire, and an AP [Associated Press] guy," recalls photographer Vinnie Zuffante. "We wait for her to come out, and we hear she's with Michael Jackson. We didn't believe it. So we see them, and they're walking out, and the maitre d' says, 'No, wait, I don't want them getting any pictures.' Both Madonna and Michael said, 'It's O.K.—no problem.' He said, 'No, not at my restaurant.' He takes Michael Jackson's hand, walks Michael Jackson to his limo. He goes back, gets Madonna, walks Madonna to the limo. He has the waiters come out, and the busboys, holding up tablecloths, and putting menus in our faces, so that we couldn't get pictures. So I hit him in the head twice with the camera—the maitre d'. Madonna says, 'It's O.K., you don't have to do this,' and the maitre d' is saying, 'Not in front of my restaurant.' He's hitting me, I hit him in the head with the camera. Madonna starts laughing. It was crazy."[149]

Word leaked out the next week that the reason for the meeting was that Michael wanted to ask Madonna to record a duet with him on his forthcoming album. She liked the idea, but would only agree if she liked the song. According to her at the time, "I'm not going to get together and do some stupid ballad or love duet—no one's going to buy it, first of all."[206]

She also bragged how she wanted to turn Michael over to her dancers Jose and Luis, and their whole House of Extravaganza for a week-long makeover session. Explaining her master plan, Madonna intimated that Michael was a closet homosexual who needed to be dragged out of the closet. "I keep telling Michael Jackson, 'I'd love to turn Jose and Luis on you for a week. They'd pull you out of the shoebox you're in. Anybody who's in a shoebox in the closet cannot be in one after hanging around with Luis and Jose—or me for that matter. I have this whole vision about Michael."[206]

It's pretty hard telling what this vision might be. Suddenly she's taking on the biggest, most elusive male media star in the world and proclaiming that she is going to drag him out of the closet! There truly is no stopping her.

Much to everyone's disappointment, when Michael's *Dangerous* album was released later in the year, their collaboration was quite a nonevent. Briefly joined on the potentially exciting cut called "In the Closet," Madonna and Michael perform the whispery love song about secret love. Neither sexually revealing, taboo-shattering, nor lyrically exciting, the song's only saving grace is its infectious beat. Madonna's name doesn't even appear on the liner notes, as it is billed as a duet between Michael and a "Mystery Girl." For all of the wasted anticipation, this song could have stayed in the closet.

Meanwhile, on February 13 the Academy Award nominations were announced, and the Sondheim tune "Sooner or Later (I Always Get My Man)" from *Dick Tracy* was up for the Best Original Song award. It was announced that Madonna was going to perform it on the prestigious annual telecast, March 25. Since she had broken up with Tony Ward, she found herself without a beau. Their breakup might have had something to do with the false tabloid reports that he had gotten married in August 1990, right before they started dating.

She later explained about the termination of their affair, "He was a complement, but I insist that whoever complements me has his own identity."[235] By her thirty-third birthday in August, she and Tony were back together again.

For whatever reason, at the end of March she found herself without a date for the Oscars! What an outrageous thought: Madonna was the most talked-about woman in Hollywood, and she didn't have a date for the Academy Awards!

Anyway, said Madonna of Jackson, "We started working together, and I didn't have a date for the Academy Awards, and Michael said, 'Well, who you gonna go with?' And I looked at him and I said, 'I don't know, you wanna go?' And he said, 'Yeah, that'd be great.' "[233]

Naturally, when the Oscars roll around every year, every paparazzo in Los Angeles is staked out at the Dorothy Chandler Pavilion with several cameras and dozens of rolls of film. According to Vinnie Zuffante, although they were both already on the premises, the superstar couple was originally going to stage their arrival for the cameras, but that move was nixed by ceremony organizers. Says Zuffante, "Madonna and Michael wanted to make the entrance, but they were warned by the Academy not to. They had all the security. What the Oscars did was tell all the fans they can't have any signs, they can't have any cameras, and they can't have any binoculars. They were doing that for security reasons, and mainly because Michael Jackson and Madonna were going to go through. But the Academy realized that Madonna and Michael were going to get more publicity than anyone else going there, and they didn't want that to happen. They weren't nominees. If Madonna and Michael walked through the front, every magazine would have had that picture on page one, instead of Kevin Costner with his Oscar. And when the Academy found out about that, they told them not to do that. They said, 'You'd better not go in the front, go in the back,' and they did go in the back. But at all of the parties they made the entrances, and let everyone get the pictures, so that's where all of the pictures are from."[149]

Madonna's performance of "Sooner or Later" at the Oscars became the most talked about segment of the entire show. Dressed in the low-cut Bob Mackie gown she wore on the cover of *Vanity Fair* and $20 million worth of diamonds on loan from jeweler Harry Winston, her hair in a platinum blonde Marilyn Monroe style, Madonna looked every inch a movie star from the fifties. In a white ermine stole, with elbow-length evening gloves, Madonna's bumping and grinding version of the song caused several jaws to drop. Although in reality Madonna looked more like Jayne Mansfield than Marilyn Monroe, she certainly made her point.

Amid her performance of the song, Madonna ad-libbed, "Talk to me, General Schwarzkopf, tell me all about it," directly mimicking Marilyn's reference to Harry Winston in "Diamonds Are a Girl's Best Friend."[236] In the following morning's edition, *USA Today* referred to her as a "Monroe Wanna-be." The song "Sooner or Later" ended up winning Best Song, but Sondheim wasn't there to pick up his Oscar.

After the show, Michael and Madonna proceeded to superagent Swifty Lazar's annual post-Oscar bash at Spago. Once there, Madonna and Michael chatted and laughed together, while mingling with the star-studded crowd. Madonna ended up at Warren Beatty's table, and Michael had Diana Ross perched on his lap at one point. After the party was over, Michael and Madonna went over to Madonna's house, where they looked at her photography books and chatted until the early hours of morning.

Everyone knew instantly that they were just friends. *People* magazine called the duo's night on the town "about as romantically valid as taking your cousin to the prom."[237]

Imagining what Madonna and Michael's conversations must be like, Coati Mundi laughs, "Madonna comes from the streets, and has a really 'street' sense of humor, so she's probably pulling his leg all the time!"[150]

Jokingly describing a night out with Michael Jackson, Madonna herself laughingly claims, "First I beg him not to wear his sunglasses, and of course he complies, because I'm stronger than he is. Then we exchange powder puffs—we both powder our noses—and we compare bank accounts."[233]

The one-time flirtatious boy toy had that night at the Academy Awards staked her claim as *the* blonde bombshell of the nineties. With her role as Breathless Mahoney and her glamorous appearance in the "Justify My Love" video, she now suddenly looked every inch a movie star. In a year of brilliant career moves, she eradicated the memories of her last three cinematic disasters. She was no longer a pop singer playing at acting, she was finally a movie star—now she just needed a movie.

That's where *Truth or Dare* came into play. When she started filming the on-stage and backstage scenes from her 1990 Blonde Ambition tour, no one suspected that it was going to become the movie that would really label her as a bankable film star. In it, she played the most outrageous, the most glamorous, and the most totally entertaining character of her career: herself.

If someone were to script the final print version of *Truth or Dare* and present it as a work of fiction, no one would believe that such a character could exist. And yet, in this film, the Madonna you see on the screen is a character who is wilder, more shocking, and more liberating than any screen heroine since Sally Bowles and Auntie Mame. In the masterful *Truth or Dare*, Madonna isn't just a synthesis of those two outlandish characters; she is also equal parts Isadora Duncan, Glenda the Good Witch, and Dorothy—all rolled up into one.

It all started with a young director named Alek Keshishian. While he was a student at Harvard, he took $2,000 and staged an imaginative theatrical production of *Wuthering Heights,* in which the principal characters mimed the voices of pop singers. Explained Keshishian, the voice of Cathy was sung by Kate Bush until the point where she marries Linton, then Cathy's singing voice changes to Madonna. The show became a huge hit on campus, and he videotaped a performance to preserve a record of it.

After he graduated from college, Alek moved to Los Angeles, where he became the director of music videos. His directing credits included Bobby Brown's "My Prerogative," Vanessa Williams's "He's Got the Look," and Elton John's "Sacrifice." Through a college friend who had begun working for the CAA talent agency, he met Madonna's agents. When agent Jane Berliner set up a viewing of Alek's *Wuthering Heights* for Madonna, she said she was impressed, but he never heard from her after that.

Up until that point, Madonna had made arrangements for David Fincher to film her concert tour, but he dropped out at the last minute. It was already March of 1990, and with just three days before the tour started in Japan, Madonna called Alek and asked him to join her there. He agreed and began filming the Tokyo dates. When he and Madonna ran through the dailies, they realized the project could emerge as much more than just an on-stage documentary about a rock and roll tour.

He wanted to film her in every possible setting. He told her, "I'll film you without makeup. I'll film you when you're being a complete bitch. I'll film you in your room after the show when you don't want anybody around. I'll film you in the morning before your sleeping pill's worn off."[238]

What started happening on the road was something unique. Madonna and her troupe of backup singers and dancers actually became a tightly bonded family backstage—a family that loved each other, fought with each other, and ultimately said good-bye to each other.

"It's something that I felt compelled to do," she says of the project. "I was very moved by the group of people I was with. I felt like their brother, their sister, their mother, their daughter—and then I also thought that they could do anything. . . . When I started looking at the footage I said, 'This is so interesting to me. There's a movie here. There's something here.' "[239]

She felt so strongly about it, in fact, that she spent $4 million of her own money to complete the film, with herself as executive producer. What started out as a routine concert film became an amazing chronicle of a slice of her life. Ultimately the backstage story proved more riveting than the story onstage. After viewing the behind-the-scenes footage, she realized, "I couldn't give a shit about the live show. This is life! This is what I want to document."[206] It turned out to be her most brilliant career move. Through it she ultimately found that people would rather see Madonna as Madonna than some fictional character. After all, truth *is* stranger than fiction.

Many of the true-to-life events that happen in the finished version of *Truth or Dare* became actual subplots to the film. First of all, there were the conflicts between six of the male dancers who were openly gay, whom Madonna refers to as "queens on the rag."[206] The seventh dancer, Oliver, was straight and constantly at odds with the others. Madonna became a mother hen to all of them, smoothing ruffled feathers, and occasionally cracking the whip.

The behind-the-scenes views of Madonna showed her off as the ringleader with her two female backup singers. Together they occasionally seemed like schoolgirls off on a round-the-world field trip. There are also revealing scenes with the co-stars of Madonna's life—both famous and previously unknown. Warren Beatty is visibly uncomfortable with the ever-present Alek and his camera. In the most famous Warren scene in the film, Madonna is seen in her Manhattan apartment getting a throat examination by a doctor. When the doctor asks Madonna if they should talk about her throat off camera, Beatty snaps, "She doesn't want to live off camera, much less talk." When Sandra Bernhard visits with Madonna in a Paris hotel, the girl talk is about an unnamed woman in Sandra's life. "Are you still sleeping with her?" Madonna asks Sandra.[240]

Probably the most surprised participant in the film is Madonna's childhood friend Moira McFarland. Madonna discloses on camera that it was Moira who taught her many things in life, like how to use a

tampon, shave her legs, and get "finger-fucked." "I remem
at her bush," Madonna reveals in her typically unembarrassed

To turn the revelation into a full cinematic moment, Alek arr
for a surprise reunion with Moira. She tells Alek on camera that s
was doing so many drugs when she was younger, if she did indeed
"finger-fuck" Madonna, the drugs wiped the memory away. When they
are reunited, Madonna is in a hurry and acts awkward. It is a touching
and telling part of the film.

Some of the between-show antics reveal Madonna and her troupe
as being bound so close together that they would do anything to shock,
startle, or get a laugh out of the other members of the group. Playing
the game Truth or Dare, the performers especially let loose. When
Madonna dares Slam to French-kiss Gabriel, the two dancers go into a
tongue-exchanging extravaganza. Not one to be outdone, when she is
dared to demonstrate her fellatio technique on a water bottle she manages
to show off dramatically.

Hosting a slumber party in her bed, she insists that garments be
removed upon command. Groping one dancer's body she laughingly
commands, "Get out of my bed until your dick is bigger!"[240]

Madonna took great delight in watching the two dancers French-
kissing. "That's my favorite scene in the movie. I love that people are
going to watch that and go home and talk about it all night long. I live
for things like that," she claims.[234]

Ultimately, the film has become the most popular rock and roll
documentary since *Woodstock*. With *Truth or Dare*, Madonna was finally
able to do something that her other films hadn't: inspire the moviegoing
public to buy tickets specifically to see her up there on the screen.

The fact that the concert footage was filmed in color, and the
backstage footage in grainy black and white, only accentuates the movie's
Wizard of Oz feeling. In the color sequences, no problem is unsolvable
and life is glitteringly glamorous. But in the black and white real world,
life is often traumatic and depressing. Madonna, however, is colorful
no matter what film stock she is captured on. She is simply larger than
life just the way she is.

When the film debuted in May 1991, Madonna flew across the globe
for each gala premiere. In Los Angeles she hosted a star-studded night

ising dance at the Arena club. Dressed in a
n-Paul Gaultier outfit, her hair dyed a dark
ance, party, and sweat, and she happily did
y raised by the $100-a-ticket event went to
ost of media stars turned up to help her kick
Lang, Sandra Bernhard, Vanilla Ice, and
nded premieres in New York and in Cannes.

In Europe, the film was called *In Bed with Madonna*, and although it was not officially entered in the annual Cannes film competition, it was screened at the Cannes Film Festival. Madonna became the toast of the entire week-long event. As though the drama of it all wasn't enough, her ex-husband, Sean Penn, was also present at the festival to show off his directorial debut with *Indian Runner*. In the two and a half years since their divorce, he had been having an affair with actress Robin Wright, with whom Penn had a baby girl they named Dylan. What an odd turn of events, indeed, especially since Madonna referred to Sean as the main love of her life in her film.

One point Madonna stressed while doing the publicity for *Truth or Dare* was her feelings about gay rights. This really marked the first time that a mainstream performer catered to a gay audience, raised money for AIDS research, and went on to champion the cause. In 1990 Madonna lost two more friends to AIDS: Keith Haring and Christopher Flynn.

In two May issues of the fortnightly gay national magazine, *The Advocate*, Madonna presented herself as someone so super-confident with herself, that she claims to want other people to love themselves more as well. She said, "I feel that most gay men are so much more in touch with a certain kind of sensitivity that heterosexual men aren't allowed to be in touch with—their feminine side." She further stressed the point by stating, "Straight men need to be emasculated. . . . Every straight guy should have a man's tongue in his mouth at least once." Taking it a step further, she also announced in the magazine that "My brother Christopher's gay, and he and I have always been the closest members of my family."[206]

A more dramatically militant gay weekly called *Outweek* refers to her as "the Queen of Queers, who's done more for fag and dyke visibility than any star since [the] Stonewall [riots]."[241]

What other star of her magnitude has stood up for gay rights? Several other stars, who wouldn't have a career if not for devoted gay followers, have turned their backs on them. When born-again Christian Donna Summer made a statement in the early eighties about AIDS being somehow retribution for evil-doing, her career reached a sudden end. Another once-huge star, Diana Ross, has never given a concert to benefit anyone but herself and has never lifted a finger for AIDS.* Madonna, on the other hand, faces the controversy head on and instinctively follows her heart.

She has taken many causes to her cone-covered breasts and made them her own. AIDS, saving the rain forest, and protecting the constitutional right of freedom of speech are three of her favorite causes. Speaking out against anything she sees she can make a difference in has never frightened her.

Continuing her unflagging support of gay causes, on April 21 Madonna went to the Fourth Annual AIDS Dance-A-Thon. Niki Harris, who had a song with Jellybean on the charts called "What's It Gonna Be" was there that night to perform it. Madonna showed up and introduced Niki and danced on-stage for an hour.

Madonna's AIDS awareness vocalizing reached a new peak when in December 1991 gossip columnists buzzed with rumors that the diva herself had tested positive with the HIV virus. To nip the rumor in the bud, Madonna issued a statement flatly denying the allegation. Later that month she became the first recipient of the AmFAR Award of Courage for her charitable work and AIDS awareness efforts.

When *Truth or Dare* opened in May of 1991 Madonna made the rounds of television talk shows, including "Good Morning America," MTV, "Regis & Kathie Lee," and a special guest spot on "Saturday Night Live." For the latter three appearances, she insisted that her segments be filmed in black and white, to simulate the look of her movie.

On each of the shows she appeared to be calm and confident about her recent career moves. She was so calm, in fact, that she could have named her film *Take It or Leave It*. She knew that a certain percentage of the population was going to love the film, and a certain percentage

*The only benefit concert Diana ever gave was to fund "The Diana Ross Playground" in New York City's Central Park. The disastrous 1983 free concert ended up costing the city a small fortune.

be appalled by it. She was prepared to let the chips fall vould.

Her most amusing performance was a pre-taped segment for "Saturday Night Live" on May 11. It was part of a recurring skit called "Wayne's World." The premise of "Wayne's World" is that it is a cable access show that two high school kids host from Wayne's parents' basement. In this particular episode, Wayne (Mike Myers) and his friend and sidekick Garth (Dana Carvey) are ranking the "top ten babes of all times." True to the teenage nonsense of the show, the list was insanely eclectic, including Kim Basinger, the Flintstones' cartoon neighbor Betty Rubble, "Beverly Hillbillies" Granny (Irene Ryan), and actress Julia Roberts. The number one "babe" turned out to be Madonna. When Wayne announces, "I've had her" to Garth, the duo amusingly go into a black and white dream sequence, supposedly transpiring in Madonna's bedroom.

The actual scene was taped in Los Angeles, in a suite at The Four Seasons Hotel. In the skit, Wayne and Garth are visiting Madonna and playing a round of her now famous game of challenges, Truth or Dare. When a seductive Madonna lounges on her bed and challenges nerdy Garth to truthfully tell her if he has ever made love to two women at once, his reply is yes. Rolling her eyes, Madonna says, in "Wayne's World" lingo, "I believe you—NOT!" When he insists that it is true, Madonna deadpans, "Yeah, you might, and monkeys might fly out of my butt!" He then "dares" her to kiss him. When she accepts the dare, the music of "Justify My Love" starts playing, and the skit becomes a riotous takeoff on her naughty French hotel video of the same name. The dream gets out of control when a Prince lookalike and a pair of forceful-looking dominatrixes appear in the room, ready for a wild sex scene. As the dream sequence ends, Madonna bids the teenagers farewell in "Wayne's World" lingo: "Party on, Wayne! Party on, Garth!"[242]

The funniest aspect of the appearance on the show was that Madonna is so confident about her artistry that she is the first to poke fun at herself. She still has an unhalting drive that fuels her career, but she seems finally to be relaxing into the character and phenomenon she has created. At last she is really having fun with it.

When *Truth or Dare* opened at theaters across America, it was an instant hit at the box office and with critics. Richard Corliss in *Time* called it "Epically entertaining . . . a spectacular dare!" Peter Traver in *Rolling Stone* referred to it as "Outrageously funny . . . and revealing." In *USA Today*, Edna Gundersen wrote that it was "Exhilarating . . . Madonna is never short of riveting." Madonna finally had a movie with the words *must see* stamped on every frame.

One of the most hysterical outgrowths of Madonna's *Truth or Dare* documentary came later that year when comedienne Julie Brown starred in a deft takeoff called *Medusa: Dare to Be Truthful*. Originally produced for the Showtime cable network, the spoof found Brown acting spoiled and self-absorbed as controversial rock star Medusa amid her "Blonde Leading the Blonde" tour. Instead of performing fellatio on a water bottle, Medusa chose a watermelon. Doing direct parodies of Madonna songs, Julie Brown performed concert versions of the lampoon hits "Like a Video," "Expose Yourself," and "Vague."

Since *Truth or Dare* has restored her box office magnetism everyone still believes that *Evita* is destined to become her greatest screen role. Yet the fate of *Evita* is still up in the air. "Every day is a different story," explains Madonna. "It's a really big production, and Hollywood's really clamping down on budgets these days. Glenn Caron wrote a brilliant script for it, and you can't make *Evita* for the small amount of money Disney is saying they want to make it for. They wanted Jeremy Irons to play Juan. All the things they want that would make it incredible cost money. So where do you draw the line? I don't want it to be a mediocre rendition of *Evita*. It has to be grand. It's an epic thing. If there is an *Evita*, I contend that I will be her."[206]

If not Eva Peron, than perhaps the life story of Martha Graham or painter Frida Kahlo is destined to be embodied on screen by Madonna. Both women were legendary nonconformists with whom Madonna is fascinated. Kahlo was the wife of famed Mexican mural painter Diego Rivera, and she had a tormented life that spilled out on her unconventional canvases. Her bizarre self-portraits comprise her most compelling work. *The Two Fridas* (1939) depict Frida sitting next to herself, a pair of scissors in her hand. There is blood on her dress, as she has just performed open-heart surgery on both of her images and linked their exposed hearts with a vein she has pulled from her own body. *The Little Deer* finds Frida's head on the body of a deer in the forest, with antlers protruding from her head and the bleeding wounds of hunters' arrows

)ody. One of Madonna's most prized possessions is an
painting that hangs in her Hollywood hills home. It is
th, depicting an adult Frida's head emerging from her
opened vagina. Madonna has already purchased the film
rights to Kanlo's life story.

Since she became as wealthy as she is famous, Madonna has been
collecting art. She not only has an original Kahlo, her house is a veritable
museum of paintings and photography. She also has an original Rivera,
several Tamara de Lempicka paintings, and a Langlois that was originally
painted for Versailles. Her collection of original photographic prints
includes those of Lartigue and Man Ray. However, it is the Kahlo that
intrigues her the most. If someone doesn't like the painting she knows
that that person can't be her friend.

For Madonna, life is one big piece of art. There is never a question
of "Is there more to come?" Rather it is "What canvas will I choose
next?" Film? Theater? Music? Something multimedia?

Without missing a beat, in mid-1991 Madonna was already two
movies ahead of her last release. She spent several weeks in Chicago
at Wrigley Field filming a supporting role in Penny Marshall's film about
a female baseball team, called *A League of Their Own.* Unlike her
personal life, Madonna has learned to become a team player on film.
Since her success in *Dick Tracy* she has discovered that she is much
more effective as part of an all-star ensemble. Co-starring with Geena
Davis and Tom Hanks in the 1940s baseball film, Madonna portrays the
role of Mae, a girl with a fast reputation and a razor-sharp tongue.

While filming *A League of Their Own* in Evansville, Indiana, later
in the year, Madonna found herself bored to tears when she wasn't on
the set. "I may as well have been in Prague," she bitched to one
reporter—complaining that she had spent three months without MTV!
Unthinkable torture for the video prima donna. She did however fit in
a highly publicized date with rap star Vanilla Ice. According to her, "I
always like to befriend the underdogs."[243]

While she has achieved the kind of fame that is in the upper
stratosphere of stardom, life has not mellowed Madonna, nor has success
erased any degree of her pushy, bratty attitude. Career-wise, she can
write her own ticket in Hollywood, but among her peers, Madonna isn't
winning any popularity contests. In the summer of 1991, while being

interviewed on the CBS television show "This Morning" Cher went so far as to call her a "cunt." The word was naturally bleeped off the audio track on the air, but it was easy to read her lips. Said Cher, "There's something about her that I don't like. She's mean, I don't like that. I remember having her over to my house a couple of times, because Sean and I were friends, and she was just so rude to everybody. It seems to me that she's got so much, that she doesn't have to act the way that she acts, like a spoiled brat all the time. It seems to me when you reach the kind of acclaim that she's reached and can do whatever you want to do, you should be a little more magnanimous and a little bit less of a cunt."[244] In a rare 1991 interview, Barbra Streisand recalled her 1983 dinner with Madonna, Jellybean, and Jon Peters. She commented that Madonna had a lot of gall seeking out the most expensive thing on the menu to order for dinner, and she found her overall nerve appalling. Likewise, grand diva Patti LaBelle complained on the Joan Rivers show that Madonna had stepped on her foot at the American Music Awards and never so much as uttered the words *excuse me.*

On one hand, Madonna has made inroads in showing her public what her personal life is all about. Through *Truth or Dare* she let the world in on several of her family secrets, like her brother Martin's alcoholism, her brother Christopher's homosexuality, and her occasional bouts with loneliness and depression. But the secret sharing is still carefully controlled. While she can talk for hours about her favorite subject—herself—she is defensive when anyone else talks out of turn. She is truly the divine ruler of her own empire, and as time goes on she controls it with a tighter reign. Dreading the idea that any of her employees may eventually make money off their association with her, she has begun signing them to confidentiality agreements. Fearing that if they spoke out of turn about her they would never work with her again, several of Madonna's current associates refused to be interviewed for this book. Madonna relishes the idea of always having the last word.

She continues to titillate her public for sheer shock value. Ever since she started hanging out with Sandra Bernhard, the whole question of lesbianism seems an ever-present theme. Smashing the taboo of homosexuality seems to be one of her strongest personal crusades. When Carrie Fisher interviewed Madonna for a 1991 article in *Rolling Stone*, Carrie asked her if women kissed better than men. "Sometimes better," she answered, "I've only *kissed* women though. I've had fantasies of women, but I'm not a lesbian."[245] Knowing what we do about Madonna, if she ever did decide to make love to another woman, she would probably videotape it, write a song about it, and sell a million copies!

To push the issue of lesbianism further, the first part of the *Rolling Stone* piece was accompanied by a photo essay by photographer Steven Meisel called "Flesh or Fantasy." The black and white photographs were inspired by and mimicked Brassaï's controversial *The Secret Paris*, of the 1920s and 1930s. Brassaï was fascinated with brothels and gay and lesbian life in Paris. In Madonna's takeoff on *The Secret Paris*, she was photographed in male drag groping a woman's buttocks on a dance floor and cavorting in a hotel room with men in garter belts, black silk stockings, and high heels. In another controversial frame, Madonna is seen in a slip and garter belt, passionately kissing another woman. In a solo shot she posed in her underwear on an upright dining room chair, her knees a yard apart from each other, drinking from a glass she holds with her feet.

In the context of Carrie Fisher's chatty interview with Madonna, she casually mentions that her father, Eddie Fisher, once slept with androgynous film legend Marlene Dietrich. Replied Madonna with jealousy, "Really? I wish I had slept with her."[245]

The tables have already been turned a couple of times on Madonna with regard to who is or isn't sleeping with her. In 1987 Manny Parrish had a hit record in England called "Male Stripper" (from *Man-to-Man Meet Man Parrish*). When he stepped off the plane in London to promote the single, his record company's publicity director told him that he had arranged a press coup by claiming that Parrish was having an affair with Madonna. Fearing a backlash from the press, Parrish played along with the charade. Based on Parrish's fictitious story about how Madonna longed to have his baby, the story made headlines on both sides of the Atlantic.

Similarly, in 1988, an Italian stud named Ettore Santinello sold a story to a British newspaper, *The Star*, about his tryst with the star during her European Who's That Girl? tour. The story was accompanied by a photo of Madonna kissing Ettore on the cheek and a publicity still autographed "With Much Love and Kisses, Madonna." When Santinello tried to turn the so-called affair into a publicity stunt to launch his own show business career, she ignored his claims, and his fifteen minutes of fame evaporated. Instead of acknowledging or denying either Parrish's or Santinello's claims, Madonna ignored them. Her entire career has been based on one sex scandal after another, and each one only makes her legend grow bigger and bigger. If Pee Wee Herman's 1991 indecent exposure plight had befallen Madonna, it wouldn't have finished her career, she probably would have sold an extra million copies of her latest album!

In January 1992, three of Madonna's *Truth or Dare* dancers—Oliver, Kevin, and Gabriel—filed a lawsuit against her, claiming they hadn't signed releases for their part in the film. Madonna was amused—NOT! Remaining in the news, she took her lumps when *Shadows and Fog* opened in Paris and at the Berlin Film Festival in mid-February. *Daily Variety* dismissed her role as a "murky cameo." Madonna was already at work on her next trio of projects: her own record label, Home; her starring role in the suspense film *Body of Evidence;* and a pictorial project involving Steven Meisel, Vanilla Ice, and several male strippers—in an erotic Madonna photo book on sex—how apropos! The Madonna machinery simply never stops.

Marketing *is* where her true genius lies. She is at such a confident plateau at the moment that she is destined to continue producing one form of art or another. Jean Harlow and Marilyn Monroe died at the pinnacle of their fame, but Madonna's survival instinct is too strong for that. Brigitte Bardot couldn't sustain it. Undoubtedly, this is not a fate Madonna will encounter—she's too hyperactive, and far too in love with being in the center of the spotlight to ever give it up.

Obviously there is more great music brewing in her. But, since she doesn't do the obvious, one never knows where her next inspiration will come from. After popularizing the whole vogueing phenomenon, there is no telling which segment of society—or herself—will pique her interest next. Whatever it is, it will undoubtedly be promoted to the hilt, as only Madonna can.

At this point Madonna's celebrity is so strongly established that she will be a media star for life. Images of Mae West still come to mind, because it is her sexy audacity that Madonna most closely resembles. When West was in her eighties she had the insight, audacity, and humor to star in a film called *Sextette,* in which she played a femme fatale who was plagued by a horde of suitors less than half her age. Like Mae, Madonna will never mellow with age. If she lives to be a hundred, we can still expect her to be shocking us with her actions and her pronouncements.

Madonna has created the perfect existence for herself. She is able to flit back and forth from New York to Los Angeles with ease. Those two cities match her energy level, and with two permanent residences, she can switch back and forth between them according to her whims. It depends on what kind of a mood she's in. If she wants to be left alone, she stays in L.A. And, if she wants to stir up some trouble, she goes to New York.

What is Madonna going to do to startle us next? This is probably the biggest unanswered question in her career. She shocks us. She provokes us. She mesmerizes us. And she manipulates us. She is more of a brilliant marketing genius than a gifted performer. She herself admits that she is neither the greatest singer nor the best dancer. But she has something more elusive: a magnetism that makes us want to know all we can about her every move.

She has harnessed the world's media more fully than any other star in history. She *is* an artist, and a great one, and her medium is the popular media. She has manipulated the massive forces of television, radio, film, magazines, newspapers, books, videos, and, of course, records, CDs, and cassettes, with an instinctual adroitness no other performer or politician comes close to matching. To Mae West and Marilyn Monroe, two obvious leaders on Madonna's list of inspirations, should be added Andy Warhol, the painter who introduced the world to the idea that in the media age, celebrity itself is an art form.

To further prove her business savvy, in April 1992 Madonna announced the finalization of her mammoth $60 million deal with Time Warner, Inc. Under the company name of Maverick, Madonna becomes a showbiz mogul unto herself with a record company, music and book publishing wings, and fully funded television, film, and merchandising divisions.

Saint, savior, sinner, siren, slut—Madonna is *all* of these. Love her, hate her, worship her, idolize her, or despise her—the only thing you cannot do is ignore her. She is rude, she is pushy, she is lewd, she is liberated, she is beautiful, she is audacious. Like it or not, thanks to the magic of electronic media, she is destined to be remembered as the biggest female star of the twentieth century.

The New World Madonna—With a Golden Touch

Though I have fears, I think truthfully I'm going to live to be a very old age. If what I've gone through hasn't killed me yet, nothing's going to. (246)

Throughout the 1990s, Madonna continued her track record for high-profile multimedia creativity, shocking pronouncements, and unpredictable antics—ultimately becoming heralded at the millennium by the press as being one of the most memorable women of the twentieth century. She also continued to question and confound society's morals and mores through her creative projects, statements, and artistic endeavors.

From 1992 to 2000, Madonna recorded one of the finest albums of her career, starred in a film that makes the rest of her movie roles forgettable, and won a major film award for her acting. On the other side of the coin, Madonna grabbed negative headlines with her controversial book, *Sex,* set the record for the number of times the word "fuck" could be said on network television in one half-hour appearance, and recorded an embarrassingly crude song about cunnilingus. Just about the same time that the world's shock reflexes thought that Madonna could finally surprise them no more, she announced that she was pregnant—for real this time!

During the same era, several pop singers who were once Madonna's prime competition on the record charts have seriously veered off course and/or stagnated. Prince changed his name to some ridiculous symbol and has continued to release forgettable albums comprised of previously unreleased cuts from his golden era of the 1980s. Michael Jackson's career skidded to a complete halt when a lawsuit claimed that his interest in underage boys reached beyond a normal concern for children: he kept them around him at all times. Boy George is in rehab, and in spite of periodic comebacks like his hit song "The Crying Game" (1992), he is no longer in Madonna's league of popularity or success. And, although Cyndi Lauper had released some critically acclaimed albums in the 1990s, she finished the decade as Cher's opening act and seemed to lose her once-sharp cutting edge.

Unlike many of her rivals, Madonna has only one thing on her mind at all times: herself. She never loses sight of her goals. During the 1990s, the fiercest competition that she confronted in the musical arena came from Whitney Houston and Cher. Whitney has also made the transition from recording star to movie star. It was a truly incredible feat when she took her recording of "I Will Always Love You" from her debut film, *The Bodyguard,* and turned it into the longest-running Number One hit of the century. Fortunately for Madonna, Whitney can't act convincingly either—*Waiting to Exhale* confirmed that fact. She is great to watch when she sings, but she can't deliver believable dialogue on camera to save her soul. Houston has also garnered a reputation for having a surly attitude, and her marriage to often drunken and disorderly singer Bobby Brown is as bizarre and tabloid-worthy as Madonna's marriage to Sean Penn. One of the main parallels between Whitney and Madonna is that they both change and develop with each album. However, Madonna has the most in common with Cher. Although Cher seemed to disappear from the forefront of high-profile projects during the middle of the decade, she became 1999's greatest comeback story with the song "Believe," which went to Number One in dozens of countries.

Comparing Madonna's career activities to those of her contemporaries, it is fascinating to note that she never really disappears from the spotlight for long. Even when her latest projects are labeled artistic "bombs," she still continues to make headlines. As always, she is as well known for her soap-opera personal life as she is heralded for her music or her acting career.

In the summer of 1992, it appeared the Madonna was debuting a new, mellower, more sensitive persona. On movie screens that season, her brief appearance as Marie in Woody Allen's black comedy *Shadows and Fog* was about as fleeting as that film's box-office life. She was next seen as a supporting player in the Penny Marshall–directed film about a woman's baseball team, *A League of Their Own*. It was a wise choice for Madonna. Not only did it put her in a box-office hit film, but through it she became very close friends with one of her costars, Rosie O'Donnell. It was stand-up comedienne O'Donnell's first major movie role, and on the set she and Madonna found that they had much in common, including the fact that both of them had lost their mothers to a fatal illness at an early age.

On radio airwaves Madonna logged her tenth Number One pop hit with the song "This Used to Be My Playground," written by Madonna with Shep Pettibone and used in *A League of Their Own*. A sentimental ballad regretting the passage of time, it is still one of Madonna's most memorable and beautiful recordings. As a further goodwill gesture, that summer the only album that the song was featured on was the official album of the 1992 Olympics, *Barcelona Gold*.

Also, keeping consistent with her career-long AIDS awareness stance, and her on-going assistance to AIDS-oriented organizations, she contributed a song to the 1992 album *Red, Hot & Dance*, which also featured music from George Michael, Lisa Stansfield, and Seal. Her song was "Supernatural," written by Madonna with Patrick Leonard and re-mixed by the Jamaican musical team of Sly & Robbie. Instead of giving the album a techno or house-music cut, her "Supernatural" is a sparse but percolating bossa nova number.

That summer, between her charming performance in *A League of Their Own* and the beautifully emotional ballad "This Used to Be My Playground," a kinder, gentler side of Madonna was finally emerging, like a delicate flower after the rain. True to form, Madonna was simply setting herself in an innocent light to throw her fans off guard, in preparation for launching two of her most ambitious and overtly sexual creations: the *Sex* book and the equally shocking *Erotica* album.

The minute that summer ended, Madonna was back to showing her true colors—and her bare breasts. On September 24, the second day of autumn, during an AMFAR AIDS–benefit fashion show in Los Angeles, entitled "Jean-Paul Gaultier at the Shrine Auditorium," Madonna strode onto the runway in a striped suspendered pant suit with her perky breasts fully exposed. As the photographers' cameras flashed like lightning during a desert storm, she stole the show. Who remembered the clothing designs after that? Only Madonna could turn an all-star celebrity fashion show into a night at Hooters and get away with it.

From a publishing and media-hype standpoint, Madonna's debut book was a smashing success. From the day it was released, *Sex* disappeared from book stores at an astonishing rate. Instantly selling out everywhere, it lodged itself at Number One on *The New York Times* best-seller list. At the time of its publication, with over a million copies of its first edition printed, *Sex* set the all-time record for an initial print-run of a book. Reportedly, it sold an astonishing 500,000 copies during the first week of its release. Physically, it was also an ambitious book to touch and behold. An unconventionally oversized photo book measuring 13³/₄ by 11 inches, *Sex* featured embossed stainless steel covers, a metal spiral binding, and a CD included on the inside of every book. In addition, each copy was numbered with a stamped steel numeral on its cover. The contents were so controversial—and guarded—that each book came sealed in a silver mylar outer wrapper, with an overexposed life-size photograph of Madonna on the outer side of it, appearing to be writhing in sexual ecstasy. Inside, the 120-page book included arty brown cardboard end-pages and an eight-page photographic comic book.

After receiving extensive prepublication publicity, *Sex* was the "must see" item of the season when it appeared in stores on October 21, 1992. "Have you read Madonna's *Sex* book?" became the cocktail party question of the month, as the limited-edition book disappeared from bookshelves. Bookstores at shopping malls across America had store copies available for perusal only for persons over the age of eighteen. Another safeguard, insuring that the book would not be for children's eyes, was the book's steep cost, which sold briskly at $49.95.

Sex is a book dealing with sexual activity in every configuration: men having sex with Madonna, women having sex with Madonna, men having sex with men while Madonna watches, Madonna having sex with herself, even Madonna in a sexually suggestive pose with a dog. A plotless picture book, some pages contain text in the form of poems, sexual fantasies, and ponderings about sex. Some of it is very sexy, some of it is lewd, some of it is purposely unsettling, and some of it is embarrassingly silly. Several of the pages feature Madonna in sexual situations, with largely pornographic text superimposed over the image.

A calculatingly naughty art book, *Sex* was photographed by Madonna's pal Steven Meisel, who has photographed her through much of her career. Some of the shots feature Madonna at her most beautiful. Photographed mainly in black and white, some of the pages were printed with different colors of ink to convey different moods. *Sex* must truly have been an art director's dream to work on.

Opening the stainless steel cover of *Sex*, the first thing that pops out is the exclusive mix of the song "Erotic," which was naturally Madonna's latest single release. It comes packaged in a silver mylar zip-lock bag, purposely looking like a large sealed condom.

On the inside of the brown cardboard end page Madonna writes, "This is a book about sex. Sex is not love." She then goes on to say that if she were to perform any of the "fantasies" that take place in the book, her sex partner would assuredly be wearing a condom. She ends the introduction to *Sex* with the disclaimer, "Nothing in this book is true. I made it all up." (247)

One of the things that she made up for the *Sex* book was the dominatrix named "Dita." As Madonna's sexual alter ego, Dita crafted handwritten messages to her fictional boyfriend Johnny. In these letters she talks about having sex with her girlfriend Ingrid, and how they both long to have sex with Johnny again.

One of the first photographs of Madonna features her in a pair of crotchless leather panties, a nipple-revealing black-leather studded bra, and a leather eye mask on her face. The middle finger of her left hand is in her mouth, and the middle of her right hand disappears deep in the crotch of her panties. On the facing page are the words: "I'll teach you how to fuck." Any questions?

Progressing into this photo essay of a book, the first section is filled with full-page photographs of Madonna romping with two intimidating-looking, shaven-headed, nipple-pierced lesbians. On one page the lesbians have Madonna tied to a chair with rope. On another, Madonna, in leather, straddles a drinking fountain while one of her butch lady friends drinks from it. The next section takes place in a male-and-female S&M dungeon. Bare-breasted, Madonna whips a woman's behind, has oral sex performed on her while her legs are in the air in a sling, and has intercourse on a jukebox. Handwritten messages from "Dita" deal with the merits of "ass fucking."

There is a disturbing photo of Madonna in a Catholic school-girl's skirt being raped by two skinheads, as well as images of her licking a man's ass and tugging on his jockstrap, putting lipstick on a pretty boy she has in bed, shaving someone's pubic hair off, and sucking on a man's big toe.

One page contains a five-sentence memoir about discovering masturbation. The episode ends with the phrase, "honey poured from my 14-year-old gash and I wept." (247) Opposite it, there is a photograph of Madonna, shaded in the screen of a baby crib, sucking her thumb. It is more embarrassing than erotic.

Another segment depicts a glamourously dressed Madonna and a tuxedo-wearing male date attending a male strip show, and finally having sex with the strippers. Throughout the book, some of the photography is beautiful, including a nude of Madonna straddling a giant sculpture of a fish that spouts water into a swimming pool. There are also photographic guest stars in various states of dress and undress, including Naomi Campbell, Vanilla Ice, Big Daddy Kane, and Isabella Rossellini. Also featured are the women and the man with whom Madonna was personally involved at the time: Ingrid Casaras and Tony Ward.

Probably the most famous shot from the book is one of Madonna stark naked—except for a pair of high heels, a purse in her hand, and a cigarette dangling from her mouth—hitchhiking on a Miami street in broad daylight. From Vanilla Ice with his hand down Madonna's pants, to Isabella Rossellini in male drag fondling Madonna, to Big Daddy Kane and Naomi Campbell forming a sexual Oreo-cookie threesome with creamy white Madonna in the middle, *Sex* thrust itself right in America's face, flaunting sexual activity in every possible variation. According to Madonna, this was a book with a statement. She referred to it as "a challenge to the hypocrisy of the world." (246) Whatever.

Explaining her visual influences, Madonna claimed, "In the *Sex* book, we [she and photographer Meisel] were influenced by everything from Visconti to Warhol to a kind of *Valley of the Dolls* aesthetic—you know, the sort of drunken, bored housewife wandering naked down a street hitchhiking in her high heels. I pushed that as far as I could." (246) And *push it* she did.

Although it was a huge hit at bookstores for several weeks, the critics were less than kind. Richard Harrington of *The Washington Post* laughingly called it "an over-sized, overpriced coffee-table book of hardcore sexual fantasies sure to separate the wannabes from the wanna-be-far-aways. . . . Is *Sex* shocking? Not really. Mostly because it's Madonna, and in a way we've come to expect this from her. . . . Is *Sex* boring? Actually, yes." (248)

Ever the cross-promoter, Madonna simultaneously released her ninth album, *Erotica*. The cover duplicated the same monochromatic blue-ink cover shot of Madonna that appeared on the mylar cover of *Sex*, and the back cover of *Erotica* featured the photo of Madonna sucking a man's big toe. Echoing the themes and stylistic mood swings of the *Sex* book, *Erotica* follows much the same path. Some of it is artistic yet suggestive, some of it is genuinely sexy, and some of it is lewd and musically unappealing.

The title cut, "Erotica," is similar to "Justify My Love"—dark, rhythmic, with a pumping beat. The song is an offshoot of the poem by her sexual alter ego, Dita, which was printed in the *Sex* book. Madonna's version of the old Peggy Lee hit, "Fever," with a new, sexier beat, follows it. "Fever" is an appealingly sexy song about desire that was a great song for her to cover. Several cuts on the album recount stories, like "Thief of Hearts," in which Madonna tells off a boyfriend-stealing woman, and "In This Life," a song about the AIDS-related death of her beloved dance instructor, Christopher Flynn. "Rain," one of the most beautiful pop ballads that Madonna has ever recorded, takes its sexual meaning from another song on the album ("Where Life Begins") that likens rain to vaginal wetness.

This was the first (and so far only) Madonna album to carry a printed warning on the cover: "Parental Advisory: Explicit Lyrics." She had been suggestive in her music in the past, but never before had she been so blatant. The disclaimer was put there because of two specific songs on the album, "Where Life Begins" and "Did You Do It?" From the minute the song "Where Life Begins" starts, Madonna sings about receiving oral sex from her male partner, complete with crude in-your-face metaphors.

Only the pubescent masturbation fantasies she wrote about in *Sex* rival the song's silliness. The song "Did You Do It?" features Mark Goodman and Dave Murphy carrying on a rap-style conversation in which they brag about their sexual exploits, while Madonna bleats the chorus of her song "Waiting for You" in the background. It sounds something like a joke without a punchline, and is neither amusing nor tuneful.

One of Madonna's main promotional ploys—a scandalous video— naturally fanned the flame of her biggest sex escapade to date. The video version of "Erotica" was so steamy and so laden with S&M fantasies that MTV would air it only after midnight. It was just another publicity "ace" perfectly played.

To further assure the success of both *Sex* and *Erotica,* Madonna threw a huge sex-themed, by-invitation-only party in a lower Manhattan loft on October 15, 1992. The 800 guests included filmmaker Spike Lee, who saluted Madonna's "courage" for publishing *Sex;* ex-Van Halen lead singer David Lee Roth; TV personality Robin Leach; and Rosie O'Donnell, who praised her pal for being "a genius at marketing herself." (249)

One of the party's prime amusements were living theater tableaus being performed during the evening. One actress in lingerie relaxed in a bathtub filled with caramel-coated popcorn, while other groups in leather and chains whipped each other in sadomasochistic scenarios. However, the rumor circulating at the party was that the guest of honor, Madonna, was going to enter the party totally nude. In a typical about-face Madonna looked more like Heidi of the Alps, with her braided hair wrapped in buns atop her head, and a low-cut Bavarian-style dress with piping and rickrack sewn to it. To complete this bizarre shepherdess get-up, Madonna arrived with a stuffed toy lamb under her arm. When it comes to dressing for attention, Madonna is a pro.

The neighborhood that night was teaming with uninvited Madonna onlookers who lined the streets, waiting for a glimpse of the former Material Girl in her new persona as sexual guru. Located in the meat-packing district of Manhattan—a neighborhood normally frequented by drag queens and hustlers—that night around the loft it was impossible to tell the party-goers from the local sex trade.

At over 2,000,000 copies sold, *Erotica* was the least commercially successful of her releases to date. It did reach Number Two on *Billboard*'s album chart, but by Christmas had fallen to Number 25. This was not typical chart activity for a Madonna album. The X-rated subject matter and the off-putting photo of her sucking a man's toe on the back cover were elements that were a bit too much, even for some of her fans.

Erotica spent over a year on the *Billboard* charts and spawned three hit singles that kept Madonna and her whole *Sex/Erotica* publicity machinery in everyone's eyes throughout the next year. The 1992 singles from the album were "Erotica" (peak American pop-chart position Number Three) and "Deeper and Deeper" (Number Seven). In 1993 she released the songs "Bad Girl" (Number 36) and "Rain" (Number Fourteen).

Instead of making the rounds of the television shows in the fall of 1992, Madonna remained silent about her *Sex* book and *Erotica* album. She let the product, and the resulting music videos, speak for her. Television programs like *The Joan Rivers Show* and *Maury Povich* based whole shows and/or segments around the theme "Has Madonna gone too far?" As usual, Madonna was laughing all the way to the bank. Since *Erotica* was her first album release on her own Maverick Records label, a 2,000,000-selling album and four Top 40 singles were great to start.

Not until four years and three albums later was she willing to discuss the project with a sense of perspective. According to Madonna: "Sexuality has always been forced down our throats, but it's always been from a male point of view. The woman is always objectified. And in this circumstance it was the opposite. I think that not only men but women responded in a really hostile way. People didn't attack me in a personal way before the book. After the book, they did. I'm talking about criticizing everything from my choice of men to my body—things that have nothing to do with my work. I also found myself the subject of almost any interview anyone did with a female. Writers used to just throw my name up there just to get six paragraphs of sensationalist journalism." (250) Did she think that she could actually release an album with songs about "eating out" a vagina, and a book that romanticized sadomasochism, and *not* be the subject of criticism?

She later whined to *Time* magazine that her witty sense of humor was simply misinterpreted. "If you read the text [of *Sex*], it was completely tongue-in-cheek. It was a joke. Unfortunately, my sense of humor is not something that a mainstream audience picks up. For me, all it did was expose our society's hangups about our sexuality. Yes, I took a beating, and yes, a lot of things that were said were hurtful and unfair. And, yes, it did make my life really difficult for a while. But there were no mistakes. It was a great learning experience." (251) Some lessons in life are harder learned than others.

Four years after *Sex* was released in bookstores, she was still trying to justify her love of shocking people. She claimed, "Most people want to hear me say I regret putting out my *Sex* book. I don't. What was problematic was putting out my *Erotica* album at the same time. I love that record, and it was overlooked. Everything I did for the next three years was dwarfed by my book." (252) It was true. With *Sex*, she had lowered the benchmark in an effort to turn controversy into a huge profit.

While this was percolating in her career, her personal life was rather colorful as well. Madonna dated not one—but *two*—of the most high-profile black basketball players in sports: Charles Barclay and Dennis Rodman. Flamboyant Rodman—known to dye his hair cherry red, orange, and lime green—has been photographed in drag and is excessively tattooed and pierced. He seemed like the perfect match for Madonna. However, after several months of an on-and-off affair, they parted under less-than-friendly terms.

Meanwhile, during the same time period that the *Sex* and *Erotica* controversies were raging, Madonna was still struggling to be taken seriously as a film actress. In 1993 she released two separate films in which she starred. One was a dreadful bomb, despite its high-profile release. The other was so awful it went almost instantly to video, and to this day few people even know it exists.

The first film, *Body of Evidence*, starred Madonna as Rebecca Carlson, an oversexed vixen on trial for murder. The role certainly seemed tailor-made for her new sexual-guru persona. In the plot, Rebecca is accused of killing her rich lover via too much rough sex. While defending the case, her laywer (Willem Dafoe) becomes involved with her emotionally and physically. The most famous scene in the movie, involving hot candle wax and steamy sex, made more audience members squirm in their seats than get turned on. Legally, Rebecca gets away with murder. However, the acquittal proves a dark useless victory: during the film's final moments someone kills her. The film was so awful that Rebecca's demise caused some audience members to cheer. Despite a fine supporting cast, including Anne Archer, Frank Langela, and Joe Mantegna, this cinematic effort was a sheer disaster.

$$Epilogue$$

Evidently, in the original script Madonna's character lived to cherish her wrongful acquittal, but this was changed at the last minute. Such treatment wasn't half as severe as the way film critics slaughtered *Body of Evidence*. *People* magazine referred to the film as "Madonna's Movie Misadventure"; Susan Stark, in *The Detroit News*, denounced it as sheer "trash"; Roger Ebert awarded it half a star; and, according to one review, in the middle-American city of Peoria, Illinois, "52 people gathered in a 237-seat theater and giggled." (253)

Speaking of *Body of Evidence*, Madonna later lamented, "In all the movies of the '40s, the bad girl has to die. What I loved about the role was that she didn't die. And in the end, they killed me. So I felt that I was sabotaged to a certain extent. For some reason, when that movie came out, I was held responsible for it entirely. It was my fault, which is absurd, because we all make bad movies. I mean, *Diabolique* [1996] came out and Sharon Stone was not held responsible for the fact that it was a crap movie." (251)

Watching her second film of 1993, *Dangerous Game*, is similar to undergoing Chinese water torture—it never seems to end. The saddest part about this film is that Madonna spent her own money to star in this tale of a director (Harvey Keitel) whose latest film, concerning the demise of a marriage, parallels his own failed relationship with his wife (Nancy Ferrara). In the film, Madonna's character just happens to be sleeping with everyone but the director's wife. The ironic aspect of this film is watching Madonna—a famous celebrity whom critics have claimed "can't act"—portray a fictional actress of whom everyone in the film seems to have the same opinion. This is truly a case of art imitating life, imitating art, imitating entertainment.

Longtime Madonna pal Marlene Stewart designed the costumes in *Dangerous Game*. The singer's manager, Freddie DeMann, was credited as one of its Executive Producers, while Madonna's Maverick Productions got all the blame for this mess. The original shooting title was *Snake Eyes*, and the director was Abel Ferrara. Madonna's best scene depicts her telling a series of "blonde" jokes at a restaurant. It seems to be the only one in which she doesn't look like she's acting. The movie's funniest line comes from actor James Russo, who says of Madonna's character, Sarah Jennings, "We both know she's a fucking whore and she can't act."

The film is moody, much of it shot either in a film noir fashion or a

stark documentary style. The action is nothing more than rambling improvisation, with Madonna, Keitel, and the rest of the cast pointlessly chatting and complaining. Madonna seizes several opportunities to undress in
this film, and does so with nonchalance. She laughs, she cries, she does
drugs, and in the end her screen husband in the film-within-the-film
(James Russo) blows Madonna's brains out. The sex is violent, but the
plot sags. Ultimately, you don't care what happens to any of these people
or their dysfunctional relationships.

Madonna thought she had a winner on her hands. She certainly had
a worthy director—or so it seemed. Abel Ferrara had received rave notices for his 1992 police drama, *The Bad Lieutenant*, starring Harvey
Keitel. Madonna complained that her best work ended up on the cutting-
room floor. According to her: "The movie had such a different texture and
meaning and outcome for me. When I went to see a screening of it, I
cried, because I really think I did a good job as an actress. I don't think
it should be called *Dangerous Game*. It should be called *The Bad Director*." (251)

In the June 1993 issue of *Interview* magazine Madonna comically
pondered future movie roles with friend and celebrity interviewer Mike
Myers, of *Saturday Night Live* and *Wayne's World* fame. According to her:
"I have this idea that we should do a remake of *Some Like It Hot*, only
with you and Garth [Dana Carvey] playing the Tony Curtis/Jack Lemmon
parts. Sharon Stone should play the Marilyn Monroe part and I'm gonna
play the bandleader. Only I want to change it slightly. I'm going to fire
the Marilyn Monroe character for being unprofessional, and then we'll
see what develops from there." (254)

While her two 1993 films were playing to lukewarm movie audiences, Madonna was playing live to ecstatic concert audiences and rave
reviews. In October she launched her first tour in four years, the elaborate
production known as *The Girlie Show Tour*. The twenty-date, four-conti-
nent tour included dates in Toronto, Detroit, New York, and Sydney. A
costume-filled *Ziegfeld Follies* kind of show, it presented Madonna at her
brazen best. Critic Richard Corliss in *Time* magazine claimed: "Her current caravan . . . is a smash. Biggest thing since the Who tour . . . biggest
thing since the Rolling Stones. . . . Madonna, once a Harlow harlot and
now a perky harlequin, is the greatest show-off on earth." (255) The
concert itself was a heavily choreographed extravaganza. Even "Justify

My Love" received a black-and-white costumed production treatment, emerging as a 1990s take-off on the "Ascot Gavot" number from *My Fair Lady*. A highly successful international concert extravaganza, the event was captured on video and is currently available on DVD. Taped in Australia, the release title is *The Girlie Show—Live Down Under*. It encompasses some of her biggest hits as well as new material from *Erotica*.

One of the most amusing and insightful things that Corliss said in his *Time* article was the statement, "It's tough to stay on top by spanking somebody's bottom. In her recent work, Madonna has pursued dominatrix fantasies until she may be the only one getting off on them." (255) This fact was painfully evident; her recent erotic attempts were viewed as blatantly silly.

Madonna actually seemed surprised that her most supportive critics had taken their fill of her antics, blasting her *Sex* book and *Erotica* album. On March 31, 1994, Madonna guested on the popular CBS-TV *Late Show with David Letterman*. The episode unpredictably became her most infamous appearance on that show since she and Sandra Bernhard had teased the audience (and Letterman) with their supposed lesbian affair in the 1980s.

Proving that she had not yet had her fill of being crude and lewd, Madonna strode onto the Letterman set wearing a clinging black velvet dress and black combat boots, her hair slicked back and dyed black. Smoking a cigar, she immediately caught David off guard by handing him a pair of her panties and demanding that he smell them. From the minute the interview started, she proceeded to speak her mind on a number of topics, denouncing Letterman as "a sick fuck." She chided him for being obsessed with her sex life, claiming, "You can't get through a show without talking about me."

Then she accused him of kissing the rear ends of his guests. "You used to be real cool," she said, "[now] you just kiss up to everyone on your show."

Quick on his feet, Letterman laughingly replied, "I can suspend that behavior tonight if you want."

Continuing her tirade, Madonna puffed her cigar and proceeded to pepper her dialogue with the word "fuck" twelve more times during the interview, until David finally cried out in mock horror, "She can't be stopped! Something's wrong with her."

She replied, "Something *is* wrong with me—I'm sitting here." (256) At that point the studio audience actually began to boo her, yelling out for her to leave the set.

Among the topics she discussed were why it is good to urinate in the shower. When the interview finally ended Letterman said to her, "Thank you for grossing us all out." (256) The totally bizarre appearance gave the Letterman show huge ratings for that episode and landed Madonna in the punchline of dozens of jokes spoofing this high-profile misadventure. According to *Time* magazine, "If basketball groupie and sometime pop singer Madonna was hoping to remind the world of her randy reputations, she succeeded." (257) Matt Roush in *USA Today* said, "Madonna reclaimed her title as the raunchiest act on TV with a bizarre, combative and shock-a-minute appearance." (256)

Reflecting from a 1998 perspective on this strange moment in broadcast history, she told *TV Guide* magazine, "That was a time in my life when I was extremely angry. . . . The press was constantly beating up on me, and I felt like I was a victim. So I lashed out at people and that was one of them. And I am not particularly proud of it." (258)

After a bestselling book about sex, a double-platinum album about sex, two disastrous films about sex, and her verbal-fuck fest on the Letterman show, she lost some of her appeal and her audience. However, ever the phoenix, Madonna spent the rest of 1994 creating a huge splash on the music charts. She had a hit single from a new soundtrack album, and she launched a great new album that dealt with sex and love in a more appealing fashion. Her first entry onto the pop charts that year was the song "I'll Remember," featured on the soundtrack from the film *With Honors.* The triumvirate of Sire Records, Warner Brothers Records, and Madonna's own Maverick Records released the LP.

Beautiful and sentimental, "I'll Remember" continued her romance with radio programmers and record buyers alike. For all her shocking pronouncements and controversial dance songs, Madonna proved once again that she could do an about-face from time to time and deliver a moving ballad. It went to Number Two on the *Billboard* charts, inaugurating a year in which she placed four consecutive singles in the Top Five, a feat she had not accomplished since her *True Blue* era of 1986–1987. In a marketplace in which record companies were complaining about the decreasing sales of singles, "I'll Remember" sold over a million copies.

The material found on *Bedtime Stories* was more appealing than that on *Erotica*. Instead of tackling sex head on, this time Madonna is actually sexy in a musically seductive fashion. *Erotica* more closely represents musical masturbation, while *Bedtime Stories* enticingly invites the listener into the action.

Critics, as well as her fans, loved *Bedtime Stories*. Edna Gundersen in *USA Today* called it "Gorgeously romantic. . . . This time, S&M means silky and mellow. . . . A solid creative effort." (259) Jim Farber in *Entertainment Weekly* observed, "More than any previous Madonna album, the latest finds her telling us the truth about her life. . . . A sustained mood suite for the boudoir. . . . Madonna's lyrics mingle sex and romance in more personal ways than ever." (260)

The infectious and snappy beat of "Secret" is one of her best recordings of the 1990s. Her dominatrix-stance on the frank "Human Nature," as well as her sentimental and exotic "Take a Bow," make this an appealingly varied album. To her credit, she has always had a knack for aligning herself with brilliant collaborators. The song "Bedtime Story," written by Nellee Hooper and Icelandic innovator Björk, is the album's centerpiece.

It was also a star-studded album. On the song "Sanctuary" Madonna worked with Herbie Hancock; the haunting "Forbidden Love" and "Take a Bow" she wrote, sang, and coproduced with Kenny "Babyface" Edmonds. Me'Shell NdegéOcello (whom Madonna had signed to Maverick Records) played bass on several cuts, while Sting and Babyface contributed synthesizer and drum programming. Once again, Madonna had an album that found her in top form.

She also managed to snipe at the press and the public outrage over her *Sex* book and *Erotica* album. On the song "Human Nature," she sings about being "punished" for telling us her "fantasies." Madonna actually displays a fleeting touch of believable vulnerability here, making *Bedtime Stories* a warm and snappy album.

Her music also benefits from bringing in some of the new hit makers on the mid-1990s charts. According to her: "The idea was to juxtapose my singing style with a hard-core hip-hop sensibility. I began by meeting with hip-hop producers whose work I most admire." (261) Her coproducers included Dallas Austin, Babyface, and Dave Hall.

According to Austin, 22 years old when he worked with her on *Bedtime Stories:* "Madonna is the kind of artist you really have to hang out with and get to know before you can start working with her. Because she's who she is, she might otherwise be sort of intimidating if you don't establish yourself with her beforehand. So we hung out, went to some ballgames, that sort of thing, before we started working. In the studio she could actually be very relaxed and playful, but also very outspoken about what she wanted." (262)

Bedtime Stories debuted at its peak chart position of Number Three in *Billboard,* ultimately selling over 2,000,000 copies in America. The single "Secret" hit number three; "Take a Bow" went all the way to Number One. With "Take a Bow," Madonna became the first solo female artist to log eleven number one hits, putting her in fifth place behind Elvis Presley, the Beatles, the Supremes, and Michael Jackson. After seven weeks at number one, "Take a Bow" became the longest-running, chart-topping single of her career ("Like a Virgin" had been Number One for six week).

In 1995, when she released the fourth single from the album, the title cut "Bedtime Story" had an accompanying video that was one of the most visually elaborate and special effects–filled videos productions ever. At a cost of $2 million, it also set the record as the most expensive music video of all time. The pulsing song—on which Madonna repeats over and over, "Let's get unconscious"—is a 1990s techno masterpiece.

To assure the album's continued success, Madonna made several high-profile appearances on television programs and at televised awards shows. She and Babyface performed "Take a Bow" on *The American Music Awards* on January 5, 1995. One of her most talked-about TV appearances came on February 13, when Madonna appeared on the *Late Show with David Letterman* to make amends for her raunchy guest spot the previous April. She brought Dave a box of Valentine's Day candy and a bouquet of long-stemmed roses as peace offerings. Her hair was back to platinum blonde. She wore a black Gaultier halter-top dress, and seemed more at ease with herself. "I'm a changed woman," she proclaimed. However, proving that she was sorry—but not too sorry—she announced on camera, "I'm not going to say *fuck* anymore." (263) That Madonna: always a lady.

A week later, on February 20, she opened the fourteenth Annual BRIT Awards at Alexandria Palace in London by singing "Bedtime Story." In March she appeared before an audience of 1,500 pajama-wearing fans and read aloud the children's bedtime story *Miss Spider's Tea Party*. The event, held at New York City's Webster Hall, was broadcast live on MTV.

While she was busy logging four hugely successful, consecutive chart singles, her catalog of past albums and videos continued to sell. Her recent chart successes spurred the Recording Industry Association of America (RIAA) to announce in September 1994 that her video compilation, *The Immaculate Collection*, was certified Gold for having sold over 300,000 copies. In February 1995 the RIAA acknowledged her album *True Blue* for having sold 7,000,000 copies and *Like a Virgin* for 9,000,000 copies sold. In March the RIAA announced that her greatest hits collection, also entitled *The Immaculate Collection*, was certified six times Platinum for having sold 6,000,000 copies in America alone.

The fifth single from *Bedtime Stories*, "Human Nature," with its sadomasochistic video, became the first Madonna single that failed to crack the Top 40 in *Billboard*. It peaked at Number 46 in April 1995.

On May 29, 1995, while Madonna was away from her elaborate fortress of a home in Hollywood Hills, her security guard, Basil Stephens, shot and wounded an intruder attempting to scale the wall of the house. The wounded man was 37-year-old Robert Hoskins. In the struggle he had attempted to grab the security guard's gun. Recovering in Cedars-Sinai Hospital, Hoskins was booked on stalking charges. Wishing to avoid a media circus, Madonna first declined to testify when the case went to trial. However, Judge Andrew Kauffman threatened to arrest her if she didn't comply. Hoskins had a previous criminal record, and the judge wanted to make sure that this latest charge stuck. On January 3, 1996, Madonna did indeed testify. Because of her testimony, and the other criminal charges, Hoskins was convicted, sentenced, and imprisoned.

Meanwhile, Madonna was appearing in three new films, released in 1995 and 1996, and preparing her next album release. Because she had been lambasted by critics for starring in *Body of Evidence* and *Most Dangerous Game*, Madonna wisely chose supporting roles to build her list of on-screen credits. Although these subsequent three films all starred top-notch actors, the general public had very little knowledge of these titles or of Madonna's appearance in them.

The first was 1995's *Four Rooms*. A small film with an impressive cast, the movie's four segments each had different directors and different casts. The exception was the central character, Ted the bellman. Working at a seedy Los Angeles hotel called the "Mon Signor," Ted is involved in four different scenarios in four different rooms on one single misadventure-filled New Year's Eve night. The directors were Allison Anders, Alexandre Rockwell, Robert Rodriguez, and Quentin Tarantino. *Four Rooms* featured an A-list of actors, including Antonio Banderas, Jennifer Beals, Marisa Tomei, Valeria Golino, and an unbilled appearance by Bruce Willis.

The episode that Madonna appears in is called "The Missing Ingredient," and stars Sammi Davis, Amanda de Cadenet, Valeria Golino, Ione Skye, Lili Taylor, and Alicia Witt. It turns out that these women are witches who are renting the room to cast a spell. However, much to their surprise, they have forgotten one of the main ingredients: a man's semen. Surprisingly, Madonna isn't pressed into duty to gather the missing liquid. Instead, they simply contact Ted, the unsuspecting bellman, to supply them with what they need. The segment is amusingly funny, although the movie itself drags in several points. Madonna, as Elspeth, is stunning in her low-cut, skin-tight, black vinyl dress. The film came and went without much notice. Movie critic Leonard Maltin labeled it a "bomb," claiming it was "embarrassingly awful . . . what a cast . . . what a waste!" (264) It actually has some funny moments but is somewhat uneven.

Blue in the Face, also released that same year, resembles a giant improvisation by some of the biggest Hollywood names in the 1990s, including Lily Tomlin, Lou Reed, Michael J. Fox, Mira Sorvino, RuPaul, Jim Jarmusch, Roseanne, Harvey Keitel, and Madonna. Written and directed by Wayne Wang and Paul Auster, it is a film in search of a script. In this sequel to the 1995 film *Smoke*, Keitel again appears as Augie, the manager of a Brooklyn cigar shop frequented by an ethnically varied mix of odd characters. Lily Tomlin, dressed as a male bum, stands outside the smoke shop dreaming of Belgium waffles. Roseanne visits to complain about her lover. Toward the end of this meandering film Madonna comes to deliver Keitel a singing telegram. She is made up like a tart and wears a short little Rockettes-like costume and a pillbox hat. After she performs her singing message, for the grand finale she bends over and moons him with her buttocks barely covered in panties and fishnet stockings. The film also intersperses documentary footage of actual colorful Brooklynites talking about their beloved, conflict-filled borough.

Although shown at the 1995 Berlin Film Festival, *Blue in the* ▮ failed to find an audience. This film also suffers from its lack of plot ▮ character development. Leonard Maltin condemned this one, too, calling it an "overindulgent mess." (264)

The one good role that Madonna did choose was in Spike Lee's 1996 film *Girl 6*. Although this wasn't one of his biggest box-office hits, it is well-acted, well-plotted, and thoroughly entertaining. The film recounts the story of a girl, played by Theresa Randle, whose acting career is floudering. Needing a paycheck, she goes to work for a telephone sex service. An imaginative actress, she becomes wildly successful at the service but finds herself getting too involved in the soap-opera lives of some of her customers. Randle is beautiful, vulnerable, and very appealing to watch. Seeking a change of pace, she interviews with another service that would allow her to make the calls from her home. Madonna, playing the owner of that particular service, looks wonderful and speaks confidently. Made up and lit beautifully, she is seen squeezed into a tight red sweater and wears several gold bangle bracelets.

In *Girl 6*, Madonna has an amusing scene with Randle, in which they discuss the sexual fetishes of some of her clients. "Shitting is really big right now, don't ask me why," Madonna says with a straight face. Although her appearance is extremely brief, she makes the most of it. The film also features Ron Silver, Naomi Campbell, Debi Mazar, Jennifer Lewis, Quentin Tarantino, Halle Berry, Richard Belzer, and Spike Lee himself. Unfortunately, this entertaining film was in and out of theaters, despite a great cast and a snappy all-Prince soundtrack.

In November 1995, Motown Records released a tribute album, *Inner City Blues—The Music of Marvin Gaye,* that featured Madonna's interpretation of Gaye's song "I Want You," which she recorded with the group Massive Attack. That same month, she released her own album, *Something to Remember.* Somewhat of a "greatest hits" package, it featured only her favorite ballads from 1984 to 1995, plus three new cuts. The album included two versions of "I Want You," which neatly bookended the other twelve selections, one percussive, and one orchestrated. "You'll See" was the album's other new cut.

One of the funniest understatements in this album package is Madonna's comment in her liner notes. Introducing this ballad hits package she begins, "So much controversy has swirled around my career this past

tle attention ever gets paid to my music." No kidding?
1at situation?

ecent sexual antics, *Something to Remember* is a beau-
d with a strong unifying feeling in the ballad realm.
My Playground" makes its Madonna-album debut here,
and it ___ at next to her ballad classics from years past, including
"Crazy for You," "Live to Tell," and "Rain."

The album debuted in England at Number Three and in America at
number six, marking its peak on both charts. Ultimately, it was certified
Platinum for selling over a million copies in the United States. The single
"You'll See" hit Number Five in England and Number Six in America. A
second single was released from the album, the remixed version of "Love
Don't Live Here Anymore," which had originally appeared on her *Like a
Virgin* album in 1984. That particular song stalled at Number 78, becom-
ing by far the least successful single of her career.

Something to Remember was something of a crossroads album for
Madonna, a chance to reflect on her career and to review some of the
songs that defined her legend. In Madonna's view:

> Listening to this record took me on my own journey. Each song is like
> a map of my life. . . . I don't really listen to my records once I've
> done them. I'm onto the next thing. And I think most of the time when
> my records come out, people are so distracted by so much fanfare and
> controversy that nobody pays attention to the music. But this is, for
> the most part, a retrospective, and I just wanted to put it out in a very
> simple way. The songs, they choke me up, and I wrote them. Isn't
> that weird? I can't tell you how painful the idea of singing "Like a
> Virgin" or "Material Girl" is to me now. I didn't write either of those
> songs, and wasn't digging deep then. I also feel more connected emo-
> tionally to the music I'm writing now, so it's more of a pleasure to do
> it. (265)

Two of the most successful and touching songs included on that
album were "You'll See" and "One More Chance." Like so many of Madonna's projects, the writing and recording of these songs overlapped with
another career milestone. She was about to head into her most challenging
project, and these two compositions benefited from that anticipation. "If
you listen to those songs," she explained at the time, "you can hear how

I was trying to absorb and utilize what I was learning from the recording of *Evita*." (266)

Everything Madonna had done in the past ten years was based on her fame and her position in show business. She had been cast in movies and stage shows solely on her notoriety and her marquee drawing power. She had done entire films based completely on her ability to bankroll them, and had been cast in others simply for the controversial value of her name. This time around she would not be in control. She couldn't use her millons of dollars to buy her way into *Evita*, nor could she simply charm her way through it.

There was no more perfect a vehicle to turn her into a legitimate film star, and there was no more challenging role for her. Up to this point in her career she had a track record for being breathtakingly stunning in song-length music videos and painfully horrendous as a dramatic actress (*Shanghai Surprise, Speed the Plow, Body of Evidence*). Since *Evita* was a complete opera, with every line either sung or lyrically recited, this was her one opportunity to shine on screen. This epic came to be known as the longest music video ever filmed, and she knew that she was ready for the challenge.

The last time Madonna had been considered for the role of Evita Perón, it was in the mid-1980s. However, the production never fully seemed to get off the ground. At first it looked as if Meryl Streep was going to be Madonna's top competitor for the role; in 1987 it looked like Oliver Stone was going to direct. Throughout the entire process Madonna had coveted the role. Finally, in 1994, it was announced that Alan Parker would direct the film for Hollywood Pictures, and the award-winning *Evita* was green-lighted again. Parker had scored huge critical successes with *Mississippi Burning, Midnight Express*, and *Angel Heart*, so his presence at the helm assured that *Evita* would be handled with dramatic and historic scope.

According to Madonna at the time: "I remember sitting down during Christmas of '94 and writing an impassioned four-page letter to the director, Alan Parker, listing the reasons why I was the only one who could portray her, explaining that only I could understand her passion and her pain. I can honestly say that I did not write this letter of my own free will. It was as if some other force drove my hand across the page. Soon afterward I heard from Alan and, following several nerve-racking meetings, the part was mine." (267)

This extravagant $59 million production was a huge risk for everyone involved. Not since the days of *Grease* (1978) and *Hair* (1979) had there been a hit musical film adapted from a Broadway musical—let alone one of epic proportions. Film producers and movie studios rarely wanted to bother with them. Appearing as the focal point of almost every scene, Madonna had to deliver the goods this time around, or her cinematic ambitions could be derailed permanently.

Fortunately, Alan Parker also directed *Bugsy Malone* (1976), *Fame* (1980), *Pink Floyd—The Wall* (1982), and *The Commitments* (1991), so he had a deep understanding of the musical-film genre. He knew how to mix drama and music, and he understood how to make a show-stopping number have grandeur and impact.

Whatever Madonna said in her four-page handwritten letter, she certainly made an impact on him. Although he had already had a few conversations with actress Michelle Pfeiffer, he was also seriously considering Madonna for the part.

"I just knew that no one could understand what she [Eva] went through more than I," Madonna proclaimed. "I related to her commitment, discipline, and ambition [and] that bravery required for a girl of fifteen to come from the pueblos and go to Buenos Aires to find her way in entertainment and later in politics. Her suffering as a child was a catalyst to make a better life. I understood that." (252)

According to Parker, "Madonna promised me from the very beginning she would give her all, and she has kept her promise. She's given herself to the film and to me." (246) She wanted the movie role so badly that she accepted a flat fee of $1 million, foregoing a percentage of the profits. By the superstar standards of the 1990s, that was a bargain.

Madonna, who had begun her career donning crucifixes as a fashion accessory, suddenly found herself shifting from a sexual to a spiritual energy mode. Just as devotedly as she had thrown herself into producing and promoting her *Sex* book, she immersed herself in the life of Eva Perón. "I see this role as being my destiny," she claimed. "I don't think anyone could have prayed as hard as I did for the film to go ahead. I put on amulets, lit candles—even consulted fortune-tellers." (268)

She became actively involved in making certain that she not only portrayed the role with dignity, historic correctness, and believable compassion, but that the production succeeded on all levels. When the production company was denied the permit to film the famed "Don't Cry for Me Argentina" balcony scene at the Casa Rosada, where the real Eva Perón addressed her people, it was Madonna who made it her mission to try and charm the president of Argentina into changing his mind. As usual, she was successful in her endeavor.

The similarities between Madonna and the real-life Evita, two of the most famous and written-about women of the twentieth century, abound. At the beginning of Madonna's music career, she became notorious for flirting with and dating men who could help her get what she wanted. She would promptly cast them aside when they were no longer useful. She didn't stop until she was at the top of the entertainment business. Struggling actress Eva Duarte dated the right men who could move her career forward in 1930s and 1940s Argentina. She too discarded them when they had served their purpose. She didn't stop until she was the first lady of the country, and an icon of power and glory who became known as the beloved Evita. Many in Argentina regarded her as a traitor and an opportunist, but even more regarded her as a modern-day saint.

The stage musical *Evita*, written by Tim Rice and Andrew Lloyd Webber, has a unique and involved history of its own. Like their earlier masterpiece, *Jesus Christ Superstar*, *Evita* began as an operatic concept album. The original 1976 album starred Julie Covington as Eva. Covington originated roles in shows like *The Rocky Horror Picture Show*, and in the 1970s hit TV miniseries *Rock Follies*. Her whispery alto voice was especially effective on Eva's poignant ballads.

The first staged version of *Evita* premiered on London's West End in 1978, and starred Elaine Paige, who brought fiery bravado and brassiness to the role. The following year *Evita* opened on Broadway, with Patti LuPone as Eva Duarte Perón, winning Tony Awards and Grammy Awards. It was LuPone's show-stopping rendition of "Don't Cry for Me Argentina" with which American audiences were most familiar, as for several years Patti sang the song on just about every variety or awards telecast. LuPone's strong and forceful Broadway delivery became widely associated with the show and particularly with the portrayal of Eva.

A wide number of female vocalists during this era, including Karen Carpenter and Donna Summer, recorded the dramatic ballad "Don't Cry for Me Argentina." When the news became known that Madonna had indeed been awarded the role of her lifetime, one of the most frequently asked questions was whether or not she had the powerful voice to compete with all of the previous Evita interpretations.

Madonna also had to compete with her own legend. She had spent the last four years promoting an overheated image of overt sexual antics with men, women, and their house pets. Stylistically, Madonna may have felt flexible enough as an actress to make the transition from recording songs about cunnilingus, writing and appearing nude in an arguably pornographic photo book, and starring in movies about women who kill their lovers with too much rough sex, to portraying the famous first lady of Argentina. However, not everyone shared her opinion.

Politically, Eva Perón and her husband, Juan Perón, made sweeping changes and improvements in Argentina in the late 1940s and early 1950s. However, they also moved millions of dollars from the country's treasury into their own Swiss bank account. Not long after Eva's untimely death in 1952, Perón fell out of power in Argentina, and anti-Perónists denounced his wife's memory. Even their house had been demolished. In the 1970s public opinion changed, and Evita was again revered as a national heroine. In Argentina the prospect of Madonna—of *Sex* and *Erotica* fame—portraying her on screen was far from popular.

In a public statement Argentine president Carlos Menem scoffed, "I don't see Madonna in the role. I don't think Argentina's people, who see Evita as a true martyr, will tolerate it." (269) Madonna's track record for challenging Catholicism and Christian mores didn't win her any points either. Even the archbishop of Buenos Aires harshly condemned the casting decision: "Madonna is pornographic and unsuitable." (268)

Madonna was the first to note the striking similarities between Evita and herself. Said Madonna of Eva, "Because of her enormous impact, her detractors tried to tear her down and desecrate her image. People were frightened of the power she had, and undermined her accomplishments by calling her a 'whore.' I can certainly relate to that. People intimidated by me feel the need to denigrate me." (252)

In Madonna's favor, a talented cast of supporting actors surrounded her. In the crucial role of Ché, the musical's narrator, Antonio Banderas, was cast to add a sexy male presence to the film. Jonathan Pryce, who won a Tony Award for his performance in *Miss Saigon*, was signed to play

Juan Perón, Eva's husband and political partner. And British singer Jimmy Nail brought a dapper darkness to his portrayal of the tango singer Migaldi, who first "discovered" young Eva Duarte. Before filming began, the complete soundtrack had to be recorded. For the entire filming, the cast would be lip-synching their own prerecorded voices, making sure every gesture matched the music.

Knowing that all ears would be evaluating her vocal ability to interpret the familiar score, before she even entered the recording studio Madonna worked with vocal coach Joan Lader for several months. The role was extremely daunting, and Madonna knew it. "*Evita* is the first movie big enough to contain me," she said at the time. "I know I have a very big presence. If I overpower the movie, the movie fails." (252)

Alan Parker also knew that the film's success or failure would rest mainly on the merits of its star. According to the director, "The hardest work that anyone had to do was obviously by Madonna. She had the lion's share of the piece, singing as she does on almost every track. Many of the songs were comfortably within her range, but much of the score was in a range where her voice had never ventured before. Also, she was determined to sing the score as it was written and not cheat in any way." (266)

During preproduction Alan Parker recognized one major weak point in the shooting script. When Eva Perón knew she was dying, her dictator husband bluntly ignored her. Reportedly, Juan Perón couldn't stand the smell of the cancer on his wife, and his only visits to her tended to consist of walking by her room and waving. The original stage musical never slowed down long enough to acknowledge this moment. Parker felt that another song might best touch on this sad fact. Unfortunately, the show's creators were still in the midst of a long-standing feud and had not collaborated with each other in years. It became Parker's quest to reunite the composer and lyricist and to convince them to write one more song—especially for the film. Miraculously, he was able to do just that.

According to Parker, "Getting the two of them in a room to collaborate after all these years wasn't easy, but they finally succumbed. Madonna loves this song the most. She sings it so beautifully, it becomes hers, and hers alone." (266) The new song was entitled "You Must Love Me."

On her very first day in the studio Madonna recorded the most important and most famous song from the movie. "I had to sing 'Don't Cry for Me Argentina' in front of Andrew Lloyd Webber," she recalled. "I was a complete mess and was sobbing afterward. I thought I had done a terrible job." (266)

Reportedly, the first day of recording the soundtrack in the studio was a disaster in the first degree. The members of the 84-piece orchestra had never played together before, and Andrew Lloyd Webber was upset with them. Parker was jittery, and Madonna indeed went home in tears. The orchestra was fired, and Webber brought in a new conductor.

According to Madonna, "I was so nervous, because I knew that Andrew had had reservations about me, and here I'm singing the hardest song in the piece. All of a sudden there, with everybody for the first time, it was really tense." (251)

Instead of copying the actresses who had previously sung the part of Evita, Madonna chose to interpret the material in her own way. Anyway you sliced it, this was a score that required singing unlike any she had done in the past. "Because the entire movie is sung instead of spoken," she explained, "it has an operatic quality, which inspires over-the-top delivery. I was going after something much more naturalistic. We had to make an intimate, emotional connection at the same time that we were acting and trying to hit our notes. It was an experience that I think has had a real impact on the other aspects of my singing." (266)

With *Evita*, Alan Parker not only had a dramatic musical, but he also had a political story fueled by power and passion. Both the music and the action had to mesh perfectly. No one was more acutely aware of this necessity than he was. "We were all daunted by the mad mountain we had all decided to climb," said Parker. "All of us came from very different worlds—from popular music, from movies, and from musical theater—and so we were all very apprehensive." (266)

The shooting schedule was expected to encompass 85 days in Buenos Aires, Budapest, and London. Budapest, unlike many of the more celebrated European cities, is known for not having its classic architecture compromised by modern glass and steel towers. For this reason, it is a favorite location for films set in pre-1950s' European capitals or in European-styled cities like Buenos Aires.

Madonna, too, had to undergo her own metamorphosis. In *Evita*, she had to age from a young ambitious brunette into a glamorous blonde icon. Madonna also had to contend with an astonishing 84 costume changes.

For the first time in her erratic fifteen-film acting career she really had to inhabit a role, to become Eva Perón in her attitude, manner, and look. One of the things that had to be altered was her famous gap-toothed smile. To eradicate the trademark space in her front teeth Madonna had to wear special dentures over her own teeth to replicate Evita's famous smile. She also had to wear brown contact lenses to match Eva's own eye color.

While Madonna's team of loyal Argentine fans were thrilled that their idol was coming to Buenos Aires, the devoted Perón supporters were appalled that an American sex object like Madonna brazenly thought that she could portray their beloved Evita. Upon arriving in Buenos Aires, Madonna found that Argentina was ready for her. On the drive from the airport to her hotel she saw graffiti that read, "Evita Lives, Get Out, Madonna."

When the film was released later that year, it proved to be a media blitz for Madonna. One of the most exhaustive magazine cover stories spotlighting Madonna appeared in *Vanity Fair*'s October 1996 issue. The 25-page article not only featured photos of the *Erotica* diva glamorously coiffed and dressed in 1940s fashion à la Eva, but also included an exhaustively detailed account of the filming experience, entitled "The Madonna Diaries." This account of her *Evita* experience featured a lot of Madonna whining, bitching, and complaining. It also found her in some rare, self-reflective, insightful moments and, overall, illustrated her single-minded devotion to making this the cinematic experience of a lifetime.

Madonna knew that her reputation was truly on the line with *Evita*. If this movie was a colossal "bomb," it could be the end of her film career. If she was not a sympathetic Eva, she could forget about ever going back to Argentina, as they would surely build a retaliatory bonfire out of her albums and videos.

Throughout the production, she had truly been a team player in a theatrical sense. She had made bonds with the majority of the cast and crew, and came to regard them as part of her *Evita* family. She had nothing but good things to say about director Parker. According to her, "Alan was very supportive during the shooting. He let me sort of follow my own instincts in a lot of cases. We had both been prepared to expect the worst from each other. And then we got together, and it was probably the smoothest working experience I've ever had in terms of a collaboration." (251)

It was rather ironic that her so-star in *Evita* was none other than the same Spanish actor, Antonio Banderas, whom she proclaimed to have a crush on in *Truth or Dare*. He was also one of her co-stars in *Four Rooms*, although their segments were filmed completely apart from each other.

Since Banderas spent the majority of his time during the shooting with his then-pregnant girlfriend Melanie Griffith, he and Madonna did not become especially warm or friendly. In her exhaustively detailed *Vanity Fair* diary, she mentioned him only in passing. She did note that the press was making a big deal about the probability that she would be competing with Melanie Griffith for his attention. With regard to this notion, Madonna dismissed it by stating that she would never date a man who wore cowboy boots.

On the other hand, Banderas had nothing but glowing praise for Madonna. "It was absolutely professional," he said about their relationship during the filming process. "She was so focused, so obsessed with this movie and what it represents to her in terms of her career as well as the personal commitment to this character. I never did sit down with her and say, 'Madonna, what is this that you have for Eva Duarte?' But there was something there. She got pieces of truth in this movie that she's never gotten in even the best video she's done. For the first time—and this is a subjective opinion—she's an actress." (270)

While busy filming *Evita*, Madonna was far from absent from the gossip columns and newspapers. Only weeks after news of her pregnancy had leaked to the press during the filming of *Evita*, she was once again splashed all over the media, thanks to basketball star Dennis Rodman and the publication of his sizzling autobiography, *Bad As I Wanne Be*, which spent eight weeks at Number One on *The New York Times* bestseller list.

According to Rodman in *Bad As I Wanne Be*, when he and Madonna got together, she demanded that he perform oral sex on her. That chapter became one of the most talked about aspects of the entire book, second only to the cover shot of him stark naked on top of a motorcycle. Inarguably, Madonna had met her match this time around. Unfortunately, Rodman's book came out at a time when she was trying to clean up and sophisticate her act. The book's publication resurrected the *Erotica* Madonna, a persona from which she needed to distance herself in order effectively launch *Evita*.

Madonna claimed to be incensed by Rodman's betrayal. "It's not the first time I feel he's exploited his very brief relationship with me," she said at the time. "When I first knew him, I sent him a few very silly faxes with really childish drawings on them, and months after I'd stopped seeing him, they appeared on [the tabloid TV program] *Hard Copy*, and I thought, 'This is only the beginning.' . . . It really wasn't much of a 'relationship,' which is why it astonishes me that he's gotten so much mileage out of it. I'm sure somebody wrote the book for him, and I can only imagine they urged him to be as imaginative and juicy as possible and to make things up and maybe offered him more money if he would talk about me." (246)

Speaking of Rodman, Madonna said, "He is actually someone I would classify as a borderline psychotic personality. He is a very exciting person to be around, like most crazy people, and during the whole two months I dated him—and that was not on any sort of regular basis—it was like this fun adventure, and then I soon discovered that he was a seriously damaged person, and I really couldn't get away from him fast enough. . . . Much as I should hate him, I actually feel compassion for him. This is a person with a few screws loose." (246)

Despite her disclaimer, Rodman's account of their relationship was the talk of all the gossip columns for weeks. "First of all, it was untrue information," Madonna countered. "Second, I felt violated because I did consider him to be a friend, as crazy as he may appear. I know his depiction of our sex life was probably one reason the book sold so well, and that is highly irritating." (252)

Naturally, when Madonna's pregnancy became front page news, the first question on everyone's lips was, "Who is the father?" It turned out to be hunky Carlos Leon, a personal trainer whom Madonna had met during a jog through New York City's Central Park.

One of the first things that the outspoken Madonna announced was that matrimony was strictly out of the question. "I don't see the need. I'm perfectly happy with the way things are," she proclaimed. (252)

In 1998, explaining their short-lived relationship, Madonna said of Carlos, "I was in love with him. A lot of people think I walked out on the street and looked at him and said, 'You're going to be my sperm donor.' I

with him for two years. We were together for three. . . .
[ ] with him. I still have a relationship with him. We are
[ ]." (258)

[ ]alamon, a reporter from *Vogue* magazine, interviewed
[ ] 1996 issue, she pressed Madonna: had Carlos visited
her often on the *Evita* set? The pregnant Ms. Ciccone snapped back, "It's
such a long trip and he has his own work, and I'm not someone who needs
my boyfriend around all the time. I'm not Melanie Griffith!" (246)

It was undeniably odd that, of all the people in the world with whom
Madonna could have had a child, she chose her trainer. On the other
hand, it was perfectly in character for her to have a child with a man she
could dismiss whenever she wanted. Particularly irritating was the fact
that she had to defend what she had done: "It is perfectly socially accept-
able for a man to find a beautiful girl who hasn't accomplished the things
that he's accomplished, and make a life with her. Why does the man
always have to be the one who makes more money? It's pathetic and
sexist and disgusting, and if people don't change the way they view this
thing—the man and woman's place in society—nothing's ever going to
change." (246)

She was equally combative about the public's moral laxity surrounding former husband Sean Penn, who had two children out of wedlock
since she had divorced him. According to her:

> I can give you this whole thing about me being pregnant and not
> being married or living with the father of my child. Does anybody say
> a damn word about my ex-husband having two children with Robin
> Wright and not living with her for five years and having a number of
> girlfriends in the interim? Did anyone say a word about it? He is a
> celebrity, and people pay attention to the things he does. . . . I know
> that up until two weeks before the marriage he had another girlfriend.
> Actually, I thought the marriage was some sort of knee-jerk response
> to me, if you must know, when it was revealed that I was pregnant.
> My reaction was, this is Sean trying to be dramatic. (246)

Sean finally married Robin Wright, but it was not an option for Madonna: "I think that everyone should get married at least once, so you
can see what a silly, outdated institution it is." (254)

Her impending motherhood was bound to change her life in many ways. For one thing, upon learning of her pregnancy, Madonna promptly put her garish Hollywood Hills mansion up for sale. She then moved to a single-story home in the Los Feliz neighborhood that writer James M. Cain made famous in his film noir novel *Double Indemnity*. Apparently, she wanted a more baby-friendly layout, and the 1926 Spanish-style mansion she found fit her perfectly.

Her pregnancy caused her to reevaluate her life. The birth experience and *Evita* transformed her into a more philosophical person than she had been. "I waited so long for this movie, and it finally happened. I wanted so badly to have a child, and I got pregnant while making the movie. Suddenly, God gave me two gifts that were very important to me." (252)

Control freak that she is, this was probably the first aspect of her life that Madonna did not scheme to obtain since having become an international singing star. According to her, "You have no control with being pregnant. Things just happen and you have to hope for the best. I had to do that with Alan. I have approached work from a completely different, more submissive point of view. In the beginning I really forgot it, and finally I realized that I had to have a heap of faith. It was a real letting-go process for me. It's prepared me for having a child." (246)

Of all the times in Madonna's life, how ironic it was that the baby would compete with the single most important project of her career. It could have turned out quite disastrously, but it didn't. "I never had morning sickness," she proudly proclaimed. "A couple of times, I got dizzy and a little nauseous. I attributed that to the incredible heat in Argentina and the long hours. It was gone by the time I found out I was pregnant. I was more worried about my stomach showing. My only sense of terror was, 'I'm not going to fit my [*Evita*] costumes!' " (252)

However, once the movie wrapped, she relaxed and concentrated on her pregnancy. "It was cool to eat whatever I wanted. It was nice to have that freedom." (252) Still, her pregnancy forced her to remove the gold navel ring from her belly button. For a couple of months Madonna did the unthinkable: she withdrew from the public eye to relax and enjoy her pregnancy. Her close friend Rosie O'Donnell gave her a baby shower. Otherwise, Madonna awaited the birth of her child and the release of *Evita*.

Although she longed to be taken seriously, critics dogged her constantly about her motivation for having a baby at this time in her life. She complained, "People have accused me of getting pregnant for the publicity, because I've run out of things to do." (246)

Predictably, the press had a field day with Madonna's pregnancy. Jay Leno joked about it on TV's *Tonight Show*. Newspaper cartoonists had a fine time drawing cone-shaped brassieres that were designed for nursing. Madonna complained in her *Vanity Fair*–magazine *Evita* diary that social critic Camille Paglia wrote that the pregnant Ms. Ciccone was unable to sustain a serious bond with any man, and that the public's concern for the child was legitimate. According to Madonna, "Everything I do is scrutinized, so I shouldn't be surprised that it continued when I was pregnant. I try to have a sense of humor about it, but it does irritate me. . . . My having a child is not for public consumption. It's not a career move. It's not a performance to be judged and rated. Nor is my role as a mother." (252)

Of all possible methods of childbirth available to Madonna, so-called "natural" childbirth was not an option. "My sister had natural childbirth, no drugs, and she doesn't pretend it was a fucking day at the beach," she explained. "I'm not interested in being Wonder Woman in the delivery room. Give me drugs. Sometimes I get really wimpy and think I'm just going to have a C-section. I don't want to go through all this." (246)

On October 14, 1996, having experienced her first labor pains at 3:30 in the morning, she checked into Good Samaritan Hospital in Los Angeles. By noon, the only thing she had experienced was ravenous hunger. Waiting for the baby to arrive, Madonna groaned, "I just want some French fries from McDonald's." (271)

Finally, by 3:30 that afternoon, her doctor suggested that a Caesarean section be performed, since she was in pain and had not gone into labor. The Material Girl agreed. While being rolled into surgery, heavily sedated, she quipped in true Hollywood fashion, "Goodbye, everyone. I'm going to get my nose job now." (271) Soon after, doctors delivered her daughter. Weight: six pounds, nine ounces. Name: Lourdes Maria Ciccone Leon. According to Madonna, "This is the greatest miracle of my life." Proud father Carlos Leon said "She's the most beautiful baby." (271)

Epilogue

Madonna, who the church had nearly banned in the past, pondered little Lourdes' spiritual upbringing: "I'll teach her about Catholicism, but also about all religions, especially Buddhism, Judaism, and the Kabbalah [ancient Jewish lore]. My own religion combines all those. I would rather present the Bible to my daughter as 'Some very interesting stories you could learn from,' rather than 'This is the rule.' " (252)

Never one to follow in anyone else's footsteps, Madonna had already decided to do things uniquely her way. "The last thing I'm going to do is raise my children the way I see a lot of celebrities raising their children now. I don't want to traipse around with nannies and tutors. I think it's really important for children to stay in one place and to socialize with other children. I had that, and I want my child to have it. I'm not saying I don't want to go on tour or make movies anymore, but I realize I'm going to have to make a lot of compromises, and I'm comfortable with that." (246)

Leaving the hospital with Lourdes, Madonna announced, "I just can't wait to wear anything with a waistline." She also wanted to keep press photographers away from her new baby girl. She issued the edict, "I won't be doing anything in public with my daughter until she's much older."

Although she kept little Lourdes out of the scrutiny of press photographers, her media extravaganza was just beginning as the premiere of *Evita* swiftly approached.

In October 1996, the month Lourdes was born, the first single from the *Evita* soundtrack was released. It was the new composition "You Must Love Me." According to Madonna at the time, "It's my favorite song from the movie. It's just so beautiful." (266)

On record, as in the movie, *Evita* allowed Madonna to step out of her bigger-than-life persona. She turned both the soundtrack album and all three of its singles into hits. The somber but touching "You Must Love Me" peaked at Number Eighteen and received a lot of solid radio airplay. As the only new song written for the movie, it was the only song eligible for an Academy Award nomination. "Don't Cry for Me Argentina" peaked at Number Eight, making it her 33rd Top-10 single on the American Pop charts in twelve years. The lushly orchestrated two-disk original sound-track album premiered on *Billboard*'s album chart at Number Six, ultimately peaking at Number Two. It was certified double Platinum in the

United States for sales in excess of two million copies. A maxi-single disco version of "Don't Cry for Me Argentina" was also released and quickly became a Number One hit on the Dance charts. In addition to Madonna singing a half-Spanish-language version of the song, it was re-mixed in six different versions and sung in a completely different tempo than the highly orchestrated, original-soundtrack version. In Europe only, a third single, "Another Suitcase in Another Hall," was also released and made it to Number Seven in England. A single made in Germany put all three of Madonna's *Evita* hits ("Another Suitcase in Another Hall," "You Must Love Me," and the "Miami Mix Edit" of "Don't Cry for Me Argen-tina"), along with a fourth cut from the film, "Hello and Goodbye," on one single disk.

Like an elaborately wrapped Christmas present laid under a holiday tree, the film *Evita* was released on December 25, 1996, in New York City and Los Angeles. It opened across the country on January 10, 1997, just in time to qualify for that spring's Academy Awards nominations.

No one was more proud of the job she had done in *Evita* than Ma-donna herself, to the point of being very vocal about it. "There's such a fleshed-out story now that the film barely resembles the stage production, and thank God," she said.

> I was actually enraged by the play, because I felt it was only the British-aristocracy point of view and portrayed Eva as this one-di-mensional ambitious bitch. It's as ridiculous as portraying or thinking of me that way. People don't accomplish by being one-dimensional or power hungry. She affected too many people. So it was really impor-tant for me to do the research I did to give her a humanity I don't think Andrew Lloyd Webber and Tim Rice gave her in the musical. (246)

With rare exception, the film *Evita* remains faithful to the original Broadway production, except that Madonna sings two more songs than Patti LuPone sang. Not only does Madonna have "You Must Love Me," but the third most famous song of the score, "Another Suitcase in Another Hall," was given to her as well. Originally, the song was sung by Perón pre-Eva mistress, as she is dismissed from his life. In the film Madonna sings it earlier, to underscore her breakup with Migaldi. When the other mistress is seen, she sings only one line of the song that once belonged to her character. This was clearly Madonna's movie, and all of the most memorable songs were hers.

A couple of lines of the song "Rainbow Tour," which had been part of the Broadway soundtrack, were scissored from the movie. They addressed Evita's disdain for the British and the insult of having tea in some "tin pot castle." The word in Buenos Aires was that this inflammatory, unflattering passage was removed as part of Menem's agreement to let the Casa Rosada be used in the film.

There were also some ironically amusing "Madonna" moments in the film. In one scene Eva Perón meets with the Pope in Rome. That one brief moment, amidst the Rainbow Tour segment, was worth a chuckle, because that is about as close to an audience with the Pope as the real-life Madonna will ever come. Then there is the scene where Madonna, as a cancer-stricken Eva, faints in a church, and for a quick flash it is a déja vu reminder of her "Like a Prayer" video. And the "Rainbow High" number is just a 1940s version of "Vogue" revisited.

Ask any three people their opinion of Madonna in *Evita*, and chances are that you will receive three different answers. One will love it, one will hate it, and the third will say, "Well, she didn't ruin it." For Madonna's fans, *Evita* was the ultimate star vehicle for her, and she made the most out of it. Madonna is more focused and fascinating than she has ever appeared on screen. She is glamorously photographed throughout, especially in the middle segments, where she brings to life Eva Perón's ascension up the social ladder. Her tango dancing is lively and exciting, and in *Evita* she does some of the best singing of her career.

For many, her singing never approached the fiery Broadway bravado of Patti LuPone. And for some, it was impossible to forget Madonna was singing about Eva Perón without ever convincingly becoming her. Leonard Maltin's *Movie & Video Guide* called *Evita* "the world's longest music video," complaining that "as a pageant, it works, but there is no emotional center, leaving the viewer aloof from its leading character from start to finish." He went on to point out, "Madonna parades (and sings) well enough," but that Pryce and Banderas "bring it to life." (264)

Yet, *Q* magazine's Paul Du Noyer proclaimed, "If there was ever an ideal vehicle for Madonna's dream of transcendent stardom, this must be it. . . . The soundtrack carries some of her most commanding vocal efforts so far. Cleverly, her singing develops with the plot. When she's a callow showgirl, hustling her way from the pampas to Buenos Aires, you hear the old Ciccone squeak. But there is maturity and richness in her rendition of the dying Evita's swan song." (268)

Siskel and Ebert gave the film "two thumbs up." ABC-TV in New York called it "unforgettable," while *Newsweek* referred to it as "spectacular." *Time* magazine, ABC-TV, and *The Boston Globe* all listed it on their year's "Ten Best" films. Even the country music magazine *Twang* declared, "Madonna has finally become a movie star, and, because of her, *Evita* is a smash. . . . She has not only landed the role of a lifetime, she charges it with lively conviction." (272)

Time magazine's Richard Corliss gave a glowing review entitled "You Must Love Her" in its December 16, 1996, issue. "It's a relief to say that Alan Parker's film, which opens on Christmas Day, is pretty damn fine, well cast and handsomely visualized—easily the best adaptation of a Broadway-style musical in decades. . . . Madonna once again confounds our expectations. . . . She does a tough score proud. Lacking the vocal vigor of Elaine Paige's West End *Evita*, Madonna plays Evita with a poignant weariness. . . . She has more than just a bit of star quality. . . . Love or hate Madonna-Eva, she is a magnet for all eyes. You must watch her. . . . You must see *Evita*." (273)

In January 1997 the nominations for the Golden Globe Awards, presented annually by the Hollywood Foreign Press Association, were announced. Miracle of miracles—after years of dreadful movies, and only an occasional flash of cinematic brilliance, Madonna was nominated as Best Actress in a Musical or Comedy for her performance in *Evita*. That distinction alone was worth all of the effort she had invested, beginning with her unflagging campaign for the role. When she actually won the award, it was a diamond in her crown of achievements.

As usual, the Academy Awards were a whole other story. Since the Foreign Press Association nominated five actresses for drama and five actresses for musical or comedy, the potential field of nominees was immediately cut in half. And since most of the old-guard Hollywood royalty—who still make up the bulk of Academy voters—viewed Madonna as less than a class act, she and *Evita* were roundly snubbed in the major categories. The one shining moment of the telecast came when "You Must Love Me" won the Academy Award for best song. Naturally, Madonna performed the song on the awards telecast, so it was almost like getting an Academy Award for her performance of it. Of course, the award really went to the songwriters, Webber and Rice.

After the Academy Awards nominations had been announced, writer Bruce Handy penned an article in the February 24, 1997, issue of *Time* magazine entitled "Crying For Madonna, Experts Explain Why Oscar Snubbed the Studios," in which he surveyed the choices that the Academy had made that year. Handy interviewed several industry insiders, identified by occupation alone. The dialogue that appeared included: "Publicist: 'There was Madonna backlash and maybe Andrew Lloyd Webber backlash—and the movie was horrible. This is the second year in a row that the Golden Globe–winning actress—last year it was Nicole Kidman—didn't even get a nomination.' Former studio head: 'I don't think there was a backlash. If anything, I think there was sympathy for the movie. It took a lot of guts to make an all-out musical.' " (274)

Amid the *Evita* media whirl, Madonna was at her most contained and least controversial. One of her appearances was the 1997 TV special *Happy Birthday Elizabeth: A Celebration of Life,* commemorating Elizabeth Taylor's birthday. It was Taylor's last performance before undergoing brain surgery, so it was an emotion-filled, concert-type event, with Elizabeth in the front row of the audience being honored in song and with comedy acts.

Clearly, the spirit of Eva Perón, and her channeling of it on screen, had somehow changed Madonna and her outlook on life: "*Evita* gave me time off from being me. And so it was a really great relief. It gave me a whole new perspective on everything. I just stopped feeling sorry for myself." (258)

Suddenly, Madonna desired to make more meaningful statements than she had at the beginning of the 1990s. If there had been any message associated with her *Erotica* era, it would have been have sex with anyone or anything if it feels good. Now, between *Evita* and motherhood, she started seeking more substance.

Three years shy of the dawn of the new millennium, publications were already logging exhaustive lists of the century's best in various fields. There was no question that Madonna's name would be bantered about in one way or another. In its May 15, 1997, issue, *Rolling Stone* magazine named *Like a Prayer* one of the "200 Best Albums Ever Made."

The year 1997 was truly one of bizarre occurrences, and the second half of it seemed to be a particularly rough one for celebrities. In July 1997 fashion designer Gianni Versace was murdered outside of his Miami home by a psychopath who committed suicide before the police found him. Having frequently worn his designs, Madonna was crushed when she found out about Versace's death.

The most symbolically tragic event of the 1990s was undoubtedly the sudden death of Princess Diana of Wales in August 1997. Only days later, when Madonna was on stage in Radio City Music Hall as a presenter for the annual *MTV Video Music Awards,* she condemned the paparazzi photographers of the world, whom it seemed had caused the death of Princess Diana. This sentiment was indicative of her new and more serious life stance.

Indeed, Diana's death had caused press photographers to stop and reevaluate their insane quest for the perfect shot. According to Madonna at the time, "Since Princess Diana's death, I have to say I've had a lot more freedom. I spent two weeks in New York right after it happened and I haven't had so much freedom in, like, ten years. I went to the park almost every day with my daughter and pushed her in a stroller and nobody bothered me. And I was in shock. Except for one day, I never saw paparazzi." (250)

Madonna also had a new way of looking at herself and her career: "The act of writing music or singing it or performing is much more exciting than trying to be beautiful. Ever since my daughter was born, I feel the fleetingness of time. And I don't want to waste it on getting the perfect lip color." (250)

She credited much of her shift in outlook to Lourdes: "I think [motherhood] made me face up to my more feminine side. I had a much more masculine view of the world. What I missed and longed for was that unconditional love that a mother gives you. And so, having my daughter is the same kind of thing. It's like that first, true, pure, unconditional love. It is the first time it has happened to me that I am aware of. The love you get from your father isn't the same." (258)

Motherhood also changed her circle of friends. "I do have a close set of women friends now," she announced in *Rolling Stone* magazine in 1997. "I'm much closer to women who have children now; I'm drawn to them. Being surrounded by good friends always helped. But having my daughter helps me deal with [the celebrity spotlight], because everything else pales in comparison anyway." (250)

By now, Carlos Leon was out of her life, with the exception of unlimited visitation rights to their daughter. As far as a future with him, apparently he was not "Y2K-compliant."

All kinds of news items about Madonna having found religion were circulating during this era, including the bizarre announcement that she was studying the Kabbalah, an ancient form of Judaism. "It is not about religion. It is sort of a manual for living," Madonna explained. "It has nothing to do with dogma. It is the mystical interpretation of the Old Testament. How has it changed me? It's helped me stand up and take responsibility for everything to do with me. To stop saying, 'You did this to me,' or 'They did this to me. It is their fault.' It has taught me to take responsibility and look at everything that is happening to me and be grateful for even the painful things." (258)

Another major change in her life involved her former fitness-freak exercise-and-jogging routines. Pumping iron was out, yoga was in. "I guess everybody associates me with this incredible sort of workout ethic," she explained. "Well, I used to do that. I am here to say it is a huge waste of time. I didn't have to push myself so hard, and I didn't know it. . . . I was hooking into aggression. Now, with yoga, I have to look inside and deal with the stillness." (258) Obviously, her self-imposed maternity leave had wrought several major changes in her life. "Now that I've had the baby, I feel liberated in a sense. I don't feel I have to be a certain size or have perfect abs. I still exercise, but I don't care as much." (252)

In the March 1998 *Vanity Fair,* Madonna unveiled little Lourdes in an exclusive photo shoot. Also in March, she was set to release her latest album, *Ray of Light.* Coincidence? Or typically careful planning from Madonna Command Central?

On January 23, several weeks before the official release of *Ray of Light,* the Singapore Madonna Link, an unauthorized web site, allowed Internet explorers to download a preview of the song "Frozen." The site reportedly received 140,000 hits in three weeks. A press controversy exploded over this issue: Was it an act of piracy, or a planned publicity stunt? Either way, the Madonna frenzy was in full swing.

On February 14, 1998, Madonna showed up at the Roxy, a dance club/roller disco on West 18th Street in Manhattan, at 2:00 A.M. to debut three songs from her forthcoming *Ray of Light* album. Reviewing the performance, her first live concert in four years, *Rolling Stone* magazine condescendingly described her performance: "Dress globally, talk snobbily, sing wobbly." (275)

Upon its release, many critics felt that *Ray of Light* was truly a case of Madonna Light, similar to what the Beatles *Magical Mystery Tour* was to their career.

Explaining her new awareness to *The New York Times*, she said, "As my body was opening up and I was going into places that had been locked for so many years, it was releasing emotional things. I'd be lying in *sivasana* [a prone corpse-like position] and I'd be weeping. Or I'd do a forward bend and tears would come to my eyes. I'd sort of get embarrassed and think, "Why is this happening to me? But I realized that I was going through a catharsis." (276)

She even admitted that her established audience might not be ready for this sudden mood swing:

> There are still a lot of people who are really uncomfortable with these topics, and they're going to go, 'We liked her better when she was hitchhiking naked in Miami. Where's the fun Madonna?' But I think that I have the ability now to have more fun and be happier than I ever have in my life. . . . People have always had this obsession with me, about my reinvention of myself. I just feel like I'm shedding layers. I'm slowly revealing who I am. (276)

She told *Billboard* magazine: "This album is reflective of where I am in my life right now—in terms of my musical interests and in terms of my personal beliefs. I feel like I've been enlightened, and that it's my responsibility to share what I've learned so far with the world." (277)

For a two-week period, you couldn't walk into a bar in Manhattan without overhearing someone asking, "Have you heard the new Madonna album? Do you like it?" Critics didn't take so long to make up their minds. *Rolling Stone,* seriously questioning her musical choices, stated, "Frankly, *Ray of Light* could have been a lot more fun. . . . Madonna's prayers and sermons, heavy with Indo-Hollywood spirituality and new motherhood, are serious verging on severe." (275)

Ann Powers, coeditor of *Rock She Wrote,* pondered in *The New York Times,*

Madonna has always encouraged her fans to express themselves. *Ray of Light* asks them to do it again on a new plane. . . . *Ray of Light* is at its weakest when Madonna gets showily 'personal.' The ruminations on fame in 'Drowned World' and the lover's farewell in 'Power of Goodbye' come off as a stilted exclamation of a drama queen. . . . 'Mer Girl' is a more interesting mess. . . . In such moments, Madonna comes perilously close to New Age gobbledygook. (276)

Time's Christopher John Farley claimed, "Unlike some of Madonna's previous hot and sexy albums, this one is resolutely frigid—if you licked this album, your tongue would stick to it. . . . However, the contrast between the chilly surface and the confessional nature of many of the lyrics creates a tension, even a passion." (278)

Billboard reported, "Much has already been made of the pop chameleon's foray into electronica, and it deserves every prerelease accolade it's gotten—and them some. Easily her most mature and personal work to date, *Ray of Light* finds Madonna weaving lyrics with the painstaking intimacy of diary entries. . . . A deliciously adventurous, ultimately victorious effort from one of pop music's most compelling performers." (279)

Some of the tracks were more musical melodies with electronic touches on which her poems of ponderance floated. As she explained, "I had been listening to a lot of electronica and trance music. It was just this blank canvas, a mood thing. It occurred to me that you could take it to another level by actually investing it with emotion." (276)

"I've been a fan of all kinds of electronic music for many years, and I wanted to incorporate that sound into my music," she stated at the time. Like her creative collaboration on *Bedtime Stories*, she aligned herself with a producer/writer who excelled at this new wave of 1990s music. She found the perfect partner for this project in William Orbit. "I love the haunting, trance-like quality of his records," she said. "I've also found something melancholy about his music. Since I'm attracted to that sound, and since I tend to write a lot of sad songs, we seemed like a good match." (277)

Their creative colloboration began with Orbit handing her a tape with five different instrumental tracks. "It basically was a sketchbook of fantastic ideas. Every track was so inspiring. I took them and gave them structure," she explains. (277)

One of them, "Swim," about the consequences of bad karma, really touched her. "It gave me shivers the first time I heard it. We both knew we were onto something special." (277)

The thirteen-track album begins with the song 'Drowned World/Substitute for Love." The song starts with Madonna announcing that she has "traded fame for love." As if that announcement isn't jarring enough, a careful examination of the album liner notes reveals that the song samples excerpts from a Rod McKuen/Anita Kerr composition called "Why I Follow the Tigers." Madonna sampling Rod McKuen? What is the world coming to?

The song ponders the hollowness of fame, but in many ways could easily be interpreted as singing about embracing film. In the song she renounces handsome strangers, ferris wheel rides, and artificial drugs for what she has now found. Indeed, there is a new Madonna for premillennium spiritual seekers.

On "Swim" she sings about diving into the ocean and washing away all of the sins of the 1990s: killings by children, rape, and the hypocrisy of modern-day preachers and churches. "Swim" was actually recorded on the day Gianni Versace was killed. Madonna went into the recording studio knowing that her friend had just been senselessly murdered on the streets of Miami—a city she now called home for part of the year. According to her, "I think that explains why the track has an emotional resonance to it. It was intense to record." (278)

"Ray of Light," with its danceable beat, sounds more like the old Madonna. She sings of the unbridled energy that has come with her new enlightenment. Then there are songs that make no earthly sense, except what they say at face value. "Candy Perfume Girl" is one of those songs. To me, it sounds like a billboard in Tokyo written in the English language and losing linguistic correctness in the translation.

On "Skin," Madonna longs to make a human connection, commanding one to put one's hands on her skin like a faith healer. On "Nothing Really Matters" she confesses her obsession with making herself happy. On "Sky Fits Heaven" she expounds about not judging others and making it her life's motto for the future—that and following her own instincts.

On the Far East India-sounding song "Shanti/Ashtangi," Madonna actually sings in the ancient lost language of Sanskrit. If anyone could have predicted this at the dawn of the 1990s, they would have been laughed at as a heretic, a drunk, or a nut. What's next for her, an album in Croatian? In the song she quotes traditional Sanskrit text, part of which reads, "I worship the guru's lotus feet." As Christopher John Farley in *Time* wryly pointed out, "Madonna in only six years has gone from sucking on feet to using them as catalysts for spiritual revelation." (278)

In "Frozen," Madonna sings about opening one's heart, or else all emotions are "on ice." According to her, the song's initial recording went on and on. "It's totally out of control, the original version is well over ten minutes long. It was completely indulgent, but I loved it. It was heartbreaking to cut it down to a manageable length." (277) The finished product logged in at six minutes and twelve seconds. When it was released as a single, four separate mixes were included, tallying 31 minutes and 36 "Frozen" seconds.

"Retaliation, revenge, hate, regret, that's what I deal with in 'Frozen,' " Madonna explained. "Everybody's going to say, 'That's a song about Carlos,' but it's not really; it's just about people in general." (276)

"The Power of Goodbye" deals with knowing when to turn one's back on a person or a phase in one's life, and walk away. "To Have and Not to Hold" is about being unable to capture another's affections. "Little Star" represents finding renewed meaning in life from someone's presence—little Lourdes is the likely inspiration for this song.

The album ends with "Mer Girl," a song with rambling narrative verse, in which Madonna sings about running from her house as though in a dream. Her dead mother, her insomniac daughter, and other aspects of her real life are all discussed as the singer claims to be running and running and running in the quest of some sort of unattainable truth. Referring to "Mer Girl" in a *TV Guide* cover story, Madonna explained, "That is an encapsulated view of me and my life." (258)

Ray of Light is a deeply personal album for Madonna. Upon initial listening, it does leave a chill. However, with subsequent listenings, it grows on one and becomes a thought-provoking milestone in a career that seems to know no boundaries.

Thanks to her *Evita* experience, and all the work she did to stretch and train her voice, she brought to *Ray of Light* a new, more finely tuned instrument. "Training my voice has opened me up immeasurably, and it's allowed me to do things with my voice that I never thought were possible. I'm so proud of the way the album came out. But for a moment, after I first finished it, I thought, 'What have I done?' Emotionally and sonically, it went in such a different territory for me." (277) However, risk-taking was a trademark Madonna move by now.

A haunting album of over an hour of music, *Ray of Light* was inspired by as many ideologies as Madonna had explored over the last few years. In her quest for spirituality she examined the teachings of several Far Eastern cultures. Her subsequent videos and television performances in which she promoted this album reflected the cultures of several of these Asian countries.

According to William Orbit, there was actually another whole album's worth of tracks left on the editing room floor, so much in fact that it was under consideration to release an album of unreleased Madonna out-takes. "It would be like the play *Rosencrantz and Guildenstern Are Dead.* You'd see the original album from a slightly different angle." (278)

Among the songs missing from *Ray of Light* is "Has To Be," a haunting Madonna-William Orbit-Patrick Leonard composition, which finds the singer pondering the existence of God and contending that there has to be "someone out there" watching life on Earth. The song's only appearance is as the "B" side on the single CD of "Ray of Light." Although it is much too slow to be a hit single, "Has to Be" makes one wonder what other goodies were omitted from this undeniably creative album.

Regarding the somber nature of the material on *Ray of Light,* Madonna proclaimed in her typically blunt fashion, "You can't help being sad and lonely when you're going through self-examination. Because, at the end of the day, you're going to be buried alone." (276)

Ultimately, *Ray of Light* hit Number Two on the *Billboard* LP chart, and tallied a triple platinum certification for sales of more than three million copies in the United States alone. She continued her magic for pulling one hit single after another from the album: "Frozen" peaked at Number Two on the singles charts in America, followed by "Ray of Light" (Number Five), "The Power of Goodbye" (Number Nineteen), and "Nothing Really Matters" (Number One).

Ever the promoter, Madonna kept herself in the public eye. On April 12, 1998, she starred in the hour-long VH1 special *Madonna Rising.* The documentary, in which she and her new best friend, gay British actor Rupert Everett, and a video cameraman visited New York City, brought back memories of her early days in Manhattan.

To usher in the new album and her new-found religious philosophies, the first video from *Ray of Light* was "Frozen," which added a whole new "look" to Madonna's sketchbook of styles. Dressed in something that looked like it came from a Goth-Girl—long black hair, mehndi henna tattoos on her hands, and severe black nail polish—this was a look radically different for Madonna.

In August 1998 Madonna reached a major milestone in her life: she turned forty. Reaching this dramatic birthday slowed neither her pace nor drive. For many media stars of the twentieth century, their forties often became their most productive artistic period. Madonna was determined to maintain her breakneck pace of producing albums, videos, and movies.

When pressed about reaching an age where playing comedy ingenue roles would become increasingly difficult, Madonna snapped, "It's not like I'm in a position where I go, 'Oh God, in a couple of more years I'm not going to be able to get those parts,' and I wouldn't want them. I'm not insanely jealous of the movies that Sandra Bullock and Demi Moore are making. What is that anyway? It's not acting, it's not cinema, it's not art. In the end, the art I make is the art I make." (246) Unlike wine, time will never mellow the outspoken Madonna.

Having already embroiled herself in controversy in the past with her response to the Catholic church, Madonna's *Ray of Light* musings providing an excellent opportunity to challenge and outrage religions. In September 1998, appearing on the annual *MTV Music Video Awards* telecast, with the help of four dancers positioned behind her, Madonna performed a song from her latest album as the multi-armed Indian goddess Shiva. To complete the look, her hands were temporarily henna tattooed. This time around, the Vatican didn't care less, however the Hindu group, World Vaishnava Association, demanded that she apologize publicly. Instead, she blasted back, "If they're so pure, why are they watching MTV?" (275)

Regardless of her critics, Madonna was winning popularity awards hands down. That night at the *MTV Music Video Awards*, she walked away with an astonishing six awards, including Best Video of the Year for "Ray of Light." *Ray of Light* was not only a testament to her newfound spiritual awareness, it was also creating a watershed of acceptance for her.

When Cher's *Believe* album became the comeback recording of the decade, everyone was listening with fascination. Cher publicly admitted that she too was amazed at suddenly having the biggest-selling single and album of her long career. It was also announced that Madonna was in love with the Spanish Flamenco, guitar-driven dance song "Dov'e L'Amore" from Cher's 1999 hit album. According to Cher, Madonna approached her and said that she was interesting in directing a video version of it, which sounded like a great idea at the time, as Madonna is certainly a pro when it comes to music videos. However, it never transpired.

In the past Madonna had been the queen of MTV, winning one video award after another, demonstrating her creativity and, most of all, her popularity. While selling millions of records, in the past Madonna had been largely overlooked by the Grammy Awards. Although nominated for eight Grammys, thus far, her only trophy was the Best Long Form Video in 1991 for *Madonna Blonde Ambition Tour Live.* Apparently, many Grammy Award voters viewed her as a studio-created pop phenomenon; her recordings and her career in general did not seem to win the respect of her peers. All this changed in 1999.

When the nominations were announced in January 1999, Madonna was up for five separate awards, including top prizes: Record of the Year and Album of the Year. Her other nominations were for Best Dance Recording, Best Pop Album, and Best Short Form Music Video for "Ray of Light."

Grammy Awards/Recording Academy president Michael Greene, in a press release on *www.grammy.com* said, "Madonna has always been a trendsetter, a risk taker and multifaceted performance artist. The Recording Academy is very proud of her contributions to music and is looking forward to what promises to be a dynamic and exciting appearance on the 41st Grammy awards telecast." (280)

Madonna opened the 1999 Grammy Awards show with "Nothing Really Matters." Having mined just about every other Asian culture for fashion ideas for her *Ray of Light* videos and performances, this time around she performed the number with a decidedly Japanese flair, in a bright red kimono, Oriental makeup, and straight black hair right out of Tokyo.

At the Shrine Auditorium that night, when the Grammy Awards took their first commercial break, all anyone in the star-studded live audience could talk about was, "What's up with Madonna and that kabuki number?" It certainly attracted everyone's attention.

Despite the success of her *Ray of Light* LP, critics still ripped into her as a performer who took herself way too seriously. In an amusing piece from the next morning's *Detroit Free Press*, entitled, "Lauryn's Sermon, Madonna's Misfire," writer Kelley L. Carter claimed, "It's official. If there was any doubt Madonna's singing voice is miserably flat, her show-opening song, 'Nothing Really Matters,' blatantly exposed her off-key warble to the world." (281)

That evening she won three separate Grammy Awards in the latter three categories. Album of the Year went to Lauryn Hill for *The Miseducation of Lauryn Hill,* and Record of the Year went to Celine Dion for "My Heart Will Go On." However, Madonna was bowled over by her achievement, especially the Grammy for Best Pop Album. She felt like she had truly won the respect of her peers and was proud that this very personal album had done it for her.

Besides Madonna's kabuki production number on the Grammy Awards telecast, the most talked-about event that evening was the explosive reception that Latin superstar Ricky Martin garnered, performing his song "The Cup of Life." After wowing the audience with his Spanish-language hit, backstage he felt a pair of hands covering his eyes from behind. The cheery "guess who" that accompanied the gesture came from none other than Madonna. That particular performance on the Grammy telecast made Ricky Martin an overnight superstar, and Madonna recognized it instantly. Martin was just finishing up recording his first English-language album for Columbia Records, and he asked her to perform a duet with him on the album. Not only did she agree, but she and William Orbit wrote a song especially for the occasion. The song, "Be Careful (*Cuidado Con Mi Corazón*)" is one of the highlights of the album.

It was fascinating to see that Madonna knew exactly whose rocket to hitch herself to and at exactly the right moment. The resulting *Ricky Martin* album went all the way to Number One in *Billboard,* selling in excess of six million copies in the United States alone. In other words, twice as many people heard Madonna singing with Ricky Martin on their duet than those who purchased *Ray of Light.* Even when she shares the spotlight, Madonna is always working overtime for Madonna.

Speaking of incredibly good instincts, while all of these endeavors were netting her millions of dollars annually, her own record label, Maverick, was something of a 1990s success story as well. The most notable person she had signed to Maverick Records was Canadian singer/song-writer Alanis Morissette. Her album *Jagged Little Pill* has sold 27 million records worldwide (as of January 2000), surpassing Madonna's *Like a Virgin* LP. She always knew a winner, and in Morissette she found exactly that.

According to Madonna, she has a very "hands on" working relationship with her label and the artists she has signed. "I asked for a record company," she explained. "I'm not going to be invisible or simply phone in my partnership. There's no honor or satisfaction in palming off the work to someone else." (282)

In 1997 Madonna's good friend Mike Myers scored a huge box-office hit with *Austin Powers: International Man of Mystery*. The James Bond/*In Like Flint* parody of spy films of the swinging 1960s ushered in a whole new array of sayings ("Do I make you horny, baaaby?"/"Let's shag!"), and a ton of cross-merchandising. In the summer of 1999 a sequel to the original Austin Powers movie was released *Austin Powers: The Spy Who Shagged Me*. Again, it was filled with a cornucopia of late 1960s non-sense. Since the soundtrack to the original movie had been a hit too, the soundtrack to the sequel was also largely touted, eventually selling over one million copies in America alone. Not only did Madonna's personal record label, Maverick Records, issue the soundtrack album to *Austin Powers: The Spy Who Shagged Me*, but Madonna was the hit-making star of the album. Her fun and swinging '60s composition, "Beautiful Stranger," became a Number Nineteen hit in America and catapulted the album to Number Five in *Billboard*, giving it million-selling Platinum status. In fact, it was such a success that a sequel was released, entitled *More Music from Austin Powers: The Spy Who Shagged Me*. Madonna was again the star of that album, as it included a remixed version of "Beautiful Stranger."

With her own movie career revitalized by *Evita*, speculation centered on what her next cinematic venture would be. It was announced in 1998 that she would star in a glitzy film based on the hit Broadway musical, *Chicago*, in the role of murderess Roxy Hart. Further casting was announced, claiming that Madonna's pal Rosie O'Donnell would be cost-arring as lesbian prison matron, Mama Morton. However, the film never seemed to get off the ground.

Finally, Madonna decided on a comedy entitled *The Next Best*

Thing, costarring her buddy Rupert Everett. In December 1999 Madonna was in the studio recording her version of the 1970s Don McLean hit "American Pie," to be included in the film's soundtrack, both with early 2000 release dates.

Just in time for the 1999 Christmas season, Madonna released the video and DVD entitled, *Madonna: The Video Collection, 1993–1999,* taking her right up to her newest 1999 shag-a-delic release, "Beautiful Stranger."

Throughout the year, Madonna had remained very high-profile. When *People* magazine published its "Best & Worst Dressed '99" celebrity issue, Madonna and her running mate Cher were both in the Top-10 tally of tackiest dressed superstars. The article hysterically claimed of Madonna, "In recent months the 41-year-old singer has been stumbling down roads leading to India, Transylvania and all points in between. No wonder we can't keep up." One of the critics who was polled in the issue said of Madonna's fashion sense, "She's way over the top." (283)

As the 21st century dawned, Madonna was very much in the news. When it came time for magazines to announce the biggest, best, and most defining events and creative products of the 20th century, Madonna was right there. *Newsweek*'s "Voices of the Century" issue (June 28, 1999) saluted her "ruthless edge" for having turned herself into one of the century's most fascinating celebrities. *People* called her their number three "Favorite Female Singer" of the century, behind Aretha Franklin and Barbra Streisand (December 31, 1999). Even *The New York Times* (January 3, 2000) claimed that her *Immaculate Collection* was one of the definitive album releases of the century.

In December 1999 there was speculation that she would move to London. It was rumored that she was contemplating making a down payment on an $8 million mansion in the British Isles. She ended up purchasing the mansion and then promptly put the house back on the marketplace when she found out that the building represented a possible security risk. After her notorious bout with one stalker, the risk seemed too great for her to chance it. There was also talk about Madonna starring in an upcoming screen adaptation of Noel Coward's *Quadrille.*

In fact, she has been raving about England ever since she filmed *Evita* there. She spoke of her new quest, and her new outlook: "It's just an evolution, really, since I made *Evita.* Because going down to South

America and getting beaten up the way that I was in the newspapers every day—and sort of living vicariously through what happened to Eva Perón—then finding myself pregnant. Going from the depths of despair and then coming out on the other side . . . you know, becoming a mother, I just have a whole new outlook on life. I see the world as a much more hopeful place. I just feel an infinite amount of compassion towards other people. That's the effect that she has on me—in addition to many others. It happened before she was born. The peace began once I left Argentina and went to London." (250) Madonna was ready for London, but was London prepared for Madonna?

Madonna spent New Year's Eve 1999 in Miami. She and her date for the evening, director Guy Ritchie, attended Donatella Versace's millennium bash at the Versace mansion. Gossip columns were abuzz with rumors of Madonna's snub of actress Jennifer Lopez at the party. Apparently, when Jennifer Lopez and her date arrived, Madonna loudly announced that, for her, the party was now over, and with that she swept out of the mansion. Madonna and Ritchie later partied at Ingrid Casares's club, called Bar Room, located in South Beach.

On January 4, 2000, the 42nd Annual Grammy Award nomination were announced. Madonna's "Beautiful Stranger," and the soundtrack album from which it had been taken, were both nominated. Madonna found herself competing against Christina Aguillera, Sarah McLachlan, Britney Spears, and Alanis Morissette in the category of Best Female Pop Vocal Performance. The *Austin Powers: The Spy Who Shagged Me* album was nominated for Best Soundtrack Album; she and William Orbit were also nominated in a third category, as writers of "Beautiful Stranger." Now that she had broken her previous Grammy streak of being largely ignored, she was thrilled to be perennially considered Grammy-worthy. When the Grammys were handed out on February 23, 2000, she ended up winning the latter award, for songwriting, along with Orbit.

The first week of February 2000, one of the most highly anticipated recordings of Madonna's career was released—her version of Don McLean's "American Pie." The original 1971 hit was an 8-minute, 27-second ode, a tone poem about the plane crash of Buddy Holly, Richie Valens, and the Big Bopper. "American Pie" became one of the most known rock anthems of the 1970s during its initial release.

According to Madonna, it was Rupert Everett's idea to have her record the song. "At first I was like, 'Don McLean? No way!' " she claims. "But Rupert kept bugging me and bugging me. So finally I embraced the idea."

She was so convinced of his decision that she invited him to be her background singer on the track. "Yup, he's my back-up singer," she explained. "Honestly, he's good. You know, he made a couple of records somewhere in his career. So, he can carry a tune." (284)

Not everyone connected with the project was equally as enthusiastic. When she asked her newest collaborator to produce the musical tracks for her, William Orbit thought she was joking. "When she called up about it, I wasn't really sure it was a serious proposition," he explained. "I thought it was one of these ideas that might go away if I didn't do anything about it. Then she called back and said, 'Have you started on it yet?' " (285)

The original treatment of the script for *The Next Best Thing* called for the use of Patti Smith's song "Easter" in a funeral scene. Rupert Everett thought that "American Pie" would better fit the segment in the film, because it was more upbeat than "Easter."

Madonna explained, "There is a scene where a boyfriend of one of the lead characters dies, and at his funeral we all start singing his favorite song, which is 'American Pie.' The song becomes a kind of theme song of rebellion and nostalgia throughout the movie." (285)

Rupert additionally felt that the song was a great one for Madonna to sing at this point in her recording career. "To hear that and imagine her looking back on her career, the 1990s, the 1980s, all that she's done. And it's just a great millennium song." (285)

Even Don McLean was enthused to hear that Madonna would be singing her version of his signature song. "I'm delighted she has decided to record it," he said prior to the song's release. "I'm a fan of hers, and I think she is a colossal performer and presence in the music business. . . . I'm sure whatever she is doing with the song is exciting and appropriate." (285)

Originally, Madonna intended to premiere "American Pie" on the pregame telecast of the January 30, 2000, Superbowl football game, traditionally the most watched TV event of the year. In other words, it was the perfect "kickoff" for her latest hit. However, she ended up backing out of the show. When the song was released to radio stations later that week, it was an instant Top-40 hit.

Naturally, Madonna's rendition is much more danceable than McLean's guitar-driven original. Instead of recording the full-length version of the song, Madonna chose to cut the story section which speaks of rock 'n' roll's most infamous airplane crash. Her 4-minute, 33-second "American Pie" makes the most of the choruses about driving a Chevy to the levee. Reviewing the song, *USA Today* awarded the recording four stars (out of four), and reviewer Edna Gundersen glowed, "Madonna devises a universal but personal message that addresses turn-of-the-century angst and her own odyssey: 'I knew if I had my chance that I could make those people dance.' Her voice is angelic yet bittersweet, imbuing a playful tune with sad undercurrents." (286)

The video version of "American Pie" features Madonna dancing in a pair of well-worn, bell-bottom blue jeans, and a cobalt-blue cotton top with shoulder straps. Upon her head she has a rhinestone tiara, as though she is the "Miss American Pie" mentioned in the lyrics. While she sings in front of a huge America flag, snapshots of Americana flash behind her.

"American Pie" peaked at Number 29 in America. However, it became a huge global smash, hitting Number One in England, Germany, Spain, Switzerland, Canada, and Australia.

When *The Next Best Thing* opened, on March 3, 2000, critics roundly panned Madonna's acting as being stiff and uncomfortable to watch. For once, her presence didn't devour the film. Since the film co-starred close friend Rupert Everett, their scenes come across more naturally than any of her other attempts at the genre, dating back to *Who's That Girl*. The plot of the film concerns an unmarried woman who gets pregnant from one drunken sexual encounter with one of her gay friends (Everett).

In the first screenplay treatment of *The Next Best Thing*, Madonna's character, Abbie, was written as a swimming instructor. To make the film closer to her own character, Abbie was rewritten to become a yoga instructor.

In the plot, Abbie is painfully aware that her own biological clock is ticking. In an attempt to drive this fact home, Madonna is given one of her most amusing scenes. Standing before a mirror, she lifts her own breasts up to a more elevated position on her body, and announces,

"1989." Dropping her breasts back to where gravity has now taken them, she deadpans, "1999."

Discussing the similarities in their screen characters, Rupert Everett admitted, "I don't think the characters are exactly us, but I think there's certainly—from my perspective—a lot of myself accessed in it. Like in our friendship—the particular kind of banter we have."

According to Madonna, "There are definite similarities between the characters and us." (287) After working so hard to mentally become Eva Perón in *Evita,* for Madonna, filming *The Next Best Thing* was much more of a breeze. Perhaps she should stick to musicals like *Evita* to define her cinematic presence in the new century.

In the year 2000 Madonna began her third decade as an international multimedia superstar. Although some things had changed, some things remained the same. She still whined about the price of fame, while single-handedly doing everything she could to maintain it.

After the scalding reviews of her *Sex* book, and the blood, sweat, and tears that she had invested in *Evita,* she felt that she was more able to accept criticism, and then simply move onward. "I don't take it as personally as I used to. I'm a much more forgiving person now. I'm sure my daughter has had a lot to do with it. But I feel much more compassion toward people who have hostile feelings towards me. Because I know that it's coming from the opposite place than it appears to be coming from. And once you accept that format and learn to forgive people . . . it's just been a lot easier for me. Everything. Being famous has been a lot easier." (250)

Madonna has begun her career begging for, demanding, and ultimately commanding fan worship. From the beginning, that seemed to be the only thing she truly desired from life. Now she appears to see everything in a new light. According to her, the birth of her daughter changed everything. Comparing the love of her fans and the love of her daughter, Madonna said, "There is no comparison. They don't love me in an unconditional way. My daughter does. Just looking into her eyes, I know it is not based on me being fabulous or rich or famous or talented or successful. It's just having a soul connect for the first time in my life." (258)

In March 2000, Madonna confirmed that she was pregnant again. This time around, the father was Guy Ritchie. No wedding plans were announced at that time.

Regardless of what it is that she does next, Madonna is now a fixture in the history books, as one of the twentieth century's most written about, most photographed, and most discussed women. What does the future hold for her? "Though I have fears, I think truthfully I'm going to live to be a very old age. If what I've gone through hasn't killed me yet, nothing's going to. That's my fucking opinion," she proclaimed. (246)

Always outspoken, always brilliantly cross-promoting, and always brashly unpredictable, Madonna continues to grow and evolve. Singer, actress, record company president, erotic sex goddess, mother, spiritual guru, and media icon, she never seems to tire of astounding the public. Love her or hate her, you cannot ignore her, even if you try. She has somehow managed to take a portion of talent, along with several freight trains full of determination and drive, and has turned it into the most successful example of blonde ambition in the history of mass media. She is a force to be reckoned with. She is Madonna.

MARK BEGO
Tucson, Arizona
May 2000

Madonna Discography

Albums

1. *Madonna*
   (Sire Records / July 1983)
   1. "Lucky Star"
      (Madonna)
   2. "Borderline"
      (Reggie Lucas)
   3. "Burning Up"
      (Madonna)
   4. "I Know It"
      (Madonna)
   5. "Holiday"
      (Curtis Hudson / Lisa Stevens)
   6. "Think of Me"
      (Madonna)
   7. "Physical Attraction"
      (Reggie Lucas)
   8. "Everybody"
      (Madonna)

2. *Like a Virgin*
   (Sire Records / November 1994)
   1. "Material Girl"
      (Peter Brown / Robert Rans)
   2. "Angel"
      (Madonna / Steve Bray)
   3. "Like a Virgin"
      (Billy Steinberg / Tom Kelly)
   4. "Over and Over"
      (Madonna / Steve Bray)
   5. "Love Don't Live Here Anymore"
      (Miles Gregory)
   6. "Dress You Up"
      (Peggy Stanzaile / Andrea La Russo)
   7. "Shoo-Bee-Doo"
      (Madonna)
   8. "Pretender"
      (Madonna / Steve Bray)
   9. "Stay"
      (Madonna / Steve Bray)

3. *True Blue*
   (Sire Records / June 1986)
   1. "Papa Don't Preach"
      (Brian Elliot / additional lyrics Madonna)

2. "Open Your Heart"
   (Madonna / Gardner Cole /
   Peter Rafelson)
3. "White Heat"
   (Madonna / Pat Leonard)
4. "Live to Tell"
   (Madonna / Pat Leonard)
5. "Where's the Party"
   (Madonna / Stephen Bray /
   Pat Leonard)
6. "True Blue"
   (Madonna / Stephen Bray)
7. "La Isla Bonita"
   (Madonna / Pat Leonard /
   Bruce Gaitsch)
8. "Jimmy Jimmy"
   (Madonna / Stephen Bray)
9. "Love Makes the World Go
   Round"
   (Madonna / Pat Leonard)

4. *Who's That Girl?*
   Movie Soundtrack
   (Sire Records / August 1987)
   1. "Who's That Girl?"
      (Madonna / Patrick Leonard)
   2. "Causing a Commotion"
      (Madonna / Stephen Bray)
   3. "The Look of Love"
      (Madonna / Patrick Leonard)
   4. "Can't Stop"
      (Madonna / Stephen Bray)
   [Note: the five other cuts on this
   album are by different artists]

5. *You Can Dance*
   (Sire Records / November 1987)
   1. "Spotlight"
      (Madonna / Stephen Bray)

2. "Holiday"
   (Curtis Hudson / Lisa
   Stevens)
3. "Everybody"
   (Madonna)
4. "Physical Attraction"
   (Reggie Lucas)
5. "Over and Over"
   (Madonna / Stephen Bray)
6. "Into the Groove"
   (Madonna / Stephen Bray)
7. "Where's the Party"
   (Madonna / Stephen Bray /
   Pat Leonard)
8. "Holiday" [Dub Version]
   (Curtis Hudson / Lisa
   Stevens)
9. "Into the Groove"
   (Madonna / Steve Bray)
10. "Where's the Party"
    (Madonna / Stephen Bray /
    Pat Leonard)

6. *Like a Prayer*
   (Sire Records / March 1989)
   1. "Like a Prayer"
      (Madonna / Patrick Leonard)
   2. "Express Yourself"
      (Madonna / Stephen Bray)
   3. "Love Song"
      (Madonna / Prince)
   4. "Till Death Do Us Part"
      (Madonna / Patrick Leonard)
   5. "Promise to Try"
      (Madonna / Patrick Leonard)
   6. "Cherish"
      (Madonna / Patrick Leonard)
   7. "Dear Jessie"
      (Madonna / Patrick Leonard)

8. "Oh Father"
(Madonna / Patrick Leonard)

9. "Keep It Together"
(Madonna / Stephen Bray)

10. "Spanish Eyes"
(Madonna / Patrick Leonard)

11. "Act of Contrition"
(Madonna)

7. *I'm Breathless: Music from and Inspired by the Film Dick Tracy*

(Sire Records / May 1990)

1. "He's a Man"
(Madonna / Patrick Leonard)

2. "Sooner or Later"
(Stephen Sondheim)

3. "Hanky Panky"
(Madonna / Patrick Leonard)

4. "I'm Going Bananas"
(Michael Kernan / Andy Paley)

5. "Cry Baby"
(Madonna / Patrick Leonard)

6. "Something to Remember"
(Madonna / Patrick Leonard)

7. "Back in Business"
(Madonna / Patrick Leonard)

8. "More"
(Stephen Sondheim)

9. "What Can You Lose"
Madonna with Mandy Patinkin
(Stephen Sondheim)

10. "Now I'm Following You (Part I)"
(Andy Paley / Jeff Lass / Ned Claflin / Jonathan Paley)

11. "Now I'm Following You (Part II)"
(Andy Paley / Jeff Lass / Ned Claflin / Jonathan Paley)

12. "Vogue"
(Madonna / Shep Pettibone)

8. *The Immaculate Collection*

(Sire Records / November 1990)

1. "Holiday"
(Curtis Hudson / Lisa Stevens)

2. "Lucky Star"
(Madonna)

3. "Borderline"
(Reggie Lucas)

4. "Like a Virgin"
(Billy Steinberg / Tom Kelly)

5. "Material Girl"
(Peter Brown / Robert Rans)

6. "Crazy for You"
(John Bettis / Jon Lind)

7. "Into the Groove"
(Madonna / Stephen Bray)

8. "Live to Tell"
(Madonna / Patrick Leonard)

9. "Papa Don't Preach"
(Brian Elliot / additional lyrics Madonna)

10. "Open Your Heart"
(Madonna / Gardner Cole / Peter Rafelson)

11. "La Isla Bonita"
(Madonna / Patrick Leonard / Bruce Gaitsch)

12. "Like a Prayer"
(Madonna / Patrick Leonard)

13. "Express Yourself"
(Madonna / Stephen Bray)

14. "Cherish"
(Madonna / Patrick Leonard)
15. "Vogue"
(Madonna / Shep Pettibone)
16. "Justify My Love"
(Lenny Kravitz / additional lyrics Madonna)
17. "Rescue Me"
(Madonna / Shep Pettibone)

9. *Erotica*

(Maverick / Sire / Warner Brothers Records / October 1992)

1. "Erotica"
(Madonna / Shep Pettibone)
2. "Fever"
(J. Davenport / E. Cooley)
3. "Bye Bye Baby"
(Madonna / Shep Pettibone)
4. "Deeper and Deeper"
(Madonna / Shep Pettibone / Tony Shimkin)
5. "Where Life Begins"
(Madonna / Andre Betts)
6. "Bad Girl"
(Madonna / Shep Pettibone)
7. "Waiting"
(Madonna / Andre Betts)
8. "Thief of Hearts"
(Madonna / Shep Pettibone)
9. "Words"
(Madonna / Shep Pettibone)
10. "Rain"
(Madonna / Shep Pettibone)
11. "Why's It So Hard"
(Madonna / Shep Pettibone)
12. "In This Life"
(Madonna / Shep Pettibone)

13. "Did You Do It?" Madonna with Mark Goodman & Dave Murphy
(Madonna / Andre Betts)
14. "Secret Garden"
(Madonna / Andre Betts)

10. *Bedtime Stories*

(Maverick / Sire / Warner Brothers Records / October 1994)

1. "Survival"
(Madonna / Dallas Austin)
2. "Secret"
(Madonna / Dallas Austin)
3. "I'd Rather Be Your Lover"
(Madonna / Dave Hall / Isley Brothers / C. Jasper)
4. "Don't Stop"
(Madonna / Dallas Austin / Colin Wolfe)
5. "Inside of Me"
(Madonna / Dave Hall / Nellee Hooper)
6. "Human Nature"
(Madonna / Dave Hall / S. McKenzie / K. McKenzie / M. Deering)
7. "Forbidden Love"
(Babyface / Madonna)
8. "Love Tried to Welcome Me"
(Madonna / Dave Hall)
9. "Sanctuary"
(Madonna / Dallas Austin / Anne Preven / Scott Cutler / Herbie Hancock)
10. "Bedtime Story"
(Nellee Hooper / Björk / Marius DeVries)
11. "Take a Bow"
(Babyface / Madonna)

11. Something to Remember
(Maverick / Warner Brothers
Records / November 1995)
   1. "I Want You" Madonna with
      Massive Attack
      (Leon Ware / T. Boy Ross)
   2. "I'll Remember"
      (Patrick Leonard / Madonna /
      Richard Page)
   3. "Take a Bow"
      (Babyface / Madonna)
   4. "You'll See"
      (Madonna / David Foster)
   5. "Crazy for You"
      (Jon Bettis / Jon Lind)
   6. "This Used to Be My
      Playground"
      (Madonna / Shep Pettibone)
   7. "Live to Tell"
      (Madonna / Patrick Leonard)
   8. "Love Don't Live Here
      Anymore" (remixed
      version)
      (Miles Gregory)
   9. "Something to Remember"
      (Madonna / Patrick Leonard)
   10. "Forbidden Love"
      (Babyface / Madonna)
   11. "One More Chance"
      (Madonna / David Foster)
   12. "Rain"
      (Madonna / Shep Pettibone)
   13. "Oh Father"
      (Madonna / Patrick Leonard)
   14. "I Want You" Madonna with
      Massive Attack (orchestral
      version)
      (Leon Ware / T. Boy Ross)

12. Evita: The Complete
Motion Picture Music
Soundtrack
(Warner Brothers Records /
November 1996)
[Note: only songs by or including
Madonna are listed]
   1. "Oh What a Circus"
      (Tim Rice / Andrew Lloyd
      Webber)
      Antonio Banderas, Madonna
   2. "Eva and Magaldi / Eva
      Beware of the City"
      (Tim Rice / Andrew Lloyd
      Webber)
      Madonna, Jimmy Nail,
      Antonio Banderas, Julian
      Littman
   3. "Buenos Aires"
      (Tim Rice / Andrew Lloyd
      Webber)
      Madonna
   4. "Another Suitcase in Another
      Hall"
      (Tim Rice / Andrew Lloyd
      Webber)
      Madonna
   5. "Goodnight and Thank You"
      (Tim Rice / Andrew Lloyd
      Webber)
      Madonna, Antonio Banderas
   6. "Charity Concert / The Art of
      the Possible"
      (Tim Rice / Andrew Lloyd
      Webber)
      Jimmy Nail, Jonathan Pryce,
      Antonio Banderas,
      Madonna
   7. "I'd Be Surprisingly Good for
      You"

(Tim Rice / Andrew Lloyd
Webber)
Madonna, Jonathan Pryce

8. "Hello and Goodbye"
(Tim Rice / Andrew Lloyd
Webber)
Madonna, Andrea Corr,
Jonathan Pryce

9. "Perón's Latest Flame"
(Tim Rice / Andrew Lloyd
Webber)
Antonio Banderas, Madonna

10. "A New Argentina"
(Tim Rice / Andrew Lloyd
Webber)
Madonna, Jonathan Pryce,
Antonio Banderas

11. "Don't Cry for Me
Argentina"
(Tim Rice / Andrew Lloyd
Webber)
Madonna

12. "On the Balcony of the Casa
Rosada 2"
(Tim Rice / Andrew Lloyd
Webber)
Madonna

13. "High Flying, Adored"
(Tim Rice / Andrew Lloyd
Webber)
Antonio Banderas, Madonna

14. "Rainbow High"
(Tim Rice / Andrew Lloyd
Webber)
Madonna

15. "Rainbow Tour"
(Tim Rice / Andrew Lloyd
Webber)
Antonio Banderas, Gary
Brooker, Peter Polycarpou,
Jonathan Pryce, Madonna,
John Gower

16. "The Actress Hasn't Learned
the Lines (You'd Like to
Hear)"
(Tim Rice / Andrew Lloyd
Webber)
Madonna, Antonio Banderas

17. "Partido Feminista"
(Tim Rice / Andrew Lloyd
Webber)
Madonna

18. "Waltz for Eva and Che"
(Tim Rice / Andrew Lloyd
Webber)
Madonna, Antonio Banderas

19. "Your Little Body's Slowly
Breaking Down"
(Tim Rice / Andrew Lloyd
Webber)
Madonna, Jonathan Pryce

20. "You Must Love Me"
(Tim Rice / Andrew Lloyd
Webber)
Madonna

21. "Eva's Final Broadcast"
(Tim Rice / Andrew Lloyd
Webber)
Madonna

22. "Lament"
(Tim Rice / Andrew Lloyd
Webber)
Madonna, Antonio Banderas

13. *Ray of Light*
(Maverick Records / March 1998)

1. "Drowned World / Substitute
for Love"
(Madonna / William Orbit /
Rod McKuen / Anita Kerr /
David Collins)

2. "Swim"
(Madonna / William Orbit)

3. "Ray of Light"
(Madonna / William Orbit /
Clive Muldoon / Dave
Curtis / Christine Leach)
4. "Candy Perfume Girl"
(Madonna / William Orbit /
Susannah Melvoin)
5. "Skin"
(Madonna / Patrick Leonard)
6. "Nothing Really Matters"
(Madonna / Patrick Leonard)
7. "Sky Fits Heaven"
(Madonna / Patrick Leonard)

8. "Shanti / Astangi"
(Madonna / William Orbit)
9. "Frozen"
(Madonna / Patrick Leonard)
10. "The Power of Goodbye"
(Madonna / Rick Nowels)
11. "To Have and Not to Hold"
(Madonna / Rick Nowels)
12. "Little Star"
(Madonna / Rick Nowels)
13. "Mer Girl"
(Madonna / William Orbit)

Albums Featuring Madonna

(Madonna songs listed only)

1. ### Revenge of the Killer B's

(Warner Brothers Records / 1984)

Various Artists
"Ain't No Big Deal"

2. ### Vision Quest

(Geffen Records / 1985)

Movie Soundtrack
"Crazy for You"
"Gambler"

3. ### A Very Special Christmas

(A&M Records / 1987)

Various Artists
"Santa Baby"

4. ### In the Beginning

(Receiver Records / London 1987 /
Europe only)

Madonna & Otto Von Wernherr
"Wild Dancing" (Extended
Dance Mix)
"Cosmic Climb" (Extended
Dance Mix)
"We Are the Gods"
"Wild Dancing"
"Cosmic Climb"

[Note: These are recordings done
before Madonna became a recording
artist on her own. Basically, Madonna
sang background vocals for Von
Wernherr, and when she became a
star, her background tracks were
expanded to make it sound like she is
the star or costar of these recordings.
They have been remixed and
rereleased in many different formats.
They are truly dreadful.]

5. ### Red, Hot & Dance

(Columbia Records / 1992)
Various Artists
"Supernatural"

6. Dangerous
   (Epic Records / 1991)

   Michael Jackson
   "In the Closet" (Madonna
   billed as "Mystery Girl")

7. Barcelona Gold
   (Warner Brothers Records / 1992)

   Various Artists
   "This Used to Be My
   Playground"

8. With Honors
   (Maverick / Sire / Warner Brothers
   Records / 1994)

   Movie Soundtrack
   "I'll Remember"

9. Inner City Blues: The
   Music of Marvin Gaye
   (Motown Records / 1995)

   Various Artists
   "I Want You" Madonna with
   Massive Attack

10. Women in Rock
    (Razor & Tie Records / 1998)

    Various Artists
    "Express Yourself"

11. 1999 Grammy Nominees
    (Warner Brothers Records / 1999)

    Various Artists
    "Ray of Light"

12. Ricky Martin
    (Columbia Records / 1999)

    Ricky Martin
    "Be Careful (*Cuidado Con
    Mi Corazón*)" Ricky
    Martin & Madonna

13. Austin Powers: The Spy
    Who Shagged Me
    (Maverick Records / 1999)

    Movie Soundtrack
    "Beautiful Stranger"

14. More Music from Austin
    Powers: The Spy Who
    Shagged Me
    (Maverick Records / 1999)

    Movie Soundtrack
    "Beautiful Stranger"
    [remixed version]

15. The Next Best Thing
    (Maverick Records / 2000)

    Movie Soundtrack
    "American Pie"
    "Time Stood Still"

Singles

[Note: Unless otherwise noted, peak
chart positions are as per *Billboard*
magazine's tally on the United States
Pop or Hot 100 chart]

1. "Everybody"
   (Sire Records / 1982)
   (Peak Position #103 Pop chart /
   #1 Dance chart)

2. "Burning Up" / "Physical
    Attraction"
    (Sire Records / 1983)
    (Peak Position #1 Dance chart)

3. "Holiday"
    (Sire Records /1983)
    (Peak Position #16)

4. "Borderline"
    (Sire Records /1984)
    (Peak Position #10)

5. "Lucky Star"
    (Sire Records /1984)
    (Peak Position #4)

6. "Like a Virgin"
    (Sire Records /1984)
    (Peak Position #1)

7. "Material Girl"
    (Sire Records /1985)
    (Peak Position #2)

8. "Crazy for You"
    (Geffen Records / 1985)
    (Peak Position #1)

9. "Angel"
    (Sire Records /1985)
    (Peak Position #5)

10. "Dress You Up"
    (Sire Records /1985)
    (Peak Position #5)

11. "Live to Tell"
    (Sire Records /1986)
    (Peak Position #1)

12. "Papa Don't Preach"
    (Sire Records /1986)
    (Peak Position #1)

13. "True Blue"
    (Sire Records /1986)
    (Peak Position #3)

14. "Open Your Heart"
    (Sire Records /1986)
    (Peak Position #1)

15. "La Isla Bonita"
    (Sire Records /1987)
    (Peak Position #4)

16. "Who's That Girl?"
    (Sire Records /1987)
    (Peak Position #1)

17. "Causing a Commotion"
    (Sire Records /1987)
    (Peak Position #2)

18. "Like a Prayer"
    (Sire Records /1978)
    (Peak Position #1)

19. "Express Yourself"
    (Sire Records /1989)
    (Peak Position #2)

20. "Cherish"
    (Sire Records /1989)
    (Peak Position #2)

21. "Oh Father"
    (Sire Records /1989)
    (Peak Position #8)

22. "Dear Jessie"
    (Sire Records /1989)
    ENGLAND ONLY
    (Peak Position #5)
    [as per BBC / *Top of the Pops*]

23. "Keep It Together"
    (Sire Records /1990)
    (Peak Position #8)

24. "Vogue"
    (Sire Records /1990)
    (Peak Position #1)

25. "Hanky Panky"
    (Sire Records /1990)
    (Peak Position #10)

26. "Justify My Love"
    (Sire Records /1990)
    (Peak Position #1)

27. "Rescue Me"
    (Sire Records /1991)
    (Peak Position #9)

28. "This Used to Be My Playground"
(Sire Records /1992)
(Peak Position #1)

29. "Erotica"
(Maverick / Sire Records / 1992)
(Peak Position #3)

30. "Deeper and Deeper"
(Maverick / Sire Records / 1992)
(Peak Position #7)

31. "Bad Girl"
(Maverick / Sire Records / 1993)
(Peak Position #36)

32. "Rain"
(Maverick / Sire Records / 1993)
(Peak Position #14)

33. "I'll Remember"
(Maverick / Sire Records / 1994)
(Peak Position #2)

34. "Secret"
(Maverick / Sire Records / 1994)
(Peak Position #3)

35. "Take a Bow"
(Maverick / Sire Records / 1994)
(Peak Position #1)

36. "Bedtime Story"
(Maverick / Sire Records / 1995)
(Peak Position #4)

37. "Human Nature"
(Maverick / Sire Records / 1995)
(Peak Position #46)

38. "You'll See"
(Maverick / Warner Brothers
Records / 1995)
(Peak Position #6)

39. "Love Don't Live Here Anymore"
(Remix)
(Maverick / Warner Brothers
Records / 1996)
(Peak Position #78)

40. "You Must Love Me"
(Warner Brothers Records / 1996)
(Peak Position #18)

41. "Don't Cry for Me Argentina"
(Warner Brothers Records / 1997)
(Peak Position #8)

42. "Another Suitcase in Another
Hall"
(Warner Brothers Records / 1997)
EUROPE ONLY
(Peak Position #7)
[as per BBC / *Top of the Pops*]

43. "Frozen"
(Maverick / Warner Brothers
Records / 1998)
(Peak Position #2)

44. "Ray of Light"
(Maverick / Warner Brothers
Records / 1998)
(Peak Position #5)

45. "Power of Goodbye"
(Maverick / Warner Brothers
Records / 1998)
(Peak Position #19)

46. "Nothing Really Matters"
(Maverick / Warner Brothers
Records / 1999)
(Peak Position #1 Hot Dance
Music / Club Play chart)

47. "Beautiful Stranger"
(Maverick / Warner Brothers
Records / 1999)
(Peak Position #19)

48. "American Pie"
(Maverick / Warner Brothers
Records / 2000)
(Peak Position #29 U.S., #1
U.K., Canada, Australia)

Filmography

1. *A Certain Sacrifice* (1985)
   —as Bruna
2. *Vision Quest* (1985)
   —as herself
3. *Desperately Seeking Susan* (1985)
   —as Susan
4. *Shanghai Surprise* (1986)
   —as Gloria Tatlock
5. *Who's That Girl?* (1987)
   —as Nikki Finn
6. *Bloodhounds of Broadway* (1989)
   —as Hortense Hathaway
7. *Dick Tracy* (1990)
   —as Breathless Mahoney
8. *Truth or Dare* (1991)
   —as herself
9. *Shadows and Fog* (1992)
   —as Marie
10. *A League of Their Own* (1992)
    —as Mae Morbadito
11. *Body of Evidence* (1993)
    —as Rebecca Carlson
12. *Dangerous Game* (1993)
    —as Sarah Jennings
13. *Four Rooms* (1995)
    "The Missing Ingredient"
    segment
    —as Elspeth
14. *Blue in the Face* (1995)
    —as Singing Telegram
15. *Girl 6* (1996)
    —as Boss #3
16. *Evita* (1996)
    —as Eva Perón
17. *The Next Best Thing* (2000)
    —as Abbie

Stageography

1. *The Virgin Tour* (1985)
   concert tour
2. *The* Who's That Girl? *Tour* (1987)
   concert tour
3. *Speed-the-Plow* (1988)
   Broadway play, New York City
4. *Blonde Ambition Tour* (1990)
   concert tour
5. *The Girlie Show* (1993)
   concert tour

Video Cassettes, Laserdiscs, and DVD's

1. *Madonna* (1985)
   compilation of videos
2. *Ciao Italia* (1988)
   stageshow, concert video
   [available on DVD]
3. *Madonna Live: Blonde Ambition* (1990)
   stageshow, concert video
   (laserdisc only)
4. *The Immaculate Collection* (1990)
   compilation of videos
   [available on DVD]
5. *Justify My Love* (1990)
   single selection music video,
   uncensored as banned by MTV
6. *The Girlie Show: Live Down Under* (1993)
   stageshow, concert video
   [available on DVD]
7. *Madonna: The Video Collection 1993–1999* (1999)
   compilation of her videos from the 1990's
   [available on DVD]

Notes

The information contained in *Blonde Ambition* came from hundreds of magazine and newspaper articles, personal observances, and personal interviews. The sources that follow correspond to the footnote numbers in each chapter. British publications identified by "UK."

1. Mark Bego's interview with Madonna, October 8, 1984, in Maripol's loft in New York City.

2. *Time*, May 27, 1985, "Madonna Rocks the Land" by John Skow, Cathy Booth, and Denise Worrell; and "Now: Madonna on Madonna" by Denise Worrell.

3. *The Face* (UK), February 1985, "Madonna: The Glamorous Life" by Jeffrey Ferry.

4. Bette Midler on the "Live Aid" international telecast, July 13, 1985.

5. *Nightlife*, 1984, "Madonna: On the Borderline of Stardom" by Mitchell Kozuchowski.

6. *No. 1* (UK), September 1987, "Madonna Interviewed on Fame, Sex and Sean Penn," by Jane Pauley/NBC.

7. *American Film*, July/August 1987, "Who's That Girl?" by Lynn Phillips.

8. *Weekend* (UK), February 24–March 1, 1988, "The Legend of Madonna/The Legend Starts Here" by Robert Nelson and Fred Wehner.

9. *Madonna!*, Pinnacle Publishers, New York, 1985, by Mark Bego.

10. *Bay City [MI] Times*, August 15, 1987, "Hey, Madonna, Come Visit Us" by Jeff Phillips.

11. *Interview*, May 1989, "Confessions of a Catholic Girl" by Becky Johnston.

12. *News of the World* (UK newspaper), July 21, 1985, "The Girl Can't Help It" by Simon Kinnersley.

13. *Interview*, December 1985, "Madonna" by Harry Dean Stanton.

14. *Record*, March 1985, "Maybe She's Good: 10 Theories on How Madonna Got 'It'" by Laura Fissinger.

15. *Spin*, May 1985, "Confessions of a Madonna" by Scott Cohen.

16. *Rolling Stone*, March 23, 1989, "Madonna: Candid Talk About Music, Movies and Marriage" by Bill Zehme.

17. *Interview*, April 1984, "Madonna: 'Borderline Angel'" by Glenn Albin.

18. *Interview*, June 1990, "Madonna!" by Glenn O'Brien.

19. *Star Hits*, December 1984, "Primo Madonna" by David Keeps.

20. *Star* (UK), September 9, 1985, "I Felt Just Like Cinderella."

21. *Cleveland Plain Dealer*, May 10, 1985, "A Trashy Act May Be in Jest" by Jane Scott.

22. *Palm Beach [FL] Post*, April 10, 1987, "A True-Blue Star for the '80s Opens Her Heart About Work, Love and Life" by Simon Bate.

23. *MacLean's* (Canada), June 18, 1990, "Spanking New Madonna" by Brian D. Johnson, Victor Dwyer, Anne Gregor, and Pamela Young.

24. *People*, March 11, 1985, "Madonna" by Carl Arrington.

25. *Ladies' Home Journal*, November 1990, "The Fifty Most Powerful Women in America/Madonna Flexes Her Muscles" by Richard Price.

26. *Cosmopolitan*, July 1987, "The Material Girl and How She Grew" by Chris Chase.

27. *Today* (UK), July 18, 1990, "Little Girl Lost Dances on Grave to Purge Guilt of Mum's Death" by Margaret Hall.

28. *Madonna* (magazine), Spring 1990, Larry Flynt Publishing, "Madonna: Her Life and Times, Part 1."

29. *Rolling Stone*, November 22, 1984, "Madonna Goes all the Way" by Christopher Connelly.

30. *Chicago Tribune*, July 10, 1986, "Madonna Cleans Up Act, But Her Music Remains True Blue to Controversy" by Stephen Holden.

31. *Record Mirror* (UK), May 19, 1984, "I Wanted to Be a Nun... Then I Discovered Boys" by Graham K.

32. *USA Weekend*, June 8–10, 1990, "Totally Outrageous" by Richard Price.

33. *Us*, September 7, 1987, "How's That Girl?" by Fred Schruers.

34. *Spin*, February 1988, "Madonna: Goodbye, Norma Jean. The Material Girl Is Growing Up Just Fine" by Kristine McKenna.

35. *An Ideal Husband, III*. A play by Oscar Wilde, 1895.

36. *Star* (UK), August 14, 1987, "Madonna: At the Age of 5 She Knew She'd Be a Star" by Terry Willows.

37. *News of the World* (UK), August 16, 1987, "I Groped Schoolgirl Madonna on Very First Date" by Hugh Dehn.

38. *Star*, May 30, 1989, "Madonna's Internal Affairs" by Reed Sparling.

39. *The Mirror* (UK), December 16, 1985, "Madonna's Sexy School Secrets."

40. *Highlander* yearbook, Rochester Adams High School, 1974. Courtesy of Madonna's classmate, Mark Brooky.

41. *Sunday Mirror* (UK), July 22, 1990, "Do You Want to Do It or Not?" by Peter Williams.

42. Mark Bego's interview with Mark Brooky, December 28, 1984, West Palm Beach, Florida.

43. *The Mail on Sunday* (UK), July 7, 1985, "How the Bad Girl of Rock Made Good" by Adam Edwards.

44. *The Detroit Free Press*, August 7, 1987, "Madonna: She Breaks Rules, Sheds Images, Hides Her Real Self" by Gary Graff.

45. *The Detroit Free Press*, May 19, 1985, "Madonna: She Always Knew She Would Be Somebody" by Gary Graff.

46. *Star Hits*, October 1987, "Just Like an Animal" by Nick Gillespie.

47. Mark Bego's phone conversation with Richard Maschal, March 5, 1991, re: his article in *The Charlotte* [NC] *Observer*, June 1, 1985, "I Knew Her When..." by Richard Maschal.

48. *You* (UK magazine), April 21, 1985, "Madonna: I Was Born to Flirt" by Nancy Mills.

49. *Us*, December 31, 1984, "Prima Donna Madonna" by Jill Pearlman.

50. *Penthouse*, September 1985, "Madonna: The Power and the Glory" by Nick Tosches.

51. *Playboy*, September 1985, "Madonna Nude: Unlike a Virgin... For the Very First Time."

52. *MLC: The Madonna Fanzine*, June/July/August 1987, "The Breakfast Club Is Right on Track."

53. *Star* (U.S.), July 30, 1985, "Why Madonna Posed for All Those Nude Photographs" by Brian Haugh.

54. *Star* (U.S.), May 21, 1985, "Madonna: She Plotted Career with One Goal in Mind—Superstardom" by Brian Haugh.

55. Mark Bego's telephone interview with Anthony Panzera, March 8, 1991.

56. Mark Bego's interview with Stephen Lewicki, Spring 1985, New York City.

57. Stephen Lewicki's letter from Madonna, Summer 1979.

58. *Sun* (UK), May 8, 1985, "Madonna's Sexy Image Pays Off" by Ruth Brotherhood.

59. *The Boston Herald*, July 3, 1987, "Madonna on Madonna: I Do It My Way" by Simon Bates.

60. *The Warhol Diaries* by Andy Warhol, edited by Pat Hackett, Warner Books, New York, 1989.

61. *Fame*, December 1988, "Madonna Goes the Distance" by Harry Crews.

62. *News of the World* (UK), September 1, 1985, "Boy Toy Madonna" by Camille Barbone talking to Wendy Leigh.

63. *News of the World* (UK), September 8, 1985, "Madonna: I Created a Monster" by Camille Barbone talking to Wendy Leigh.

64. *Star* (UK), July 14, 1988, "The Strange Love of Lesbian and Madonna" by Allan Hall.

65. *You* (UK), March 22, 1987, "The Empress's New Clothes" by Michael Gross.

66. Mark Bego's interview with Mark Kamins, January 18, 1985, New York City.

67. *The New York Post,* June 3, 1985, "Prima Madonna" by Pat Wadsley.

68. *Record Mirror* (UK), March 23, 1985, "It's a Mad, Mad, Madonna" by Betty Page.

69. Mark Bego's telephone interview with Bobby Shaw, March 11, 1991.

70. Mark Bego's interviews with John "Jellybean" Benitez, November 27, 1984 and February 1985, New York City.

71. Mark Bego's interview with Mary Wilson, Summer 1990, Los Angeles.

72. Mark Bego's telephone interview with David Salidor, April 1991.

73. *Us,* July 12, 1989, "Madonna Sizzles" by Carl Wayne Arrington.

74. *No. 1* (UK), February 4, 1984, "Working Holiday" by Max Bell.

75. Mark Bego's telephone interview with Manny Parrish, April 8, 1991.

76. *The Seattle Times,* April 7, 1985, "Madonna Is Foxy but Professional" by Martin Porter and Steven Schwartz.

77. *Record Mirror* (UK), January 12, 1985, "Nile Rodgers: Me and the Stars."

78. *Cash Box,* February 9, 1985, "Nile Rodgers: Juggling Superstars" by Rusty Cutchin.

79. Bette Midler on the "First Annual MTV Awards" telecast, September 14, 1984.

80. Mark Bego's interview with Maripol, December 10, 1984, New York City.

81. *Rolling Stone*, September 10, 1987, "Madonna on Being a Star/The Madonna Mystique" by Mikal Gilmore.

82. Bette Midler re: Madonna, April 30, 1985, The Improv, Los Angeles.

83. *Rock Video*, December 1984, "Madonna: She Doesn't Care What People Think" by Richard Robinson.

84. *Smash Hits*, January 1985, "I Always Acted Like a Star Even Before I Was One!" by David Keeps.

85. *No. 1* (UK), March 24, 1984, "Madonna."

86. *Penthouse* (UK ed'n.), August 1985, "Madonna" by Scott Cohen.

87. *Desperately Seeking Susan* press kit, 1985, by Reid Rosefelt for Orion Pictures.

88. Mark Bego's interview with Susan Seidelman, November 29, 1984, at her loft in SoHo, New York City.

89. Mark Bego's interview with Reid Rosefelt, January 30, 1985, in his office, New York City.

90. *L.A. Weekly*, April 5–11, 1985, "Susan Seidelman: 'Women Have Learned'" by Helen Knode.

91. *Rolling Stone*, January 17, 1985, item from the "Random Notes" column.

92. *Rolling Stone*, May 9, 1985, "Madonna and Rosanna: Lucky Stars" by Fred Schruers.

93. *The Chicago Tribune*, August 2, 1987, "The Show Goes on Without Sean" by Gene Siskel.

94. New York *Daily News*, June 2, 1985, "Material Rewards" by Fred Schruers.

95. *Company* (UK), June 1985, "Bella Madonna: The Hot New Look of Female Rock" by Jim Miller, Cathleen McGuigan, Mark D. Uehling, Janet Huck, Peter McAlevey, Jacob Young, Donna Foote, and Tony Clifton.

96. *The Music Connection*, March 28–April 10, 1985, "The Making of Madonna's 'Material Girl'" by Hugh Lambert.

97. *People*, September 2, 1985, "Madonna Lands Her Lucky Star" by Roger Wolmuth, Eleanor Hoover, Susan Peters, and Steve Walker.

98. *Cosmopolitan*, May 1990, "Madonna: Magnificent Maverick" by David Ansen.

99. *Vanity Fair*, April 1990, "White Heat" by Kevin Sessums.

100. *Rolling Stone*, May 26, 1983, "Bad Boy Sean Penn" by Christopher Connelly.

101. *Los Angeles Times*, April 7, 1985, "Material Girl on a Roll" by Patrick Goldstein.

102. *Rolling Stone*, December 20, 1984, "Great Faces of 1984." Quote by Gina Schock of the Go-Go's.

103. *Record Mirror* (UK), January 7, 1984, "Madonna: The Belly Star" by Simon Hills.

104. *People*, May 13, 1985, "That Man-Smasher Madonna! On Tour" by James McBride, Carl Arrington, and Hilary Evans.

105. *Beverly Hills (213)*, April 17, 1985, column item by Jacquelyn Nicholson.

106. *The New York Times*, April 14, 1985, "'Susan' Draws Spirit From the Sidewalks of New York" by Lindsey Grudson.

107. *Theater Crafts*, November 1985, "Programming Madonna" by Steve Pollock.

108. From the Virgin Tour of America, April to June 1985.

109. *The Hollywood Reporter*, May 1985, "Music: Madonna" by Iain Blair.

110. *USA Today*, May 7, 1985, "Madonna Wanna-Be's: Trash and Frills for Material Girls" by Karen S. Peterson.

111. *Los Angeles Times*, April 21, 1985, "Subscribers Will Sit on the Hot Seats" by Patrick Goldstein.

112. *Rolling Stone*, June 5, 1986, "The New Madonna/Can't Stop the Girl" by Fred Schruers.

113. *USA Today*, July 8, 1985, "Madonna Bares It" by Matt Roush.

114. *The Mirror* (UK), July 11, 1985, "Naughty (But Very Nice) Madonna."

115. *USA Today*, July 9, 1985, "The Naked Truth Doesn't Faze Madonna" by Matt Roush.

116. *Time*, July 22, 1985, "Like a Pinup: Navel Battle of the Newsstands."

117. *The New York Post*, various daily issues, July 1985.

118. *USA Today*, July 15, 1985, "Most Stars Checked Their Egos" by Jeffrey Peisch, Jerry Shriver, John Milward, and Dan Ehrlich.

119. Madonna on the "Live Aid" international telecast, July 13, 1985.

120. *USA Today*, July 23, 1985, "Madonna Keeps House-Hunting" by Jeannie Williams and Matt Roush.

121. New York *Daily News*, July 31, 1985, "Billing in Racy Film Makes Mad-onna" by Salvatore Arena.

122. *The New York Post*, August 2, 1985, "Madonna Loses Suit to Keep Name Off Nude Flick" by Hal Davis.

123. Mark Bego's interview with John McCormick, July 9, 1990, Los Angeles.

124. *People*, July 8, 1985, "Desperately Seeking Matrimony: Rock's Bad Girl Madonna and Her Lucky Star Sean Penn" by Carol Wallace.

125. *The New York Post*, August 13, 1985, "Madonna and Sean Get Marriage License."

126. *USA Today*, August 15, 1985, "Madonna and Sean Play Hard to Get."

127. *Sun* (UK), August 18, 1985, "Madonna & Sean: Wild Pair Spruce Up" by Martin Dunn.

128. Mark Bego's telephone interview with Maggie Hall, May 9, 1991.

129. *Star*, September 3, 1985, "Sean's Gunplay Upsets Madonna Before Wacky Clifftop Wedding" by Rod Barrand.

130. *Time*, August 26, 1985, "This Time It Was for Real" by Amy Wilentz and Barbara Kraft.

131. *News of the World* (UK) October 27, 1985, "Bride Madonna's Bizarre Bathtime" by Wendy Leigh.

132. *Us*, August 25, 1986, "Sean & Madonna: A Year in the Life" by Leslie Van Buskirk.

133. Madonna on "Saturday Night Live," November 6, 1985.

134. Mark Bego's telephone interview with Fred Zarr, April 16, 1991.

135. *Newsweek*, May 6, 1985, "Stop Pornographic Rock" by Kandy Stroud.

136. *Sunday People* (UK), August 11, 1985, "The Bad Girl Image Is Good for Business" by Douglas Thompson.

137. *Sunday Mirror* (UK), October 5, 1986, "Madonna: Now I'm Just a Sweet Little Superstar."

138. *Dallas Morning News*, July 26, 1987, "A Reflection on the Nature of Fame—To Wit, Madonna" by Elizabeth Wurtzel.

139. *Record Mirror* (UK), March 15, 1986, "Madonna: 'I Reserve My Judgement About Working Here Again . . . ' " by Eleanor Levy.

140. *Star*, February 4, 1986, "Sean's Tantrums Wreck Madonna's Paradise Honeymoon" by Steven Edwards.

141. *The Sun* (UK), October 3, 1986, "Why I Hate the Poison Penns/TV Boss Tells of Rows With Mr. and Mrs. Madonna" by Martin Dunn and Nick Ferrari.

142. *People*, March 24, 1986, "Madonna's Beatle Boss/A Hard Day's Fight" by Carol Wallace, Jonathan Cooper, Laura Sanderson Healy, and Jack Kelley.

143. *People*, November 30, 1987, "Chatter" page item by Tim Allis.

144. *Star*, April 14, 1987, " 'Lunatic' Sean Penn Pulled Gun on Me, Says Paparazzi" by Dennis Powell.

145. *Vanity Fair*, December 1986, "Classic Madonna" by Michael Gross.

146. *Los Angeles Times*, November 11, 1984, "Madonna Takes Total Control" by Robert Hillburn.

147. *People*, August 11, 1986, "Alex McArthur's Silent Sizzling in a Video with Madonna Has Women Crying 'Who's That?' "

148. The quote "for 'a sick friend'" is from a New York City newspaper, as cited in *The Warhol Diaries*.

149. Mark Bego's telephone interview with Vinnie Zuffante, April 24, 1991.

150. Mark Bego's telephone interview with Coati Mundi, April 20, 1991.

151. *USA Today*, June 24, 1987, "Bad-Boy Penn Gets 2 Months in Jail" by Lorrie Lynch.

152. *USA Today*, July 3, 1987, "Bad Boy or Bad Rap?/Sean Penn Is Off to Jail Tuesday" by Karen S. Peterson.

153. *USA Today*, February 21, 1985, "Madonna! Her Unsaintly, Sexy Image Sells Records" by Mark Marymont and Craig Modderno.

154. *Star*, June 16, 1987, "Sean Penn's Rampage over 'Lost Love' Madonna" by Lorraine Tilden.

155. *USA Today*, June 26–28, 1987, "Madonna's on the Move/She's Out to Show the USA Who's That Girl" by Lorrie Lynch.

156. *Washington Post*, June 28, 1987, "Tour Couture: Who's Madonna Wanna Be?" by Martha Sherrill Dailey.

157. *USA Today*, June 11, 1987, "Who's That Stadium Sensation? Madonna" by Susan Spillman.

158. *Time*, July 27, 1987, "How Artists Respond to AIDS" by Richard Corliss, Mary Cronin, and Dennis Wyss.

159. *People*, August 17, 1987, "Chris Finch, Madonna's High-Stepping Sidekick Who's Also a Penn Pal" by Kim Hubbard and Sandra Lyon.

160. *Orange County* [CA] *Register*, July 20, 1987, "13-Year-Old Chris Finch Becomes a Lucky Star Dancing with Madonna" by Cynthia Hunter.

161. *Time*, September 7, 1987, "People" page item by Guy D. Garcia.

162. *People*, September 21, 1987, "The Return of a 'Native' Brings Cheers in Italy from Everyone but Madonna's Family Elders."

163. *USA Today,* December 8, 1987, "Briefly . . . " column item by Lorrie Lynch, Anne Trebbe, and Stephen Schaefer.

164. *People,* December 14, 1987, "Diary of a Mad Marriage/The Divorce of Madonna & Sean/Everyone Said It Wouldn't Last" by Joanne Kaufman, Victoria Balfour, and bureau correspondents.

165. *Rolling Stone,* March 24, 1988, "Random Notes" item.

166. *Star,* November 7, 1989, "Madonna Tells of AIDS Anguish Behind Latest Movie."

167. *Vanity Fair,* April 1988, "Mamet Meets Madonna" by Stephen Schiff.

168. *People,* May 2, 1988, "While Her Sean Sizzles on Film, Madonna Takes on Broadway."

169. *Us,* April 2, 1990, "Sterling Silver" by David Kissinger.

170. *Cosmopolitan,* November 1988, "Things Change for Joe Mantegna" by Marjorie Rosen.

171. *Time,* March 14, 1988, "People" page item.

172. *Harper's Bazaar,* May 1988, "Madonna: Broadway Bound."

173. *USA Today,* May 5, 1988, "Madonna Earns Glowing Reviews from Co-Stars" by Jeannie Williams.

174. *Time,* May 16, 1988, "Madonna Comes to Broadway" by William A. Henry III and Elizabeth L. Brand.

175. *MLC: The Madonna Fanzine,* Spring 1991, "Eye on Madonna" column item by Linda Perez from an interview with Ron Silver from Canada's "E" Entertainment television network.

176. *Interview,* March 1990, "Sandra Bernhard" by Paul Taylor.

177. *BAM (Bay Area Music),* August 1985, "Weird of Mouth/Near the Top with Sandra Bernhard" by Alvin Eng.

178. *Us,* August 8, 1988, "Sandra Bernhard 'Fesses Up" by Leslie Van Buskirk.

Notes

179. *Penthouse*, November 1988, "Sandra Bernhard: The Queen of Comedy" by Richard Dominick.

180. *Fame*, November 1990, "Sean Penn: Is There Life After Madonna?" by Harry Crews.

181. *USA Today*, July 5, 1988, "Sean Penn Comes Back Kicking."

182. Madonna, Sandra Bernhard, and David Letterman on "Late Night with David Letterman," July 1988.

183. *Star*, June 28, 1988, "It's All-Girls Night as Madonna Leads Terrible Trio on Late-Night Lulus."

184. *Time*, August 22, 1988, "People" page column item.

185. *People*, January 23, 1989, "Surprise! It's Splits, Fits and Quits Again for Sean and Madonna" by James S. Kunen.

186. Mark Bego's interview with a confidential source, Spring 1991.

187. *Star*, January 24, 1989, "Sean Penn's 9-Hour Torture of Madonna" by Lorraine Tilden.

188. *USA Today*, January 11, 1989, "Madonna: Pre-Split Attack?"

189. *The New York Post*, January 6, 1989, "Madonna Sues Sean Penn for Divorce."

190. Mark Bego's telephone interview with Jerry George, May 10, 1991.

191. *Time*, December 17, 1990, "Madonna Draws a Line" by Jay Cocks.

192. Liner notes from the Madonna album, *Like a Prayer*, Sire Records, 1989.

193. *The New York Times*, March 19, 1989, "Madonna Re-Creates Herself—Again" by Stephen Holden.

194. *USA Today*, January 26, 1989, "Pepsi: $5M for Madonna's Fizz" by Stuart Elliott.

195. *The Sun* (UK), February 28, 1989, "How Madonna Earned £5m for That Ad" by Rick Sky.

196. Mark Bego's telephone interview with Bobby Glenn, February 5, 1991.

Notes

197. *USA Today*, March 9, 1989, "Boycott Aim: Pepsi/Madonna 'Ridicules Christianity'" by James Cox.

198. *Cox News Service*, wire item, March 1989, "Making Scents of Madonna."

199. *USA Today*, January 4, 1989, "Herb Ritts Focuses in on all the Real Hot Shots" by Ann Trebbe.

200. *Vogue*, March 1988, "Images" column item.

201. *MTV News*, March 1989, Madonna and Christopher Flynn addressing the APLA Dance-A-Thon, February 26, 1989. Videotape courtesy of Coati Mundi.

202. *The Sun* (UK), May 26, 1989, "Madonna and Sandra Shock Fans" by Allan Hall.

203. *People*, June 12, 1989, "Gal Pals Sandra Bernhard and Madonna Monkey Around to Save the Jungle."

204. *USA Today*, May 9, 1989, "Briefly . . . " column item.

205. *USA Today*, October 24, 1989, "Bernhard Burning over 'Sordid' Press" by Ann Trebbe.

206. *The Advocate*, two-part interview, May 7, 1991 and May 21, 1991, "The Saint, the Slut, the Sensation . . . Madonna" and "The Gospel According to St. Madonna" by Don Shewey.

207. *San Francisco Weekly*, December 27, 1989, "Sex and Sensibility/Women Rockers Discover 1980's Cool" by Ann Powers.

208. Madonna and Warren Beatty in the film *Dick Tracy*, Touchstone Films, 1990.

209. *Premiere*, July 1990, "The Magnificent Obsessions of Warren Beatty/Warren and Me" by Peter Biskind.

210. *Entertainment Weekly*, June 15, 1990, "Strip Show/The Comic Book Look of Dick Tracy" by Gregg Kilday.

211. *Premiere*, February 1991, "The Hits/Best Preservation."

212. *USA Today*, May 11–13, 1990, "*Dick Tracy*/Big Gamble for Beatty and Disney" by Susan Spillman.

213. *Daily Variety*, January 11, 1990, item from the "Auditions" column.

214. *MLC/The Madonna Fanzine*, Spring 1990, "Hollywood Hot Flashes" by Marcia Del Vecchio.

215. *Entertainment Weekly*, May 11, 1990, "Madonna Strikes a New Pose/Madonnarama" by Ron Givens.

216. *People*, December 10, 1990, "After Decking Out Madonna and Losing His Closest Friend, Jean-Paul Gaultier Softens His Fashion Cutting Edge" by Karen S. Schneider and Georgina Oliver.

217. *The New York Times*, June 17, 1990, "Video and Theater Shape a New Madonna" by Patricia Leigh Brown.

218. *People*, May 7, 1990, " 'Blonde Ambition' and Banzai Bustiers: Madonna Launches a Throbbing World Tour in Tokyo" by Montgomery Brower and Todd Gold.

219. *Los Angeles Times*, May 18, 1990, "Body by Parr" by Barbara Foley.

220. Madonna and Arsenio Hall on "Arsenio Hall," May 1, 1990.

221. Madonna from the Blonde Ambition tour, May 11, 1990, Los Angeles.

222. *MLC: The Madonna Fanzine*, Fall 1990, "Madonna Quote/Unquote" by Linda Perez.

223. Madonna from the Blonde Ambition tour, August 5, 1990, Nice, France.

224. *Newsweek*, June 25, 1990, "Tracymania" by David Ansen and Pamela Abramson.

225. *Entertainment Weekly*, December 14, 1990, "Some Like It Hot . . . Some Not/ Madonna's New Video Has MTV Bothered" by Benjamin Svetkey.

226. *USA Today*, November 30, 1990, "Who's That Girl Kissing Madonna?" by Elizabeth Snead and Ann Trebbe.

227. *The Face* (UK), February 1991, "Madonna and *That* Video/Breathless" by Sheryl Garratt.

228. Madonna on *Nightline*, December 3, 1990.

229. *Jet*, November 5, 1990, "Madonna Cites Malcolm X, Dr. King in Steamy Rap on Voting, Freedom of Speech."

230. *Forbes*, October 1, 1990, "America's Smartest Business Woman?/A Brain for Sin and a Bod for Business" by Matthew Schifrin and Peter Newcomb.

231. *Us*, November 26, 1990, "The Heavy 100/The Most Powerful People in Entertainment."

232. *USA Today*, March 7, 1991, "Madonna Justified" by David Landis.

233. Madonna on "Live with Regis & Kathie Lee," May 13 & 14, 1991.

234. *Vanity Fair*, April 1991, "Madonna: Who Can Justify Her Love?" by Lynn Hirschberg.

235. *USA Today*, May 17, 1991, "Carrie Fisher Talks to Madonna" by Karen Thomas.

236. Madonna on the Academy Awards telecast, March 25, 1991.

237. *People*, "Michael & Madonna: The Oddest Couple" by Steve Dougherty, Todd Gold, David Marlow, Robin Micheli, Andrew Abrahams, and Sabrina McFarland.

238. *Rolling Stone*, May 16, 1991, "Madonna's Favorite Filmmaker Is One Smart Alek" by Peter Wilkinson.

239. *Entertainment Weekly*, May 17, 1991, "Madonna: The Naked Truth" by James Kaplan.

240. Dialogue from *Truth or Dare*, Miramax Films, 1991.

241. *Outweek*, March 20, 1991, "Immaculate Connection/Madonna and Us" by Michael Musto.

242. Dialogue from "Saturday Night Live," May 11, 1991.

243. *TV Guide*, November 23–29, 1991, "Madonna on TV" by Kurt Loder.

244. Cher on "CBS This Morning," June 14, 1991.

245. *Rolling Stone*, June 13, 1991 (Part I) and June 27, 1991 (Part II), "Madonna: Big-Time Girl Talk" by Carrie Fisher.

Sources of Updated Material

246. *Vogue*, October 1996, "Madonna's Moment as Evita, Mother, and Fashion Force /
Madonna Moment," by Julie Salamon.

247. *Sex*, by Madonna, 1992 Warner Books, New York City.

248. *Washington Post*, October 21, 1992, "The Madonna Pornucopia: *Sex* for the Coffee
Table and *Erotica* for the Ears," by Richard Harrington.

249. *People*, November 2, 1992, "Naked Ambition."

250. *Rolling Stone*, November 13, 1997, "The Women of Rock Interviews," by Gerri
Hirshey.

251. *Time*, January 20, 1997, "Mad for *Evita*," by Richard Zoglin.

252. *USA Today*, December 11, 1996, "Face to Face with Madonna," by Edna Gundersen.

253. *The Madonna Companion: Two Decades of Criticism*, Schimner Books 1999, New
York City, compiled by Allan Metz and Carol Benson; quoted material was further compiled in the essay, "Madonna" by Steve Allen.

254. *Interview*, June 1993, "Chameleon in Motion," interview by Mike Myers.

255. *Time*, October 25, 1993, "Madonna Goes Camp," by Richard Corliss.

256. *USA Today*, April 1, 1994, "Madonna, Crass Act of 'Late Show,' " by Matt Roush.

257. *Time*, April 11, 1994, "People" section, item, "Dirty Laundry."

258. *TV Guide*, April 11–17, 1998, "Madonna Confidential," by Mary Murphy.

259. *USA Today*, October 21, 1994, "Madonna Snuggles Up for 'Bedtime' Romance," by
Edna Gundersen.

260. *Entertainment Weekly*, October 28, 1994, "Swinging a New Jack," by Jim Farber.

261. *Discover*, Fall 1994, BMG Record Service, "Madonna Bedtime Stories."

262. *Atlanta Journal Constitution*, October 25, 1994, "Pillow Talk," by Steve Dollar.

263. *USA Today*, February 14, 1995, "Madonna Likes 'Late Night' Peace," by Alan Bash.

264. *Leonard Maltin's 1998 Movie & Video Guide*, Signet Books, New York City, 1997.

265. *Billboard*, September 30, 1995, " 'Something' in the Way She Grieves," by Timothy White.

266. *Billboard*, October 26, 1996, "Radio Embraces *Evita*," by Larry Flick.

267. *Vanity Fair*, November 1996, "Madonna's Private Diaries."

268. *Q*, December 1996, "Commanding," a review of the Evita soundtrack album by Paul Du Noyer.

269. *Time*, February 12, 1996, "People: All The Rage in Argentina," by Belinda Luscombe.

270. *USA Today*, January 3, 1997, "Antonio Bandaras: 'Evita' Tests Press-Shy Star's Voice and Mettle," by Marco R. della Cava.

271. *People*, October 29, 1996, "Mama Madonna! / A Labor of Love," by Todd Gold.

272. *Twang*, February 1997, "Madonna Does *Evita*," by Mark Bego.

273. *Time*, December 16, 1996, "You Must Love Her," by Richard Corliss.

274. *Time*, February 24, 1997, "Crying for Madonna, Experts Explain Why Oscar Snubbed the Studios," by Bruce Handy.

275. *Rolling Stone*, December 24, 1998–January 7, 1999, "1998 Rock & Roll Yearbook" and "1998's Essential Records," by various writers.

276. *New York Times*, March 1, 1998, "New Tune for the Material Girl; I'm Neither," by Ann Powers.

277. *Billboard*, February 21, 1998, "WB Expects Madonna to 'Light' Up International Markets," by Larry Flick.

278. *Time,* March 16, 1998, "Heading for the Light," by Christopher John Farley.

279. *Billboard,* March 14, 1998, *Ray of Light,* album review.

280. *www.Grammy.com,* January 21, 1999, "Madonna Will Perform on the 41st Annual Grammy Awards on February 24 on CBS."

281. *Detroit Free Press,* February 25, 1999, "Lauryn's Sermon, Madonna's Misfire," by Kelley L. Carter.

282. *Billboard,* February 21, 1998, "The Lady Is a Maverick," by Larry Flick.

283. *People,* September 20, 1999, "Best & Worst Dressed '99."

284. *People,* February 2, 2000, "Chatter" section, item, "Cover Girl," by Chuck Arnold.

285. *Los Angeles Times,* January 29, 2000, "Madonna's Brand-New 'Pie' Recipe," by Geoff Boucher.

286. *USA Today,* February 1, 2000, "Madonna Serves Upper-Crust 'American Pie,' " by Edna Gundersen.

287. *Vanity Fair,* March 2000, "Madonna & Rupert Everett: Just Great Friends," by Ned Zeman.

Acknowledgments

The author would like to thank:

Norbert Alberti
Bruce Baron
Bob & Mary Bego
Jellybean Benitez
Angela Bowie
Mark Brooky
John Christe
Brad DeMeulenaere
Paul Donnelley
Jerry George
Roger Glazer
Bobby Glenn
Ron Goldfarb
Jimmy & Karen
  Greenspoon
Rob Haddix
Maggie Hall
Glenn Hughes
Mark Kamins
Rusty Kothavala
Virginia Lohle

Madonna
Maripol
Richard Maschal
Jason McCluskey
Walter McBride
Sue "Muffy" McDonald
Doug McQueen
Charles Moniz
Marie Morreale
Coati Mundi
Anthony Panzera
Manny Parrish
Michael Pietsch
Reid Rosefelt
Liz Rosenberg
David Salidor
Susan Seidelman
Bobby Shaw
Barbara Shelley
Fred Zarr
Vinnie Zuffante

Index

Index

About the Author

Mark Bego is the author of forty celebrity biographies, including books of Michael Jackson, Whitney Houston, Bette Midler, Aretha Franklin, Linda Ronstadt, Patsy Cline, Bonnie Raitt, Leonardo DiCarprio, and Cher. He has also co-written the autobiographies of Mickey Dolenz (of the Monkees), Jimmy Greenspoon (of Three Dog Night), and Martha Reeves (of Martha and the Vandellas). He lives in Tucson, Arizona.

DREAMGIRL AND SUPREME FAITH
My Life as a Supreme
Mary Wilson
Updated Edition
732 pp., 150 b/w photos, 15 color photos
0-8154-1000-X
$19.95

FAITHFULL
An Autobiography
Marianne Faithfull with David Dalton
320 pp., 32 b/w photos
0-8154-1046-8
$16.95

ROCK SHE WROTE
Women Write About Rock, Pop, and Rap
Edited by Evelyn McDonnell & Ann Powers
496 pp.
0-8154-1018-2
$16.95

GOIN' BACK TO MEMPHIS
A Century of Blues, Rock 'n' Roll, and Glorious Soul
James Dickerson
284 pp., 58 b/w photos
0-8154-1049-2
$16.95

MICK JAGGER
Primitive Cool
Chris Sandford
Updated Edition
352 pp., 56 b/w photos
0-8154-1002-6
$16.95

THE BLUES
In Images and Interviews
Robert Neff and Anthony Connor
152 pp., 84 b/w photos
0-8154-1003-4
$17.95

ROCK 100
The Greatest Stars of Rock's Golden Age
David Dalton and Lenny Kaye
with a new introduction
288 pp., 195 b/w photos
0-8154-1017-4
$19.95

SUMMER OF LOVE
The Inside Story of LSD, Rock & Roll, Free Love and High Times in the Wild West
Joel Selvin
392 pp., 23 b/w photos
0-8154-1019-0
$15.95

ANY OLD WAY YOU CHOOSE IT
Rock and Other Pop Music, 1967–1973
Robert Christgau
Expanded Edition
360 pp.
0-8154-1041-7
$16.95

DESPERADOS
The Roots of Country Rock
John Einarson
304 pp., 16 pp. of b/w photos
0-8154-1065-4
$19.95

TURNED ON
A Biography of Henry Rollins
James Parker
280 pp., 10 b/w photos
0-8154-1050-6
$17.95

Available at bookstores; or call 1-800-462-6420

150 Fifth Avenue
Suite 911
New York, NY 10011